Woodland Flowers

BRITISH WILDLIFE
COLLECTION
8

Woodland Flowers

Colourful past, uncertain future

Keith Kirby

BLOOMSBURY WILDLIFE
LONDON · OXFORD · NEW YORK · NEW DELHI · SYDNEY

BLOOMSBURY WILDLIFE
Bloomsbury Publishing Plc
50 Bedford Square, London, WC1B 3DP, UK

BLOOMSBURY, BLOOMSBURY WILDLIFE and the Diana logo are trademarks of
Bloomsbury Publishing Plc

Published with the support of the British Ecological Society

First published in the United Kingdom 2020

A catalogue record for this book is available from the British Library

ISBN: HB: 9781472949073; ePDF: 9781472949097; ePub: 9781472949080

2 4 6 8 10 9 7 5 3

Page layouts by Susan McIntyre
Jacket artwork by Carry Akroyd
Printed and bound in India by Replika Press Pvt. Ltd.

To find out more about our authors and books visit www.bloomsbury.com
and sign up for our newsletters

HALF-TITLE: Early-purple Orchids.
FRONTISPIECE: A way through the woods…

Contents

Preface

Nemophilist: one who is fond of forests or forest scenery;
a haunter of the woods.

I was born behind a pub called The Woodman, in south Essex, now just outside the M25 motorway ring, but in those days London was still some way off. It was a landscape of mixed farming, hedged fields, streams and small rivers.

The family later moved to Wheeler's Yard, a black weather-board house with a garden of rough grass, an Elm clump, several small hedges and a large Crack Willow. Elder bushes grew on what had been the house rubbish dump. Every year, by an old Ash, a small patch of Lesser Celandine and Lords-and-Ladies popped up – the first proper woodland flowers that I came to know.

In the nearby fields there were overgrown hedges with caves formed in the Bramble where cows found shade, and old pollard oaks with Rosebay Willowherb growing in the mould in their hollow trunks. Our primary school had a nature table with jars of flowers such as Greater Stitchwort and Cow Parsley. For some months we even had a carefully labelled badger skull, although it did look remarkably like part of a chicken skeleton! My early attempts at art were dominated by green and brown poster paint splodges labelled 'forest'.

Those plants of woodland and hedges are an integral part of my childhood memories, and I later had a chance to study them as part of my degree in Agricultural and Forest Sciences at the University of Oxford, followed by three years of research on Bramble growth in the nearby Wytham Woods. Wytham will feature strongly in this book because it is one of the hotspots for ecological studies on a world scale, although my efforts on brambles contributed little to this great accumulation of knowledge. I did not know what sort of career might

OPPOSITE PAGE:
Herb-Paris; a favourite plant of mine and a fine example of botanical illustration by Rosemary Wise.

7

develop from an interest in nature, but through good fortune ended up with the Nature Conservancy Council (NCC), at that time the government agency concerned with wildlife conservation.

I was apprenticed to George Peterken who developed many of the ideas that still shape woodland conservation and management today. One of the perks of the job as a forestry and woodland officer was the opportunity to visit woods, to record the flowers that grew in them. This helped me and my colleagues to understand what was happening to our woods, which was essential if we were to improve their conservation.

In 2012 retirement from NCC's successor, Natural England, gave me a chance to move back to Oxford, where I am now associated with the University's Department of Plant Sciences. I have revived my researches in Wytham Woods and had the time to write this book – a homage to the flowers in the back garden in Wheeler's Yard, and to the woods, not only those of south Essex where I played as a child, but also the many others the length and breadth of Great Britain that I have had the good fortune to visit. It is also a tribute to the people who have helped and inspired me over the years.

I hope it will encourage you to look down at the wood beneath the trees, the plants of the forest floor. Woodland plants have been part of our past lives in practical ways as food and medicines, and as the inspirations for poetry, perfume and pub signs. They tell a variety of stories about the history of woodland, its past management and how that has changed over the last century or so, not always for the better. The plants can also be a very visible sign of progress when we do get it right in terms of conserving our woodland wildlife for future generations. They turn woods into magical places for me still, and bring to mind words from the traditional ballad of Thomas the Rhymer: 'Oh, see you not that bonny road that curves about the ferny brae. That is the path to fair elfland where you and I this night maun gae.'

Acknowledgements

I am grateful to the University of Oxford's Department of Plant Sciences for the working space to produce this book; to the Nature Conservancy Council and its successors (English Nature, Natural England) who, as my employers for 33 years, allowed me to visit woods across Great Britain and occasionally abroad. Innumerable woodland owners, foresters and reserve managers shared their insights into which plants occur where and why, as well as much other useful information on woodland ecology and management.

Many people kindly provided comments on ideas and draft chapters, including Peter Buckley, Arnold Cooke, Rob Cooke, Tom Curtis, Jeremy Dagley, Nigel Fisher, Diana Gilbert, Emma Goldberg, Jeanette Hall, Ralph Harmer, Stephen Harris, Alison Hester, Della Hooke, John Hopkins, Rob Jarman, Richard Jefferson, Daniel Kelly, Jane Kirby, James Littlemore, Jim Latham, Peter Marren, Fraser Mitchell, Andy Moffat, Mike Morecroft, Suzanne Perry, George Peterken, Dominic Price, Heather Robertson, John Rodwell, Simon Smart, Tim Sparks, Jonathan Spencer, Christine Tansey, Ian Taylor, Peter Thomas, Charles Watkins, Trudy Watt, Kevin Watts and Scot Wilson. Much helpful advice came from the British Wildlife Collection's editors, Katy Roper and David Campbell, who remained calm and showed tolerance throughout the writing, and to Alison Rix who copy-edited the text. I am very grateful for all their input, but any errors or misinterpretations rest with me.

Finally, my thanks to my partner, Trudy Watt, for putting up with living with me and this project for years.

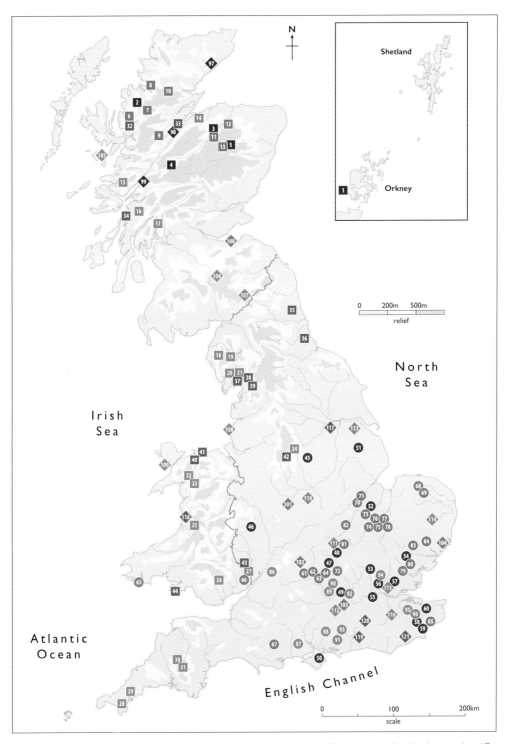

Map showing the location and type of the main woods discussed in this book. Types are described in chapters 6 and 7.

No.	Name	No.	Name	No.	Name
1	Berriedale	42	Derbyshire Dales	83	Lineage Wood
2	Talladale	43	Wye Valley, Lady Park Wood	84	Bradfield Wood
3	Cairngorms, Craigellachie Birchwood	44	The Gower Ashwoods	85	Biggin Wood
4	Creag Meaghaid	45	Sherwood Forest	86	Cotswolds Beechwoods
5	Morrone Birkwoods	46	Wyre Forest	87	The New Forest
6	Sheildaig Forest	47	Bernwood Forest	88	Chappetts Copse
7	Beinn Eighe	48	Sheephouse Wood	89	Warburg Reserve
8	Rhiddoroch Pinewood	49	Wykery Copse	90	Chilterns Beechwoods
9	Glen Affric	50	Isle of Wight, Briddlesford Copse	91	Kingley Vale
10	Alladale	51	The Lincolnshire Limewoods	92	Burnham Beeches
11	Craig Fhiaclach	52	Holme Fen	93	Ebernoe Common
12	Abernethy Pinewood	53	Wormley Wood/Hoddesdon Park	94	Epping Forest
13	Mar Lodge, Deeside	54	Chalkney Wood	95	Toys Hill
14	Cawdor, Great Wood	55	Oxleas Wood	96	Wye, Kent
15	Loch Sunart Oakwoods	56	Hainault Forest	97	Langwell Water
16	Dalavich Oakwood	57	Norsey Wood	98	Urquhart Bay
17	Lochlomondside Oakwoods	58	Orlestone Forest	99	Carnach Wood/North Ballachulish
18	Ennerdale	59	Ham Street Wood	100	Dalkeith Old Park
19	Borrowdale	60	The Blean	101	Sutton Park
20	Duddon Valley	61	Wytham Woods	102	Woodstock Old Park
21	Coniston Woods	62	Sydlings Copse	103	Windsor Great Park
22	Maentwrog Oakwoods	63	Whitecross Green Wood	104	Staverton Park
23	Coed y Rhygen	64	Weston Turville	105	Rum
24	Yarncliffe Wood	65	Orielton	106	Carrifran
25	Coed Rheidol	66	Coed Wen	107	Kielder Forest
26	Coed Deri-Newydd	67	Cranborne Chase	108	Ainsdale NNR
27	Forest of Dean	68	Swanton Novers	109	Newborough Warren, Anglesey
28	Helford Estuary Woods	69	Foxley Wood	110	National Forest
29	Fal Oakwoods	70	Short Wood	111	Milton Keynes
30	Black Tor Copse, Dartmoor	71	Bedford Purlieus	112	Swinley Plantations
31	Wistmans Wood	72	Broadbalk/Geescroft wilderness	113	Poolthorn Covert
32	Rassal Ashwood	73	Monks Wood	114	Breckland/Thetford Forest
33	Moniack Burn	74	Gamlingay Wood	115	Thames Chase
34	Ballachuan Hazelwood	75	Hayley Wood	116	Tunbridge Wells bypass
35	Cotting Wood	76	Papworth Wood	117	Hatfield Chase
36	Castle Eden Dene	77	Overhall Grove	118	Borth Beach, submerged forest
37	Roudsea Wood	78	Kingston Wood	119	Knepp Estate
38	Witherslack Woods	79	Hatfield Forest	120	Box Hill
39	Gait Barrows	80	Hempstead Wood	121	Pett Levels
40	Coed Gorswen	81	Salcey Forest		
41	Marle Hall Woods	82	Oakleigh Purlieus		

Map legend

Upland	▪	Northern birchwoods (mainly NVC types W11, 17, but some W9)
	▪	Native pinewoods (mainly NVC type W18, but patches of W4 common in hollows)
	▪	Upland oakwoods (mainly NVC types W11, 16, but patches of W7 and W9 also often common along streams)
	▪	Upland mixed ashwoods (mainly NVC types W8, 9)
Lowland	●	Lowland mixed oakwoods (mainly NVC types W10, 16)
	●	Lowland mixed ashwoods (mainly NVC type W8)
	●	Beech-Yew woodland (mainly NVC types W12-15)
Other	◆	Wet woodland (NVC types W1-7, but mainly W7 in sites listed)
	◆	Parkland
	◆	Plantations
	◆	Miscellaneous

Into the woods

O n a map showing the locations of forests in Europe, much of Great Britain is blank. There are the big 20th-century spruce and pine plantations, such as Kielder Forest or Thetford Forest, but most of our more natural woods are too small to register. Yet size is not always a guide to interest and value. Wykery Copse covers just three hectares and is now largely engulfed by the town of Bracknell, but within it you can find Early-purple Orchid, Yellow Archangel and primroses. Many other towns and cities contain small patches of woodland. However, whether in town or country, I hope this account will encourage you to explore all that your local wood has to offer.

Woods are a bit like buildings where the trees provide the walls and ceiling – so the twisted stems of a Dartmoor copse might be the equivalent of a ramshackle labourer's cottage, while a Cotswold beechwood with its soaring tree-trunk pillars is more like a Gothic cathedral. However, much of the variety is found around your feet – the wood beneath the trees. There are usually five to ten times as many species in the ground flora as there are varieties of trees and shrubs, and they – the carpets of Wood Anemone or Wild Garlic, cushions of Bilberry, curtains of Ivy and Honeysuckle hanging off the trees – provide the 'soft furnishings'.

My focus is on woodland flowers, ferns, sedges and grasses, collectively called woodland plants or ground flora hereafter. These are only part of the woodland system alongside the mosses and liverworts (which are also plants), lichens, fungi, invertebrates, birds and mammals. However, woodland plants are one of the easier groups to deal with and can be a useful way of understanding woods more generally.

OPPOSITE PAGE:
Take a look at the wood
beneath the trees.

A small wood encircled by Bracknell.

Home to Yellow Archangel, Bugle and a wide range of other woodland plants.

In this book I explore how woodland plants in Great Britain have come to be where they are, introducing some of the issues in this chapter through a look at one of our most distinctive species, the Bluebell. Later chapters touch on the work of botanists who have walked the woods in the past, collecting information on where plants occur and why. Other chapters look at how plants on the forest floor cope with living in the shade of their bigger relatives, the trees and shrubs, or the attentions of herbivores.

We will be going on walks through time as well as space, looking at the annual change in the wood through the seasons; how plants survive the woodman's cycles of cutting and tending the trees, typically between 10 and 150 years; and how plants spread to Great Britain in the distant past (over periods of several thousand years), perhaps by hitching a lift on the coat of a passing Wild Boar or in the stomach of a wintering thrush.

Forests, woods or just scattered trees – an explanation of terms

The following is based on Kirby & Watkins (2015)

- **Wood**, **woodland** and **forest** are used generally to describe tree-covered lands. Wood tends to be used for relatively small discrete areas of land; woodland and forest for more extensive tracts.
- **Forest** (capital F) is also used in a more specialised sense where it refers to land subject to Forest Law, particularly in the medieval period. Forest Law was primarily concerned with regulating hunting; the land to which it applied might or might not be covered by trees, so not all of it was forest in the modern sense.
- **Wood-pasture** refers to landscapes grazed by domestic stock or deer with an open tree cover. This includes parks whose boundaries are often marked by walls or fences as well as less well-defined areas of scattered trees.
- **Coppicing** refers to the practice of repeatedly cutting trees close to ground level, followed by the regrowth of multiple stems from the stump. These can be harvested again when they have regrown, usually after intervals of between five and thirty years.
- **Pollarding** is a similar process, but the cut is made at 2–3m above the ground so that the regrowth is out of the reach of browsing animals.

- **Plantations** are areas where most trees have been planted. They may be within existing woodland or on previously open ground. The trees may be native to the area or introductions; they may be planted in large even-aged blocks or as wide-spaced individual stems. Old plantations may be difficult to distinguish from more natural woods.
- **Ancient woods** (or ancient forests) are those where there has been continuous woodland cover since AD 1600 in England and Wales and AD 1750 in Scotland. These might be on land which was open at some time before this date as evidenced by old moats, Roman building remains or Iron Age settlements, within the current woodland boundary.
- **Ancient trees** are those old for their species with features such as cavities or a hollow trunk, bark loss over sections of the trunk and a large quantity of dead wood in the canopy. The broader term 'veteran trees' includes younger individuals that have developed similar characteristics, perhaps due to adverse growing conditions or injury.

Gnarly Oak at Black Tor
Copse on Dartmoor.

The ground flora says as much about the past as it does about present conditions, and these messages may give clues for the future as the flora faces the new challenges imposed by climate change and pollution. There may also be new opportunities for the ground flora in the drive to expand our tree cover for wood production as well as for nature conservation.

Generally, English plant names are used in the text, although the scientific name, following Stace (2010), is also given at first mention. A full list of English and scientific names used is to be found in Appendix 1.

When the population was mainly rural, most people would recognise at least the common woodland plants. Today most people still know Bluebell *Hyacinthoides non-scripta*, Dog Rose *Rosa canina*, Honeysuckle *Lonicera periclymenum* and Primrose *Primula vulgaris*. However, the opportunities to come across woodland plants are fewer than they were when I was a child. On the other hand, as a society, we are now more active in trying to conserve woods through their designation as reserves and by encouraging sympathetic management by farmers and foresters. Proposals to clear woods are likely to be met by strong opposition and Woodland Trust campaigns, with compensatory conservation packages required if the clearance goes ahead. We are finding new values for woods as places important for recreation, carbon

storage, water regulation and soil erosion control. New woods are being created where woodland plants may eventually be able to thrive.

How will our woodland flora survive under modern forestry practices?

Our woodland flora is going to change, and we cannot tell which plants will be winners, and which losers in the long-term. Some further losses are probably inevitable, but I am cautiously optimistic that we can turn things around.

Why focus on woodland plants?

We know a lot about what is needed for plants to grow and spread because they are relatively easy to study. They do not fly away or hide themselves in bushes just before you work out what they are. Most can be found throughout much of the year. There is a good variety of species to learn to identify, but not the almost overwhelming numbers of insects. For the casual botanist there is the advantage that the woodland flora has fewer species in the more difficult groups such as grasses and sedges, or yellow dandelion-type flowers such as hawkweeds, than meadows or mires. There are, admittedly, the 400 or so micro-species of Bramble, but many of us lump these together as the aggregate species *Rubus fruticosus*. As a proper taxonomist once told me: 'Don't bother to try to separate them, dear boy. No-one would believe *your* identifications!'.

Woodland plants pick up the sorts of variations in the environment that humans can easily appreciate, for example the differences between wet and dry soils (do you need wellington boots or not?). From our gardens, we know that plants such as Heather *Calluna vulgaris* like acid conditions, whilst others like Old-Man's Beard *Clematis vitalba* need more limey soils. People usually gravitate towards the sunny glades and open patches in woods where much of the floral richness lies.

Ecologists have also gained insights from woodland plants into many important woodland conservation issues. For example, surveys in the 1970s threw up anomalies in the distribution of some plants – why did Wood Anemone *Anemone nemorosa* occur in one wood but not in the similar patch across the field? – which in turn led to an appreciation of how woodland history affects modern species patterns. The lack of ground vegetation under many spruce plantations provided an easily understood message in the 1980s when many conservationists were arguing the case for not converting broadleaved woodland to conifers. The recovery of the ground flora in those same stands, now the conifers are being removed, can be used as an indication of the success of our restoration efforts. In the 1990s the trend towards earlier flowering of species such as Lady's Smock *Cardamine pratensis* became a tangible indicator of climate change. The impact of rising deer populations can be demonstrated more easily through the reduction in Bramble and increase in grasses than through the less visible effects on bird or butterfly populations. Banks of Nettle *Urtica dioica* at the edge of woods where none grew previously are a signal of possible fertiliser drift from adjacent arable fields.

Ground flora plants are not as massive as the trees and shrubs, making up less than a twentieth of above-ground weight of vegetation in a wood. However, they are critical to the way that woodland works. The ground flora can protect the soil from erosion and capture nutrients in the spring and late autumn, when the trees are generally dormant, that would otherwise be washed out of the system. Dense stands of flowers, ferns and grasses may sometimes prevent tree seedlings from establishing successfully, but in other situations can provide essential shelter to the young trees and protect them against being grazed-off by deer and sheep. Flowers produce nectar and pollen for a wide range of insects and in return benefit from the cross-pollination leading to the improved seed-set that occurs when the insects carry some of that pollen to a nearby flower. Fruits and seeds, such as blackberries, are eaten by birds and mammals, but if some

Bramble seeds were found in the body of a Bronze Age man discovered at Walton-on-the-Naze.

pass through the animal undigested they may be dispersed to new parts of the wood. The leaves provide food for many species, ranging from tiny insects that mine the cells within the leaf itself, through to our largest wild land mammal, the Red Deer.

If we are careful, we can use the woodland ground flora as a measure of how well our woods are doing. This does not mean that what is good for woodland plants is necessarily good for all the other parts of a woodland system; at times it can be the reverse. However, if we understand what is driving change in the ground flora, we can separately consider whether these same factors might be relevant to other groups of wildlife. For example, intense browsing by deer can lead to reductions in Bramble cover: this browsing is also likely to affect tree regeneration and populations of small mammals that need dense low vegetation cover; however, birds and insects living high in the trees may not be affected.

Where has our knowledge come from?

Many people have studied woodland plants, from the Greek Theophrastus, who lived three centuries before Christ and is often called the Father of Botany, through to the 16th-century herbalists such as John Gerard. However, much of our knowledge of where plants grow in Great Britain stems from the explosion of interest in natural history that occurred during the 19th and early 20th centuries. By happy chance, the herbarium of one of the most knowledgeable botanists of the late 19th century, the Oxford chemist, George Claridge Druce (1850–1932), is housed directly below the office where I now work.

This wealth of natural history data paved the way for the modern generations of botanists. The great Cambridge ecologist, Oliver Rackham, and my mentor George Peterken transformed the way we look at woods in the landscape. Others have summarised how the flora varies in woods across the country in response to differences in climate and soils (Rodwell 1991) and which characteristics help woodland species cope with stress, competition and disturbance in their environment (Grime *et al.* 2007), or varying levels of light, water and mineral nutrients (Ellenberg 1988).

Woodland plants as part of our lives

Woods long provided people with the necessities of life, such as fuel and building materials. Consequently, they had an economic value, and might be protected by a physical barrier such as a fence; incidences of trespass, theft or vandalism were treated seriously, and there are frequent mentions of woodland in historic legal documents, including wills. Some woodland plants have also crept out from under the trees and into our lives both through culture, such as art and music, and also in the form of practical pursuits such as flower-picking and foraging.

In the past, some woodland plants were considered to be magical. Fern seed (the spores), for example, might render one invisible, while in the old Welsh stories, known as *The Mabinogion*, a bride for the hero is conjured out of the flowers of the Oak *Quercus* spp., Broom *Cytisus scoparius*, and Meadowsweet *Filipendula ulmaria*. In a later ballad, Broom is used to cause drowsiness in a lover and save a lady from the consequences of an unwise wager. Banks of sweet primroses, roses and briars are a feature of many English folksongs, and Shakespeare's 'bank where the wild thyme blows' also has oxlips, violets and woodbine (Honeysuckle). Wordsworth danced with the wild daffodils *Narcissus pseudonarcissus* on the shores of Ullswater but was also so taken by the Lesser Celandine *Ficaria verna*, that he dedicated an entire poem to it! 'There is a flower that shall be mine, Tis the little celandine'.

John Clare, the 19th-century Northamptonshire peasant-poet, included violets and primroses, Woodbine, Old Man's Beard and Ivy *Hedera helix*, Pilewort (Lesser Celandine) and Bramble in his works. He also knew the hardships of a wood-cutter's life, as made clear

in the poem of that title. Edward Thomas picked up on celandines, again, but unusually includes the rather nondescript Dog's Mercury *Mercurialis perennis* in his poem *The Hollow Wood*.

Broom flowers such as these were said to cause drowsiness, as suggested in the traditional ballad *Broomfield Hill.*

Flowers used in a metaphorical sense in the Scottish ballad *The Flowers of the Forest* reflect the nobility lost at the battle of Flodden Field in 1513 (the common version of the lyrics dates from about 1756). They were also a key part of 1960s culture, and their vulnerability used as a metaphor in the Pete Seeger song 'Where have all the flowers gone?' and in reality in Wally Whyton's plea to 'Leave them a flower'.

Paintings of woodland plants range in type from detailed portraits of individual species, such as the Columbine *Aquilegia vulgaris* from the workshop of Albrecht Dürer, to the flowers in the woodland scenes of the Pre-Raphaelites. There is also a long tradition of scientific botanical drawing and painting, grouped loosely under the heading of Botanical Art, that relies on close observation of the living plant, and at its best combines precision and aesthetics.

More practically, Geoffrey Grigson's delightful written account – *An Englishman's Flora* (first published in 1958, re-published 1975) – gives local names and uses of plants that he collected just after the Second World War. People at that time were making sauces from Hedge and Wild Garlic (*Alliaria petiolata, Allium ursinum*); cooking the shoots of Bath Asparagus *Ornithogalum pyrenaicum*, Giant Bellflower

Campanula latifolia and Rosebay Willowherb *Chamerion angustifolium*; boiling up the leaves of Ground Elder *Aegopodium podagraria* or having a salad of Sorrel *Rumex acetosella*. There might be a side order of 'roots' of Silverweed *Potentilla anserina* (famine food) or Pignut *Conopodium majus* (the Nuts in May of the nursery rhyme?), and for afters a variety of fruits such as Blackberry or Bilberry *Vaccinium myrtillus*. The food might be washed down with beer flavoured with Hops *Humulus lupulus*, or in earlier times Ground-ivy *Glechoma hederacea* and Wood Sage *Teucrium scorodonia*. The dirty dishes and saucepans could be scrubbed clean using Horsetails *Equisetum* spp., although that was largely distant memory by Grigson's time.

Nettle leaves were, and still are, eaten, but a more valuable use was to provide fibres for making cloth, which could be dyed with extracts from Marsh-marigold *Caltha palustris*, Yellow Iris *Iris pseudacorus*, or Tormentil *Potentilla erecta*, then starched using Lords-and-Ladies *Arum maculatum*. Outside, the poultry could be given Chickweed *Stellaria media* or Goosegrass *Galium aparine* (also known as Cleavers), but not Gooseberry *Ribes uva-crispa* (whose name has nothing to do with geese, but derives from a Frankish word meaning crisp). The cattle got Gorse *Ulex europaeus* as a winter food provided the spines were crushed, while the pigs had their Hogweed *Heracleum sphondylium*. Bracken *Pteridium aquilinum* was used as bedding for stock.

Historically, if you were ill, woodland plants might be used to try to cure you. Sometimes this was based on 'sympathetic magic', the idea that if a plant looked like your symptoms it was good as a remedy. So, Lesser Celandine (Pilewort) was used to treat piles because it has lumps on its roots that look like them. Other plants do have real, though often dangerous, effects on human physiology, such as Foxglove *Digitalis purpurea* (the original source of the drug Digitalis used in heart complaints) and Stinking Hellebore *Helleborus foetidus*. Herbs were not just collected for personal or local use: Grigson (1975) refers to Mezereon *Daphne mezereum*, used in folk medicine against cancer, being collected from Sussex woods for sale in London markets. It is now quite a rare plant. Common Valerian *Valeriana officinalis*, taken as a tea to calm the head and prevent hysteria, was brought up to London from Cranborne Chase in Wiltshire.

One of our commonest woodland species – the Bluebell – is now used to introduce some of the major issues and ideas that run through the rest of the book.

In and out the dusky bluebells

Bluebell has just about everything going for it: attractive, easy to recognise, widespread without being too common. Moreover, we can be proud that, as a plant of the Atlantic fringe in Europe, Great Britain and Ireland probably have more bluebells than the rest of the world put together (chapter 13). It does not seem to be able to tolerate the hard winters of northern and central Europe, or the hot, dry summers of southern Europe.

In 2002 the British conservation charity, Plantlife, ran a competition to choose county flowers as part of the celebrations recognising the Queen's Golden Jubilee; the Bluebell was taken out of consideration early on, because too many counties wanted it. In 2015 it was voted the national flower for England, though beaten by the Primrose in Scotland, Wales and Northern Ireland. It is one of a handful of wildflowers commonly used as a pub sign and is much celebrated by poets. Gerard Manley Hopkins referred to 'the blue buzzed-haze and the wafts of intoxicant perfume'. Perhaps not surprisingly perfumiers have sought to capture its fragrance, as they have with other woodland plants such as Lily-of-the-Valley *Convallaria majalis* and violets *Viola* spp.

The name 'Bluebell' was popularised by the romantic poets: other local names collected by Geoffrey Grigson (45 in total) included Adder's Flower, Bell Bottle, Bloody Man's Fingers, Blue Bonnets, Blue Bottle, Blue Goggles, Blue Granfer-Greygles, Blue Rocket, Blue Trumpets, Bummuck, Crake-feet, Crawfeet, Crawtaes, Cross-flower ... Ring-o-Bells, Rook's Flower, Single Gussies, Snake's Flower, Snapgrass and Wood Bells. In Scotland it is sometimes called the Wild Hyacinth because the name Bluebell is also used for the Harebell.

Spring awakening

In early spring Bluebell leaves emerge before most of the trees and shrubs above them have broken bud (chapter 8). Rarely do you find just one Bluebell on its own. Where conditions are suitable there may be thousands and the ground becomes first a sheet of dark-green leaves and then glorious blue as the flowers open. Beechwoods are often the best places to see this effect, because there are usually few shrubs beneath the trees to distract the eye from the flowers as they stretch into the distance between the grey-brown trunks.

By emerging early, bluebells are one of a group of spring-growing species, including Lesser Celandine and Wood Anemone, that take advantage of the high light levels that reach the forest floor before the trees and shrubs above them have expanded their leaves (Blackman & Rutter 1954). The cells that form the new Bluebell leaves are largely laid down during the previous year, and their rapid expansion, driven by water uptake from the upper layers of the soil, gives rise to the plant's rapid growth and dominance of the woodland floor. The bluebell's reliance on this spring window of high light conditions is one reason they do not do well where broadleaved woods have been replaced by the dense evergreen canopy of a tree such as Norway Spruce.

Bluebell flowers provide a source of nectar for early flying bees and hoverflies, and particularly for the bumblebee queens emerging from hibernation, looking to establish new nests. Such visits may lead to pollen from one plant being transferred to another, resulting in a mixing of genes through cross-fertilisation. In cold springs the bluebells may self-pollinate, but self-pollination in plants often leads to fewer seeds being produced and less vigorous offspring.

OPPOSITE PAGE:
Massed leaves waiting to flower (top).

A Bluebell haze (below).

Seed dispersal and colonisation of new sites

During the summer Bluebell leaves die back; contractile roots pull the bulb deeper into the soil where it will be better protected against future winter frosts. However, Bluebell banks can still be picked out in late summer, by the white straw of the stems and the dead flower heads with their rattle of small black seeds. The stems blow about, fall over, or are knocked by dogs, deer and people, scattering the seeds around the parent plant (Knight 1964). In this way, gaps in the Bluebell carpets are filled up by new plants. Some seeds germinate in the autumn as the temperature drops, and the seedlings may continue to grow in periods of mild weather. Other seeds remain dormant until the following year, so that not all will be lost if a very bad winter kills off the early seedlings. It may take several years from the seedling stage until the plant is large enough, with sufficient reserves, to flower.

The seeds do not spread very far, which means that the plant is good at occupying ground but not so good at colonising new sites. A team in Belgium followed the spread of small groups of bluebells transplanted into new sites. Just under half the clumps survived after 45 years and were spreading, but only very slowly. The researchers estimated that the main population front only advanced about 14m over a 45-year period, although with isolated individuals perhaps out to 42m (Van Der Veken *et al*. 2007). This is also the sort of pattern plotted by Oliver Rackham for Bluebell spread into a patch of new woodland from its long-established base population at Hayley Wood in Cambridgeshire (Rackham 2003).

If bluebells never spread faster than this, they might never have reached Great Britain at all. About 15,000 years ago, when much of Great Britain was under ice, Bluebell and many other woodland plants survived further south, probably on the Iberian Peninsula, in Italy, or the Balkans (chapter 12). They spread back as the conditions improved after the Ice Ages ended and Bluebell pollen has been found in 7000-year-old peat remains in Great Britain. At the rates seen in the Cambridgeshire and Belgian studies, bluebells could only have covered about 10–100 kilometres northwards before rising sea levels and the consequent formation of the English Channel destroyed the direct land connection between Great Britain and the Continent. Therefore, either Bluebell can sometimes spread much faster and over longer distances than we see now, or there were refuges for woodland plants during the Ice Ages much closer than we have yet found.

Bluebell probably reached Great Britain on its own, but many other plants have been deliberately or accidentally introduced to Great Britain by our ancestors, and the process is still going on today. One such introduction, the Spanish Bluebell *Hyacinthoides hispanica*, was already being grown in gardens by the 17th century and noted as occurring occasionally in the wild, as an escape, about a hundred years ago. This species differs from our woodland Bluebell in having a less strong scent, wider leaves and flowers all around the stem, not just hanging from one side of the stalk. It hybridises easily with our Bluebell, many populations of which are within bee-flight distance of gardens where the Spanish species is growing. The hybrid is already widespread, and we risk losing some of the distinctiveness of this very British plant (Kohn *et al*. 2009).

The threat from hybridisation with garden plants affects a relatively small number of woodland species, but other impacts on Bluebell populations are common to a wider range of species. These include woodland loss, grazing by deer, atmospheric pollution and climate change.

Eaten, trampled, picked and over-fertilised!

Bluebell leaves contain poisonous chemicals, similar to those in foxgloves, which ought to make them safe from grazing animals (chapter 11). However, this taste does not seem to deter Muntjac deer; presumably either they are not susceptible to the poison, or individuals do not eat enough to get a lethal dose. These small deer (about the size of a Labrador dog) were introduced to several places including Woburn Park, Bedfordshire, and around 1925 some escaped. They have since spread through much of southern Great Britain and are moving, or being moved illegally, north and west.

A former colleague in English Nature, Arnie Cooke, spent many hours measuring the lengths of Bluebell leaves in woods where there were numerous Muntjac (Cooke 2006). He found that plants where the leaves were grazed were smaller and less likely to flower, and when they did, the flower-heads were often grazed off by deer. Fewer resources went back into the bulb, from which the following year's leaves and flowers are produced; and fewer seeds were produced to fill gaps in the stand. The bluebells in Monks Wood National Nature Reserve in Cambridgeshire went into decline.

Bluebell carpets are also attractive to Wild Boar, which, although part of the landscape that developed in Great Britain in prehistoric times, had been killed off by around the 17th century. In the last few decades, however, they have been released or escaped from boar

Wild boar among the bluebells.

farms. The abundance and density of bluebells can be very much reduced by the rootling of Wild Boar in search of the bulbs to eat, but the bluebell patches can recover (Sims *et al.* 2014). Small bulbs that are not eaten may be spread by the boar to new space, away from the main clump. The long-term effects on Bluebell and on other woodland plants of pig/boar rootling are unknown, but the dense Bluebell carpets we love may only have developed over the last thousand years as boar became less common. This does not make such carpets less valuable, but it is something we should bear in mind when deciding how we want to manage our woods in future.

Despite the fact that bluebells last for a notoriously short time as cut flowers, people have at times also engaged in a distinctive form of Bluebell grazing: in the late 19th and early 20th centuries there were special trains out of London, so that people could go and pick them. This is commemorated in the Bluebell Line steam railway in Sussex. The actual picking of the flowers may be less of a threat than the trampling of the leaves that happens at the same time. Even just a few dozen passes of heavy boots can do enough damage to the leaves that the next year's growth and seed production are reduced (Littlemore & Barker 2001), a good reason for sticking to the existing paths when walking through Bluebell woods (chapter 17).

The bigger impacts that we make on the environment around us and their effects on woodland plants cannot be so easily resolved. An insidious threat to woodland plants is the spread of nitrogen oxides and ammonium from farming, power plants, aircraft and cars, leading to the incidental fertilisation of the countryside as a by-product of modern society. Most plants grow vigorously with more nutrients, but the risk for a species like Bluebell is that taller plants such as nettles, brambles and grasses grow even faster. These competitive species could take over and shade out the low-growing spring flowers (chapter 16).

The climate is also changing and plants respond to this, each in their own particular way. Milder winters and earlier springs could mean that bluebells come into leaf earlier and may therefore have a longer growing period. More resources then become available for flowering and seed set. Climate change might open up areas in the north for some species that in the past were not able to survive there. However, Bluebell already occurs in northern Scotland and its poor colonising ability means that it may not be able to take advantage of any new sites that do become available.

Changes in rainfall amounts or patterns might also affect how well the Bluebell does in future, because it can be susceptible to both drought and waterlogging. In Hayley Wood, Cambridgeshire, the main Bluebell zone is sandwiched between the areas that are waterlogged in spring where Oxlip *Primula elatior* is abundant, and the Dog's Mercury-dominant zone on the drier, somewhat sloping, ground (Abeywickrama 1949). If we get more intense rain in late winter through to early spring and/or drier summers then Bluebell might lose out in parts of its range to other, more competitive, species.

While most people associate Bluebell with woodland, it also grows well on coastal slopes under Bracken where there may never have been much in the way of woody cover. So, what counts as a woodland plant?

What am I including as a woodland plant?

No British plant will grow only in woodland although there are parasitic plants, like Toothwort *Lathraea squamaria*, that require the presence of a particular host tree. There are many plants with 'wood' in their common name, for example Wood Sage, or with the scientific specific names *sylvestris*, *sylvatica* (derived from the Latin word for woodland), but there are far more plants found in woods than are named in this way. In fact, there are few plant species that have not turned up somewhere within woodland, if only in glades or along wooded streams.

Toothwort, a parasitic plant.

What matters for the plant is that there are the right combinations of light, soil nutrients and moisture that it needs to grow. Heather can thrive in acid woods after felling, or on the open heathland of Dorset that forms the backdrop to Thomas Hardy's novels. 'Wood' Anemone still grew in meadows next to Epping Forest in the 1950s; Lesser Celandine has invaded my urban lawn. Sometimes, but not always, woodland plants in open ground reflect where trees have been cleared away, the ghosts of woods past (Rotherham 2017b).

Descriptions of plants as woodland species, grassland species or heathland species are anyway artificial: they reflect how humans

see where the plants grow now. The mixture of plants found in a
wood, meadow or moor 200, 500 or 1,000 years ago might have
been very different to what we see in those places today. Under the
projections for climate change, our woodland flora will be different
again 100 years from now. However, over most of Great Britain the
landscape is divided up into discrete habitat patches – a wood here, a
field there, moorland over there. My woodland plant list (Appendix 1)
is therefore simply those plants that regularly occur in, or seem to
prefer, woods as they exist in current landscapes (Kirby *et al.* 2012).
It includes species capable of surviving under the shade of the closed
canopy stands in woods, species associated with woodland edges,
rides and glades, and those found in the temporary openings in
woods created by coppicing or tree-felling. A selection of species from
the full list is considered in more detail later in this book where they
are particularly linked to an idea being discussed.

Deciding what to include in the woodland-plant list

My doctoral research on brambles involved clipping all the above-
ground growth from one-metre square plots in Wytham Woods once
a month for a year. The cut material was bundled up and sorted
in the laboratory into leaves, stems, flowers and fruits. Numerous

prickles ended up in my coat pockets, which made delving for a handkerchief a risky business. During the June harvest, when the thicket was about 1–2m high, I was cutting down through the Bramble canopy when I came across a strange-looking plant. It had a single stem, four leaves coming off at the top, a few wispy threads forming the petals and the beginnings of a black berry. This patch of Herb-Paris *Paris quadrifolia* had been marked on a map by Mick Southern, an ecologist studying small mammals and tawny owls in the Woods in the 1960s, and it was still thriving in 2018.

Brambles can be called a woodland plant because they are amongst the commonest species encountered in woods, almost anywhere in the country, and in the 1970s covered about a third of the ground in Wytham Woods. However, brambles are also common along hedges, stream-sides and on any old patch of rough ground. Bracken, nettles, Ivy and other plants that are common in woods but found widely in other habitats, are what I call woodland 'generalists'. Herb-Paris is another matter. It is almost always found within woods, and usually in woods that have existed for several hundred years at least. Such plants I term woodland 'specialists' in the rest of this book. Taken as a group, the woodland specialists show distinct differences from the generalists, being more shade-tolerant for example, and in turn, woodland species (generalists and specialists combined) tend to have different characteristics and growth patterns from 'non-woodland' species.

The core of this woodland plant list comes, as did the list for another book in this series, *Mountain flowers* (Scott 2016), from surveys done in the late 1960s and early 1970s. *A nature conservation review* (Ratcliffe 1977) listed 236 ferns, grasses and other flowering plants (excluding trees and shrubs) that occurred either mainly in woodland, or with a wider range of habitats, but often in woodland as well. Ratcliffe's list was further developed by George Peterken and used on recording cards in hundreds of surveys during the 1970s and 1980s. Species were added to the list where local experience suggested these were regularly encountered in woods. Some rare species were dropped from the list because if a species occurs in only a few places it may just have survived by chance at those points which happen to be woodland.

The list has since been compared with the species found in independent survey projects across the country, such as those that underpin the National Vegetation Classification (NVC; see chapter 6). Species from my woodland list made up two-thirds of those recorded from the woodland NVC samples, but only about a third of those from other habitats. Species found in woodland but also in wetland of various sorts, include Marsh Violet *Viola palustris*, Purple Moor-grass *Molinia caerulea* and Creeping Bent *Agrostis stolonifera* (acid mires); and Greater Tussock-sedge *Carex paniculata*, Common Valerian, Bittersweet *Solanum dulcamara* and Common Marsh Bedstraw *Galium palustre* (nutrient-rich swamps). Other overlaps are between the species of upland and lowland heaths and acid woods (Bilberry, Heath Bedstraw *Galium saxatile*, Wavy Hair-grass *Deschampsia flexuosa*, Tormentil and Heather). A third grouping consists of the woodland species that may also occur in free-draining chalk and limestone grassland (Lady's-mantle *Alchemilla* spp., Common Dog-violet *Viola riviniana*, Red Fescue *Festuca rubra*, Harebell *Campanula rotundifolia*, Ploughman's-spikenard *Inula conyza*), or in moister, nutrient-rich neutral grassland (Pignut, Creeping Buttercup *Ranunculus repens* and grasses such as Cock's-foot *Dactylis glomerata*, Yorkshire-fog *Holcus lanatus* and False Oat-grass *Arrhenatherum elatius*).

Depending where you are in the country, a case can be made for or against the inclusion of particular species or for changing their allocation between specialist and generalist. I have Adder's-tongue *Ophioglossum vulgatum* as a woodland specialist because it is characteristic of rides in old woods in eastern England, but it is also common in old grassland more generally. Limestone Fern *Gymnocarpium robertianum* is classed as a woodland generalist because the specialised conditions it needs are not confined to woodland situations.

Producing the list was only possible because of the wide range of surveys that had previously been done on what plants grew in woodland and what conditions they needed. So, the next chapter explores the development of our understanding of the British woodland flora.

How many of these common woodland plants are still widely known?

Ceres

Pomona

Ecce dedi vobis omnes herbas sementantes semen, quæ sunt. Gen. 1.29.

Excideret ne tibi diuini muneris Author:
Præsentem monstrat quælibet herba Deum.

THE
HERBALL
OR GENERALL
Historie of
Plantes.

Gathered by Iohn Gerardé
of London Master in
CHIRVRGERIE

Very much
Enlarged and Amended by
Thomas Iohnson
Citizen and Apothecarye
of
LONDON

THEOPHRASTVS

DIOSCORIDES

London Printed by
Adam Islip Ioice Norton
and Richard Whitakers
Anno 1633.

Io: Payne sculps.

The wandering botanist chapter two

'The wandering botanist is naturally mistaken for a tramp off the beaten track, or for an officious inspector of something or other', wrote Arthur Church in 1922. This quotation does rather sum up my career: from scruffy student researcher, through besuited civil servant, back to the grey-haired wanderer in the woods. More serious tramps and inspectors, the professional and enthusiastic botanists (such as Church himself) recording plants over the last 600 years, have generated the knowledge on which this book is based; and people still go out to survey woods for plants to help with their conservation or just for fun.

We don't know when our ancestors first started looking at plants as more than just something to eat or to avoid, but it may have been before we were even *Homo sapiens*. From early times there must have been an appreciation of which trees made the best firewood, which greens could be eaten, which might heal the sick and which might kill. The remains of flowers have been found in prehistoric graves and ritual deposits. A considerable amount of what we would now consider basic natural history was understood in the ancient world, although this might run alongside discredited ideas such as the 'doctrine of signatures'. This last suggested that similarities between the appearance of plants and disease symptoms meant that the plant could be used to cure that disease.

OPPOSITE PAGE:
The frontispiece to Gerard's Herbal – an early guide to the identification and uses of plants.

ABOVE:
The botanist at work, reproduced from an original 1981 etching by Graham Clarke.

The Ancient Greek Tyrtamus (usually known as Theophrastus, born c.370 BC) wrote about the herbal properties of many plants, but also other aspects of their growth. For example, he reported that both male and female plants contributed to the production of seed, at least for some plants – an early appreciation of the role of pollination. Moving plants from one place to another was known to sometimes increase yields but also to cause greater vulnerability to frost – an issue for us, if we wish to translocate species in response to climate change. Stirring up soil led to new vegetation growth, from, as we now know, buried seed (Hort 1916). He referred to the problem of naming plants precisely because misidentification could have serious consequences: Theophrastus was concerned that the three plants referred to as 'strykhnos' had distinct properties: one was edible and like a cultivated plant, having a berry-like fruit; one was said to induce sleep; the third (Thorn Apple *Datura stramonium*) to cause madness or death. Even today, many of the specimens in botanical collections around the world are not correctly named. There is also a link to my doctoral research in that Theophrastus recognised the great variety of brambles and that they might spread by stems growing down and rooting at their tips, something I studied at Wytham.

The Herbalists

Much of the classical world's knowledge of plants may have been lost or corrupted in early modern Europe, but some was passed down through Arab and then medieval scholars (Pavord 2005). Those who lived and worked in the countryside might have known many locally-growing species, if they had cause to collect them for culinary or medicinal purposes, while those whose business was with other matters might know only one or two species. We see the same thing today when the first-year undergraduate students in biology come on a field trip; there are some who are already good botanists, but others struggle over anything less obvious than a Bluebell.

Gradually, herbalists such as William Turner of Morpeth (c.1508–1568) started to record what our plants really looked like, what they did, and to give them distinct names. Turner's writings include at least 250 species. The invention of printing made it possible to spread this information widely. A near contemporary, John Gerard, published his 'Herbal' (a book describing plants and their uses) in 1597. This had many errors, but after his death an 'enlarged and amended version' by Thomas Johnson was published in 1632. Thomas Johnson also produced the first plant list for England and Wales (1634, 1641), *Mercurius Botanicus* (Pearman 2018). Out of about 270 woodland plants in Great Britain for which there is a date for a first record in print, 200 were published before 1700. Our flora was becoming well-documented, although the distinctive elements of the Scottish Highland flora would not be described for another century.

Proper botany emerges

Gradually, systematic lists were produced of locations where plants occurred. John Ray (1627–1705), an early modern botanist, compiled the first regional catalogue, of the plants around Cambridge, in 1660, which was based on direct observations and collecting (Preston & Oswald 2012). Over 600 species were named, with habitat details for three-quarters of them. Crested Cow-wheat *Melampyrum cristatum*, for example, was described as growing plentifully in almost all woods; now it is a rare species that is carefully nurtured along the margins of Monks Wood National Nature Reserve. Others of Ray's notes are more practical – 'the young stems of Burdock can be eaten in salads, raw or cooked'.

The consistent naming of plants remained a problem, as it had been for Theophrastus (Pavord 2005). Ray proposed some principles for classifying plants that were simple but efficient: names should be changed as little as possible to avoid confusion; related plants should be grouped together; the characteristics of a species should be clearly defined; the minimum number of characteristics possible should be used; the characteristics should be obvious and easy to grasp (this one has been challenged by modern classification, which uses DNA analysis!). Even so, species were still usually named according to a, sometimes cumbersome, description of their characteristics. This was simplified through the development and promotion by the Swedish botanist Linnaeus (1707–1778) of the system of two-word scientific names used today.

One specimen of a plant was chosen as the 'type' specimen; its description then became the reference with which any future collections are compared. Linnaeus's collection of botanical specimens came to Great Britain after his death and is still held by the Linnaean Society in London. It includes his 'type' specimen

A portrait of Linnaeus, who developed the binomial system for naming plants, in the Department of Plant Sciences, University of Oxford.

A specimen of Twinflower collected by Linnaeus, from the Linnaean Society collection.

of the Twinflower, which was apparently his favourite plant. Twinflower was given the scientific name *Linnaea borealis* by another botanist, because it is not done to name a species after yourself!

An explosion of interest

The Apothecaries' Act of 1815 brought in compulsory apprenticeship and formal qualifications for what would now be termed medical general practitioners. They were expected to be familiar with a variety of plants used in healing, and this stimulated botanical teaching at universities. Later in the Victorian era and the early 20th century there was a more general upsurge of interest in natural history. Drawing and collecting plants became common pastimes as illustrated by Elizabeth Holden's nature notes of 1906, which became a best-seller after they were rediscovered and published in 1977 as *The Country Diary of an Edwardian Lady*.

Plant records were brought together in books that listed for each county the species found, with notes on their distribution, commonly called 'county floras'. Such collations for Northamptonshire, Oxfordshire, Berkshire and Buckinghamshire were all written by one man, George Claridge Druce (1850–1932), who was also very involved with the Botanical Society and Exchange Club of the British Isles, a forerunner of what is now the Botanical Society of Britain and Ireland (Allen 1986). Druce had trained as a pharmacist and later owned a chemist's shop in Oxford. His early interest in the plants and animals around his childhood home in Northamptonshire matured into a collection of over 200,000 specimens. Other

A low, insignificant plant?

The Twinflower *Linnaea borealis* is a common plant in the northern Scandinavian forests that Linnaeus encountered on a trip he made through Lapland in 1732. Later he described it as 'low, insignificant, forgotten, flowering for a short time; it is named after Linnaeus, who resembles it'. He may have been suffering from depression when he wrote the above comment, or was it just false modesty, since he was quite a self-publicist? The association with Linnaeus led to this being one of the most common plants in the world's herbaria, with tens of thousands of specimens collected from across its range (Stephen Harris, personal communication).

For today's botanists in Britain, Twinflower is not so insignificant, because it is one of the group of species that are largely confined to the pinewoods of Scotland, making their flora different to woods elsewhere in the country. Twinflower is found in both native and planted pinewoods, and occasionally turns up in birch–oak woods usually in light to moderate shade. Its low stature means that complete removal of grazing from sites is undesirable because the increased vigour of plants such as Bilberry may over-top it. Flowering shoots bear the eponymous two flowers, which are pollinated by solitary bees and hoverflies.

Twinflower disappeared from many sites prior to the 1930s because of woodland clearance, and it is still declining in Great Britain, both in terms of losing patches and reduction and fragmentation of individual patches. It is potentially at risk from climate change because its northern distribution suggests that it may grow less well as conditions get warmer. The main spread within a site is from shoots creeping through the moss carpet. The shoot connections eventually break down, and many apparently separate patches may be the same clone (Eriksson 1992, Wiberg *et al.* 2016).

Twinflower growing in a Scottish pinewood.

Self-fertilisation is rarely successful, so poor seed production reduces the chances that the plant can colonise new sites (Wilcock 2002, Scobie & Wilcock 2009).

To try to overcome this problem, plants from different sites which are likely to be genetically different have been planted around an existing Twinflower patch as part of conservation projects in the Cairngorm National Park. This should increase the chances of cross-fertilisation and seed set. Plants of 11 separate clones are being grown on, and four new mixed populations have been planted out at one site, with each population having a minimum of five clones to improve the chances that flowers will be cross-fertilised. The plans are to repeat this at other sites (Diana Gilbert, personal communication).

Twinflower has been recorded from time to time in northern England, but, like some other pinewood specialists, these records are usually treated as introductions, possibly associated with tree-planting. The same may be the case for some of the records from the lowlands of northeast Scotland (Welch 2003).

George Claridge Druce, botanist extraordinary, from the Fielding-Druce Herbarium, University of Oxford.

individuals and institutions built up herbaria, even if not on the scale or of the quality that Druce achieved. Many were no doubt what May Coley (1932) in her guide to botanical etiquette would call 'mournful collections', with poorly presented or incomplete specimens. The better collections are now, however, being used to explore the past distribution of species; as sources of DNA to look at the evolution of species; and also to see how flowering times have changed (chapter 16).

Collecting could be overdone. Arthur Church (1922) complained that people would 'devastate hedges and woodland, grabbing all available specimens of rarer flowers of aesthetic value for alleged decorative purposes'. He accused collectors of showing no compunction about taking rare plants for their herbaria or to exchange with other botanists. Giving the locality for a rare or interesting plant might be to sign its death warrant, although this was not a new concern. John Ray in 1660 noted that some species he listed might have been completely eradicated and carried off by root-collectors. Even today, botanists may be reluctant to publish precise coordinates for rare species, and the public records are fuzzied-up on maps.

Excessive collecting might have other consequences. May Coley wrote that 'Too much cannot be said against greedy and destructive gathering, so largely responsible for the closing of many secluded woods that might otherwise be open to the public' (Coley 1932). Certainly, in the late 19th and early 20th century the opportunities for casual botanising were starting to diminish. Common rights were being abolished, or simply not exercised, as the number of people living and working in the countryside declined. Privately-owned land became more private, particularly if game birds were involved. In the uplands the public were discouraged, even banned, from moors keepered for grouse and deer, while in the lowlands Arthur Church noted that woods were 'becoming more and more closed against the public and the favourite collecting grounds of an older generation of botanists are destroyed or are no longer available'.

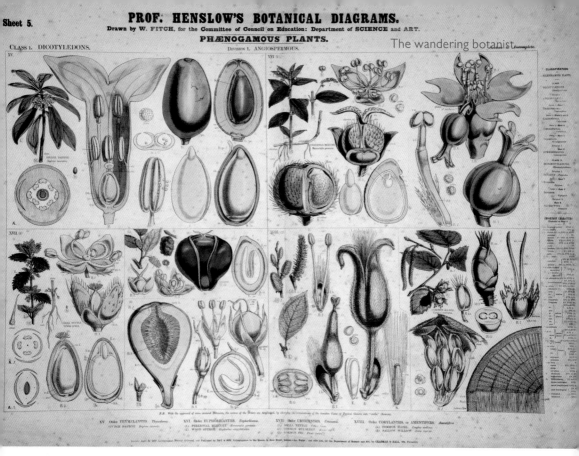

Identification guides and atlases

By the beginning of the 20th century the British flora was pretty well-defined, with fewer and fewer new species being added to the list, except amongst introductions and difficult groups such as brambles, Hawkweed *Hieracium* spp. and Dandelion *Taraxacum* spp. Identification guides allowed people to name plants through the use of keys based on descriptions, and sometimes drawings, of the species. The seventh edition of Bentham and Hooker's British Flora for example was my sixth-form biology introduction to the intricacies of the parts of a flower, the petals and sepals, stigmas and stamens, inferior and superior ovaries (Bentham *et al.* 1930).

Bentham *et al.*'s books were overtaken by Clapham, Tutin and Warburg's *Flora of the British Isles*, affectionately known amongst botanists as CTW (Clapham *et al.* 1962). This was for many people the standard work through to the 1980s. Other publication landmarks were the Reverend Keble-Martin's illustrations, Roger Phillips's series of photographic guides and Francis Rose's *The Wild Flower Key* (Keble-Martin 1965, Phillips 1977, Rose 1981, Rose &

A mid-19th-century teaching diagram showing the parts of a flower, from the Department of Plant Sciences, University of Oxford.

41

O'Reilly 2006). In recent years there has been the replacement of CTW by Stace's *New Flora of the British Isles* (Stace 2010). Plant identification often focuses on the flowers, but in woodland the heavy shade may prevent plants from producing any. Fortunately, one of the more recent guides is to plants in their vegetative state (Poland *et al.* 2009).

A different sort of landmark publication was the first *Atlas of the British Flora* produced by the Botanical Society of the British Isles (BSBI) in 1962 (2nd edition, Perring & Walters 1976), which showed the distribution of species by 10km squares (chapter 4). As with Geoffrey Grigson's study of plant names and uses, the timing proved to be critical: many of the records for where plants grew predated the effects of the post-war intensification in farming and forestry and the spread of urban development. The atlas thus acted as a baseline against which to show subsequent trends (mainly losses, but some gains) for different groups of species. A second atlas was produced for the millennium (Preston *et al.* 2002).

When the two atlases are compared, common species tend to have maintained their distribution and abundance; species that are tolerant of fertile conditions are more likely to have increased since 1962 than those found on infertile soils. Plants of shady conditions have generally done better than those of open conditions. Species associated with broadleaved woodland, for example, showed little change compared to the sharp declines for the weeds of arable fields. A third atlas project is currently under way.

My age and upbringing mean that I still mainly use books for identifying plants, but students on our first-year field course use their iPhones to pull up pictures of plants they are unfamiliar with. Photographs can be identified using apps such as iSpot, and the tedious business of plotting records by hand to produce a distribution map has been automated through use of spreadsheets, Geographic Information Systems (GIS) and Geographic Positioning Systems (GPS). Web technology has made it possible for people to access past records through the National Biodiversity Network, a partnership of organisations committed to sharing biodiversity information. It already holds more than 200 million records. However, whether you record using pen and clipboard, or hand-held data logger, identify plants from a book or the internet, you still have to go into the woods to find them.

Woodland surveys

The atlases produced by the BSBI map plant species by 10km squares and these can be used to give a national picture of species-distribution changes, but that does not tell us what has been happening to the plants in any individual wood. More detailed records are needed for that, and the simplest way of making a list is just to go on a 'walkabout' (Kirby & Hall 2019). Plot a route through the wood that aims to see as much of the ground as possible, picking up any obvious variations such as streams and glades, woodland edges, or variations up and down the slope. You can get an overview of what a wood of 20–30ha is like in a day by this method, with typically between 50 and 120 woodland species likely to be found.

A surveyor and trusty clipboard.

Species can be allocated to abundance categories such as Dominant, Abundant, Frequent, Occasional, Rare (the DAFOR scale). Most will fall into the Occasional/Rare categories, with just a few Frequent or Abundant. This system is useful, but rough and ready. It does not allow for precise statements to be made about the composition at specific points in the wood; comparisons over time between two walkabout surveys are difficult because what I call Abundant, you might call Frequent. Small, 'difficult-looking' plants may be ignored, in the hope that either they are something already recorded, or that a better specimen will be encountered later on in the walk.

Other botanists look in detail at a series of points using (usually square) plots or 'quadrats'. A fixed area of ground is defined, for example with a tape measure, and this is then systematically searched for plants. This forces you to look at the difficult areas (dense thickets) as well as easy ones, and all plants within the quadrat, even the awkward little ones, have to be considered. This standardised approach allows for quantitative comparisons to be made between quadrats placed in different parts of a wood, and between woods. In grassland, quadrats tend to be quite small, 1 × 1m or 2 × 2m, because species in grassland are usually tightly packed. This is nicely illustrated by Albrecht Dürer's famous painting *Der Grosse Rasenstück* (The Great Piece of Turf), which shows a range of grasses and herbs. In woods there are often swathes of just one species (Bracken, Bluebell, Ivy, Bilberry) or large patches of

Who chose this spot for a quadrat?

bare soil or litter in between clumps of plants. Small quadrats are not so useful, because they might contain only one or two species which would not make as exciting a painting!

Because of this, woodland surveyors tend to work with large quadrats, varying from about 4×4m as the smallest size in common use, to 14.1×14.1m or 30×30m. The larger the quadrat, the more species are likely to be found in it, but it takes more time to survey each one and there is a greater chance that species will be missed. Fewer quadrats can be recorded in a day. As a convenient compromise I usually use either 5×5m or 10×10m plots. The number of species found may not be much more than is found in the smaller areas sampled for grassland surveys, with generally fewer than 20 vascular plants in a 10×10m plot under shade and, occasionally, none at all.

The surveyor may deliberately place the quadrats to aid the description of a typical patch of woodland vegetation or a particularly unusual area. Alternatively, the quadrats may be distributed at random or as a systematic grid through the wood, so that statistically-valid analyses can be performed on the data. Other measurements such as the size and cover of the tree layer or the soil characteristics may be made at the same time as recording the ground flora. The variations in the distribution of plants can then be related to these other factors, such as the degree of shade, soil acidity, recent management, or evidence of browsing.

Quadrat recording involves more systematic and thorough recording than just listing plants seen on a walk, but a much smaller area of woodland is actually seen. Many species may not be picked up, because they happen not to be present at the spots where the quadrats have been placed. Six of us spent a good part of one spring and summer looking at how many species were found according to the number of quadrats recorded or the time spent on a walkabout through the same bit of woodland (Kirby *et al.* 1986). In Wytham we could easily pick up 80 species in the course of a three-hour walk; but to get that number of species recording quadrats through the same area took about twice as long. There was a similar result from the woods surveyed in Wales and Scotland. So, it depends on the objectives of your survey, as to which method is most appropriate, and if there is time, a combination of the two gives the best of both worlds.

If the quadrat positions are recorded precisely enough, then it is possible to return to the same spot some years later and see exactly how things have changed. I inherited from my supervisor the results from two such sets of permanent quadrats, established in the 1970s. One is at Wytham Woods, the other at the Warburg Reserve in Bix Bottom in south Oxfordshire. The first recordings were in 1973 and there have been several re-recordings since. Two overriding lessons emerge from these efforts. The first is how difficult it can be to re-find quadrats in woodland, even if you know that the quadrat is close by and that there are buried metal markers at its corners; the second is that the woodland flora can be much more variable over time than might at first be expected (Kirby & Thomas 2000).

Common plants can become rare, while rare plants may go locally extinct, and new plants may colonise a wood and start to spread. In Wytham Woods, between 1974 and 1991, Bramble went from being the dominant plant over large areas, to making an almost insignificant contribution to the structure of the ground flora. By 2018 it had recovered enough to become a trip hazard again. The grass False Brome *Brachypodium sylvaticum* was scarce in these woods in the 1970s but is now locally dominant.

The Wytham work is only one of many local and national surveys of woodland vegetation organised during the last half of the 20th century (Peterken 1993, Kirby *et al.* 2005). In the late 1970s and 1980s I spent a lot of time travelling round the country looking at woods with clipboard in hand and quadrat poles on my back. Many others were similarly engaged, as conservation organisations took advantage of funding available under the then Government's job creation programmes.

The results fed into the refinement of the woodland species list and into maps of the national distribution of species. Another major project set about looking at which species regularly grew together and how such groupings, sometimes called assemblages or communities, relate to soil conditions (chapter 5), climate differences across the country, or the effects of past management. These assemblages form what is now called the National Vegetation Classification (Rodwell 1991), described in chapters 6 and 7. However, one significant finding from the 1970s, arising from woodland surveys, was that old maps could be a useful way of identifying where rare and unusual woodland plants might be found, as discussed in the next chapter.

Historical influences and woodland plant distributions

I n the 1930s, a Norfolk landowner noticed that bluebells were concentrated in some woods but not others; he speculated that perhaps their presence was an indicator of woods that had always been there (Beevor 1925). Similarly, in the 1950s, Eustace Jones, an Oxford forest ecologist, noted that Herb-Paris was in Marley Wood and Wytham Great Wood, both areas mapped as woodland in 1780, but that the species almost never turned up in the adjacent belts of Oak and Ash planted in the early 19th century on old fields. It appeared that the range of plants to be found in a wood might be influenced by land-use history; so, could conservation priorities be developed by looking for woods that were shown on old maps (Goldberg *et al.* 2011)?

Ancient woodland indicators

In the 1970s George Peterken of the Nature Conservancy explored this link between history and plant distribution in a rather obscure part of eastern England. His work has since become a classic study and the Lincolnshire Limewoods now feature on local village signs. He found a range of species that were common only in woods present on maps since at least the 18th century (Peterken 1974). These included the grasses Wood Millet *Milium effusum* and Wood Melick *Melica uniflora*, Remote and Pendulous Sedge (*Carex remota*, *C. pendula*), and herbs such as Yellow Archangel *Lamiastrum galeobdolon*, Wood-sorrel *Oxalis acetosella* and Sweet Woodruff *Galium odoratum*. More or less independently, Oliver Rackham of the University of Cambridge found something similar in his woodland studies in East Anglia (Rackham 2003). Together they promoted the term 'ancient woodland' for those

OPPOSITE PAGE:
Goldilocks Buttercup, a plant often associated with ancient woodland.

The late Oliver Rackham, a charismatic woodland ecologist, in his element.

Andre & Chapman's 1771 map of woods around Navestock in Essex – most of which were still there when I was growing up in the 1950s.

sites that had been wooded for at least the last 300 years, Peterken adopting the threshold date of AD 1600 to define an ancient wood. Species that were common in ancient woods but found less often elsewhere came to be called 'ancient woodland indicators', and they form the core of the woodland specialist list.

Other ecologists have looked to see if there are similar 'indicator' species amongst insects, lichens and fungi, with mixed results. Bradfield Woods in Suffolk is a very well-documented ancient wood and has many ancient woodland indicator plants. However, it has almost no important lichen indicators because there are few freestanding large, old trees of the type the rarer lichens require. Nevertheless, ancient woods do generally contain more of the uncommon species, across a range of species groups, than recently-created woodland.

Ancient woodland can be identified by its occurrence on old maps and through references in historical documents. It used to be quite laborious to find and copy the relevant maps or track down the estate papers in which a wood was mentioned, but these searches have become easier now that much of the material has been digitised and is available via the internet. Geographic information systems (GIS) can be used to overlay different sources to explore the history of particular patches of ground.

Accurate large-scale maps for much of the country are only available from the early 19th century and there are very few before about 1750. Woods might only be mentioned in documents in passing and many are not referred to directly at all. Where no documentary evidence is available, then field observations of the structure of woods, their place in the landscape and the nature of any boundary banks can help to fill the gaps in a wood's history. Ancient woodland indicator plants (mentioned above) have become an important part of the evidence used.

The principle is straightforward. Take a group of woods that can be shown to have existed for several centuries from independent evidence such as maps and old documents. Compare their flora with the plants found in a similar set of woods known to have developed (through planting or natural regeneration) on open ground in the last two centuries. Species found in greater abundance in the first set may depend on a long history of woodland cover. So, the presence of these species in other woods might then suggest that that wood is also ancient, even where there is no documentary or map evidence available. In practice things are not that simple.

Species might be good ancient woodland indicators in some parts of the country, but not in other regions: Great Wood-rush *Luzula sylvatica* was largely confined to ancient woods in Peterken's Lincolnshire study but is regularly found outside woodland in western Great Britain, where it is an important component of the tall-herb community found on rock ledges. The Lincolnshire ancient woodland indicators Wood Millet and Wood-sorrel were strongly associated with ancient

Wood-sorrel: quite a good ancient woodland indicator in eastern England, but less so in the west of Great Britain.

woods in Essex and East Anglia, but Goldilocks Buttercup *Ranunculus auricomus*, Wild Garlic, Sanicle *Sanicula europaea* and Early Dog-violet *Viola reichenbachiana* were not (Rackham 2003). Before we can use plants as indicators of past landscapes, we need to understand how and why woodland history might affect current distribution patterns.

Lasting effects of woodland history

Much of Great Britain may once have been tree-covered, but now the known ancient woods cover only a few percent of the country, usually as small patches less than 10 hectares in size (Roberts *et al.* 1992, Spencer & Kirby 1992). Ancient woods often survive at the edges of parishes, on soils that were difficult or unprofitable for farming, or on very steep slopes. Species might be associated with ancient woodland simply because the plant's needs coincide with the conditions that discouraged people from clearing woodland in the first place.

Woodland generally has a more stable and more humid microclimate than the surrounding landscape. Inside a wood it is usually less breezy, cooler in summer, but warmer in winter than outside, because of the shelter from the trees and shrubs. These differences in conditions inside and outside woods are greatest in eastern England. Species may have become trapped in ancient woodland patches because they do not grow well in the drier conditions found in the surrounding open landscape. In the west of Great Britain, however, where the weather is generally milder and moister, species that are good indicators in eastern England, such as Primrose and Wood Anemone, can be widespread outside woods.

For a species to spread from an ancient to a recently-established wood, the new wood has to be within the plant's dispersal distance. Some woodland plants have seeds that spread for several kilometres on the wind, for example the downy parachutes of Marsh Thistle *Cirsium palustre*. The seeds of many ancient woodland indicators lack mechanisms to allow them to travel such long distances and rarely spread more than a few metres or tens of metres at a time (chapter 8). Some rarely set seed at all and rely on slow vegetative spread: they are unlikely to make it across a ploughed field.

If dispersal is the limiting factor, ancient woodland indicators might be expected to spread more successfully where the overall woodland cover is higher and the distances between woods are less. Indeed, in heavily-wooded areas such as the Chilterns and the Weald of south-east England, the Wye Valley or the oakwoods of the west coast of Scotland, there are fewer differences between ancient and recent woods in terms of their ground flora than in eastern England with its thin scatter of isolated woods. Ancient woodland indicators might also be expected to occur more often in new woodland that has grown up next to an ancient wood than in isolated patches surrounded by arable fields or improved pasture, which again is what research often shows (Peterken & Game 1984).

However, even if the seeds, or young plants, of ancient woodland indicators are deliberately introduced to new woods, the plants do not always prosper, particularly if the woods are growing on ex-arable fields (chapter 15). The soils in such woods are generally more fertile than those of nearby ancient woods; this allows taller, more competitive woodland generalists to thrive, outcompeting the lower-growing woodland specialists. The increased fertility is caused partly by ploughing that mixes up the surface soil layers and partly from added fertiliser. The soils of ex-grassland fields have generally been altered less by long-term farming practices, but the distribution of soil water, soil structure, organic matter and nutrients may still be different from those of nearby ancient woodland. In particular, the soil fungi on former farmland sites are not likely to be the same as those in ancient woods, which may affect whether specialist woodland plants grow well or not.

Woodland plant movement through this mixed landscape (Eastnor Park, Herefordshire) is likely to be better than in poorly-wooded areas.

Some ancient woods were once open ground, even if they have been wooded since 1600, and there may still be legacies in the soil from these past land-uses. Parts of Epping Forest overlie Iron Age encampments, for example. Similarly, Peterken (1993) noted that Papworth and Overhall Grove Woods in Cambridgeshire were ancient (pre-1600 origin) but had grown up on the remains of medieval fields and buildings. These two woods still lacked some ancient woodland plants found in other nearby ancient woods and had more Nettle, Hogweed and Cleavers. French researchers looked at forests which had grown up on abandoned Roman farms and compared them with areas that were probably woodland in the Roman era (Dupouey *et al.* 2002). Some ancient woodland plants had colonised the old farmland and were more common there, for example Goldilocks Buttercup, Wood Millet and Sweet Woodruff. Other species such as Barren Strawberry *Potentilla sterilis*, Wood Barley *Hordelymus europaeus* and Lily-of-the-valley were more common in the forest remote from the Roman settlement.

Centuries of woodland management may have impoverished ancient woodland soils. Some nutrients would have been lost from the wood when timber was taken away, or when leaf litter was removed, for bedding for livestock (chapter 5). Some ancient woodland plants may actually depend on these centuries of soil impoverishment, because they can survive better against woodland generalists in low nutrient conditions.

There is no single reason why a plant may be linked to ancient woodland, but rather it depends on the history of forest clearance in a region, how much woodland cover there is now, what is between the woods and what the soils are like. Each species will respond to a given set of conditions in a slightly different way, as illustrated by the Dog's Mercury story.

A shady history

Dog's Mercury *Mercurialis perennis*, like many woodland plants, is potentially poisonous. The 'dog' in its name suggests that the herbalists saw it as an inferior version of Annual Mercury *Mercurialis annua* that was regarded as useful for making enemas. Other local names are equally unflattering, such as Snakeweed and Boggart-posy (Jefferson & Kirby 2011). Dog's Mercury is widespread in Great Britain south of the Great Glen, predominantly on neutral to base-rich (not acid) soils (Jefferson 2008). The abandonment of coppicing in many ancient woods during the 20th century, and the increase in closed canopy high forest since the 1950s, has favoured the species because it is one of our most shade-tolerant plants. Its dense carpets can exclude virtually all other ground flora species. This makes for quick, but monotonous, plant recording.

Dog's Mercury is however susceptible to disturbance from forest management and trampling, as is evident where there are bare paths of badgers, or humans running through dense Mercury patches. In the past, pigs or Wild Boar foraging in woods would have limited its dominance, as does deer grazing now. At Monks Wood, near Huntingdon, large areas that were dominated by Dog's Mercury in the 1970s had become grass and sedge dominated by the 1990s. This was attributed to an increase in deer populations, particularly Muntjac (Steele & Welch 1973, Cooke & Farrell 2001).

The emerging bright green shoots of Dog's Mercury are one of the first signs of spring in many woods, and this early start to growth may explain its sensitivity to spring waterlogging. In Hayley Wood in Cambridgeshire, it yields to the Oxlip on the wetter central area. In the 1900s,

Despite its unpleasant taste Dog's Mercury is eaten by deer, and thrives here only in a cage.

Dog's Mercury flowers are some of the earliest to appear in spring.

at nearby Gamlingay Wood, a large area was dominated by Meadowsweet, which prefers relatively wet open woodland (Adamson 1912), but by 1991 the Meadowsweet had largely been replaced by Dog's Mercury (Rackham 2003). The changes were put down to drying out of the soils through abandonment of coppicing and the planting of conifers in parts of the wood in the 1950s.

Peterken and Game (1981) demonstrated how woodland history can affect the distribution of Dog's Mercury in their study area in central Lincolnshire. Of the 154 places where they found Dog's Mercury, 119 were in ancient woods or hedges (where the plant might have survived for centuries) with only 35 populations definitely the result of establishment within the last two hundred years. The 35 long-distance colonisations were presumably from the spread of seed, perhaps carried on the coats of animals such as deer or hares.

Once established, however, the plant can spread through underground stems to form a clonal patch. Clones are all of one sex because Dog's Mercury plants produce only either male or female flowers. Vegetative spread is relatively slow, variously estimated as about a metre or two per year, and so new populations are generally small and uniform. Over time, if a seed of the opposite sex establishes or if stray pollen blows in from another population, more mixed populations might eventually arise.

In the Lincolnshire Limewoods it was reasonable to describe Dog's Mercury as an ancient woodland indicator, but Peterken and Game noted that on drier, more calcareous soils, away from the clays, Dog's Mercury spreads more easily, making it less useful as an indicator. Merton (1970), working in the limestone woods of the Derbyshire Dales, found Dog's Mercury to be almost ubiquitous. In Wytham Woods Dog's Mercury is similarly almost as common in the recent woodland as it is in the ancient woods. Where soil conditions are favourable more seed will be produced so the chances of some of it carrying a long way are increased; clonal spread will also be more extensive under good growing conditions. This is part of the reason that ancient woodland lists need to be region-specific.

Dog's Mercury and bluebells on Rough Common (part of Wytham Woods), an area that historically has been limestone grassland, apart from a brief spell as scrub in the 1970s.

A proliferation of ancient woodland indicator lists

During the 1980s, concern about the clearance and replanting of ancient woodland became widespread. Ancient woodland indicators were seen as a simple way of identifying these valuable woods and getting them on to the county lists, being prepared by the Nature Conservancy Council, that have become known as the Ancient Woodland Inventory. People built on the work of Peterken and Rackham and developed indicator lists for their own part of the country (Glaves *et al.* 2009). Some of the lists were, like the Lincolnshire work, based on independent historical studies to test whether the distribution of a species in ancient versus recent woodland was significantly different; other lists were based on local botanists' interpretation of where species grew.

The lists produced were of very different lengths, partly because different criteria were used to judge whether a species was sufficiently associated with ancient woodland to be classed as an indicator. If the criteria were too strict very few species would qualify. In Lincolnshire, there were species, such as Common Cow-wheat *Melampyrum pratense*, recorded only from ancient woods and never from recent ones (Peterken 2000). However, restricting the list to just those few species would not be very helpful. Most ancient woods did not contain any of them because the species were uncommon in Lincolnshire generally. Bringing in species, such as Wood Anemone, which was found in most ancient woods, increased the chances that all ancient woods could be detected, but Anemone was also recorded from some recent woods. This would lead to 'false positives' – recent woods that were identified as ancient. From a conservation perspective, the risk of missing some ancient woods (by having a short, strict list) is more serious than including some recent woods through having a longer list. After all, a recent wood with a good flora may still be important for conservation.

Is there a minimum number of indicator plants that must be present for a wood to be ancient? This too is affected by the length of the list: ten species from a potential list of 20 might be considered a good score; ten out of a list of 100 would not mean as much. Castle *et al.* (2008) suggested a minimum of 25 indicator species present in a 2ha sample plot in their Welsh woodland study. In Northern Ireland sites a threshold number was devised based on the average number of indicators expected for a wood of a given size (Woodland Trust 2006).

An archetypal ancient woodland specialist – Herb-Paris *Paris quadrifolia*

This distinctive member of the Lily family has (usually) four leaves, a central flower and black berry. It is widespread across Europe, except in the Mediterranean region (Jacquemyn *et al.* 2008). Through much of England it tends to be on somewhat moist, calcareous soils, also amongst limestone pavements. There is a scatter of records from highland Scotland, including from Skye and the Black Isle, but it is largely absent from Devon, Cornwall and western Wales and it is one of the plants that seems not to have made it to Ireland.

The leaves emerge in the spring, the precise time depending on the soil temperatures, but by mid-summer they start to die back,

particularly in drought conditions. Late surveys may miss the plant altogether. There may be more flowers in the open stages of coppice woods or at the edges of stands, but it can persist under deep shade (such as in my Bramble patches in Wytham, chapter 1). Colonies of plants tend to appear in the same place every year and individual plants might live for more than a century in good conditions.

The first documented record for Great Britain was from William Turner in the 16th century who wrote about the 'Libbardsbane', also known as 'Oneberrie' from Cotting Wood on the edge of Morpeth, in Northumberland (Marren 1999). Peter Marren, then the local

Alder-Horsetail flushes at Cotting Wood, near Morpeth, sheltering Herb-Paris. INSET: A possible descendant of Willam Turner's 'Oneberrie'.

Nature Conservancy Council officer, tried (unsuccessfully) to make the site a Site of Special Scientific Interest in the 1970s because of its botanical history. I visited the wood to pay homage to this first record in 2017. The initial appearance of the wood was not promising. The flora of Brambles, Broad Buckler-fern *Dryopteris dilatata*, and Honeysuckle seemed to indicate conditions a bit too free-draining and acid for Paris; there were signs of old planting, in the form of introduced Sweet and Horse Chestnut (*Castanea sativa*, *Aesculus hippocastanum*) amongst the native oak and birch; a series of ridges and hollows across the slope might be natural slippage, but I feared they were probably past mineral working; and there were various tracks created by mountain bikers.

Dropping down the slope to the burn, the flora perked up. In the end I saw 42 species in about half an hour, including Broad-leaved Helleborine *Epipactis helleborine*, Sanicle, Primrose and Wood Anemone. There were wet alder flushes filled with large horsetails and sedges, and Hazel and Ash along the burn with Dog's Mercury, Enchanter's-nightshade *Circaea lutetiana* and Wood-avens *Geum urbanum*. Appropriately, given that Turner was a herbalist, there were patches of Goutweed naturalised on the slumping banks of the burn. Everything looked right for Herb-Paris, and eventually there it was, nestling on the edge of the horsetail flushes. The leaves were starting to go yellow, but some plants had the distinctive plump glossy black fruits.

Like many woodland plants, Herb-Paris is poisonous, which may provide some protection against grazing by small mammals such as voles. It is not generally lethal to humans and was recommended in the past as an emetic. The toxin levels are lower in the berries and these may be eaten by mammals and birds. This could help with the spread of the seed, provided either that the berries are hoarded and not subsequently eaten, or that the seed can pass through the animal unharmed. In practice, much seed is damaged and so there is little spread this way. Consequently, patches of Paris may expand by less than a metre a year.

In south-east Sweden seed was sown experimentally into unoccupied patches to test whether this slow dispersal was the problem for Herb-Paris and other similar species such as Lily-of-the-Valley and Baneberry *Actaea spicata*, or whether the soil in patches where it did not occur was unsuitable for it. The new Paris plants did establish and, although there was a gradual loss over the years, some were still present eleven years on (Ehrlén *et al.* 2006). Elsewhere seeds introduced to new patches grew better on moist sites and had greater levels of genetic variation. Dry sites were more likely to be dominated by large patches of Herb-Paris that were all one clone (Jacquemyn *et al.* 2006).

Herb-Paris does turn up naturally in new woods if the conditions are right. On the Continent, it has been found in recent scrub by rivers in the Pyrenees. Richard Mabey (1996) reported that it was spreading into deciduous plantations and self-sown woods on the Cotswold plateau, while I have seen it in alderwoods near Newbury that were mapped as floodplain meadows in the early 19th century (unfortunately a recent survey failed to find any Paris). In general, though, Herb-Paris relies mainly on persisting at one place, through being long-lived, highly shade-tolerant and poisonous. That this strategy can work well is demonstrated by its survival for nearly 500 years at Cotting Wood.

Generally, the more indicator species there are present the more likely it is that a wood is ancient, but there can be no guarantee that it is. Recent detailed historical research in Norfolk, for example, has shown that woods or parts of woods with a good range of ancient woodland indicators are not ancient according to the map evidence. D'Oyly's Grove, planted after 1767, contained Dog's Mercury, Early-purple Orchid *Orchis mascula*, Remote Sedge, Yellow Archangel, Pignut and even Herb-Paris (Barnes & Willliamson 2015). The distribution of the indicator species may help in such situations; if they are strongly clustered along one side of the woodland, this might suggest that only part of the wood is ancient, or that there has been spread in from an adjacent older wood or hedge. In one Essex wood, Oxlip was only along one side of a 19th-century plantation on old fields where it had jumped the ride from the adjacent ancient woodland.

The number of indicators present is also affected by the size of the wood. Large woods generally contain more plant species than small ones and the difference in the numbers of indicators between ancient and recent woods tends to be clearer in the larger sites. In woods around the Malvern Hills both small ancient and small recent woods (up to about 5ha) might contain as many as 20 indicators (Hill 2003). A complication is that surveys in small woods may pick up most of the indicators that are present but find only a much lower proportion of those present in a large wood, simply because it takes a lot longer to thoroughly search a large wood. So, comparing indicator numbers across woods of different sizes may be misleading because more of those in a large wood will have been missed.

Fewer vascular plant species occur on acid soils than on base-rich fertile ones, meaning that there are fewer potential indicators for acid woods. Whereas a wood on base-rich soils might have 20 or 30 species, a similar-sized wood on acid soils might only have a dozen such vascular plants. More vascular plant indicators are found in woods with a mixture of woodland types than in woods that have a uniform vegetation. Francis Rose (1999) found that the richest woods in southern England were equally split between acid and calcareous soils, because the chalk woods tended to be rather uniform, whereas the acid-clay woods often had more calcareous wet flushes in them, which added greatly to their overall richness.

The way different factors influence the number of indicators found is illustrated by the example of Sydlings Copse near Oxford. This is quite a small ancient wood that probably regenerated on open ground sometime before the 13th century. We might expect therefore only a few ancient woodland indicator plants. However, at least 43 indicator species (out of a potential list for southern England of 100 species) have been recorded (Day 1993). Its richness reflects the diversity of soil conditions found within this small valley.

Indicate with caution

If there are plants that indicate ancient woodland, are there others that occur more often in recent woodland? Rackham (2003) considered that in eastern England Cow Parsley *Anthriscus sylvestris*, Hedge Garlic, Spurge-laurel *Daphne laureola* and Sweet Violet *Viola odorata* had a definite affinity for recent woodland, only rarely occurring in ancient woods and then usually near the edges.

Peterken (1993) described the flora of recent woods in his Lincolnshire study as essentially an expanded hedgerow flora. Species that were relatively fast colonists of new woods (found in more than half of the woods that were no more than 150 years old) included Lords-and-Ladies, Herb-Robert *Geranium robertianum*, Ground Ivy and Three-veined Sandwort *Moehringia trinervia*. Other specialists, found less frequently, were Giant Fescue *Schedonorus giganteus*, Twayblade *Neottia ovata*, Sanicle and Hairy-brome *Bromopsis ramosa*. Even woods that had grown up on Lincolnshire farmland were not all nettles, Ivy and Bramble (see chapter 15).

Several decades of studies have largely confirmed Peterken's original caution: inferring woodland history from the flora is not as straightforward as it first appears. The various lists suggest that there are plants, such as Wood Anemone, that find it either difficult to move to, or establish in, new sites, but sometimes they can. At the other end of the spectrum are the woodland generalists such as brambles and nettles that are well able to colonise new woodland, as well as being common in non-woodland habitats. Generalists tend to be more common than specialist species, almost by definition, but there are other factors that influence whether a plant is common or rare (chapter 4).

Commonness
and rarity

In the late 1970s I was surveying a wood in Cumbria and picked a leaf of a plant I had not seen before, to show to my boss. To my consternation it was quite rare, Mezereon, and he wanted to know exactly where I had found it, in case it was a new record for that 10km square. If it had been (it wasn't), it would have been recorded as another spot on the map in the *New Atlas of the British and Irish Flora* (Preston *et al.* 2002). Such maps enable us to explore which are the most widespread and which the rarest of our woodland plants; the atlas also contains notes on which species are probably native to Great Britain and which may have been introduced by humans. These distinctions can shape conservation priorities and actions, with more attention focused on rare and native species than on common or introduced ones.

Common woodland plants

Michael Proctor (2013) of Exeter University used the atlas data to find the 75 species that had been recorded from more than 85% of the 2,823 10km squares in Great Britain. Many are pasture and wetland species, but 40 are on my woodland list, mostly generalists such as Bramble, Bracken, Cleavers and Nettle, but also Herb-Robert, Primrose, Dog-violet and Bush Vetch *Vicia sepium*. Not surprisingly, these plants were also generally common in a separate survey of broadleaved woods across Great Britain. Bramble, Broad Buckler and Male-ferns *Dryopteris filix-mas*, *D. affinis*, Dog-violet, Honeysuckle, Nettle, Bracken, Enchanter's-nightshade, Herb-Robert and Wood Avens were all present in at least 80% of sites; Dog's Mercury and Cleavers were in more than 70% of sites, Primrose more than 60%, although Bush Vetch only in 29% (Kirby *et al.* 2005).

OPPOSITE PAGE:
Mezereon – a rare plant: the specimen I once accidentally found in Witherslack Woods, Cumbria, had far fewer flowers.

Within any one wood there are usually only a few species that are abundant, with the rest mostly present as scattered plants or just locally common, contributing little to the overall herbaceous cover. The few generally-common species largely determine how the wood functions, what it looks like, even sometimes the appearance of the wider landscape. In 1974 I chose Bramble to work on in Wytham because it covered about a third of the ground and was the most important species in terms of the biomass of the ground flora.

The plants most likely to dominate the ground flora are Bramble, Ivy, Nettle, Bracken, and one woodland specialist, Dog's Mercury. Between them these five species cover much of the spread of soil variations found in British woods, excluding only very wet and very acid conditions. They do however have their weaknesses – Bramble and Ivy are grazed by deer, Dog's Mercury is sensitive to trampling, Bracken is not tolerant of deep shade, while Nettle needs high levels of phosphates to thrive. Different forms of disturbance, from tree-falls to trampling, and variations in conditions across a landscape ensure that there is space left for the rest of the woodland flora.

Oak over Bracken in the Forest of Dean.

Beech Fern, a north-westerly species.

Among less widespread species some common distribution patterns emerge. There are the species that are rarely found north of a line from the Thames Estuary to south Wales, such as Southern Wood-rush *Luzula forsteri* and Butcher's-broom *Ruscus aculeatus*. Others, for example Spurge-laurel and Thin-spiked Wood-sedge *Carex strigosa* extend their range through most of the lowlands to roughly a line from Durham to Anglesey, often with some gaps in central and eastern England where woodland cover is scattered. A large group reaches into the lowlands of Scotland but are largely absent from the central and northern Highlands, including Moschatel *Adoxa moschatellina* and Hairy-brome. Some species show the reverse patterns: Beech Fern *Phegopteris connectilis* and Lemon-scented Fern *Oreopteris limbosperma*, for example, show a strongly northern and westerly distribution, while a small group including Creeping Ladies-tresses *Goodyera repens* and Serrated Wintergreen *Orthilia secunda* is largely confined to the Highlands of Scotland.

Some rare woodland plants

At the rare end of the occurrence spectrum are the species whose fate is more likely to get the headlines than that of Bramble or Nettle. People often associate orchids with rarity and some of our rarest woodland plants are indeed orchids. The Ghost Orchid *Epipogium aphyllum* for example was even declared extinct in 2005 because it had not been reported since 1986, only to reappear again in the last decade (Jannink & Rich 2010). However, not all orchids are rare – the Early-purple and Common Spotted-orchid *Dactylorhiza fuchsii* are widespread across Great Britain (50% and 68% of 10km squares respectively) and can be locally common. Conversely, plants from other families such as the Starved Wood-sedge *Carex depauperata* (present in two 10km squares), or the Spiked Rampion *Phyteuma spicatum* (present in four squares) can be very rare. (The status of the latter is under review and it may end up being classed as an introduction.)

Looking at where a species occurred in the past may indicate whether it has always had a rather limited distribution in Britain, or whether it has only recently become rare. In the Fielding-Druce Herbarium in the Department of Plant Sciences, University of Oxford, are 32 specimens of the Italian Lords-and-Ladies *Arum italicum* collected in the 19th/early 20th centuries from a scatter of sites across southern England. These reflect its current distribution quite well, so it has probably never been much more common. Other species where the collected specimens largely match the current distribution include the Red Helleborine *Cephalanthera rubra* (seven specimens collected between 1799 and 1902). This is largely restricted to the western Cotswolds around Stroud, where it still just manages to hold on, with a few other records from south-east England. There are five specimens of the Large Yellow Sedge *Carex flava*, three from its current stronghold at Roudsea Wood, Cumbria; for the Coralroot Orchid *Corallorhiza trifida* there are 19 specimens from eastern Scotland and northern England (collected 1833–1916). Of more conservation concern will be those species that were once more widespread and have declined so much that they are now classed as rare, such as the Crested Cow-wheat, which John Ray had found in many local woods but is now in only a handful of sites there.

A paradox is that rare species can be extremely abundant locally. The Oxlip occurs in only 29 10km squares, tightly clustered in eastern England, but within the woods there it can occur by the thousands. The Narrow-leaved Helleborine *Cephalanthera longifolia* is more widespread, being found from Hampshire up to the west coast of Scotland, but in only slightly more (34) 10km squares than the Oxlip and in most woods only present as a few individuals.

What's so special about the Oxlip?

The true Oxlip *Primula elatior* was among many species first identified by John Ray in about 1660, from Kingston Wood, west of Cambridge. One of Ray's successors at Cambridge, Oliver Rackham (2003), became a great champion of the plant, researching its changing fortunes at Hayley Wood, near Huntingdon. Its flower is somewhere between that of the Primrose and the Cowslip, and the hybrid between the two is called the False Oxlip. Grigson (1975), rather harshly, described the False Oxlip as a 'coarse hybrid... lacking the charm of either parent or of the woodland Oxlip', but it looks attractive to me. It was probably the False Oxlip that Oberon refers to in *A Midsummer Night's Dream*: 'I know a bank where the wild thyme blows, where oxlips and the nodding violet grows' – since Shakespeare would not have come across the true Oxlip in Warwickshire. Historically, the true and the false were often confused, and only in the 19th century was it generally recognised that the true Oxlip did also occur in Britain (Christy 1897).

The true Oxlip is a long-lived herb that can be considered the Continental equivalent of the Primrose. In Great Britain the Oxlip grows on slightly less acid and more clay-rich soils than its commoner relative (Taylor & Woodell 2008), mainly in woods, particularly ancient woods, although on the Continent it is also often found in meadows and wood-pastures. It is not a rare plant on a European scale, but its British distribution is restricted to a small area of north Essex, Suffolk and Cambridgeshire. This is the part of the country closest to the Continent with respect to its climate and is also close to where there was once a direct connection via the Dogger Bank land-bridge. By contrast, the Primrose is nearly ubiquitous across Great Britain, but largely restricted to the Atlantic zone on the Continent (see Chapter 13). The two species almost never occur together.

The true Oxlip.

Within the woods where it occurs the Oxlip can be abundant, flowering profusely in recently coppiced patches. Miller Christy (1897), an early enthusiast for the plant, describes the ground as appearing yellow all round and '… by counting the number of plants growing on a typical space measuring four yards square and the number of umbels those plants bore, I was able to estimate that each acre bore about 70,000 plants … an estimate I have reason to believe was very much below the mark.'

In Hayley Wood the Oxlip occupies the poorly-drained soils, being particularly tolerant of spring-waterlogging. In hot, dry summers, the leaves die back earlier, so fewer reserves are available for producing the next year's leaves and flowers. The exceptional drought years of 1975 and 1976 contributed to a crash in its numbers at Hayley Wood, but increasing numbers of Fallow Deer also had a major impact (Rackham 1975). When deer were fenced out of the coppiced areas the flower populations recovered.

Oxlips do not have any obvious long-distance seed-dispersal mechanism, although the seeds may be moved over short distances by ants. This slow colonisation rate provided Rackham with the opportunity for another elegant conservation study. He carefully mapped the spread of oxlips from the ancient part of Hayley Wood into an adjacent triangular field that became wooded only in the 1920s, and established that by the 1970s the oxlips were most abundant close to the boundary between old and new woodland. During the 1990s they thinned out, probably because of the deer pressure, but colonisation of The Triangle continued. However, even after 80 years oxlips had not spread through the entire area.

Hempstead Wood in Essex was also noted for its Oxlip, one of the reasons why the wood was notified as a Site of Special Scientific Interest in 1973, although part of the site had been felled and replanted with conifers by the Forestry Commission during the 1960s (chapter 9). Further replanting led to reductions in the Oxlip populations from the effects of the shade and litter of the Corsican Pine. A colleague and I visited the wood in the early 1980s for the Nature Conservancy Council and concluded that we could not justify keeping it on our books, so the wood was de-notified. Following a change in forestry policy in 1985, the conifers started to be removed and coppicing was restored (chapter 18). There was an initial recovery of the Oxlip population at Hempstead, but it has proved difficult to keep the deer pressure down. Much of the ground is now covered by dense Pendulous Sedge, which can tolerate high deer levels and outcompetes the Oxlip, so they have not regained their former glory at this wood.

Oxlip is common further south in Europe and so with climate change it might be expected to benefit from warmer summers. However, its sensitivity to summer droughts may lead to more frequent population crashes. Small populations are vulnerable to further erosion by deer nibbling the leaves, which reduces the likelihood of flowering the subsequent year; scattered groups of flowers attract fewer pollinators than massed displays, which may mean less seed is set per plant. As most of its locations are in isolated woods the chances of seed spreading to new sites, or back into old sites from which it has been lost, are low. This might be a case where we should consider assisting its (re-)colonisation (chapter 19).

A widespread rare orchid

The Narrow-leaved Helleborine *Cephalanthera longifolia* is an orchid found throughout Europe, but unlike the Oxlip it tends to occur as scattered individuals or as small groups. This makes it particularly vulnerable to local extinction from even small operations in the wrong place, as when a colony was lost to roadworks in the Wye Valley (Marren 1999). In Great Britain the species declined markedly in the 19th and early 20th centuries, through collecting and the loss of the open woodland in which it usually occurs, as management such as coppicing, or the grazing of cattle in woodland, became uneconomic. More recently, flowering may be being reduced by deer grazing, as with the Oxlip.

There remains a dense cluster of records from Hampshire and Sussex. The largest individual population is thought to be at Chappett's Copse, a reserve owned by the Hampshire and Isle of Wight Wildlife Trust. Exceptionally here there are several thousand plants: they have benefited from opening-up of the canopy and reduction of competition from Dog's Mercury and Bramble through cutting. In another Hampshire wood the canopy was thinned, and autumn sheep grazing introduced, leading to an increase in both plant numbers and seed-pods per plant over a ten-year period (Ian Taylor, personal communication). More usually the orchid is found as just a few individual plants.

The species only grows on base-rich soils such as those on chalk. In limestone woods of northern England, the Narrow-leaved Helleborine was often found with Lady's-slipper Orchid *Cypripedium calceolus* in the 19th century but both have since declined in these woods. However, since the 1960s the Helleborine has been found on other types of base-rich rock along the west coast of Scotland.

Narrow-leaved Helleborine.

This was where I first came across it during surveys in Argyll and Lochaber in the 1980s. In Scotland, the semi-shaded conditions it needs occur naturally on steep rocky slopes with open tree canopy which tend to be places that deer and sheep avoid.

Seed dispersal per se may not be a problem, because, like most orchids, its seeds are small and dust-like, carried far and wide on the wind. However, such seeds contain very few reserves of nutrients because they are so small. They depend on making contact with a fungal associate from which they then derive the material they need to establish and grow. If the right fungus is not present the seedling cannot survive. This type of mycorrhizal relationship is discussed further in the next chapter.

Because of the declines in its abundance, the Narrow-leaved Helleborine was one of the species targeted for conservation efforts under the UK Biodiversity Action Plan developed in the 1990s. In southern England, its conservation is likely to depend on encouraging woodland management that creates and maintains openings in the woods, but in Scotland the emphasis is more on ensuring that there is the right level of grazing: not too much, but enough to stop the woods becoming too dense.

Oxlip outcompeted by dense Pendulous Sedge patches.

The tricky question of 'nativeness'

A common principle in British nature conservation is to give priority to native species, usually defined as those that have arrived during this post-glacial period (the last 10,000–12,000 years) without human intervention. By contrast, species such as Rhododendron, Norway Spruce *Picea abies* and Silver Fir *Abies alba*, although present in Great Britain in previous inter-glacial periods, did not (as far as we know) recolonise naturally after the last ice retreat. Rather, they have been reintroduced in historical times. More recent introductions from other parts of the world include Sitka Spruce *Picea sitchensis* from North America, Giant Hogweed *Heracleum mantegazzianum* from the Caucasus and Hottentot-fig *Carpobrotus edulis* from South Africa.

Humans, however, have been present throughout this post-glacial period, and separating introductions from native species becomes more difficult the further back in time we go. We cannot rule out the possibility that some species might have had a helping hand to get here. Rare arable weeds that are now a conservation priority were almost certainly inadvertently introduced by humans with the advent of farming. Along wood-edges White Dead-nettle *Lamium album* is an old introduction, established in the wild by 1500, as is the Field Pansy *Viola arvensis*, found along woodland rides.

A species whose origins are debatable and debated, probably because it is attractive, is the Snowdrop *Galanthus nivalis*. There have been claims that this might be native at a couple of places in south-west England, but it is absent from much of western Europe as a native species, and written references to it outside gardens are quite recent. It is now generally considered an introduction to Great Britain, but is thoroughly naturalised, that is

White Dead-nettle, an old introduction to Great Britain, now common on woodland edges.

it grows well and freely regenerates in the wild. Similar discussions have taken place over the northern Continental species, May Lily *Maianthemum bifolium*, but for this species the decision reached was that it is native in some British woods. In other locations it is classed in the *New Atlas of the British and Irish Flora* (2002) as introduced, including at one of its strongholds at Swanton Novers in Norfolk.

May Lily – a debated native.

Preston *et al.* (2002) point out that the native distributions are complicated, sometimes totally obscured by garden escapes for various species including Monk's-hood *Aconitum napellus*, Columbine, Giant Bellflower, Coralroot Bitter-cress *Cardamine bulbifera*, Pendulous Sedge, Meadow Saffron *Colchicum autumnale*, Stinking Hellebore and Butcher's-broom. Even within a region where a species may be native, there may be deliberate introductions to sites where it was not formerly present as part of efforts to create more species-rich woodland (Blakesley & Buckley 2010). Such introductions are likely to increase in future, as discussed in chapter 15.

Some species generally considered as introductions to Great Britain, such as Sycamore *Acer pseudoplatanus* (probably brought in sometime in the early medieval period), could conceivably have reached here independently. For example, a big storm, such as that of 1703 or 1987, could have blown its seeds across the Channel, and these might then have established here naturally. If this could ever be shown to have happened, would we now treat Sycamore as a native species?

Attitudes to introductions are seldom completely logical. I recently came across May Lily in a Kent wood; I assume it was planted there, but it seemed to fit just as well as if it had been a patch of Herb-Paris. Ten minutes later I came across a similar patch of introduced Small Balsam *Impatiens parviflora* and immediately felt somewhat aggrieved at this alien plant in otherwise semi-natural woodland! My woodland plant list is overwhelmingly of British natives, but a few additions have crept in because of the ambiguities discussed above.

Plant lifestyles as a key to their occurrence and abundance

During the 1970s, ecologists working in the Sheffield Unit of Comparative Ecology, led by Philip Grime, developed a way of classifying plants based around three broad strategies for survival (Grime *et al.* 2007). The first of these covers the plants that thrive in disturbed conditions, tending to grow fast, shed their seeds and die back. These plants are termed Ruderals. Woodland species with a Ruderal tendency include Annual Meadow-grass *Poa annua*, Common Chickweed, Heath Ragwort *Senecio sylvaticus* and Wavy Bitter-cress *Cardamine flexuosa*, which are usually found along paths or in new-felled areas.

The Welsh Poppy – a Himalayan outpost in Snowdonia or not?

Modern techniques, particularly DNA analysis, make it possible to explore the origins of our flora in more detail than was possible in the past, sometimes with surprising results. Welsh Poppy *Meconopsis cambrica* is a handsome plant, the core of its native British distribution being in north and central Wales, with some outliers in south-west England. It is also widely grown in gardens and has naturalised through much of central and western Great Britain as far north as the Great Glen. On the Continent its native distribution is restricted to part of northern Spain, the Pyrenees and the Massif Central in France.

All other species of the genus *Meconopsis* occur in the Himalayas, making its European distribution unusual. Preston *et al.* (2012) looked at molecular data to establish the relationships between the Welsh Poppy and the Himalayan species. They concluded that the Welsh Poppy should not actually be in the same genus as the Himalayan species after all, but rather grouped with the true poppies such as the familiar red flowers of Flanders Fields. The researchers also found that the native populations of Welsh Poppy were genetically distinct from garden and naturalised populations. The native forms were closely linked to populations from the Massif Central and western Pyrenees, but the samples from introduced populations and garden escapes showed a greater affinity to populations in the central and eastern Pyrenees.

The introduced plants seem to be thriving and spreading, but the native type may be declining. We should be concerned that there is a risk of losing some of the genetic distinctiveness of the native populations through interbreeding; but we can also celebrate that here is an attractive native species that is on the increase, albeit the populations are derived from a slightly different part of Europe. We are left though with the conundrum of why the Welsh Poppy grows in moist, shady habitats rather than dry, open conditions where most of its new relatives occur.

Welsh Poppy in Cumbria. The species is native to Britain, but this plant probably comes from a non-native source.

Secondly, there are those plants that rely on growing better than their neighbours, by being taller, more aggressive in the occupation of ground, or in getting hold of nutrients – these are called Competitors. Strong competitors amongst the woodland list include Rosebay Willowherb, Bracken and Nettle. They are often more common along woodland edges or in long-established clearings than under dense canopy.

The third strategy involves being able to tolerate poor-growing conditions where other species are unable to thrive, for example very dry places, infertile soils, or, most relevant to woodland, under deep shade. These are called Stress-tolerators and include Hard-Fern *Blechnum spicant*, Wood-sedge *Carex sylvatica*, Hart's-tongue Fern *Asplenium scolopendrium*, Sanicle and Dog-violet.

Most species do not depend solely on any one strategy, but on mixtures of approaches. They may for example have some Ruderal characteristics, but also have some characteristics more typical of Competitors: they would be called a Competitive-Ruderal species, for example Cleavers. Amongst woodland plants there is a bias, particularly amongst the specialists, towards Stress-tolerance, when compared to the strategies typical of the rest of the British flora. Many woodland species can cope with the low light levels created by the shade from the tree and shrub layers. When trees blow down or are felled, an ability to thrive under disturbance or to compete well with your neighbours becomes more of an advantage, and the plants

Hard Fern – a stress-tolerator type of plant.

on the woodland list relying on Ruderal or Competitive strategies have more chance to thrive (chapter 10).

Grime and his team also collated information on a wide range of other attributes for much of the British flora, for example on their typical height, how long their seed survived in the soil and what sorts of habitats they occurred in. Woodland generalists are more likely to be tall, vigorous species that, when conditions allow, easily outgrow and dominate the other species of the woodland floor.

Goosegrass, or Cleavers, showing its competitive spirit with Cow Parsley in this Lincolnshire hedge.

Ellenberg scores

In 1988 I first came across the work of the German ecologist Heinz Ellenberg, who produced detailed descriptions of the vegetation of central Europe (Ellenberg 1988). He also gave, for a wide range of species, a score, on a 1–9 or 1–12 scale, for how sensitive they are to shade, to drought, to soil fertility, particularly to levels of nitrogen, and to soil acidity (pH). These scores were based on his knowledge of where species occurred and how they behaved in central Europe. The scores have since been adjusted where necessary for British conditions by Hill *et al.* (2004) and new scores developed for species that Ellenberg did not assess. The light scale and examples of species allocated to different points on it are given overleaf.

Ellenberg scores for light conditions

Ellenberg Indicator Values based on Ellenberg (1988), Hill *et al.* (2004)		
L	**Light**	**Species from the woodland list**
1	Plants in deep shade	
2	Between 1 and 3	
3	Shade plants	Sweet Woodruff, Dog's Mercury
4	Between 3 and 5	Wild Garlic, Hart's-tongue Fern, Sanicle
5	Plants of half shade	Hedge Garlic, Male-fern, Greater Stitchwort *Stellaria holostea*
6	Between 5 and 7	Lesser Burdock *Arctium minus*, Common Twayblade
7	Generally in well-lit places	Wild Angelica *Angelica sylvestris*, Yellow Iris *Iris pseudacorus*
8	Light-loving plants	Silverweed, Red Fescue
9	Plants of full light	

Woodland specialists came out as being the most shade-tolerant, with nearly two-thirds having an Ellenberg score of 5 or less, an indication that they are typically found in conditions of half-shade or darker. For tolerance of different levels of soil water and nutrients woodland species tended to be more clustered in the middle of the ranges compared to those for other habitats (Hermy *et al.* 1999, Kimberley *et al.* 2013).

The scores can also be used to look for patterns in the types of species that increase and decrease in abundance over time in a wood, or when comparing the floras of different woods, to understand what may be causing these differences. For example, on the Continent, an increase in species tolerant of acid conditions, such as Wavy Hair-grass, was found in comparisons of plant lists from the 1930s–1950s and lists from the same places in the 1970s–1980s which pointed to the effects of soil acidification. Species with high Ellenberg nutrient values may accumulate at wood-edges next to intensive livestock farms that tend to give off ammonium compounds. Reductions in the more light-demanding woodland species have been linked to a decline in woodland management: if fewer trees are being felled, there will be fewer gaps in the canopy and the forest floor will be darker.

Sweet Woodruff, a shade bearer with an Ellenberg light score of just 3.

Silverweed with its yellow flower, found only in open places such as rides, which is reflected in its Ellenberg light score of 8.

Each woodland plant species has its own distinct requirements; in terms of its association with ancient woods, its ability to withstand shade and its life strategy, its needs may largely overlap with those of other species, so that some species commonly occur together. This may be because species require particular soil conditions – no surprise to any gardener – so before looking at plant communities in further detail we must first delve into the wood below ground.

A
DELINEATION
OF THE
STRATA
OF
ENGLAND AND WALES,
WITH PART OF
SCOTLAND;
EXHIBITING
THE COLLIERIES AND MINES,
THE MARSHES AND FEN LANDS ORIGINALLY OVERFLOWED BY THE SEA,
AND THE
VARIETIES OF SOIL
ACCORDING TO THE VARIATIONS IN THE SUBSTRATA,
ILLUSTRATED BY THE MOST DESCRIPTIVE NAMES.
BY W. SMITH.

THE GERMAN OCEAN

IRISH SEA

S.T GEORGE'S CHANNEL

CARNARVON BAY

CARDIGAN BAY

BRISTOL CHANNEL

THE ENGLISH CHANNEL

The wood below
the ground

chapter
five

There are a few plants, such as Mistletoe *Viscum album*, that live on trees directly. The rest have to have something to cover their roots, even if this is just a thin skim on a branch fork that allows a Polypody fern *Polypodium vulgare* to establish. Soil does not just provide mechanical support for the plants but is also the source of the mineral nutrients and water needed for growth.

Woodland soil is a complex mix of organic material (leaf litter, dead roots, faeces, living invertebrates and microbes) and mineral particles derived from the weathering of rocks locally or brought in by wind and water. The proportions of the mineral and organic components and how they are structured vary considerably (Kennedy 2002). Ainsdale National Nature Reserve, north of Liverpool, has large areas of pine planted on old sand dunes; apart from the surface litter the soil is almost entirely mineral. Conversely the Birch wood at Holme Fen in Cambridgeshire is growing on the drying peat left after the nearby Whittlesey Mere was drained in the middle of the 19th century, so it has an almost entirely organic soil. Drying, shrinkage and oxidation of the peat has lowered the soil surface by several metres over the last century and a half.

Below the soil surface, plants may have specialised roots and stems that spread out, budding-off new individuals that allow the original plant to occupy new ground. Other types of modified stem act as storage

OPPOSITE PAGE:
William Smith's pioneering map of the geology of England and Wales.

BELOW:
Common polypody fern on a low mossy branch.

77

organs, allowing the plants to survive unfavourable periods, such as summer droughts or winter cold. In some species these below-ground structures can survive for several years without producing aerial leaves and shoots. Seeds can also get buried in the soil and provide a way for plants to re-colonise areas after periods when they may have been absent above ground.

The mineral component

Our geology is extremely varied, as shown in the wonderful map produced by William Smith (1769–1839) at the beginning of the 19th century with diagonal stripes of colour across the country for the different rock types. The modern version of this is the British Geological Society's interactive website, which allows you to look at the geology in your area. In Great Britain there is a major split between the younger rocks, which generally produce more fertile soils of the south-east 'lowlands', and the 'upland' soils of the north-west, which are underlain by older, harder rocks. There are however many exceptions. Sherwood Forest in the lowland grows on acidic sands; Marle Hall Woods near Llandudno and Rassal Ashwood in Wester Ross are in the uplands of Great Britain but are on limestone, giving base-rich, fertile soils.

The effect of the underlying geology on the soil may be masked by deposits of surface drift material. During the Ice Ages as the glaciers moved down valleys they scraped off and carried with them pre-existing soil, stones and sometimes huge boulders. In the

Holme Fen woodland has developed on an almost entirely organic soil.

process stones might be ground down, first into fine gravel and then to dust. When the ice melted, this material was left behind. In the post-glacial period rock-dust and sand was blown around and some eventually accumulated in small hollows.

The soil underlying this pine plantation on Ainsdale sand dunes north of Liverpool is almost entirely mineral.

The characteristics of the mineral component of the soil are strongly determined by the size of the particles present: from sands (the largest, particles greater than 0.06mm in diameter) through silts (0.06–0.002mm) to clays (<0.002mm). If you take a piece of soil and rub it between your fingers, then a soil with a high sand content feels gritty. If the soil is moistened it does not stick together well and you cannot easily mould it into a ball between your hands. If it does stick together and you can roll the ball out into a thin worm and bend the worm into a circle without breaking it, there is a lot of clay in the soil. If the soil does stick together, but will not form a worm, and feels soapy or slippery, the dominant particles are probably silts. Clay and silt soils are often described as 'heavy', those with lots of sand as 'light'. These terms derive from the effort generally needed to plough them in the past.

The large size of sand particles is usually matched by equally large gaps between them, meaning that water tends to drain through them quickly. There is usually plenty of oxygen in these big spaces, allowing the plant roots to go down deep. The smaller the particles, the tighter they are likely to pack down, leaving smaller spaces between them. Silt and clay soils tend to hold more water and there may be less oxygen in the soil spaces. This in turn may mean that the plant roots cannot go down very far.

Most of the nutrients needed for woodland plant growth (potassium, phosphoros, calcium and magnesium plus smaller quantities of other elements) come from soil minerals. Soils derived from different rocks vary in the amount of these elements that is available for plants to take up. As a broad generalisation, sandy soils tend to have fewer available nutrients. They are therefore less fertile than clays or silts.

The other major element plants need for growth is nitrogen. This ultimately comes from the atmosphere but has to be converted first into compounds that can be absorbed by the plant roots. Nitrogen fixation is carried out by bacteria, which may be free-living in the soil or in nodules on the roots of plants of the pea family, such as the woodland vetches, and on Alder roots. Subsequently, the nitrogen compounds may be released into the soil, for example when the roots die, where they may be taken up by other species. Nitrogen oxides and ammonia may also be released into the atmosphere, but then be washed back into the soil. Additional wet and dry deposition of nitrogen compounds comes from human sources, such as farming or the exhaust gases of cars.

The elements that become available as the rocks weather also affect how acidic or alkaline the soil is. If there is a high concentration of calcium, for example from the breakdown of chalk and limestone, then the soil will be alkaline, with a pH (the scale used to measure soil acidity/alkalinity) higher than 7. Other rocks, such as slates, tend to give rise to acid soils, with a pH less than 7, perhaps going as low as 3 or 4. In very acid soils aluminium ions, which are toxic to plants, start to be released into the soil water.

The ground flora composition is affected by the available water in the soil, the nutrients that their roots can take up, and the soil acidity. Heinz Ellenberg, as well as assigning scores for shade tolerance (discussed in the previous chapter), classified species according to their ability to cope with different degrees of soil wetness, soil nutrients and soil acidity. The scores indicate where a species is most likely to be found, in the presence of competition from other plants – most will grow best in fertile, well-watered soils if growing on their own.

Ellenberg scores for moisture and nitrogen conditions

Ellenberg Indicator Values based on Ellenberg (1988), Hill *et al.* (2004)			
F	**Soil moisture (with example species for each score)**	**N**	**Soil nitrogen (with example species for each score)**
1	Plants of extreme dryness	1	Sites poor in available N (Rock Stonecrop *Sedum forsterianum*)
2	Between 1 and 3	2	Between 1 and 3 (Heather)
3	Dry site indicators (Ploughman's-spikenard)	3	More often N-deficient soils (Common Spotted-orchid)
4	Between 3 and 5 (Lesser Burdock)	4	Between 3 and 5 (Wild Strawberry *Fragaria vesca*)
5	Moist site indicators (Wood-sedge)	5	Average N availability (Wood Crane's-bill *Geranium sylvaticum*)
6	Between 5 and 7 (Toothwort)	6	Between 5 and 7 (Bluebell)
7	Damp site indicators (Wild Hop)	7	More often N-rich sites (Upright Hedge-parsley *Torilis japonica*)
8	Between 7 and 9 (Hemp-agrimony *Eupatorium cannabinum*)	8	Between 7 and 9 (White Dead-nettle)
9	Wet site indicators (Lesser Pond Sedge *Carex acutiformis*)	9	Extremely rich N soils, for example cattle resting places (Broad-leaved Dock *Rumex obtusifolius*)
10–12	Flooded/aquatic conditions		

Lesser Pond Sedge – a species of wet soils.

Purple Moor-grass – a species of wet, acid places with an Ellenberg nutrient score of 2.

There are few woodland species associated with either very low or very high soil moisture scores compared to the rest of the British flora: in very dry conditions woodland tends to give way to scrub and savanna and there are not many floating woods! However, Royal Fern *Osmunda regalis*, Common Marsh Bedstraw and Lesser Spearwort *Ranunculus flammula* are placed at 9 (needing wet conditions) on the moisture score, contrasting with Wood Sage, Harebell, or Old-man's Beard (score 4), which grow better in free-draining soils.

There are also relatively few woodland species with very low Ellenberg nutrient scores compared to those in non-woodland habitats. Species can withstand low-fertility levels in high light conditions but not many are able to cope with the double stress of both low light and low fertility. Species tolerating low-nitrogen conditions are usually also associated with acid soils, for example Purple Moor-grass and Tormentil (score 2 on the nutrient score), while at the fertile end of the nutrient spectrum (score 8) are Cleavers, Hedge Woundwort *Stachys sylvatica* and Hedge Garlic.

The organic contribution

Water and nutrient availability are also affected by the nature and distribution of the organic component of the soil. In a wood, organic material is most obviously added to the soil surface in the autumn in broadleaved woods, through falling tree leaves, or dying

Bracken fronds. There are other, less noticeable, contributions through the rest of the year: the bud scales as the tree leaves emerge in spring, the dieback of the Bluebell leaves in early summer, the petals from the Bramble flowers. Sometimes you can hear it happening: the gentle pitter-patter of caterpillar frass (their faeces) falling from the canopy in summer. There are occasional more dramatic additions as when a deer dies, or a tree falls. Organic matter is also being added below ground as plant roots die and decay.

Earthworms play a key role in organic matter decomposition and soil structure development.

In the ground, bacteria, fungi and invertebrates, from earthworms to tiny springtails, break down the material by physical and chemical means. The relative importance of different species groups in the decomposition process can be observed by placing a fixed amount of litter into mesh bags, where the size of the mesh allows access to small organisms but excludes larger ones such as worms. Some of the carbon and nutrients is incorporated in the cells of the decomposer organisms themselves, some is incorporated into the soil, where it may remain largely inert for periods from a few years to centuries or more.

These mesh bags have been filled with litter to test which species are most important in its breakdown. Different mesh sizes exclude larger invertebrates such as worms from some bags but let through smaller beasts.

Elm, Alder, and particularly Ash, leaves tend to break down rapidly; most have gone by the following summer. Other tree leaves

such as those of Sycamore and Lime may take two years to disappear; Oak and Beech three years, and some of the conifers even longer (Ellenberg 1988). The woodland ground flora produces a smaller mass of leaves and stems each year, but this is generally broken down more easily than the tree leaves, so the nutrients in them are recycled more quickly. Where there is Bracken, though, and, to a lesser extent, grasses growing in open glades, the dead leaves and fronds can build up as a thick mat. Bramble thickets also accumulate large amounts of standing dead stems that remain separate from the soil for some months because they are held up by the subsequent year's living stems. Such stems may make up a third of the mass of dense thickets.

As leaves, stems and twigs decay, some of the carbon is added to the upper soil layers. Provided the soils are not too acid, earthworms will drag leaves and other organic material down into the soil so that the carbon is quite deeply distributed through the soil profile, leaving perhaps only a thin layer of surface litter. These are called mull humus soils, and the richest vascular plant communities tend to be associated with such soils.

In acid soils, there are fewer deep-burrowing earthworms to mix the surface layers with the mineral soil below. Litter builds up at the soil surface and fungi play a bigger role in breaking down the material. There can develop a sharp line between an upper organic zone and the mineral soil beneath – this is known as mor humus type. Iron compounds are leached out of the upper mineral layers by organic acids formed by the breakdown of the litter, leaving a greyish-white sandy layer. Sometimes this iron is re-deposited lower down as an impervious iron-pan that limits the rate at which water can drain away.

In British forests the action of earthworms in incorporating litter to the mineral soil is seen as positive, to be encouraged in both gardening and farming generally. It was a surprise to me, on a trip to the north-eastern United States, to discover that, there, deep-burrowing earthworms are invasive species: fishermen use worms as live bait and may discard any unused ones at the end of the day (Bohlen *et al.* 2004). These abandoned worms are changing the nature of some American forest soils. In the natural absence of deep-burrowing worms many American hardwood forests had developed deep surface organic layers. The invasive worms change the decomposition processes, eating their way through these layers and dragging some remains down into their burrows. The greater mixing of organic and mineral layers facilitated by the worms can lead to less carbon being stored in the soil, changes to the patterns of nutrient cycling, and also in the diversity of both the above-ground vegetation and the buried seed flora. Rich herb communities can be reduced down to just one or two species. Some of the smaller trees are left on little pedestals of twisted roots as the worms eat the forest floor out from underneath them. Earthworms also change the fungal communities that thread their way through the forest floor, decomposing the litter (Dempsey *et al.* 2013).

A pit dug to show the soil profile in an acid oakwood. At the top is a thin dark organic layer, then a grey mineral upper zone, above the orange-brown subsoil.

Underground connections

Some fungal threads (hyphae) invade the roots of plants to form what are called mycorrhizae – plant–fungus interactions. The host plant (usually) acts as a source of carbon compounds, derived from photosynthesis, for the fungus, but the host benefits from increased availability of water and nutrients such as phosphate absorbed initially by the fungal hyphae system. It has long been recognised that most trees have mycorrhizal roots; on species such as Oak, for example, the fungus forms a distinct sheath around the fine roots, from which the hyphae then spread out through the forest floor, connecting with other trees. However, more recent research has shown that under natural conditions most woodland ground flora plants also have mycorrhizae (Harley & Harley 1987). The links are not as obvious as with the fungal sheaths on many tree roots, because the fungus grows into the roots and forms structures within the host-plant cells themselves.

The movements between the components of the system are more complex than just the transfer of sugars from the plant to fungus, and water and mineral nutrients from the fungus back to the plant. Some of the sugars moving into the fungus from one plant may end up in other plants connected via the fungal hyphae, meaning that there is a transfer of energy from plant to plant, possibly from one species to another (Wohlleben 2016). The dynamics of the relationship between the fungus and the host-plant can change over

This solitary Fly Agaric toadstool is just the visible part of a vast below-ground web connecting nearby woodland plants via their roots.

time. If the host-plant is weakened the fungus may end up killing the host, but the so-called host can be the freeloader as well. The early growth of most orchids relies on carbon from the fungus as well as mineral nutrients, because the dust-like seeds of orchids contain too few reserves to grow a stem and leaves on their own. For several years the orchid is in effect a parasite on the fungus. The fungus in turn draws on carbon from its connections to adjacent trees, so a three-way relationship is formed.

If the fungal partner is adversely affected by a change in environmental conditions, this could have knock-on effects for the host-plant's growth. Fungi are more sensitive than most vascular plants to increases in heavy metals and nitrogen deposition to British woodland soils from air pollution, and so some of the pollution impacts that we see may be indirect responses to the disruption of the below-ground relationships.

Roots and their roles

I dug up some Bramble plants in Oxfordshire as part of my doctoral research, tracing their roots for about a metre, but in Australia, where introduced brambles are a major weed, their roots have been followed down for over four metres. Developing a deep-root system might initially seem like a good strategy for a plant as it opens up a larger volume of soil for extraction of water and nutrients. However, deep roots are at risk from waterlogging and they may be costly to produce in terms of the plant's photosynthesis output. Other woodland plants (Wood Anemone, Wood-sorrel, Germander Speedwell *Veronica chamaedrys*, Hairy Violet *Viola hirta*) have only relatively shallow roots but this makes them vulnerable to summer droughts.

Even trees have much of their feeding root-system in the upper part of the soil because that is where most of the available nutrients tend to be concentrated. This is often very apparent when trees blow over: the uplifted root plate is seldom more than a metre deep. This means there is a lot of below-ground competition in the humus and upper mineral layers. If this competition from the tree roots is reduced, for example by digging a trench around a plot, severing the tree roots from their parent stem, there is usually an increase in the ground flora growth within the trenched area.

Roots provide the water and nutrients from the soil needed for plant growth, which is usually fastest in the spring and early summer. At this time, there is a surge in nutrients in the soil as rising temperatures increase the microbial activity. Deciduous trees have not developed their full canopy and therefore are not so active, at least in the early spring. There can be a second, smaller, peak in autumn as the trees lose their leaves. The ground flora may play an important role at these times in reducing the amount of soluble nutrients such as nitrates that would otherwise be washed out of the soils. Capturing nutrients that might otherwise be lost is also an important role for the ground flora after the trees have been felled and so no longer have active root systems. Foresters may therefore create strips of dense ground vegetation along streamsides to help reduce run-off from felled areas.

A wind-blown Beech showing the shallowness of its rootplate, from which a Birch is now growing.

Soil seed banks, the plants we don't usually see

Roots are not the only part of a plant that may be hidden in the soil: there are seeds as well. If you spread out soil from a woodland as a thin layer on a tray with a good supply of light and water, the seeds it contains start to grow. Stir it around from time to time to expose any seeds that may be at the bottom and more plants will appear.

Usually what comes up is a very different mix to the species that are growing above ground (Brown & Warr 1992). In one study less than 40% of the seedlings grown from the soil under neglected coppices in East Anglia were of species found in the surface vegetation. Many species typical of the shaded conditions in woods, such as Wild Garlic, Wood Anemone, Enchanter's-nightshade, Bluebell, Sanicle and Dog's Mercury, are rarely found in the buried seed bank. Either they do not produce much seed because their flowering is suppressed under shade, or else their seed does not survive for long in the soil. There may be small amounts of some specialist species such as Wood-sedge, Hairy Wood-rush *Luzula pilosa* and Yellow Pimpernel *Lysimachia nemorum*, but the buried flora largely consists of the more light-demanding non-woodland species and woodland generalists such as Soft Rush *Juncus effusus* and Bramble.

Some of the buried seed may germinate each year, but under shade the seedlings rapidly die. Only when conditions are more favourable do they survive long enough to grow and be noticed. Disturbance of the soil surface during coppicing brings other buried seed to the surface where increased warmth, light or a change in the ratio of red/far-red light wavelengths may stimulate them to sprout. Equally, new seeds are added to the seed bank each year and gradually buried as leaf litter builds up on top of them. Some seeds may be dragged down along with leaves by earthworms; small seeds may get washed down to deeper layers in the tunnels created by the worms.

Once buried, the clock starts ticking; the seed numbers start to decline as they rot or get eaten. The longer the time before the soil is disturbed again, the fewer the seeds that are likely to still be alive, to germinate and appear above ground. For much of the buried flora the critical period seems to be about 40–50 years (Brown & Warr 1992). When most ancient woods were managed as coppice the rotation lengths were almost always less than 30 years, which allowed for a strong showing from the species in the soil seed bank after each cut.

Some rare species such as Tintern Spurge *Euphorbia serrulata* may rely on buried seed to tide them over difficult shady periods. Tintern Spurge had been recorded from a South Wales wood, Coed Wen, but declined there in the post-Second World War period. When coppicing was resumed at the site in the 1980s, the plant reappeared in abundance (Marren 1992). Its seeds had been buried, lying dormant, until the soil disturbance and increased light brought them to the surface and encouraged their growth. Its more common relative, Wood Spurge, behaves similarly.

Soil patterns and woodland conservation

If the woodland ground flora has sometimes been overlooked in woodland conservation thinking, this applies even more strongly to the woodland soil. Yet it literally underlies many aspects of current conservation concern. Our ancestors were aware of, and exploited, different soil types. The free-draining chalk and sandy lands of southern England were extensively used by Mesolithic, Neolithic and Bronze Age peoples (chapter 12). Many such areas were cleared of trees early in prehistory; some heavily-used regions on the Wiltshire chalk around Stonehenge may never have developed much of a tree cover at all (Allen 2017). The wetter clay soils presented a more difficult challenge to our ancestors and these were often where woodland survived longest, or which recolonised first, whenever human pressure lifted. This effect is still partly reflected in the current distribution of ancient woodland, which has generally survived better on soils that were difficult to farm or gave only poor yields.

Good farming areas such as the Lleyn Peninsula, much of Essex, and Aberdeenshire tend to have few ancient woods compared to the steep Maentwrog Valley in Gwynedd, the stiff clay of the Weald or high cold ground of upper Deeside (Roberts *et al.* 1992, Spencer & Kirby 1992). At a local level around Wytham Hill, the ancient woodland survives in a band around the lower slopes of the hill on the hard clay soils. By contrast the fertile alluvial soils of the floodplain were used for grazing or hay-making. The upper slopes on free-draining sand and limestone provided common grazing until the 19th century; they had been cleared by the medieval period and have traces of earlier occupation.

Changes in soil nutrients occur all the time. In some places more nutrients are entering the soil than leaving it (through, for example,

A splurge of Spurge

Wood Spurge *Euphorbia amygdaloides* has a low-density but persistent seed bank that results in a fine show in recently-cut coppice or where ride edges are cut back (Buckley *et al.* 1997). It is associated with ancient woodland, but in a study in Picardy the species was found more often in ancient woods that had been occupied in the Gallo-Roman period than forests which showed no such history (Plue *et al.* 2008). This may indicate that it does depend on some regular disturbance of the soil, such as comes with felling or coppicing, to persist over the very long term.

Once established, it can persist for some time, its thick stock producing tufts of stems. These bear only leaves in the first year, but in their second year are topped by a cluster of yellowish-green flowers. Like others of its family it produces a milky latex when cut and this may make it unpalatable to grazing animals, so it can be widespread in some wood-pastures such as the New Forest.

Wood Spurge is largely restricted to woods and hedges south of a line from the Wash to the Wirral, on dry, slightly acid to neutral soils. In Europe generally, it appears to be limited towards the north and east by winter temperatures and frost damage. This could mean it will benefit from warmer winters under climate change scenarios. Predicting the future distribution of Wood Spurge in Great Britain is however complicated because a vigorous sub-species that has been cultivated in gardens for a century or so has started to appear in the wild. Rather, as with the Welsh Poppy, we may see more occurrences but from a different gene pool.

LEFT: Wood Spurge.
BELOW: A mass of Wood Spurge in the New Forest.

increased nitrogen compound deposition from car exhausts) and the soil is said to be becoming eutrophic. There are then likely to be changes in the flora with an increase in tall, competitive generalists such as nettles and brambles (see also chapter 16).

There have also been times when more nutrients were removed each year than were added through the weathering of rock, and in this case the soils could become impoverished. High nutrient loss might occur where twigs and Bramble stems were collected and bound into faggots for firing ovens off-site, or where Bracken and leaf litter were gathered for use as animal bedding. (In the 1980s I saw pine needle litter being collected for this purpose from forests on the Canary Island of Tenerife). Oliver Rackham (2003) suggested that this nutrient depletion might have slowed the regrowth of the coppice over time, leading to longer rotations becoming necessary. Reduced soil fertility would tend to favour the more specialist woodland flora over competitive generalists: woodland management, through its effects on the soil, may therefore have biased the composition of the woodland flora that we have inherited (chapter 9).

It is, however, the variations in soil composition and structure across the country that have the more obvious effects on which species grow in any particular wood, with dramatic differences sometimes visible over the space of a few metres. At the north end of the Witherslack Woods in Cumbria, for example, a footpath by the roadside starts on acid soil. Here there are tall Oak and Birch, over Wavy Hair-grass, Bilberry, Heath Bedstraw, Wood-sorrel and Bracken. The ground is uneven and, in the hollows, wet Alder woodland has formed with Meadowsweet, Water Mint *Mentha aquatica*, a variety of sedges and rushes, and small herbs such as Yellow Pimpernel and Common Marsh Bedstraw. At the base of the steep limestone slope there is a sharp change to Ash-Hazel woodland with scattered Small-leaved Lime *Tilia cordata* and Elm, over Dog's Mercury, False Brome, Lords-and-Ladies, Barren Strawberry, plus rarer species such as Wood Fescue *Festuca altissima* and Mezereon. Similar types of pattern can be found in lowland oakwoods, where Bracken and Bramble on free-draining slopes give way to dense sedge stands in wet valley bottoms. Finding a way to describe such variations in a consistent way was one of the reasons for developing the National Vegetation Classification, which is described in the next chapters, 6 and 7.

Types of British woldland: the north and west

In woods near Bath you may see Bath Asparagus; almost certainly you will find Nettle in woods around Nettlecombe and Bramble near Bramblecombe. No two woods contain the same range of plants with the same abundance, but some patches of woodland are clearly more similar to one another than to others. Just as books are put into rough categories (thrillers, historical, fantasy) or breeds of dog (poodle, Labrador, boxer) to simplify describing them, ecologists have defined types of woodland vegetation by looking for species that tend to occur together in particular situations.

A typical wood in the Chilterns, for example, might be composed of Beech with a ground flora of Dog's Mercury, Sanicle, Wall Lettuce *Mycelis muralis*, perhaps with some Ivy. In the Maentwrog Valley we see Oak with Wavy Hair-grass, Bilberry, Bracken and plenty of ferns. Bilberry, Bracken and Wavy Hair-grass are also likely to turn up under Scots Pine on Deeside, but along with Cowberry *Vaccinium vitis-idaea* and Chickweed-wintergreen *Trientalis europaea*. Having a standard set of woodland types makes it easier to map and describe woods. We can judge whether the woods chosen as nature reserves cover the full range of woodland variation in a region. We can see how our woods differ (or not) from woods on the Continent, which may in turn affect what priority we place on their conservation. If we want to know how woods might respond to a change in their management, we can look for examples where this has already been tried in a wood with a similar composition.

Various ways of categorising woods were developed during the 20th century (Tansley 1939, Peterken 1981, Bunce 1982), but I will mainly

OPPOSITE PAGE:
Bath Asparagus, or Spiked Star-of-Bethlehem.

use that developed for the Nature Conservancy Council from 1975 onward as the National Vegetation Classification, usually shortened to NVC (Rodwell 1991, Hall *et al*. 2001). It is not appropriate for all purposes: for example, the structure of a wood is often more important than detailed botanical composition in determining what insects and birds are present. However, the NVC is currently the most widely used classification in Great Britain and is most relevant here because the ground flora features strongly in how its types were defined. The vegetation types produced by this project largely reflect the variation in climate across Great Britain (broadly-speaking, warmer and drier in the south-east; cooler and wetter in the north-west) and differences in soil types within these broad climatic regions.

Climatic influences on our woods

The average July temperatures in Great Britain vary from about 21° Centigrade on the south coast to about 13° in Orkney. The growing season in the south may be one to two months longer than in the north. The warm ocean current, the Gulf Stream, moderates our climate so that we have milder winters than might be expected for our latitude: the 50-degree latitude line, which passes close to Helston in Cornwall, cuts through northern Newfoundland on the other side of the Atlantic. The range of temperatures over the year in Great Britain is very much less than in central Europe on the same latitude, where summers may be hotter, but winters much colder. Our islands lie just off a large continent to the east, with a large ocean to the west, leading also to a gradient in annual rainfall from east to west. This can be less than 500 millimetres in parts of East Anglia, similar to the mean rainfall for Syria or Israel, to over 2,500mm down the west coast, a temperate rainforest climate.

By chance, Great Britain also spans a major Europe-wide vegetation transition linked to climate. To the south are the temperate broadleaved forests of Beech, Lime, Maples and Oaks that run through central and southern Europe, while to the north are the boreal forests of predominantly coniferous trees such as Spruce and Pine, with some Birch and Aspen. The flora in our woods includes species with affinities to those in Scandinavia, such as Chickweed-wintergreen; species having their strongholds in central Europe, such as Yellow Archangel; and even a few outliers of the Mediterranean zone such as Wild Madder *Rubia peregrina*. The link to climate is explored further in chapter 12.

The origins of the National Vegetation Classification (NVC)

Between 1975 and 1986 thousands of plant species lists were collected and analysed from across Great Britain and the results summarised in five volumes describing different plant communities. These descriptions are the most comprehensive account to date of the vegetation found in semi-natural habitats across Great Britain, including in woodland. They allow our vegetation to be compared with that on the Continent, where similar types of classification had been used since the early 20th century (Proctor 2013). The system has proved reasonably robust (Goldberg 2003), although, as with any such exercise, one clear result has been to highlight the ways in which it was incomplete! Since its publication in 1991, people have found examples of woodland vegetation that do not fit in well, and at some stage the classification will need to be revised and updated.

The woodland part of the classification is based on over 2,700 samples, the largest such collation ever undertaken in Great Britain. The woodland samples were grouped, according to the similarity of the plants that had been found in them, into 18 main woodland types and 7 scrub communities, with the more variable communities

The most northerly semi-natural wood in Britain at Berriedale on the Island of Hoy.

further divided into sub-communities (Rodwell 1991). The main woodland types are described below along a meandering route from north-west Scotland down to the English Channel and summarised in the 'dartboard' diagram.

The National Vegetation Classification Woodland Dartboard

The relationships between the main 18 woodland types in the National Vegetation Classification are set out below. The outermost ring on the 'dartboard' gives their code number (W1, W2 etc); the next ring in indicates whether they are mainly in the warmer, drier south and east of the country (SE) or the cooler, wetter north and west (NW); the third ring indicates the most commonly found tree species in the canopy; and the innermost ring whether the soils on which they are found tend to be wet, or, if dry, acidic or basic. The accompanying boxes round the edge include the most common ground flora species found with the type; (M) after the name means that the species is a moss.

W17 Sessile Oak–Downy Birch–*Dicranum majus*
Sessile Oak, Downy Birch, Rowan, Wavy Hair-grass, Bilberry, *Rhytidiadelphus loreus* (M) *Polytrichum formosum* (M). Very acid, often shallow soils in cooler and wetter parts of GB.

W16 Oak–Birch–Wavy Hair-grass
Silver Birch, Oak, Wavy Hair-grass, Bracken, Bilberry, Broad Buckler-fern.

W15 Beech–Wavy Hair-grass
Beech, Pedunculate Oak, Holly, Bracken, Wavy Hair-Grass, *Dicranella heteromalla* (M). On base-poor soils in the southern lowlands of GB.

W14 Beech–Bramble
Beech, Holly, Bramble, Bracken, *Mnium hornum* (M). Base-poor, slightly poorly-drained soils, mainly in south-east GB.

W13 Yew
Yew, Whitebeam, Elder, Dog's Mercury, Old-man's Beard. Mainly on shallow, dry base-rich soils in the south and east of GB, but occasional stands occur on other soil types elsewhere.

W12 Beech–Dog's Mercury
Beech, Ash, Dog's Mercury, Bramble, Ivy, False Brome. On free-draining, base-rich soils, mainly in the south-east of GB.

W11 Sessile Oak–Downy Birch-Wood-sorrel
Downy Birch, Sessile Oak, Rowan, Sweet Vernal-grass, Wood-sorrel, Common Bent, Wavy Hair-grass. On moist but free-draining, base-poor, acidic soils, mainly in the north and west of GB.

The rest of the chapter looks at the woodland types found mainly in the north and west (W3, 4, 7, 9, 11, 17, 18 on the dartboard), starting in the far north of Scotland and then coming down the west coast of Great Britain. The types found more commonly in the south-east are considered in the next chapter.

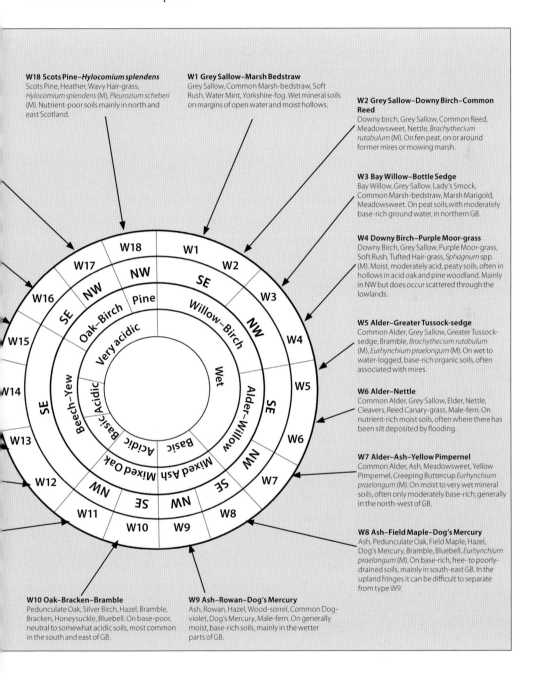

W18 Scots Pine–*Hylocomium splendens*
Scots Pine, Heather, Wavy Hair-grass, *Hylocomium splendens* (M), *Pleurozium scheberi* (M). Nutrient-poor soils mainly in north and east Scotland.

W1 Grey Sallow–Marsh Bedstraw
Grey Sallow, Common Marsh-bedstraw, Soft Rush, Water Mint, Yorkshire-fog. Wet mineral soils on margins of open water and moist hollows.

W2 Grey Sallow–Downy Birch–Common Reed
Downy birch, Grey Sallow, Common Reed, Meadowsweet, Nettle, *Brachythecium rutabulum* (M). On fen peat, on or around former mires or mowing marsh.

W3 Bay Willow–Bottle Sedge
Bay Willow, Grey Sallow, Lady's Smock, Common Marsh-bedstraw, Marsh Marigold, Meadowsweet. On peat soils, with moderately base-rich ground water, in northern GB.

W4 Downy Birch–Purple Moor-grass
Downy Birch, Grey Sallow, Purple Moor-grass, Soft Rush, Tufted Hair-grass, *Sphagnum* spp. (M). Moist, moderately acid, peaty soils, often in hollows in acid oak and pine woodland. Mainly in NW but does occur scattered through the lowlands.

W5 Alder–Greater Tussock-sedge
Common Alder, Grey Sallow, Greater Tussock-sedge, Bramble, *Brachythecium rutabulum* (M), *Eurhynchium praelongum* (M). On wet to water-logged, base-rich organic soils, often associated with mires.

W6 Alder–Nettle
Common Alder, Grey Sallow, Elder, Nettle, Cleavers, Reed Canary-grass, Male-fern. On nutrient-rich moist soils, often where there has been silt deposited by flooding.

W7 Alder–Ash–Yellow Pimpernel
Common Alder, Ash, Meadowsweet, Yellow Pimpernel, Creeping Buttercup *Eurhynchium praelongum* (M). On moist to very wet mineral soils, often only moderately base-rich; generally in the north-west of GB.

W8 Ash–Field Maple–Dog's Mercury
Ash, Pedunculate Oak, Field Maple, Hazel, Dog's Mercury, Bramble, Bluebell, *Eurhynchium praelongum* (M). On base-rich, free- to poorly-drained soils, mainly in south-east GB. In the upland fringes it can be difficult to separate from type W9.

W10 Oak–Bracken–Bramble
Pedunculate Oak, Silver Birch, Hazel, Bramble, Bracken, Honeysuckle, Bluebell. On base-poor, neutral to somewhat acidic soils, most common in the south and east of GB.

W9 Ash–Rowan–Dog's Mercury
Ash, Rowan, Hazel, Wood-sorrel, Common Dog-violet, Dog's Mercury, Male-fern. On generally moist, base-rich soils, mainly in the wetter parts of GB.

Woods at the extremities

The trees that dominate semi-natural woods throughout much of Great Britain, such as Oak, Ash and Elm, become increasingly scarce, and even Scots Pine struggles to survive, in the far north of mainland Scotland and on the Scottish islands. Woodland is often found only in small patches in gullies or amongst rocks. These woods do not always fit well into the classification scheme: they have similarities to Oak and Ash woodland types in terms of their ground flora (W11, W9 further south) but lack these tree species.

At some point in the past, there were trees, and probably woods, on Shetland, and some woodland plants even made it to St Kilda (Sarker 2014). Around the abandoned village Lady-fern, Polypody and Broad Buckler-fern can be seen on old walls, with Lesser Celandine, Common Dog-violet, Creeping Buttercup and Heath Bedstraw in the grassland. The riverside adds Wild Angelica and Primrose, with Slender St John's-wort *Hypericum pulchrum* in an old quarry. There are little patches of woodland tucked in sheltered ravines on the Island of Hoy in Orkney. The canopy is rather open, the woodland floor scattered with boulders in narrow ravines. In Berriedale and nearby valleys the richest patches have Birch, Sallow, Aspen and Rowan (Prentice & Prentice 1975). Great Wood-rush is the main dominant in the ground flora, with a mixture of tall herbs (Wild Angelica, Water Avens, Marsh Thistle), ferns (Broad Buckler, Scaly Male and Lady Fern *Athyrium filix-femina*), grasses (Tufted-Hair-grass *Deschampsia cespitosa*, Sweet Vernal-grass *Anthoxanthum*

Inside Berriedale, showing dense stands of Great Wood-rush.

odoratum, Yorkshire-fog) and small woodland plants (Primrose, Selfheal *Prunella vulgaris*, Common Dog-violet). Much of the west of the island is now managed by the Royal Society for the Protection of Birds, and sheep grazing has been greatly reduced. Willow and Birch scrub is now developing in many of the small gullies further north than Berriedale, threatening its claim to be the most northerly natural woodland in Great Britain!

More extensive areas of woodland, mainly of Birch and Willow, occur on the Scottish mainland. Heather, Bilberry and Bracken are abundant where the soils are shallow and acid, whereas Birch woods on base-rich soils have a richer flora. For example, the sub-alpine Morrone Birkwood above Braemar (Huntley & Birks 1979) has Melancholy Thistle *Cirsium heterophyllum*, Wood Crane's-bill, Globeflower *Trollius europaeus* and Dog's Mercury. Many of these species are vulnerable to grazing and are most vigorous in the shelter of large Juniper bushes, or in deer-proof exclosures erected to protect tree regeneration.

Boreal outliers

The native pinewoods (W18 on the dartboard) in the Highlands of Scotland are the westerly outpost of the great boreal forests that spread across Eurasia (Rodwell 1991; Steven and Carlisle 1959; Hill *et al.* 1975). The typical image of a native pinewood, such as Abernethy (Summers 2018), or Mar Lodge on Deeside, is of rather open landscape with scattered 'granny' pines (old open-grown trees with many low branches). This reflects centuries of grazing by cattle, sheep and deer, but in fact these woods can be much more varied in both structure and composition.

Grazing has probably reduced the numbers of broadleaved trees mixed with the pine, because broadleaves tend to be more palatable to animals than Scots Pine. Birch and Aspen would once have been more common, with Alder and Willows along streams and on floodplains. At Rhiddoroch Forest, near Ullapool, there are remnants of such a pattern with Alder and Birch on the lower ground, while Pine is mainly on the upper slopes. In north-east Scotland at Cawdor Great Wood and along the River Darnaway, there are hints as to what woods in the transitional zone between those dominated by Scots Pine and those dominated by Oak might have been like.

Where there has been heavy grazing under the trees the ground flora may be uniformly close-cropped Heather, Hard-fern and Bent grasses. Where grazing is only light there are large hummocks of Heather, Cowberry and Bilberry that can be up to a metre high. The Bilberry is a particularly important component in the diet of our largest grouse, the Capercaillie. The leaves and fruit are eaten by the adults through the summer and autumn, supplementing their main food of pine needles. Meanwhile the chicks are feeding on the insects – caterpillars, ants, beetles and flies – associated with the Bilberry areas (Summers *et al.* 2004).

Scattered through most pinewoods are peaty hollows filled with Purple Moor-grass and Sphagnum moss (W4), sometimes grading into more extensive bog vegetation with Cross-leaved Heath *Erica tetralix* and Hare's-tail Cotton-grass *Eriophorum vaginatum*. Stunted, scattered Pine may grow across the surface of the peat, making it difficult to say where woodland ends and bog begins. In one or two sites in north-east Scotland, such as Moniack Burn, near Inverness, there are traces of a more herb-rich pinewood vegetation, similar to that seen in parts of Scandinavia, but generally pinewoods have not survived on such fertile soils in Great Britain. Intriguingly, recent research from Ireland suggests that Scots Pine may have survived in the Burren among the hazelwoods on limestone (Roche *et al.* 2018).

OPPOSITE PAGE:
Native pinewood (W18) with hummocky Heather and Bilberry in Rothiemurchus Forest, Speyside (top).

Alder on the floodplain below Pine and Birch woodland on the slopes along the Rhiddoroch River near Ullapool (below).

In winter the pale dead leaves of Purple moor-grass pick out the boggy Sphagnum–Birch woodland (W4) in Glen Affric pinewood.

Pinewoods are home to a subspecies of Bracken *Pteridium aquilinum* ssp. *latiusculum* that is widespread in boreal conifer forests elsewhere. The fronds of this Northern Bracken are smaller, and patches of it tend to be more open than with the common form. In autumn and winter the dying leaves have a cinnamon-red colour. Northern Bracken may once have been more widespread than it is today but has lost out in some places to its more aggressive cousin (Page 1988). For the wandering botanist, however, a more distinctive feature of the pinewoods is the scattered occurrence of small herbs seldom encountered elsewhere in the country or in other types of woods. They include Linnaeus's favourite, the Twinflower, little wintergreens *Pyrola* spp., Creeping Lady's Tresses, Lesser Twayblade *Neottia cordata* and the somewhat more widespread Chickweed-wintergreen.

A northern speciality

Chickweed-wintergreen *Trientalis europaea* is a plant of moist, acidic, but often rather fertile, soils and has its heartland in the central and eastern Highlands. It has been recorded from northern England, although there it has declined because of woodland clearance and moor-burning. It is mainly associated with pinewoods but can sometimes be found in open birch and oak woods, as well as on moorland.

The leaves form an apparent whorl at the top of the stem; the flowers are white on long stalks. Seed set is rare and local spread is mainly by underground stems. The plants are somewhat vulnerable to grazing in that the whole of a shoot tends to be taken or broken off by trampling. Shoots that regrow from any surviving fragments are smaller than those from the parent plant. Patches where Chickweed-wintergreen is abundant may be widely separated from each other by apparently suitable habitats (Hiirsalmi 1969) because of this slow rate of spread.

A Swedish study showed an unusual interaction between the grazing effects of voles and a smut-fungus disease that affects the Wintergreen. Voles tended to eat more of the diseased plants, so there could be circumstances where the losses to voles are offset by the remaining plants being less disease-prone (Ericson & Wennstrom 1997).

It is not always clear why some species thrive in the cooler north but are not able to grow well in the south of Great Britain. In the case of Chickweed-wintergreen, however, it fixes carbon best at relatively low temperatures (Taylor *et al.* 2002), so its growth slows if it gets too warm. It may then be overtopped by faster-growing species.

Chickweed-wintergreen, one of the special pinewood plants.

The Atlantic zone

Moving from the northern and eastern Highlands across to the west coast of Scotland, for example around Loch Sunart, Birch remains common, but Oak replaces Scots Pine as the main tree in semi-natural woodland (types W17, W11). Such oakwoods are also found through Borrowdale in Cumbria, the Maentwrog Valley in North Wales, Coed Rheidol in Ceredigion to the Exmoor coombes, the fringes of Dartmoor and the cloaked valley-sides of the Helford and Fal estuaries in Cornwall. They have been called temperate rainforests and they can certainly be very wet. In the highest rainfall areas, the mosses and liverworts, which depend on year-round high levels of humidity, cover the ground, rocks and tree bases (Ratcliffe 1969, Rodwell 2005). The woodland plants that are the focus of this book are more limited – mainly Wavy Hair-grass, Bilberry, Heather and Heath Bedstraw. In Coed Deri-Newydd, an 18ha ancient wood in south Wales, Oliver Rackham found just eight species of herbs and grasses on a visit in the 1980s. On a visit with the Woodland Trust in 2016, we managed to push the list up to 26. The sheep grazing had been reduced during the intervening years and one or two gaps had formed in the canopy, which allowed more light to reach the ground layer. Even this total was however less than you might find in a 15 × 15m square in richer types of woodland.

Coed Deri-Newydd in Glamorgan, an ancient oakwood notably poor in vascular plants.

Herb–grass–bracken oakwood (WII) on Loch Lomondside.

Where the soils are deeper, the mosses and liverworts are less abundant, but ferns may be more common, along with grasses such as Sweet Vernal, Creeping Soft-grass *Holcus mollis*, various species of Bent, plus herbs such as Bluebell and Bramble. Tittensor and Steele (1971) describe such heathy and mossy woodland through to more herb-rich and grassy areas from the woods along Loch Lomondside. The balance between grasses and herbs often depends on the intensity of sheep grazing; the grasses tend to be more abundant where the grazing pressure is high, while Bramble and ferns are more common where grazing is less intense. Very palatable species may be confined to rock ledges or small islands in lochs, out of reach of hungry mouths. These oakwoods also harbour more unusual species, such as the Filmy Ferns *Hymenophyllum* spp., and the Hay-scented Fern *Dryopteris aemula*, and include the handful of sites for Irish Spurge *Euphorbia hyberna* in the south-west of England.

Pockets of diversity

Most upland oakwoods are not quite as species-poor as Coed Deri-Newydd, because they occur with other woodland types. There may be peaty hollows with Birch above Purple Moor-grass, Soft Rush and Marsh Violet (W4), as in the pinewoods. Where the oakwood on the

An Atlantic speciality

Hay-scented Fern *Dryopteris aemula* looks a bit like the common Broad Buckler-fern, but the crisped-up edges to the leaves give it a distinctive appearance. The fronds are said to smell of new-mown hay, although I cannot say I have ever noticed this.

The Hay-scented Fern is found in parts of North-western France, Galicia, The Azores and Madeira, but its world headquarters are Great Britain and Ireland, where it grows on moist, but well-drained and generally somewhat acidic soils. The fronds are slow to harden-off in the autumn and remain winter-green: its restriction to the Atlantic zone may be because this remains largely frost-free (Page 1988).

In Great Britain it is strongly associated with the western woods, but it is also found in north Yorkshire and the Weald of Sussex and Kent. Some other moisture-loving plants, including rare mosses and liverworts, show

Hay-scented fern.

a similar distribution pattern. Damp porous sandstone, often combined with the humid, shaded microclimate of steep-sided wooded valleys, may offset the generally drier climate of eastern England. Given that it is a species whose distribution is focused on Great Britain, Hay-scented Fern deserves to be better known.

slope meets the wet valley bottom, small patches of willow may be found. In the uplands these tend to be Bay Willow and Eared Sallow (W3) rather than the Grey Sallow commonly found in the lowlands. Common tall fen-herbs, such as Meadowsweet and Wild Angelica, are joined by species with a more north-westerly distribution, such as Marsh Hawk's-beard *Crepis paludosa*. Coralroot Orchid, a plant largely of eastern Scotland and the county flower of Fife, is associated with this community. This species is parasitic on its associated fungi and lives mainly as underground rhizomes, only appearing while flowering in July and August. It may have been under-recorded in the past, because new sites have been found recently.

Richer, moister soils along streamsides may have Alder with Meadowsweet, Yellow Pimpernel, Creeping Buttercup, Opposite-leaved Golden Saxifrage *Chrysosplenium oppositifolium*, various sedges and grasses, particularly Remote Sedge and Tufted Hair-grass (W7). Where there are many small streams or springs, the Alder spreads

out over much of the hillside. George Peterken (1993) categorised such sites as Slope Alderwoods. Often the alders appear to have been cut 2–3m above the ground as pollards, and the woods have been grazed by cattle and sheep. These upland wood-pastures can be found from Wales through northern England, to Langwell Water in Caithness. At Carnach Wood near the entrance to Glen Coe, and in the woods above North Ballachulish, on the other side of Loch Leven, the Ash and Alder have been managed as irregular coppice, but the woods have a similar open structure. The combination of an open canopy and a mixture of dry and wet soil conditions makes for a species-rich flora.

More species may be added to the plant list for the wood where fertile soils occur in shallow valleys or towards the base of slopes. These areas are often picked out in spring by grey stripes where the pale bark of the Ash contrasts with the olive green of the Oak and reddish tinge of the Birch canopy. Wych Elm used to be common in such situations and often still survives as regrowth following attacks of Dutch Elm Disease. In England and Wales Small-leaved Lime may be present, usually only in the form of a few old trees. It is found for example in Roudsea Wood on the edge of Morecambe Bay, which had something like the current mix of tree species even some 5,000 to 6,000 years ago (Birks 1982). Lime is often considered a tree from the past, found mainly in ancient woods, because it rarely set seed, particularly in northern England. However, with recent

Yellow Pimpernel, a species often found in upland alderwoods.

warmer summers Small-leaved Lime regeneration is less unusual and perhaps its days as an ancient woodland indicator will be numbered. Sycamore, probably introduced to Great Britain in the early medieval period, has found its natural home in many of these upland Ash woods, mirroring situations where it occurs in northern France. There is a strong case that it should be accepted as part of the future composition of such stands, as a replacement for Elm and Ash, where these are subject to disease.

The fertile soils of these upland Ash woods (W9) allow herbs such as Dog's Mercury, Wild Garlic and Water Avens *Geum rivale* to flourish alongside a range of tall grasses (Giant Fescue, False Brome and Wood Millet). Extensive areas of this type are found on limestone outcrops in northern and western Great Britain, from the Gower Peninsula, through the Peak District and Yorkshire Dales to Skye. A locally rare species in these woods across northern England, often on limestone pavement, is Baneberry *Actaea spicata*. Elsewhere in Europe it is also found under conifers on base-rich soils. This is a long-lived plant and its populations are generally stable. Its black berries, as its name implies, are poisonous to humans. They fall close to the plant, leading often to clusters of plants, but some may be dispersed further by birds or small mammals (Eriksson 1994). In ungrazed, or only lightly grazed, woods, flowers such as Globeflower, Melancholy Thistle and Wood Crane's-bill put on a fine show, as they also do in some northern hay-meadows (Peterken 2013).

Wood Crane's-bill

Wood Crane's-bill *Geranium sylvaticum* has a distinctly northern distribution in Great Britain and is found in open, dry to moist damp woods and meadows on moderately fertile soils (Averis 2013). It is a tall perennial plant with striking purplish-pink to mauve flowers, which may have earned it the name Kingshood (Grigson 1975). It has declined at the edges of its range because of the agricultural improvement of grassland through ploughing or fertilisation. During habitat surveys in Cumbria we would sometimes come across largely-improved fields with just the odd clump of Crane's-bill surviving at the margins. While it can survive and spread clonally under low grazing intensity, summer grazing may reduce or prevent seed production.

Sensitivity to grazing (chapter 11) may be why it is often only found on inaccessible rock ledges in grazed woods. Rock ledges may also

Wood Crane's-bill – a component of ungrazed ashwoods in the north and west.

be less shaded, an additional benefit to the plant as its flowering is reduced under tree cover. Because of its northerly distribution, it is one of the species whose distribution is likely to contract if conditions get warmer with climate change.

Atlantic hazelwoods

Along the west coast of Scotland the windswept conditions make it difficult for tall-growing trees to thrive. Fragments of hazelwood on rocky outcrops and in ravines with fertile soils might then be considered a form of ash-type woodland (W9), but this does not do justice to their interest.

While working for the Nature Conservancy Council in the 1980s, our local officer, Peter Wormell, suggested we look at a wood on Seil Island, Argyll. Hazel *Corylus avellana* bushes formed a tight cloak around a low coastal hill. The western slope was nearly vertical while the top of the hill was open with grass and Bracken glades. The Hazel was up to about 6m high in sheltered places, but only about 1–2m high where it faced the full force of the westerly wind. There were few other shrubs, apart from Eared Willow which formed a fringe along the wetter ground at the base of the hill. The British Lichen Society had identified the wood as something special, but what impressed me was the huge variety in the ground flora. Under the trees, Creeping

Soft-grass and Bluebells were abundant, with Pignut and Greater Stitchwort *Stellaria holostea*; flushed areas had much Wild Garlic, while fern-banks covered the rocky areas.

The site was proposed as a Site of Special Scientific Interest (SSSI) and added to the Nature Conservation Review list of nationally important sites. Unfortunately, the designation process was sidelined with the break-up of the NCC in 1991. The site is now managed as a reserve by the Scottish Wildlife Trust as Ballachuan Hazelwood. Other patches of hazelwood along the west coast have also been surveyed and found to be equally species rich (Coppins & Coppins 2012).

Ballachuan Hazelwood, with Hazel on the slopes and with a lower fringe of Sallow.

These Atlantic hazelwoods could be looked on as analogues of the Hazel forests that were widespread across much of Great Britain in the early post-glacial period, but it seems unlikely that they have never been cut at some time or other. On the top of the hill at Ballachuan are some old Beech, probably from the early 19th century. Might whoever planted the Beech also have been managing the Hazel on the slopes?

A rich Ash–Hazel woodland flora at Ballachuan, but without any Ash!

Types of British woodland: the south and east

The woods of the south and east have a warmer, drier climate than those of northern and western Great Britain. Because of this, mosses, liverworts and ferns that depend on humid conditions are less abundant and there are fewer species of these groups present. On the other hand, the herb and grass components have a higher diversity because there are more vascular plant species found in southern than northern Great Britain. South-east England also has the greatest area of surviving ancient woodland, which may contribute to the overall richness of the woodland ground flora. Woodland types commoner in the south and east include various Oak and Ash woodland types, Beech and Yew woods and some wet woodland communities (W1, 2, 5, 6, 8, 10, 12–16 on the dartboard).

Lowland oakwoods

Oak and Birch are usually common in the canopy on acid soils in the lowlands, as they are in the uplands (Rodwell 1991). Many woods on these soils, such as Sherwood Forest, have a long history as wood-pastures and are primarily of conservation interest for their old trees and their associated invertebrates. At Sherwood Forest these include the largest British pseudoscorpion, all of about 8mm long! If some northern limestone woods can be seen as hay meadows with trees, these oakwoods are lowland heaths with trees. The vegetation under the oaks is generally dominated by Wavy Hair-grass and Bracken, with some Bilberry and Heather (W16). Where the soils are slightly richer, Bramble and Wood Sage start to come in, with Purple Moor-grass found where the conditions are wetter.

OPPOSITE PAGE:
The Major Oak in Sherwood Forest.

On the deeper, more fertile, brown-earth soils, Oak may still be common in the canopy but with a Hazel coppice understorey (W10) and some combination of Bramble, Bracken or Honeysuckle abundant in the ground flora. This is probably the commonest type of broadleaved woodland in the lowlands. On ancient sites there may be displays of Bluebell and Wood Anemone in spring, or dense stands of Wood Spurge in recently coppiced areas. Locally, other trees, such as Lime or Hornbeam *Carpinus betulus*, may predominate. Many of the Lincolnshire Limewoods studied by George Peterken (1993) are of this type, while Hornbeam is particularly common in a ring of woods around London that once supplied firewood to the city.

The mixed woods just outside Canterbury known as The Blean (mainly Oak, Hornbeam and Sweet Chestnut *Castanea sativa*) have large areas of Bramble, Bracken, Honeysuckle, Wood Sage and Ivy (Holmes & Wheaten 2002). Woodland specialists present include the Hairy and Great Wood-rush, Wood Millet, Butcher's-broom and Goldenrod *Solidago virgaurea*. The most important plant in The Blean is however the Common Cow-wheat, because it is the food plant for one of our rarest butterflies, the Heath Fritillary (chapter 9).

OPPOSITE PAGE:

Oak over Wavy Hair-grass (W16) in a wood near Sheffield (top).

Creeping Soft-grass on the slope under Hornbeam (W10) in Wormley Woods, Hertfordshire (below).

A green and white carpet of anemones at Chalkney Wood, Essex.

Wood Anemone or Windflower

Late in the season, Oak, Hornbeam, Sweet Chestnut and Lime stands can be quite dull with large expanses of bare leaf litter, but in spring, these areas may be a mass of Wood Anemone *Anemone nemorosa*. It is second only to Bluebell in the way that it can carpet spring woods, with shimmering displays of white starry flowers and the occasional dash of the purple variant.

William Turner, in 1562, described Wood Anemone as 'Ranunculus …the fourth kinde with a white floure' which 'groweth in woddes and shaddish places in April'. Windflower, an alternative name, picks out the way in which the petals tremble in a light breeze, making them difficult to photograph. Other local names reflect the colour of its flowers (Drops of Snow, Moon-flower, Granny's Nightcap) or spring appearance (Cuckoo-flower) (Grigson 1975).

Anemones can be found throughout Great Britain except for the Fens of Eastern England and the far north of Scotland. They persist in grassland and heath and are less dependent on woodland in the north and west of Great Britain (Shirreffs 1985). On moist to wet soils their shallow rooting system allows them to survive short-term waterlogging. They are however at risk of suffering from summer drought, so potentially under threat from climate change.

An Anemone plant can spread slowly outwards, at about 2–5cm a year, through growth of stems just below the surface of the soil. These stems, connecting the different parts of the patch, break down after about five years, or if they are damaged by trampling, with the result that patches of apparently independent plants may all be genetically the same. Individual patches may die out, but the clone can survive for hundreds of years. This carpet growth allows Anemone to shade out smaller competitors, but it may itself be pushed into secondary place by taller species such as Dog's Mercury or Bluebell. Donald Pigott (1982) at Lancaster University showed that if the Bluebell leaves were held apart to stop them shading the Anemone it was able to spread more and produce more flowers.

The association of Wood Anemone with ancient woodland in the south and east is probably linked to this slow rate of vegetative spread and low levels of seed production and dispersal. For seed to be set, pollen from one plant must be carried by bee or beetle to a genetically different plant. Even then, the seed is not always viable. Wood Anemone has no special adaptation to help the seeds disperse, although they may be spread short distances by ants. Once a seedling has established, it may be many years before it flowers. This is a plant that takes its time in all aspects of its ecology!

Wood Anemone, also known as Windflower.

Similar woods on the north side of London were studied by Edward J. Salisbury, one of the pioneering ecologists working at the beginning of the 20th century, who later became Director of the Royal Botanic Gardens, Kew. His descriptions of the Oak–Hornbeam woods of Hertfordshire showed areas dominated by Bramble and Honeysuckle, Creeping Soft-grass and Wood-sorrel. In the drier areas Bluebell dominated, whereas in the damper zones Wood Anemone was abundant (Salisbury 1916, 1918). After the Second World War large parts of these woods were felled and replanted with conifers, but Wormley Wood and Hoddesdon Park were later bought by the Woodland Trust and the conifers are now being taken out again.

Lowland mixed ashwoods

Lowland mixed ashwoods (W8) are widespread in the lowlands on fertile soils. They usually have some Field Maple *Acer campestre* and Hazel in the understorey, but the proportions of the three species vary in different woods. In addition, some Elm, Small-leaved Lime, Spindle *Euonymus europaeus*, Dogwood *Cornus sanquineus*, Privet *Ligustrum vulgare*, Hawthorn *Crataegus* spp., Wayfaring Tree *Viburnum lantana* or Wild Service *Sorbus torminalis* is often present. Typical examples include the Cambridgeshire boulder-clay woods described by Oliver Rackham and the richer examples amongst the Lincolnshire woods studied by George Peterken (Peterken 1993, Rackham 2003).

Other plants, such as Lords-and-Ladies, Yellow Archangel and Bugle, found under Ash–Dog's Mercury woodland (W8).

Dog's Mercury is generally the most widespread ground flora species, but Wild Garlic, Nettle and False Brome can also be locally abundant. Other species may become common, depending on small variations in soil or light conditions as recorded in vegetation maps for Monks Wood near Huntingdon (Steele & Welch 1973), or those for Hayley Wood near Cambridge (Rackham 2003). This is the richest woodland type in terms of woodland specialist plants. The differences between ancient and recent woods can be very marked, with recent woods often dominated by just Nettle and Bramble, or, if the wood is very shady, by Ivy.

Ivy: friend or foe?

Ivy *Hedera helix* is mainly found in the south and west of Europe, becoming much less common, particularly as a climber, in central Europe. It shares this strongly Atlantic distribution in Europe with the two other plants closely associated with Christmas – Holly and Mistletoe. In the past Ivy was valued by countryfolk for keeping evil off milk, butter and animals, and whooping cough away from children (Grigson 1975).

The plant is common throughout Great Britain, except in northern Scotland, on dry to moist, generally fertile, soils (Metcalfe 2005). Its thick stems climb straight up or round trees and branch out to form a dense evergreen canopy within that of its host, but it can also spread across the woodland floor as a dense carpet. In eastern England these carpets are most often seen in recent woods, but they are common in many beechwoods and in ancient ashwoods in the west, provided the woods are ungrazed. Ivy has been important since Neolithic times as

winter fodder for livestock, although it can be toxic if too much is eaten at a time. If they are not eaten, the lower leaves can last for three or four years. Unusually for British plants there are two forms of leaf: those low down (the juvenile foliage) are lobed, while those higher up on the flowering branches are oval and unlobed.

Ivy is becoming more common, especially in eastern, and parts of southwest, England. The shift to mild winters favours it, as do increased levels of nitrogen compounds deposited from the atmosphere (see chapter 16). Ivy is also tolerant of wind-borne dust, from bare fields and roads, and is abundant in the woods and hedges near limestone quarries.

Many people think that such 'ivy-infestations' kill trees (Patch 2004), and I often come across Ivy stems cut through at the base by guerrilla conservation action, even on nature reserves. The winter foliage area of an ivy-grown tree can increase the risk that the tree will blow over in a storm, but vigorous trees should be able

Ground-carpeting Ivy with lobed leaves.

Ivy fruits.

to withstand this pressure. Ivy is only likely to outgrow its host's canopy if the tree is already weakened by some other factor. For example, elms killed by Dutch Elm Disease often became covered by Ivy and stood out starkly in the hedges, before they fell. We may see a similar thing happening over the next few years with dying Ash, as the Ash Dieback disease spreads across the country.

Campaigns against Ivy should be countered by its high conservation value, as the food plant for the summer generation of Holly Blue butterflies (the spring generation feeds on Holly). The stems and leaves provide shelter and foraging potential for small birds. Its fruit contributes to late winter/early spring food for thrushes, robins, blackcaps and starlings, which may help to disperse the seeds, although wood-pigeons take the unripe Ivy berries, thus destroying much of the crop. Ivy is a critical source of late pollen and nectar for bees, butterflies and moths, both in terms of the numbers of species for which it provides, and the numbers of individuals that congregate

around a flowering branch (Elton 1966). However, Ivy honey can set like rock in the comb, making it difficult to extract. Some say Ivy honey has a somewhat unpleasant taste, but also multiple therapeutic properties (perhaps on the principle that anything that tastes nasty is good for you!), and it does make good mead.

Ivy on ruins is often thought to add to their romance, as reflected in early descriptions of Tintern Abbey, Monmouthshire. A programme of Ivy removal was then instigated by the Ministry of Works in 1914. More recently I was persuaded to clear it from the walls of my terrace in Peterborough when I wanted to sell the house. In fact, while Ivy roots do enter existing cracks and weaken old mortar, solid walls should not be damaged. Moreover, its web of dark green leaves can protect walls against pollution damage and act as a 'thermal shield', insulating brick or stonework from the extremes of temperature and moisture that themselves cause cracks (Sternberg et al. 2010, 2011). So, cling on to your Ivy.

Beechwoods on chalk and limestone

Just as the pinewoods are outliers of the European boreal forests, our beechwoods are the westerly outpost of the central European Beech forests. The tree casts a deep shade and its shallow roots compete with those of the ground flora for nutrients and water, so the large areas of deep leaf litter often found under Beech can appear rather dull botanically at first sight.

Beech woodland is strongly associated with the chalk and limestone of southern England. The woods of the Chilterns and the Cotswolds in particular were the subject of studies by A.S. Watt, a lecturer in Forestry, later Forest Botany, at Cambridge. Watt's beechwood studies are summarised in Sir Arthur Tansley's (1939) *The British Islands and their Vegetation*, the first attempt at a comprehensive account of our woods, grassland, wetland and coast. Richard Fortey (2016) provides a recent description of one such Chiltern beechwood in his book, *The wood for the trees: the long view of nature from a small wood*.

Common species in chalk and limestone beechwoods include Dog's Mercury, Ivy, Sanicle and Wood Melick (W12), with Bramble where there is sufficient light, for example under canopy gaps. The continental affinities of this woodland type are indicated by species that are much more widespread through central Europe, such as Coralroot Bitter-cress and Wood Barley. The beechwoods are also noted for their orchids, such as the White Helleborine *Cephalanthera damosonium* and Red Helleborine (this last only found in Great Britain in a handful of sites). Less rare, but with an unusual lifestyle, is the Yellow Bird's-nest.

ABOVE:
Beech over chalk (W12) with Dog's Mercury.

RIGHT:
Coralroot Bitter-cress
– an uncommon plant of
Chiltern beechwoods,
but more common on
the Continent (as here
in Italy).

Living off others

Yellow Bird's-nest *Hypopitys monotropa* is part of the Heath family, but it has given up on leaves and photosynthesis. Instead it is parasitic on a fungus that is associated with its roots. The fungus is in turn linked to the beech-roots and derives its energy from the tree, some of which is then siphoned off by the Yellow Bird's-nest (Björkman 1960). The fungus absorbs minerals from the breakdown of leaf litter and other organic matter in the soil, so there is an element of two-way exchange in its relationship with the tree. However, the Yellow Bird's-nest appears to be contributing nothing to the party.

The plant occurs mainly in southern England, generally under Beech, although sometimes associated with Hazel or Pine. A colleague of mine reports seeing it in abundance among young pines at Newborough Warren on Anglesey. It only appears above ground for a few weeks each year when it flowers. The short fleshy stems, bent over at the tip, give rise to one American name, Dutchman's Pipe, for such plants. The species may be in decline and many sites for it were lost before the Second World War. However, its largely invisible lifestyle means it is easily overlooked.

Although Yellow Bird's-nest had been reported from Wytham Woods, for example, no-one had seen it there since the 1950s. Then we came across a reference in Charles Elton's diaries. Elton was one of the founders of community ecology in Great Britain and a leading figure in promoting research programmes in Wytham Wood in the 1950s.

A specimen of Yellow Bird's-nest collected from Wytham Woods in the 1950s.

Beech on acid soils

Despite its association with chalk and limestone landscapes, Beech also grows well on acid soils, for example in the New Forest and Burnham Beeches, as long as these are reasonably free-draining. The flora may again be sparse, particularly where Holly develops as an understorey. Bramble, Bracken and Wood-sorrel can be abundant (W14). In Wytham Woods the best displays of bluebells tend to be under the Beech that have been planted on a band of acid sandy soil between the clay at the bottom of the hill and limestone on the top. At the right time in spring these stands become a blue lake that stretches off into the distance.

His diaries contain a wealth of information about those early years (Kirby 2016), including where he had found the Yellow Bird's-nest: '25/7/1953. In the beech wood south of the path (above the swimming bath, where *Cephalanthera damasonium* site is) was a great outburst of the Bird's-nest (*Monotropa hypopithys*) growing in scores under the beeches, on the barish-ground or litter, parasitizing the roots… we have a specimen previously from this Belt'.

A live plant seen in the same place in 2014.

The belt of woodland referred to (Brogden's Belt) is only a couple of hectares in extent and the White Helleborines are still there. Re-finding Yellow Bird's-nest should have been straightforward, but first attempts failed. After an hour's searching, I gave up and started to walk out of the Belt, only to see the plant less than a metre from a well-used path! The species has also been relocated at the second place noted in the Elton records, appropriately enough during a tree-planting event by Elton's family. Richard Fortey describes similar excitement at finding Yellow Bird's-nest in his wood in the Chilterns. We have seen the plant in Wytham each year since its rediscovery. Its apparent absence in Wytham since the 1950s could have been put down as another effect of our changing woodland environment. In fact, it was more that surveyors often do not see plants that they do not expect to be there!

On these more acid soils there are fewer orchids, but one of the other oddities of our flora, the Butcher's-broom, may be present (Thomas & Mukassabi 2014). This is a small spiky shrub, but it is usually included with the ground flora as it seldom gets more than about a metre and a half tall. It is a member of the Lily family and what look like oval leaves are not leaves at all but modified flattened stems. This becomes apparent when the small greenish flowers and later the red berries appear from the middle of them.

Where Beech grows on even more acid soils the ground flora is similar to that of acid Oak and Pine woods, with Wavy Hair-grass, Bilberry and Heather (W15). Which of the three ground flora species is

ABOVE:
Butcher's-broom flowers and fruit.

BELOW:
Beech over Bilberry (W15) in the New Forest.

most abundant depends in part on the degree of shade, with Heather only in the most open places. As in acid oakwoods, Bilberry cover may be reduced by heavy grazing.

In woods in central Germany, acid-loving plants sometimes unexpectedly turn up around the base of Beech trees growing on limestone soils. Rainwater falling on the trees is channelled back along the branches and runs down the trunk. The water becomes more acid from pollutants that have been deposited on the leaves and bark and this changes the chemistry of the soil immediately around the tree base (Wittig & Neite 1986). The species that need more alkaline soils such as Wood Meadow-grass *Poa nemoralis* are only found well away from

the trunks. This effect can sometimes be seen around old beeches in Great Britain.

Beechwoods are only considered native in southern Great Britain. However, Beech grows and regenerates well much further north. Tansley (1939) includes an account and photograph of beechwoods studied by A.S. Watt in Aberdeenshire. Here, the flora included not only woodland specialists such as Wood-sorrel and Wood Anemone, which are found further south, but also Chickweed-wintergreen, very much a northern species. Generally, these northern stands are acid beechwood types, but I have been shown a mature beechwood on limestone near Port Appin (Argyll), which had a rich flora, including Bird's-nest Orchid *Neottia nidus-avis*, Spurge-laurel and Narrow-leaved Helleborine. A challenge for the conservation sector is whether or not to treat these northern beechwoods as part of the future natural range of Beech (Wesche *et al.* 2006). The woods are planted (or have regenerated from planted trees), but Beech might have spread into Scotland naturally over the last few thousand years, even in the absence of humans.

Beech woodland beyond its traditional native range, near Nairn in north-east Scotland.

Woods without a ground flora!

The flora under Beech may sometimes be thin, but there are some native woodland types that are distinguished by an almost complete absence of ground flora. Yew woodland (W13) is the most distinctive example, found for example on the southern chalk, in the limestone woods around Morecambe Bay and in the Durham denes. Box scrub, found on Box Hill, at Boxwell in the Cotswolds and on the Chequers Estate in Buckinghamshire, is equally effective at eliminating most of the ground flora below. A third native evergreen, Holly, is much more widespread, and commonly occurs as an understorey species to Oak or Beech. Where Holly is increasing its cover, the ground flora declines and may be wiped out completely (chapter 11). Conservation managers need to decide if they are prepared to let this happen or to control Holly spread, as they do for the non-native evergreen Rhododendron.

Remnants of our wetland woods

Most woods in the lowlands occur on relatively dry ground, but 7,000 years ago there would have been a rich variety of wet woodland and scrub in and around extensive areas of swamp and bog. Taller forests would have formed galleries along the meandering channels of the river valleys. Virtually all of this has disappeared because the land has been cleared and drained. However, where wet ground is left alone, we can start to get a feel for what we have lost.

Goat Willow *Salix caprea* and Grey Sallow *Salix cinerea* often form a fringing zone on the edge of ponds, lakes and large rivers. They may be early invaders of neglected wet corners of fields, silted-up pools or old canals. Large patches have developed on the former tin-streaming areas at Goss Moor in Cornwall since the Second World War (Southall *et al.* 2003) as grazing on these areas has declined. Willow stems tend to collapse and then regrow, creating a great tangle of branches. Common Marsh Bedstraw, Soft Rush and Water Mint are the most frequent ground flora species, but there may be much bare, rather uninviting, black ooze in the summer when the water level is low (W1). A colleague reports seeing the introduced (and invasive) American Skunk Cabbage *Lysichiton americanus* growing on this black ooze in the kind of niche it occupies in British Columbia.

In lowland fens and mires, such as around the Norfolk Broads or the meres of Cheshire and Shropshire, Grey Sallow, mixed with Birch

and Alder, forms part of the woodland associated with tall reeds and sedges (W2). Often it has developed through the invasion of fens or mown marshes when the management stops (Wheeler 1980). Tall fen-herbs such as Meadowsweet, Nettle and Hemp-agrimony are common. These herbs start to thin out where there is dense shade. Rare species associated with this type include Marsh Fern *Thelypteris palustris* and Elongated Sedge *Carex elongata*. This latter is scattered through southern Great Britain and into lowland Scotland, including on the banks of Loch Lomond. It forms loose tussocks that have a somewhat precarious existence. The plant needs wet conditions, yet at the same time cannot tolerate continuous waterlogging or much competition from other species. So, for example, it does not colonise newly exposed mud where it would have the waterlogging but avoid other plants. One place it can grow is on collapsed Alder and Willow branches, where these are just above the flood level but with easy access to water for its roots (David 1978). Many locations for this species were lost in the early 20th century through drainage and wetland improvement.

Alder woods often form in the lowlands on base-rich organic soils, on the edges of standing or slow-moving water. The tall Tussock-sedge, herbs such as Yellow Loosestrife *Lysimachia vulgaris*

Beware the poisonous Hemlock Water-dropwort.

and the sprawling Bittersweet give these stands a distinctive appearance (W5). A plant to watch out for though is Hemlock Water-dropwort *Oenanthe crocata*; it is one of our most poisonous species, but, fortunately, also quite easy to recognise. A further type of alderwood is common but can be rather dull. At the upper margins of the flood-line there may be stands of Cleavers, Bramble and Broad Buckler-fern (W6). Often too, there is an accumulation of washed-up litter, both natural debris such as the dead stems of Common Reed *Phragmites australis* or Hemlock *Conium maculatum*, and human rubbish in the shape of plastic bottles, bags and bits of old rope. These sites are often rich in nutrients, making them one of the more natural habitats for Nettle.

But my wood's not like any of these!

The descriptions and lists of species found in the National Vegetation Classification (Rodwell 1991) are based on an amalgamation of samples from across the country: any individual wood is unlikely to contain the full range of species listed. Even some of the species most common for that woodland type generally may be absent from your particular wood. Conversely you may have species that are abundant but are shown as scarce in Rodwell's lists. For example, Great Wood-rush is sometimes almost dominant in ungrazed oakwoods, but usually is present only as scattered patches, so it does not feature in the general oakwood descriptions. The maps of where different types of woodland occur must also be treated with caution. They show only where woodland types have so far been recorded; new records help to fill in gaps and sometimes to extend the range. I did however (correctly as it turned out) question a report of montane willow-scrub (W20) in a wood on Humberside, barely above sea level!

Another complication is that the bulk of the NVC records come from mature stands. Recently coppiced or felled areas have a different flora, as do rides, which usually contain many species more typical of grassland and other open habitats. In addition, botanists tend to put more effort into describing rich and interesting woods, so the variation sampled for the production of the NVC was largely that shown in woods that were still semi-natural and long-established, if not always ancient. Less recording has been done in the new woodland growing up along railway lines, planted in field corners, or the great dark plantations created mainly in the 20th century.

A tale in the sting

Stinging nettles are found throughout the country on waste ground and corners of gardens and farmyards where they cover 'many springs, the rusty harrow, the plough long worn-out' as Edward Thomas put it in one of his poems written in the early 20th century. The ubiquity of nettles is partly because they can be spread by animals, as well as more commonly on the wind. Many seeds do not germinate immediately but become a major part of the soil seed bank, to reappear in future years when the ground is next disturbed.

In woods, Nettle picks out places rich in phosphates (Taylor 2009), such as around the remains of old buildings, but also where the soil has been disturbed by the digging of badgers or rabbits, or where there is an accumulation of bird droppings, for example below heronries. In the Białowieza Forest in Poland, I once saw a neat line of nettles marking what remained of a rotting log. Birds perching on the log, plus the small mammals running along or hiding underneath it, had left their droppings and raised the local nutrient levels.

Nettles are therefore common in recent woods planted on former farmland, where the

fields have a legacy of phosphates from past fertiliser application, and also along hedges and wood edges (often hiding a ditch) where they benefit from high light conditions and fertiliser inputs from the adjacent fields. They are, however, also a component of ancient woodland vegetation where the soil is naturally disturbed, such as along the base of limestone slopes and at the edges of wet woods.

As one of our tallest herbs, typically around a metre high, with a dense root system that may spread up to 50cm in a year, nettles are a strong competitor, and there may be few associated species other than Rough Meadow-grass *Poa trivialis*, Ground Ivy and Cleavers. Nettles are however not very tolerant of dense shade, so this may limit how far patches can spread. Nettles do also provide food for a wide range of insects, including the caterpillars of Peacock and Small Tortoiseshell butterflies.

Nettles are wind-pollinated, the pollen release reaching a peak in the June–August period – as hay-fever sufferers become all too aware. Nettle pollen was common in the early post-glacial period, about 10,000 years ago, then declined somewhat during the period when tree cover is thought to have been highest (about 7,000 years ago), before rising again from the Neolithic period onward as farming spread. Such a widespread, large and useful plant must have attracted the attention of our ancestors from very early times and is still collected today. Young leaves are nutrient-rich and can be made into soup; fibres can be extracted from the stems and turned into string and cloth. Even the stings have their uses as a possible cure for rheumatism, as a less stringent beating than Birch twigs in saunas, and in children's fighting games.

Nettles.

These new woods cover such a large (and increasing) area that they tend to be what many people are most likely to encounter. Under the trees there are usually large areas of bare leaf litter and twigs, or extensive stands of just one or two common species – Nettle, Bramble, Broad Buckler-fern and Bracken – which do not fit the classifications very well. Yet even such new woods are not without potential for woodland plants, given the right treatment. If we do not try to improve them, we are condemning the next generation to a legacy of dull woods (see chapter 15).

Classifications are also only ever a snapshot of what woodland was like when the surveys were carried out. Yet the woodland flora is not static but constantly changing, both through the seasons, as considered in the next chapter, and through the less predictable disturbances that help to maintain its variety (chapters 9, 10 and 11).

For everything there is a season

'When Gorse is out of bloom, kissing is out of season', the traditional saying goes, but fortunately, the odd Gorse flower can be found at almost any time of year. Otherwise, the marked seasonal differences in the growth and flowering of woodland plants are one of the delights of living in Great Britain. Many of these differences are linked to the amount of light, warmth and water that plants forming the woodland flora receive, which in turn is influenced by the nature of the trees and shrubs above them. On any one day, for example, a Primrose under the shade in a wood experiences a different microclimate to that of a Daisy in a nearby meadow. If the Primrose is in an ashwood it will have a longer growing season than one in a beechwood because Ash is generally later to produce its leaves than Beech and more light gets through an ash canopy than a beech canopy. Then there are the changes through the year.

In spring the woods are generally getting warmer; light levels are high in broadleaved woods because the leaves on the trees have not yet opened. Soil moisture is also usually quite high because the trees have not been using much water over the winter. Summer sees warmer temperatures overall. The expanding tree leaves cut out some of the warmth as well as much of the light, so it is cooler under the canopy than outside. Rainfall is less than in winter and some of what there is never reaches the ground because it is caught on the tree leaves and is evaporated back into the atmosphere. Below ground there is more competition from the trees for water, meaning that there is increased risk that the ground flora will suffer from drought.

Light levels start to rise again in the autumn as the trees drop their leaves, but the days are getting shorter and temperatures declining, so growth conditions are not as favourable for the ground flora as in

OPPOSITE PAGE:
Waiting for the sun.

131

the spring. Soil moisture starts to be recharged. Low-growing plants, such as Violet and Wood-sorrel, may be at risk of being smothered by leaf litter. Eventually comes winter, when plant growth is mainly limited by low temperatures and there is a risk of frost damage to above-ground stems and foliage. For much of our woodland flora, spring tends to be the season of peak flowering, summer the main vegetative growth period, autumn a time of dispersal of seeds and fruits, while winter is a time of rest.

Spring – the season of flowers

'Tis the first time of the year, now the violets do appear; Now the rose receives its birth and pretty primroses deck the earth.' (Staines Morris, traditional).

Along with the violets, spring is marked by new shoots pushing through the leaf litter, in the form of the delicate fronds of Wood Anemone and the coiled leaves of Lords-and-Ladies, or the unfurling croziers of young ferns. There is a freshness to the new leaves on the Bramble stems, unsullied by the tears or holes of the dark, ragged and blotched survivors that they replace. In acid woods there are the opening buds of Bilberry, and the bright green leaves of Purple Moor-grass showing amongst the loose dry hay from the previous year's growth.

As the year progresses there is a rough sequence to flowering which is especially marked in lowland mixed woods. A wood's appearance

Green Hellebore, an early flowering species.

The Cuckoo, inspiration
for many local plant names.

can change dramatically over the space of a few weeks. In January
and February, the first flowers may be the rather insignificant green of
Dog's Mercury and Spurge-laurel, with perhaps the odd Wild Daffodil
or Primrose. Things really get going in March and April with the
hellebores, violets, wood-anemones and lesser celandines, but most
obviously a rush of bluebells. Other spring flowers include the little
woodland buttercup known as Goldilocks, Early-purple Orchid, and
the intricate delicacy of Moschatel *Adoxa moschatellina*. In the acid oak
and pinewoods, where they are not bitten back by deer or sheep, the
pink flowers of Bilberry and white of Wood-sorrel emerge.

Spring is also the season when there is the influx of birds, migrating
north to nest in our woods. Thomas Hardy, in his poem *Weathers*,
writes 'This is the weather the cuckoo likes, And so do I'. Grigson
(1975) recorded a wide range of plant names associated with this
herald of spring, in most cases because their flowering more-or-less
coincided with the cuckoo song period. Bugle *Ajuga reptans* in Dorset
and Harebell in Devon were simply Cuckoos: in Wiltshire Wood
Anemone could be Cuckoo-spit; Cuckoo's-meat was the Greater
Stitchwort in Buckinghamshire, but Common Sorrel *Rumex acetosa*
in Cheshire. This could go with Devon's Cuckoobread for Wood-
sorrel and Donegal's Cuckoo-potato for Pignut. Dog-violets were the
Cuckoo's-stockings in Caithness; Burdock in Somerset the Cuckoo-
buttons; Bluebell in Shropshire Cuckoo-boots; Wild Daffodil in
Devon the Cuckoo-rose. Some names however, such as Cuckoo-pint,
an alternative for Lords-and-Ladies, have more earthy derivations.

The smell of spring

There are not many plants in Great Britain that you can smell long before you see them, but Wild Garlic *Allium ursinum* or Ramsons is one – you can sometimes smell it just driving past the wood in a car. It is so distinctive, at least in spring, that a Wild Garlic wood (*hrameslea*) is mentioned in a charter of AD 944 as one of the features used to define the boundaries of a land grant from King Edmund to Bishop Aelfric (Mabey 1996).

Aside from the smell (which can be overwhelming) it is an attractive plant for a short period, with broad bright green leaves and a cluster of white star-shaped flowers on a separate stalk. En masse these can form sheets of white under the trees to rival Wood Anemone. However, the leaves die back quite quickly, leaving a messy, slimy mix of yellowing leaves and pale flower stalks.

Wild Garlic is widespread throughout the temperate zone in continental Europe (Ernst 1979), being particularly abundant in damp, nutrient-rich soils, almost always in woodland, because it may suffer from drought in the open. It has been suggested as an ancient woodland indicator in parts of Great Britain, which might imply that it does not spread very well, although it is good at taking over its local neighbourhood. The seeds generally fall close to the parent plant so one plant becomes a small clump, then a bigger clump and eventually a whole swathe of green and white. Over 2,000 plants per square metre were counted in a wood in northern Germany (Ernst 1979). Once established, it holds its own, possibly helped by the effect of the rapid decay of the leaves in mid-summer, which may inhibit the growth of other herbs. In late summer there can be strips of woodland, often by streams, that are just bare litter, but dig down a few centimetres and you will find the bulbs.

In Wytham Woods there is evidence for recent longer-distance spread. In the 1950s Mick Southern, who worked in the Bureau of Animal Population under Charles Elton, drew up a map showing *The distribution of certain plants in the Woods*. Eight of the nine species are still rare or uncommon in Wytham, making it logical for them to be mapped in this way: Toothwort, Common Twayblade , Bird's-nest Orchid, Common Gromwell *Lithospermum officinale*, Columbine,

Wild Garlic on the northern slopes of Wytham as far as you can smell.

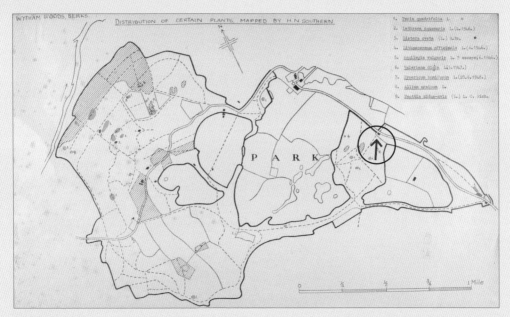

Yet Mick Southern's map from the 1950s shows Wild Garlic at one point only as indicated by the arrow on the right of the map.

Marsh Valerian *Valeriana dioica*, Trailing St John's-wort *Hypericum humifusum* and Herb-Paris. The final species on Southern's list was Wild Garlic.

This was shown as present only in one place in Marley Wood and not at all on the north slope, more than a kilometre away, which is now a Garlic stronghold. There are dense carpets of the plant dominating sight and smell for a couple of months each year. As you move away from the places where it forms solid sheets, the patches get smaller and more dispersed. They become small circular clumps where it looks like just one or two seeds have established and then started to spread. Recent increases in garlic abundance were also seen in the results from a survey of woods across Great Britain where plots first looked at in 1971 were surveyed again in 2001. Wild Garlic had increased its cover and occurrence, unlike many other species (Kirby *et al.* 2005).

Perhaps the seeds are being spread around more in damp soil on the fur, or in the hooves, of deer, whose numbers have increased. Many woods have also become shadier in recent

decades and Wild Garlic has a high tolerance of shade, reflected in its Ellenberg light score of 4 (= plants of shade, rarely in full light). Our woods have also been subject to increased nitrogen deposition (Wytham for example is downwind of a dairy farm and close to a major road) and Wild Garlic has an Ellenberg nutrient score of 7 (more often found in places rich in nitrogen). Wild Garlic is vulnerable to disturbance, for example by heavy trampling, but there has generally been less forestry management activity in broadleaved woods in recent decades than previously. Whatever the reasons, there seems little doubt that Wild Garlic is doing well at the moment.

Wild Garlic is collected by foragers. It is surprisingly mild in flavour and Oliver Rackham used to say it went well with peanut-butter sandwiches. It would be best not to eat too much, however: the 16th-century herbalist, Gerard, noted that a sauce to go with fish may be made from the leaves 'for such as are of a strong constitution'.

The pollination game

Spring flowers, such as the white stars of Wild Garlic, are there for a purpose – to be pollinated so that seed can be set (Proctor & Yeo 1973). Generally, there are benefits for species' survival from combining genes from a different individual, through cross-fertilisation, in order to maintain the potential for adaptation to changing conditions and longer-term evolution. For cross-fertilisation to occur, pollen needs to get from the male anthers on to the female stigma of a flower on a different plant.

Some plants simply cast their fate and pollen to the wind, a strategy used by many of the trees that dominate the forests of Europe and North America and the grasses of prairie and steppes. Wind-pollinated woodland ground flora plants include various grasses, sedges, rushes and two of our commonest flowers of fertile soils, the Stinging Nettle and Dog's Mercury. Such flowers tend to be on flexible stalks that are shaken by the slightest breeze and are usually insignificant, green or brown in colour, because there is no advantage in investing in showy petals. Below the tree canopy is not a good environment for wind dispersal because wind speeds are less than in open grassland. Large amounts of pollen have to be shed into the atmosphere, in order that a little reaches its target. An alternative approach is to use animals as carriers, which in the tropics includes birds and bats, but in Great Britain the pollinator partners are almost entirely invertebrates, particularly insects.

Large coordinated displays of flowers such as the spring masses of Lesser Celandine, Wood Anemone and Bluebell may bring in more insect visitors than if the flowers are scattered (the same is true for human visitors). This is particularly important in early spring when not many flying insects are about. Yellows and white predominate amongst insect-pollinated woodland flowers, followed by blues and purples – red woodland flowers are rare. However, how we see the flowers and how an insect does may not be the same. What to us are pure white flowers can appear strikingly marked if viewed under ultra-violet light. Insects can see these nectar guides and by following the guide-marks they enter the flower inadvertently in the way most likely to pick up and deposit pollen to achieve successful fertilisation.

Insects can also be attracted to plants by scent, which may be better for dusk- or night-flying insects. Again, our ideas of an attractive smell differ from those of an insect: Stinking Iris *Iris foetidissima* (a rather beefy smell) may be rose-sweet to the flies that visit its flowers. The attraction of insects to bright colours, sweetness and strong smells has long been used by entomologists as the basis for various collecting techniques. Yellow bowls filled with water are put out during the day to attract insects that then fall in the water; sugar solutions, perhaps mixed with a drop of rum, painted on to tree trunks are used to attract moths at dusk. Other collectors hover around patches of dung and carrion on paths, waiting for butterflies to come down to collect the salts in such material.

Cup- or saucer-shaped flowers such as Bramble, or the multiple small flowers forming the head of Hogweed, are accessible to a wide range of flies, wasps and bees, beetles and butterflies. This makes them important fuel stations for insects. A sheltered, sunny Bramble bank in mid-summer can be literally a-buzz with excited bees. Having a lot of insect visitors may increase the chances that one of them goes off and spreads pollen to the next Bramble or Hogweed, but much of the pollen may still be wasted because it ends up on a different, but equally promiscuous, species of flower.

More complicated flower structures limit the types of insects that can access the nectar or pollen and hence pollinate them; in return the successful insects have more exclusive use of this resource (Proctor & Yeo 1973). The hanging bells of Bluebell favour bees that are willing to cling on from below; the tubular flowers of the Solomon's-seal *Polygonatum* spp. or the deep spurs of Columbine mean that only long-tongued species can reach the nectar. Even more complex mechanisms can be found, for example that of Lords-and-Ladies. Insects, particularly flies of the genus *Psychoda*, are attracted on the first day that the flower opens by scents produced from the spadix – the spike in the flower's centre. The flies fall into the chamber below but are unable to climb out round its sides because the surface of the chamber walls is slippery. Instead they must climb around over the female flowers, which are receptive at this stage to any pollen that the flies have picked up from a previously-visited plant. On the second day the hairs that prevented the flies walking out up the spadix wither and they can escape that way. In doing so they become dusted with pollen from the now ripe male flowers and this pollen will be carried across to the next Lords-and-Ladies flower that they visit.

Honeysuckle attracts its pollinators through a combination of colour, scent and flower shape. The buds open in the early evening. At this stage the flowers are a clear creamy-white, which is easily seen in the dusk. The flowers give off a powerful scent until after

Lords-and-Ladies, one
of the most complicated
flower structures among
our woodland flora.

nightfall to attract long-tongued moths, such as the Silver-Y, that
can reach deep into the long flower-tube to find the nectar at its base.
Moths visiting on the first night pick up pollen from the anthers, but
the stigmas are not receptive at this stage. The next day the flower
becomes more yellowish and the stigma becomes receptive to any
pollen that is brought in by moth visitors from a flower at the white-
petal stage.

Even more infamous for their apparent luring of insects to 'mate'
with them, and in the process transfer pollen between plants, are
some of the orchids (Proctor & Yeo 1973). The Fly Orchid *Ophrys
insectifera*, which in Great Britain should really be called the Wasp
Orchid, is found at woodland edges on chalk soils. Solitary wasps
of the genus *Argogorytes* are attracted to the plants, initially by scent,
then by sight. The male wasp settles on the flower and makes various
movements that might be seen as a mating attempt, before going off
to try another flower. However, for all this effort, the proportion of
flowers pollinated may be quite low.

The Primrose family illustrates another mechanism, with the
pollen-producing anthers generally set at a different level in the tube of
the flower to the stigmas that receive it (Jacquemyn *et al.* 2009). Some
have the stigmas at the top of the tube and the anthers developing
half-way down – so-called 'pin' flowers; in others, the positions are
reversed ('thrum' plants). If a bee visits a pin type flower and picks up

pollen on its body this will be transferred to the stigmas of a thrum plant but will be in the wrong position if the next flower visited is another pin flower; and vice versa. Occasionally individuals occur where anther and stigmas are at the same level – these plants are self-fertile. This form, found mainly in Somerset and North Dorset, does set more seed than normal plants when pollinators are scarce, but has not spread widely through the Primrose populations, suggesting that there are generally more benefits from cross-fertilisation.

Honeysuckle flowers.

Some plants retain the option of self-fertilisation for occasions when cross-fertilisation becomes unlikely. In late spring Sweet Violet produces small flowers that do not open, but within which self-fertilisation can occur; Wood-sorrel does the same in late summer. Regular self-fertilisation may also have arisen in some Helleborines that tend to flower in dark shady areas where insect pollinators are few.

Some plants have gone one stage further and produce seeds without even a semblance of the need for fertilisation. The process, known as apomixis, is common in the dandelions, lady's-mantles and brambles. Each plant breeds true to itself and this can lead to the creation of many micro-species, with over 400 brambles and over 200 dandelions. This raises conservation questions around whether it is important to maintain all these different variants, with the same diligence as might be applied to Wood Avens or Sanicle. For brambles and dandelions, it is perhaps more important to concentrate on maintaining the

Dandelion.

conditions that promote the formation of new micro-species rather than worrying about every last micro-species itself.

Discussions on pollination are often viewed from the perspective of the plant: that is, what is the most efficient way of achieving fertilisation? However, the insects concerned are in the business of collecting pollen and nectar as food for themselves and/or for their larvae, for the minimum of effort. The concentrations of flowers, for example along woodland rides and glades, are more attractive foraging zones for nectar feeders than where the flowers are scattered. Areas rich in insect pollinators then also attract predators such as wasps and the dragonflies that may be seen hawking up and down woodland rides. Entomologists focus on such areas as well, not least because nectar plants can be important food for the adults of many beetles and flies whose larvae live in dead and decaying wood. Finding the adult insects when they are visiting flowers is generally easier than finding their larvae in logs or large hollow trees.

Plants that flower early in the year are particularly significant from the insects' point of view because there are fewer alternative sources of food for them. Queens of 11 species of bumblebee have been recorded visiting White Dead-nettle in the early part of the year. Later in the year, the scarcity of flowers providing nectar during the shaded stages of the woodland cycle may explain why specialist woodland butterflies also seek nutrients from sap, mud and dung.

Summer – the season of leaves

The glories of the spring flora fade, with the yellowing leaves of Lesser Celandine, Bluebell and Wild Garlic. The expanding leaves on the trees begin to cut back the light available to the ground flora and also restrict how far you can see in the wood. This can create interesting encounters as you round a path corner and nearly bump into a deer. As the woods become darker and more humid, tall plants such as Bramble, Nettle and Bracken reach their peak, so you can't move so easily off the paths. Grasses in glades and ride edges flower in profusion, bringing on hay fever; horseflies and ticks add to the distractions. High summer is not my favourite time in the woods.

On the plus side there is the emergence of the stately Nettle-leaved Bell-flower *Campanula trachelium* and its northern giant counterpart to look for. Scattered through the woods may be patches of white Sanicle and Enchanter's-nightshade, yellow Wood Avens and various St John's-worts *Hypericum* spp. More exotic-looking flowers such as Bird's-nest Orchid and the Greater Butterfly-orchid *Platanthera chlorantha* begin to show, as do the northerly woodland specialities, the wintergreens, Twinflower, Globeflower, Stone Bramble *Rubus saxatilis* and Melancholy Thistle. In open woods on acid soils Heather flowers turn purple; Ragged-Robin comes into flower along ditches; while

Ragged-Robin in June at Beinn Eighe.

Meadow Saffron, a late summer plant.

Meadow Saffron pokes up in grassy glades. Great Horsetails *Equisetum telmateia* in woodland flushes, some a metre high, remind us of their ancestors (real giants) that formed fast-growing, bamboo-like forests up to 20m high in the Carboniferous period (*c.*330 million years ago).

For many species summer is the critical time for building up reserves to see them through the winter and to support the following year's growth. Summer plants depend less on growth from resources carried over from the previous year in bulbs or other below-ground storage organs and more on the photosynthesis from the current year's leaves. While spring plants are often quite short in stature, the summer flowers have more time to grow and include species such as Rosebay Willowherb and Great Willowherb *Epilobium hirsutum* that may be over a metre tall. Summer is also the season for consolidating a plant's position in tussocks and clumps, by extending creeping roots and stems, or developing tall arching thickets that sprawl over their neighbours.

Tussocks, clumps and patches

The ability to form tussocks and clumps is one way that plants can occupy a small patch of ground more-or-less to the exclusion of other species. Grasses such as Tufted Hair-grass and Purple Moor-grass illustrate this approach, as do the three common sedges found in woodland – Remote Sedge, Wood-sedge and Pendulous Sedge – and the Great Wood-rush. Most ferns show a tussocky, or clumpy, formation. The leaves of such plants tend to grow vertically at least initially and then flop to the side. Interspersed between the tussocks or clumps there may be space for other smaller woodland flowers, or there may just be moss and bare litter. This hummocky structure provides plenty of opportunities for invertebrates to shelter among the cracks and crevices in the vegetation at the base of the clump.

Species spreading by underground horizontal stems, or surface-creeping ones, form more solid patches as the advancing growth spreads through or over the soil en masse. Nettles and Dog's Mercury put up vertical shoots at regular intervals so that a continuous canopy cover is formed. Bracken and Bilberry do something similar on acid soils. Ivy creeps above ground, to equal effect, to form solid patches of shiny green. This leaves little space for other species.

Some species creep around in a more dispersed way, such as Yellow Archangel, with stretches of runner-stem between the individual plantlets. This way of the plants spreading, albeit slowly, to exploit locally variable conditions has been termed 'foraging'.

Clumps of Broad Buckler-fern.

Gill-creep-by-the-hedge or Blue Runner

Blue Runner, or Ground-ivy *Glechoma hederacea*, as it is more commonly known today, is widespread, both in Great Britain and across the Continent, on fertile soils, mainly in lightly-shaded places in woods and hedges. The blue flowers appear early in the year, but the leaves reach their maximum in the summer and it remains winter-green. The old names highlight its characteristic growth form that enables it to spread rapidly by means of horizontally-growing stems, for example after coppicing. These stems can infiltrate dense stands of other plants such as Dog's Mercury.

Mike Hutchings and colleagues at the University of Sussex looked in detail at the relationship between the parent and daughter plants of Ground-ivy and have shown that there is movement of material along the runners towards the plants at the tip. Where a plant grows in a variable environment with both high and low nutrient conditions there is a greater concentration of rooting by the daughter plants in the rich patches, so that the necessary minerals are taken up more efficiently. Daughter plants in patches with high light levels may specialise more in carbon assimilation. This division of labour allows the whole runner to grow more vigorously (Hutchings & Elizabeth 1999).

Ground-ivy's strong-smelling leaves were one of the chief bittering agents used in making beer prior to the 16th century and were also used in tea as a remedy for coughs (Grigson 1975). It can though be toxic to livestock and the taste or smell may make it less palatable to deer, allowing it to increase at the expense of more palatable species. As a low-growing plant Ground-ivy also benefits when deer take out taller shade-casting species such as Bramble.

Ground-ivy creeping around.

Scramblers, sprawlers and climbers

Various woodland species gain competitive advantage by scrambling or sprawling over their lower-growing neighbours. For example, each year new canes of Bramble push through the litter, sometimes reaching several metres in length. The new canes intertwine with the previous year's growth to create the familiar bramble patch. The flowering branches on the previous year's growth themselves may be up to a metre long. As a result, the summer canopy of Bramble leaves may be held a metre or more above the ground, well above the height of most of the rest of the woodland flora. Creating long canes early in the year comes at a cost, though, as reserves need to be built up the previous year and stored over winter, ready for the spring push. There are gaps between the rootstocks of Bramble plants which other species may be able to occupy; maintaining leaves over winter makes Bramble vulnerable to deer grazing. Wild Rose can form free-standing thickets similar to Bramble and are just as unpleasant to move through, although people usually find roses more attractive.

The sprawling Hedge and Field Bindweeds are pests in gardens, reflected in their local names, such as Devil's-guts. My mother remembers Bindweed being so abundant in weedy wheat fields in the 1930s that it wrapped around the sails of the reaper-binders

Hedge Bindweed – almost tropical in its exuberance.

Old-Man's Beard lianas, an invitation to swing?

and broke them. Yet as part of wood-edges and wet woodland their large trumpet-shaped flowers give something of a tropical feel to the vegetation. Other species, such as Bittersweet, White and Black Bryony (*Bryonia dioica*, *Tamus communis*), scramble across logs, stumps, and up the stems of shrubs such as Hazel or Hawthorn.

Honeysuckle, Ivy and Old-Man's Beard take the sprawling approach to new heights, climbing up from the ground flora, through the shrub and into the tree layers of a wood. Old-Man's Beard (also known as Traveller's-joy) is a plant of scrub and open woodland on chalk or limestone and the nearest thing we have to a tropical liana. Well-grown plants can have stems several centimetres in diameter, trailing in great loops that tempt you to swing on them. Their weight can be enough to bend over young trees, so that even if the tree survives it does not grow with the straight stem desired by timber merchants. John Workman, a noted forester in Gloucestershire, whose woods grew very fine Beech, gleefully told me how he pulled up any Old-Man's Beard that dared to poke up through the leaf litter. Honeysuckle can also deform hazel shoots, but in this instance, the candy-stick twists produced are highly valued for making walking sticks.

A pair of mandrakes

White and Black Bryony are summer flowering sprawling plants, but they are actually unrelated taxonomical oddities, being the only British representatives of the Cucumber and Yam families respectively. The medieval herbalists sometimes used them as substitutes for the Mandrake *Mandragora officinalis*. The root of that plant was said to be man-shaped with many magical properties; it would scream when it was pulled up; and it might drive you mad. Real Mandrake root was expensive, so home-grown Bryony tubers were sometimes trimmed into roughly human shapes and sold instead.

White Bryony *Bryonia dioica* is a climbing plant of well-drained, base-rich soils, generally in hedges and at the edges of woods. It has a bias towards southern and western Europe and, in Great Britain, is largely confined to lowland England. The leaves are deeply lobed, somewhat like a large Field Maple leaf, and the flowers are greenish-white, from which forms a red berry. The whole plant is dangerously poisonous, especially the roots, although in the past it was sometimes used as a purgative.

Black Bryony *Tamus communis* is similarly poisonous, but its bright red berries were at one time preserved in gin or brandy for use against chilblains (Grigson 1975). It is also found on neutral to calcareous, well-drained soils, although its deep roots make it vulnerable to waterlogging in wet woods. Its distribution is a little wider than that of the White Bryony, occurring in Wales and England north to the Lake District and Durham. It is often commonest in ancient woodland within this range, although it grows well in tall shady hedges. Like White Bryony it is a climber, but the leaves are simple, broadly oval with a heart-shaped base, and often a somewhat glossy, shiny look.

White Bryony.

Black Bryony.

Both plants have large tubers that increase in size with age, though I doubt that any now approach the half hundredweight (25kg) claimed for one White Bryony tuber by the herbalist John Gerard.

Autumn – the season of fruits

Summer growth may be slowed by droughts, but even if water remains abundant there comes a point where falling temperatures signal another shift in plant activity in woodland. There is a constant movement in the air as leaves start to drop and the ground turns red and rich brown. Lines of toadstools appear where last week there were none. The bright colours of fruit replace those of the flowers – the lurid pink of Spindle berries or the yellow rings of fallen crab apples around a tree. The ground flora also contributes through the reds of rose hips and the berries of Bittersweet, the blue-black of Bilberry and the red-through-black of Bramble. Woodland flowers are in decline, but Ivy remains a major nectar source through the shortening days for late-season insects, not just the bees thinking 'warm days may never cease' (Keats, *Ode to Autumn*).

The fruits and seeds that plants produce in the autumn enable the plants to colonise new places within a wood, or spread to new woods, where their offspring can grow and flower in turn. Understanding movement of plants around the landscape, by what means, how fast and how far helps us to reconstruct the ways plants moved back into Great Britain after the last Ice Age (chapter 12). Poor colonisation ability partly explains why some plants are common in ancient woods but not in recent woods (chapter 3). Dispersal rates could also be

Rose hips.

Seeds may be dispersed by ants over surprising distances.

critical to identifying which species are going to be able to respond well to future climate change (chapter 16).

Plants certainly turn up in unexpected places. For nearly 30 years I lived within Peterborough city limits. My garden had been enthusiastically dug-over by the previous occupants, but I left it largely to its own devices. False Brome established, probably brought in as seed on my socks, because it is a common plant in many of the sites I visited. Butcher's-broom might have come from a fruit that embedded itself in the tread of my wellington boots, but more likely came in with bird droppings, under my neighbour's Leyland Cypress hedge. Other plants spread their seed in a variety of ways, including the wind, the activities of ants, hitchhiking on and in mammals, or the explosive expulsion of seed from pods. There are also woodland flowers for which there is no apparent special mechanism – the seeds just fall and take their chance, somewhere close to the parent plant.

Wind-dispersed species tend to have very small seeds or spores that can be carried easily in the air. This approach has evolved in ferns, horsetails and orchids. Large numbers of seeds and spores are released and can travel long distances. However, each seed or spore contains very few reserves, so where they land must be favourable for them to survive and establish. Woodland grasses such as Wood Millet and Wood Meadow-grass, and several of the St John's-worts, have bigger seeds that are more likely to be able to germinate and grow where they land, but heavier seeds fall out of the sky more

Old-Man's Beard, waiting to be blown away.

quickly so travel less distance. A third group of wind-dispersed plants also have relatively heavy seeds but have increased their dispersal potential through the addition of a 'parachute' to slow their fall. Such parachutes include the beard of the Old-Man's Beard and the downy hairs on Marsh and Spear Thistle *Cirsium vulgare* seeds.

Wind dispersal, as with wind pollination, is less reliable for woodland flowers than for plants growing out in the open, because wind speeds are lower below the canopy. An alternative is to make use of the mammals that pass through the woods – including woodland surveyors. Seeds or fruits of plants such as Burdock, Cleavers, Giant Fescue and Sweet Woodruff have extensions, hooks or angles that catch in fur (and boot socks), allowing them to be carried to another part of wood or to a new wood altogether. Wild Boar carry seeds in the soil that sticks to their coat after they have been wallowing in mud (Schmidt *et al*. 2004, Von Oheimb *et al*. 2005). A concentration of a species along woodland paths may be a sign of animal transfers.

Theo Heinken, a German researcher, looked at what plants he could find in the fur of his dog on nearly 50 occasions, after it had been taken on its evening walk through a wood. He found, as expected, mainly species with spines or hooks, such as Enchanter's-nightshade, Wood Avens and Sanicle (Heinken 2000). These were not always the most common plants in the wood, illustrating that the species that are spread by this means are only a subset of those present.

Non-specialised seeds may also get a helping hand from animals. G.H. Knight (a teacher at Leamington College) looked at dispersal of the smooth round seeds of bluebells in a Warwickshire wood. He found that rabbits contributed to accidental movement of the seeds through their scufflings. Badgers also included the dead flower stalks with attached seed amongst their bedding and moved material 30–40 metres (Knight 1964).

Knight also looked at seeds on his boots, but even when Bluebell seeds were found they were usually damaged. Trouser turn-ups had more potential – between 20 and 80 seeds might be found in them at the end of a four-hour woodland walk. The Reverend Woodruffe-Peacock (1918) identified seeds or fruits of Burdock, Hairy-brome, Cleavers, Wood and Water Avens on a fellow shooter's clothes and socks. At the next meet they made the chap turn out his pockets and added Enchanter's-nightshade and Creeping Soft-grass to the list. Changes in botanist fashion mean that this form of dispersal is less important than in the past.

In the past, seeds might be spread from wood to wood in the mud on the wheels and bottom of carts. One study of the modern equivalent, the mud on the underside of cars, had seeds of 124 species, including 29 woodland or woodland edge species.

The fashions of past botanists may have provided more scope for seed dispersal.

These were mainly common generalist species including Rough Meadow-grass, nettles, creeping buttercups, Ground-ivy, Self-heal and Tufted Hair-grass (Schmidt 1989).

Seeds may be moved around inside other animals after being eaten, provided they can pass through the gut unharmed. Germination may even be improved by the process and the seeds will be deposited with their own supply of manure. Fleshy fruits such as Bilberry and Bramble are eaten by foxes and martens and the seed subsequently deposited in their dung. Species detected in the dung of larger mammals, such as deer and boar, are usually generalist woodland plants such as rushes, Nettle, Common Chickweed, Tufted and Wavy Hair-grass (Schmidt *et al.* 2004, von Oheimb *et al.* 2005). Woodland specialists, such as Remote Sedge, are only occasionally reported as spread in this way. However, these studies are usually conducted in landscapes of mixed woodland and open farmland, where the animals are feeding preferentially outside the woods. In a densely wooded landscape, more woodland plants might be eaten and hence more seeds dispersed.

Birds contribute to the spread of berry-bearing plants such as Ivy, the bryonies, Bramble and Raspberry, roses, Honeysuckle and some lower growing woodland plants, for example Lords-and-Ladies, Mezereon, Wild Strawberry and Red Currant (Snow & Snow 1988). Wet woodland plants may be spread by ducks and other waterfowl, including tall herbs found in fens such as Gypsywort *Lycopus europaeus*, Purple-loosestrife *Lythrum salicaria*, Great Willowherb and Yellow Loosestrife. Weedy species such as docks, Common Chickweed and Silverweed from the disturbed open ground at the woodland/wetland interface can also be dispersed in this way. The seeds may be in the mud on the webbed feet of water-birds, but often it is through the seed being eaten and then excreted elsewhere.

Woodland plants thought to be dispersed by ants include woodland specialists such as Primrose, Dog's Mercury, Wood and Mountain Melick *Melica nutans*, Hairy Wood-rush and Yellow Archangel. Sometimes these plants have a special nutrient-rich appendage on the seed, called an elaiosome, which is particularly attractive to the ants. A study of Liverleaf *Hepatica nobilis*, a plant of Continental woods, but naturalised in a few woods in Gloucestershire and Yorkshire, found that, other things being equal, seeds with large elaiosomes were taken first (Mark & Olesen 1996). In a German study seeds of Common Cow-wheat were dusted in fluorescent powder and set out close to a

major ant foraging trail (Chlumský *et al.* 2013). The researchers then went back at night looking for the seeds with ultra-violet lights: within seven hours some seeds had been moved up to 36 metres.

Seeds of Purple-loosestrife, a water-edge species, may sometimes be spread by wildfowl.

Ants tend to like warm, dry sites in woodland – they are often found on or close to the edges of rides. Yet there are moist dark woods where ants may be rare but 'ant-dispersed' species common. In these situations, and possibly elsewhere, slugs may be more important than ants. Slugs, like ants, are attracted to the elaiosome and may only eat that. Even if the seeds are swallowed, some pass through the slug and remain viable. In a study of 105 German beechwoods there was a better relationship between 'ant-plant' abundance and slug presence than with ant presence (Türke *et al.* 2012). In Great Britain slugs are thought to disperse the spring-flowering Moschatel (Jefferson & Kirby 2018). The scope for long-distance dispersal of seeds by ants or slugs is less than that by wind or Wild Boar, which might partly explain why some plants seem to be more linked to ancient rather than recent woodland. Ant-dispersed species do include some strong ancient woodland indicators like Wood Anemone and Wood-sedge, but other ant-dispersed species such as Sweet Violet and Ground-ivy can be widespread in new woodland.

Moschatel, or Town-hall Clock, thought to be dispersed by slugs.

The average distance seeds spread each year may be less important than the occasions when a few seeds go very much further, or the exceptional year when good conditions allow lots of seedlings to establish successfully. Such rare or long-distance events, for example the appearance of the Butcher's-broom in my Peterborough garden, may do more for range expansion over centuries than incremental spread by a few tens of metres a year. The study, mentioned above, which looked at the movement of seeds of Common Cow-wheat by ants, also found that the seeds could pass through the gut of cows. The long-distance spread needed for Cow-wheat to have reached Great Britain after the last Ice Age might perhaps have been via the dung-pats of the Wild Ox, before it finally became extinct in 1627. However, more attention has recently been paid to the study of the current local distribution patterns of the plant in relation to its associated butterfly – the Heath Fritillary.

Winter and a time of waiting

Nowadays, autumns seem to be stretching out more, with trees regularly holding leaves into November. Then there comes a gale, a spell of frost, some drippy fog-days, and suddenly most of the wood looks bare. From being the back end of summer, autumn becomes

Common Cow-wheat

Common Cow-wheat *Melampyrum pratense*, though scarce in central England, is generally widespread through most of Great Britain. Its leaves look somewhat like those of Greater Stitchwort, but it has distinctive deep yellow to whitish flowers. It is found on nutrient-poor soils, mainly in woods but also on heaths, and is somewhat northerly in its distribution across Europe. Common Cow-wheat gets some of its nutrients through parasitism on the roots of other species via its fungal mycorrhizal links.

Cow-wheat is an annual species. In the past, on suitable sites it would come up in abundance following woodland disturbance, such as coppicing. Coppice management was abandoned in much of southern Great Britain in the early 20th century and the species declined, although the survival of the plant was not itself threatened. However, the reduction in its abundance in woodland had serious implications for the Heath Fritillary butterfly, for which Cow-wheat is a food plant.

One of the last strongholds for the butterfly in Kent became the Blean Woods north of Canterbury. Martin Warren, for his doctoral research, established that there the butterfly only laid eggs on Cow-wheat that was growing in large open areas; it would not use plants growing in shade. Patches of Cow-wheat in newly cut-over areas were only suitable for the butterfly for a few years, until the coppice grew and started to shade that patch. The butterflies then had to move on, but they tended not to move very far. Suitable open Cow-wheat patches had to be within about 300m of an existing population for Heath Fritillaries to stand a good chance of establishing a new colony (Warren 1991). Managers of the Blean Woods now try to ensure that new-cut areas are large enough and close to others or to wide rides that contain Cow-wheat along their edges. The butterfly's future in the Blean is now more certain, and it has also been introduced to coppiced woods in South-East Essex where it is also flourishing, an example of assisted long-distance dispersal.

Common Cow-wheat may once have been spread by wild cows.

the harbinger of winter. The bright reds and golds of the fallen leaves turn to mucky browns and black as they gradually disintegrate. Winter has arrived.

Despite winter's bleak reputation, woods become lighter and on bright days the low sun slanting through the trees gives them a magical feel. You can see much further, appreciate the architecture of the trees, the folds and hollows across the slopes, and the banks and ditches, some of which are medieval, some more modern.

Many ground flora species disappear from above ground completely and survive the difficult winter months as buried seed, bulbs or other structures hidden in the soil, to reappear again the following spring. Some, such as Purple Moor-grass and Bilberry, are deciduous, losing their leaves as do most broadleaved trees, but retaining an above-ground presence. There are, though, still some green plants on a woodland floor, and provided it is warm enough they may be able to photosynthesise, building up resources for the growth that is to come next year. Common winter-green species include Wavy and Tufted hair-grasses, wood-rushes, Pendulous Sedge, some ferns and Bramble (on its first-year canes) as well as smaller rosettes of Self-heal, Red Campion *Silene dioica* and Stitchwort (Grime *et al.* 2007). However, the plants are vulnerable to snowfalls that flatten down tall plants and to hard frosts that may leave ferns looking blasted and black.

Increasingly with climate change (chapter 16), there is not much of a gap between the time when conditions become too cold and dark for the flora, and the spurt of activity as the next spring arrives. The regular annual cycle is also disrupted when gaps appear in the canopy as a result of woodland management (the next chapter) or more natural disturbances (chapter 10).

OPPOSITE PAGE:
The lack of ground flora in winter reveals surface features such as these WWI practice trenches (top).

Snow flattening brambles, an increasingly rare occurrence in Wytham Woods, Oxfordshire (below).

Mind the gap: the woodcutter's legacy

W oods are often presented as stable and unchanging places. Yet for the plants of the woodland floor conditions are variable and uncertain. The amounts of light and warmth reaching the ground level change over the year, as discussed in the previous chapter, and there are more dramatic effects when a tree is cut, falls or loses a major branch. Suddenly there is more direct light, warmth and rainfall reaching the ground even during the summer. Some ground flora plants might wilt if the temperature rises too much, but for most these increases in resources will be beneficial.

The plants under the gap can grow more leaves, increase their flowering and seed set, but the new resources are not theirs alone. Other plants, perhaps less good at surviving under the shade, may now be better competitors under these improved growing conditions. Felling a few trees to make a canopy gap allowed my Bramble patches to increase their leaf cover by about 50%, and the thicket height increased from about 35cm above the ground to 55cm in just two years.

The extra warmth and light under a gap can stimulate germination of seeds buried in the soil, including some species not seen above ground since the previous gap closed over (see chapter 5). These buried-seed species grow fast and tall because they depend on getting a new batch of seeds back into the soil before the tree canopy re-forms and they are shaded out again. Seeds of other species come in from other temporary gaps and the more permanent open spaces, such as rides, where they have been growing in the wood (see chapter 14). The plants already on the ground have a head-start on the incomers but their lead is soon eroded. The initial free-for-all species richness drops back after a couple of years as the biggest, most competitive species take control of the ground.

OPPOSITE PAGE:
Woods are shaped by their past management.

Columbine flowering in a gap.

During these early years after gap formation, tree and shrub seedlings are vulnerable to competition from this increased ground flora growth. Saplings and stump regrowth that already have a well-established root system have a better chance of getting away. Eventually some tree and shrub growth over-tops even the Bramble and Bracken and gradually dense shade is re-established. Those ground flora species that cannot tolerate dense shade die back. Shade-tolerant species are left to stick it out until the next disturbance.

No two gaps are the same, but the general pattern of exuberant initial growth and slow decline is seen where trees blow over, die from disease, or are burst by lightning strike. The changes have however been most often studied in Great Britain in the context of traditional management practices such as coppicing or in the more infrequent and larger gaps created by clear-felling.

Coppicing – woodland management with a long history

Our distant ancestors would have noted that cutting down our common broadleaved trees does not kill them: a new crop of poles starts to grow the next spring from buds just under the bark of the stump. Let these poles grow to a usable but manageable size

(5–20 years, depending on how big a stem you want and can carry) and then harvest them again. The tree still does not die but throws up another lot of poles from a somewhat larger stump. Repeat more or less *ad infinitum* and you have the coppice cycle.

Casual cutting as and when required developed into increasingly organised forms of management. There are Roman descriptions of how it should be carried out, and many medieval accounts also. Within an individual wood one patch would be cut this year, another the next and so on, resulting in a patchwork of different age classes. A scatter of trees, usually Oak, might be left as 'standards' to be harvested on a longer rotation of perhaps 60–120 years. The standards provided bigger timbers when required, for example to repair the great hall, the church or the village windmill. Rates of cutting might go up when demand for wood was high, or patches might be left uncut for longer when the markets were not so good.

Coppice management was common across Europe, and artists used it to provide a background to their main subjects. The Frontispiece to Oliver Rackham's great work *Ancient Woodland* (Rackham 2003) shows a medieval hunting scene by a Flemish artist set against a recently-cut coppice stand; Bellini has woodmen cutting coppice, apparently oblivious to the brutal *Assassination of St Peter, Martyr* (*c.*1505–7), that is taking place in the picture in front of them. In theory coppicing was meant to be well controlled and lawsuits followed where the rules were not obeyed. For example, in 1555 there was trouble in Wytham

Illustration of tree cutting, drawn by 13th-century Benedictine monk Matthew Paris.

Woods. George Owen (the King's Physician to whom parts of the Woods had been granted) opened proceedings in the Star Chamber against Lord Williams who was accused of causing his tenants to cut wood on Owen's land. A writ was issued against Lord Williams to the effect that he should stop this practice. One of the areas mentioned was Cowley Copse; it is still there today as Cowlease Coppice (Grayson & Jones 1955).

Coppices provided a convenient supply of small-sized wood for domestic and industrial fuel, poles and stems for fencing and building material. More specialised markets included wood for the cogs of windmills, charcoal for gunpowder and oak bark used as a source of chemicals for tanning leather, and it could be big business. *The Gentleman's Magazine* from 1803 noted that land-owners in Colton in the Lake District 'had ceased to breed sheep, so far were they involved in the cultivation of coppices'. Iron-working in the Weald, and then in Cumberland and Argyll, required large amounts of charcoal derived largely from oak coppices; the leather industry, meanwhile, needed plenty of oak bark for tanning. However, cheap imported timber from the Empire, cheap pottery replacing wooden bowls, and coke replacing charcoal as an industrial fuel, gradually drove coppice into decline during the latter part of the 19th century.

The Duddon Valley Iron Furnace in the Lake District was one of the last to still use charcoal from coppice in England.

Despite this, coppice was still a familiar sight in the first quarter of the 20th century. Arthur Ransome included descriptions of oak coppicing and charcoal-making in the Lake District in his *Swallows and Amazons* books. Similarly, in 1949 the first management plan for Wytham Woods had 57 hectares (about 15% of the woodland) allocated to coppice because there was still thought to be a market for local products. Yet just ten years later this was no longer the case, and coppicing was abandoned.

Ecological studies of coppice floras

The distribution of different woodland plants, and their response to coppicing, were captured in papers by early ecologists. Adamson (1912) describes the changes through the coppice cycle at Gamlingay Wood, a mixed ash-maple-hazel coppice in Cambridgeshire. Prior to cutting, 'the light is so much reduced that the ground flora is very scattered and does not form a continuous carpet' but 'great changes take place immediately afterwards owing to the sudden increase of light and of the evaporation rate. Plants from surrounding cornfields and pastures find admission in the sparsely populated soil thus exposed, but apart from these the vegetation becomes very mixed.'

Grasses increased. Adamson lists Tufted Hair-grass, Sweet Vernal-grass, Hairy-brome, Giant Fescue, False Brome, Wood Meadow-grass, Rough Meadow-grass, Common Bent *Agrostis capillaris* and Cock's-foot. Dewberry *Rubus caesius* and Wild Rose spread quickly, the former often 'nearly choking out the existing vegetation'. Common Centaury *Centaurium erythraea*, Great Willowherb and Prickly Sedge *Carex muricata* were more abundant in the coppiced areas, and some species were only found there, including Perforate St John's-wort *Hypericum perforatum*, Square-stalked Willowherb *Epilobium tetragonum*, Welted Thistle *Carduus crispus*, Wild Teasel *Dipsacus fullonum* and Field Forget-me-not *Myosotis arvensis*. Spring flowers, such as Oxlip, Bugle, Ground-ivy and Wood-sedge increased in quantity and abundance for the first two or three years 'but as the shade begins to be reformed many of the species become enfeebled and are crowded out by more tolerant forms... Thus by the gradual elimination of sun-plants and intolerant species the shade phase is again reached'.

Another early ecologist, E.J. Salisbury (1916, 1918), gives a similar account for the coppice flora of the Hertfordshire Oak–Hornbeam woods. After the shrub layer is cut 'firstly there is a great addition

to the number of species occupying the areas formerly shaded; secondly the species already present exhibit an increase both in the number and vigour of individuals'. The maximum development of the ground flora was again usually seen in the second or third year after coppicing. Species already present, but increasing a lot after coppicing, included Bugle, Three-veined Sandwort, Wood Avens, Yellow Archangel, Ground-ivy, Sanicle, Germander Speedwell and Violet. Salisbury, like Adamson, noted that the flora of a coppiced area was made up of different components: the original shade-flora, the species formerly occupying the margins of woods and rides, and weeds. Over half the species recorded in the coppices came from the wood-margin and ride category.

Interest in the sequence of changes in the flora of coppice was rekindled in the 1970s and confirmed these earlier observations. The flora under different ages of mixed Ash–Field Maple–Hazel coppice was surveyed in Foxley Wood in Norfolk (Ash & Barkham 1976). About 10 species, mostly shade-tolerant or shade-avoiding, such as Common Dog-violet, Lesser Celandine, Dog's Mercury, Honeysuckle, Wood Avens, Wild Strawberry and Bluebell, were found in areas around 17–33 years after coppicing. By contrast, over 30 ground flora species were detected in the first year after coppicing. The bulk of the increase in the early years was of species associated with open or

disturbed conditions (Salisbury's wood-margins and weed categories) – Common Bent, Mouse-eared Chickweed *Cerastium fontanum*, Spear and Marsh Thistle, Broad-leaved Willowherb *Epilobium montanum*, Hogweed, Meadow Buttercup *Ranunculus acris* and Common Figwort *Scrophularia nodosa*.

A sparse ground flora under mature coppice.

In Ham Street Woods in Kent, Ford and Newbould (1977) measured the above-ground weight of ground vegetation per hectare for patches 1 to 15 years after coppicing. Peak biomass was recorded in the second year after cutting, at about 2 tonnes per hectare, a hundred times that found under the dense shade of 15-year-old coppice. Just a handful of species – Wood Anemone, Bluebell, Bramble, Bracken, Wood Sage and Rosebay Willowherb – contributed the bulk of the biomass in each age class.

Species richness increased, as in the other studies, and was highest (30 species) in the fifth year after cutting. By this time the coppice layer had partially regrown, reducing the growth of field layer in the immediate vicinity, but there was still enough open ground in between the stools where invasion of new species could take place. Thereafter species richness declined to only 8 species recorded in the plots under fifteen-year-old coppice regrowth.

Rackham (1975, 2003) developed Salisbury's classification of the different types of plants found in coppiced areas based on his observations in eastern England. He distinguished spring-flowering persistent perennials such as the Oxlip and Bluebell; summer-flowering persisters such as Meadowsweet; seed-bank species such as Wood-spurge; mobile plants that move around the wood from one coppice area to another such as Thistles and Willowherbs; casual species that came in sporadically from outside and were not sustainable within the wood, such as Borage *Borago officinalis*; and species that sometimes declined after cutting.

Coppicing affects the abundance of other groups of plants and animals both directly and through its effects on the vegetation structure and composition (Buckley 1992; Buckley & Mills 2015b). The richness of mosses and liverworts may decline after cutting because they are less able to cope with the warmer, drier conditions of the new-felled patch. Spiders that rely on plant stems to anchor the threads of their webs are similarly disadvantaged. As the coppice shoots regrow, the dense thickets that shade out the ground flora provide good nesting and foraging areas for many of our summer migrant birds, notably Nightingale, Blackcap and Willow Warbler. The interlocking shrub canopy creates aerial pathways for dormice. However, it was the declines in some of our violet-feeding woodland butterflies that highlighted why maintaining coppice management might be particularly important for wildlife conservation in Great Britain.

What changes when coppice is cut?

Levels of light and warmth at ground level change when coppice is cut, but Adamson (1912), in his study of Gamlingay Wood, pointed out that also less water is lost because transpiration from the tree and shrub canopy is reduced. The water table rises and species typical of damp or wet soils increase, such as Ragged-Robin *Silene flos-cuculi*, Meadowsweet, Soft Rush and Water Avens, even Flote-grass *Glyceria* spp. in the ruts or wet hollows. There may be more leaf-litter breakdown with the higher ground temperature, creating more bare soil. Disturbance to the ground surface during the felling and extraction of the timber favours establishment of the Ruderal/weedy species, such as Three-veined Sandwort, Burdock, Marsh Thistle, Common Hemp-nettle *Galeopsis tetrahit* and Broad-leaved Dock.

The reduction in the quantity of leaf litter might also be due to its collection by villagers from the coppice plots as bedding for animals. The effect of such leaf-litter removal was tested in a 16-year experiment in a Polish Oak–Pine forest. In the control plots, where litter collection ceased, nutrients increased, along with plants such as Bramble and Wood Millet that prefer such conditions, whereas Bilberry and May Lily declined. These latter, acid-loving, species maintained their abundance where the litter was removed (Dzwonko & Gawroński 2002). I am not aware of any similar experiment being carried out for so long a time in Great Britain. A small trial under way in Wytham Woods has only been going for five years and, as yet, has produced no obvious change in the ground flora.

There is nowadays little use for small twigs or leaf litter, and they are no longer removed after the coppice is cut. During the 1980s, unwanted branchwood was often burnt where coppicing was done on nature reserves, attracting Fireweed, another name for Rosebay Willowherb. This is now discouraged because fires release carbon dioxide back into the atmosphere, may scorch and damage adjacent trees, and kill roots and microbial life in the soil immediately below the fire. An alternative approach is to heap up the branches to act as habitat for insects and other invertebrates. This keeps the nutrients on-site and concentrates them into small, enriched areas that may later be colonised by nettles.

Weather conditions, levels of deer browsing, competition within the ground flora, even just the way in which the cutting and extraction are carried out, can also affect which species grow after a coppice cut. The ground flora response to coppicing may therefore differ from one cut to the next (Rackham 1975), but overall, the shifting mosaic of conditions creates a rich diversity of plant communities across the woodland.

Reviving coppice has been strongly promoted in writings about woodland conservation in Great Britain over the last 40 years, for example Fuller & Warren (1993), Rackham (2003), Steele & Peterken (1982). However, coppicing on the ground has tended to decline. In 1947 a survey of the state of British woodland (HMSO 1952) recorded 141,000 hectares as coppice or coppice-with-standards. By 2003 the worked area had shrunk to less than a fifth of the 1947 figure, to about 23,000 hectares (Forestry Commission 2003). These estimates for current coppice may be on the low side. Coppicing is generally a small-scale activity. Coppice workers and coppice woods often slip under the radar of official surveys. Even so, it is clear from the large stems on old coppice stools found in many woods that they have not been cut for about 70 years or more. There are far fewer coppice stools than there were, and the poles on the surviving stools have grown up to form a dense upper canopy layer, a form of high forest.

Cooling violets and shrinking butterfly populations

Violets are a popular plant, associated in the Victorian language of flowers with a restrained, modest kind of love. The Sweet Violet *Viola odorata* was encouraged for its scent and used in posies to disguise less attractive odours; the two common 'Dog' Violets *Viola riviniana* and *V. reichenbachiana* are unscented.

Violet species are well represented in woodland (Grime *et al.* 2007, Preston *et al.* 2002). The Common and Early Dog-violet can tolerate shade across a wide range of soil conditions. They usually grow as scattered low tufts that may be hidden below the taller species such as Bramble. They are winter-green and contribute to the early spring flowering displays. The number of flowers produced increases considerably after coppicing. Hairy Violet *Viola hirta* tends to be common on base-rich soils in more open conditions, while Marsh Violet *Viola palustris* is found, as the name suggests,

on wet, usually acid, sites. Sweet Violet is also a plant of more open conditions, sometimes, like Snowdrop, a sign of old gardens. The Field Pansy *Viola arvensis* occurs on well-drained soils in open areas, such as disturbed patches of woodland rides and tracks.

The Marsh Violet has lost some ground because of the draining of wet places, and the Field Pansy has become less common, outside woods because weeds in arable crops, one of its other habitats, are controlled by herbicides. Woodland violets remain common but the butterflies that rely on them as food plants for their caterpillars have not done as well. For example, the Pearl-bordered Fritillary and Small Pearl-bordered Fritillary have been lost from many sites in south-east England since the Second World War, even though this remains the region with the greatest density of ancient semi-natural woodland in England.

Dog violets.

The conditions in which the violets grow are no longer right for the butterflies. The butterflies prefer to lay their eggs on violets growing in the first few years after coppice has been cut, when the vegetation cover around the plants is still sparse (Warren & Thomas 1992). The bare soil and litter absorb more heat from sunlight than tall vegetation, creating a warm microclimate around the flowers, and this enables the caterpillars to grow faster because their metabolic rate is linked to temperatures. After a year or two, the growth of other ground flora plants overtops the violets, and the cooler conditions in the shade are less suitable for caterpillar growth.

When most woods were still being coppiced, there would usually have been another recent coppice-cut close by to which the butterflies could migrate to find hot violets. However, as coppice has declined, there are now fewer patches where the violets are in a suitable state and those there are, are more spread out, meaning that the butterflies are less likely to find them in time. Gradually, wood by wood, the butterflies have disappeared.

Some of our rarest plants have declined in a similar way, probably due to a reduction in coppicing or similar forms of woodland management (Preston et al. 2002). These include Spreading Bell-flower Campanula patula, Wood Calamint Clinopodium menthifolium, Crested cow-wheat, Bastard Balm Melittis melisophyllum, Fly Orchid, Irish Spurge, Upright/Tintern Spurge, Spiked Rampion, Suffolk Lungwort Pulmonaria obscura, Starved Wood-sedge and Narrow-leaved Helleborine. Climate change might improve conditions for some of these species in the longer term, but not if we are unable to keep their populations going in the meantime.

Pearl-bordered fritillary butterfly – a violet-feeder.

The shift to high forest

'High forest' is the term used by foresters for woodland in which trees grow as single stems. It started to be strongly favoured over coppice across Europe in the 19th century and became the most common form of woodland management in Great Britain during the second half of the 20th century. This is understandable, as high forest management produces the uniform-sized trees that suit most modern markets for timber. Under this system the trees are grown for longer than in coppice; for example, from 50 to 150 years before they are felled. The canopy may be kept quite closed for much of the time and there is a preference for stems that have grown up as single stems from seedlings, not multiple stems off one stump which are more likely to have rot at the base of the trunk.

Blocks of high forest stands may be cut at one go, potentially over many hectares, a practice known as clear-felling. Alternatively, harvesting may be done in small groups of less than half a hectare, or even by just removing single trees to create a patchwork of small gaps. In the gaps left between the main felling, the canopy may be thinner, due to the removal of overhead branches, but the light at ground level may still not increase much, because any gaps rapidly close over through the growth of branches from the surrounding trees. In high forests, tree regeneration is generally through planting in large gaps, with reliance on natural regeneration in the smaller-scale interventions.

Around 2001 a survey was carried out of 103 woods spread across Great Britain that had first been looked at in 1971 (Kirby *et al.* 2005). Many of these were former coppices that were developing into high forest. The overall species richness of woodland plants in the plots recorded was lower in 2001 than in 1971, with woodland specialists being more likely than other species to have thinned out in the plots. The decreases were associated with the increase in density of the trees in the woods, and the flora also showed, unsurprisingly, a shift towards a more shaded character. In a coppice the same patch might be cut every 10–20 years, but it might be cut only every 100 years in a high forest. The proportion of the woodland that is at the open stage in the forest cycle is therefore much lower in high forest than in coppice.

The different patterns of gaps and shade created under high forest management affect the ground flora, even if the main tree species remain the same as in coppice. In practice, the shift to high forest has often also involved a change in the main tree species, with severe consequences for the ground flora where broadleaved trees are

replaced by conifers. The scale at which felling takes place and the way felling is done also tend to cause more disturbance to the flora under high forest management.

In coppices. the area immediately around a stump is partly protected from disturbance and plants may survive there because vehicle movement and timber extraction are likely to work around the stumps that are the source of the next crop poles. In a high forest the stumps are generally smaller than those in coppice; they are not the source of the next generation of stems, so there is little incentive to avoid running over them. The trees harvested are bigger, the machinery is bigger and the ground is more disturbed. Nevertheless, the flora of clear-fells shows some similarities to that of recently-cut coppice. There is an increase in species richness and cover, mainly of woodland generalists and non-woodland species, followed by a decline in both as the tree and shrub layers reform. The new species come from the soil seed bank and by spreading in from other felled areas or permanent open areas.

Oak high forest in Wyre Forest, Worcestershire.

The ground flora regrowth in a clear-fell may initially be similar to that after a coppice cut.

In a study in the 1980s I found that recently-felled areas generally have one-and-a-half to two times as many species in a plot as those in closed canopy areas (Kirby 1988). Grasses and brambles tend to dominate after a year or two. Shade-tolerant woodland specialists are usually present, but their abundance declines through competition with other species if the stand remains open for more than a few years. Light-demanding species associated with new-felled areas depend for their survival more on the permanent open spaces such as rides than in coppice, because the temporary gaps after felling are fewer. However, the rides may be less suitable for them because they are more shaded, for a given width, as the adjacent trees are taller than in coppice.

Some Continental studies have found a decline in woodland species (Broad Buckler-fern, Hairy Wood-rush, Great Wood-rush, Wood-sorrel, Wood Anemone) in clear-fells compared to the surrounding forest (Godefroid *et al.* 2005), but there was subsequent re-invasion from the surrounding woodland if the areas were small. However, over several rotations, large clear-fells could lead to a cumulative loss of species. Soil seed bank species may decline because the time between replenishment of the seed bank during the gap phase is greatly increased, potentially well beyond the 50 years or so that most buried seed lasts (Brown & Warr 1992).

The shade-tolerant species that persist through the coppice phase, such as Primroses, may not do as well in high forest. The gap phases when they can flower and build up reserves will come less frequently, and individual plants are more likely to be damaged/destroyed during the harvesting process. Tall, summer-leafing species such as Bramble increase, compared to under mature coppice, because more light may get through in summer in high forest where there is no shrub layer.

At Salcey Forest (Northamptonshire), it was found that from 1983 to 2014 species richness declined in old broadleaved high forest, particularly amongst the more light-demanding species, for example Marsh Thistle, Lady's Smock, Bittersweet, Hedge Woundwort (Kirby et al. 2017). Rackham (2003), who re-surveyed the areas in Gamlingay Wood (Cambridgeshire) that Adamson had described in 1911, similarly found that the flora had changed in the areas that had remained broadleaved but had not been coppiced. The area dominated by Meadowsweet declined through increased shade and the drying-out of the soil through increased transpiration by the high forest.

The push for more wood production: from light to dark woods

The First and Second World Wars highlighted Great Britain's dependence on imports of food and wood which left us vulnerable to naval blockades (Gambles 2019, Tsouvalis 2000). After 1945 there was a push to increase food from our own resources, leading to farm intensification and increases in farm productivity. In forestry, a parallel drive to increase home-grown timber production was aimed at building up the strategic timber reserve. The programmes of large-scale afforestation of open land that had begun after the First World War continued, but a new emphasis was put on more productive management of the broadleaved woods, many of which had been heavily cut over. The 1947 forestry census recorded almost a quarter of the area as recently felled, or devastated, the latter being where most usable timber had been removed, but there was no restocking with young trees (HMSO 1952).

Meadowsweet, or Courtship and Marriage

Meadowsweet *Filipendula ulmaria* is a tall herb with dark-green, pinnate leaves, found in most 10km squares in Great Britain, and distributed widely across Europe. Its name derives not from the word meadow, though it is found in them, but from its use to flavour mead. The froth of creamy-white flowers has a strong scent, which in dense stands can be somewhat overpowering. Gerard, in his herbal, regarded it as one of the best 'strewing herbs' to mask unpleasant smells. The Yorkshire name of Courtship and Marriage (Grigson 1975) is said to contrast this sweet smell of the flowers with the more bitter scent of the crushed leaves! It has long been used as a healing herb and the flowers do contain salicylic acid, the basis of aspirin. In modern times biochemists have investigated potential uses of other chemicals in the plant.

Meadowsweet grows on damp or wet, moderately fertile, soils, although it is more tolerant of drought than most wetland species and can be found where there is no obvious wetness (Grime *et al.* 2007). Under favourable conditions it forms dense stands that dominate the vegetation of fens and open woods, but its growth and flowering are much reduced by shade. Hence it tends to increase after areas are coppiced because there is more light and a higher water table. A shift to more shady conditions associated with high forest, and particularly the replanting of ancient woods with conifers after the Second World War, will have reduced its abundance, as at Gamlingay Wood. It is also sensitive to grazing, and so further reductions are likely from the increase in deer populations.

Meadowsweet.

The wartime fellings were not in themselves a problem for the flora; many of these woods had been managed as coppice in the past and so periods of large-scale opening up of the canopy were not unprecedented. Coppicing had been in decline in the first half of the 20th century and this burst of activity in the woods may have given species that depended on open conditions an unexpected chance to flourish on a grand scale. Left to their own devices, the devastated woods could, and many did, regrow without further intervention, but a lot of the regrowth was initially of Birch, Hawthorn and Blackthorn. Such regrowth was classed as unproductive scrub according to the forestry views of the time, not what was wanted when there was a greater demand for softwoods, such as pines, spruces and firs.

Owners were encouraged to plant these conifers either pure or in mixture with broadleaves. Commonly, 3–5 rows of (say) Norway Spruce were alternated with 2–3 rows of Oak; the Spruce was to be thinned out over the first 50 years, leaving a final crop of Oak to go on for another 50–100 years. A belt a chain (roughly 20m) wide of broadleaves was sometimes left round the edge of the stand to hide the young mixed-growth within. These belts still survive in places such as Salcey Forest in Northamptonshire and Orlestone Forest in Kent. Similar practices were introduced to Wytham Woods in the 1950s, where the University of Oxford's Department of Forestry aimed to show students what modern forestry was all about. Radbrook Common, an area of rough grass, Bracken and scattered scrub, was planted-up and mixed conifer–broadleaved crops were established in the gaps created by wartime fellings.

As ideas on warfare changed, the need for a home-grown, strategic timber reserve faded. Forestry was to be justified on economic grounds, and this favoured the conifer element even in mixed crops. In well-tended woods, there were some temporary increases in cover and richness of the ground flora following thinning. There might also be some species surviving where broadleaved trees remained from the mixed planting or survivors from the previous crop, and in the patches where the conifers had not established. However, in general the more acid nature of the litter from Pine, Fir and particularly Spruce, and the heavier shade cast by their canopies compared to the common broadleaves such as Oak and Ash, started to cause widespread decline of the woodland flora.

The species richness under dense-shading conifers such as Norway Spruce, Lawson's Cypress or Western Hemlock is often less than

half that of broadleaved stands of a similar age (Kirby 1988). Pine and Larch crops usually have higher ground flora cover and can be quite rich, although even here, the dense blanket of conifer needles suppresses some smaller woodland plants. We do not know whether the changes seen, generally towards more uniform, less rich, and more shady floras, will be repeated in the next rotation because almost certainly the way the forests are managed will change, as it has done over the last 70 years.

Since 1945 there has been a transition from felling by axe and extraction with horses, through the introduction of chain saws and tractor-extraction, to the development of machines that can cut and load a tree without the operator leaving the cab. Large clear-fells were initially favoured but are increasingly seen as undesirable for a variety of different reasons to do with landscape, carbon sequestration and water management objectives. Since 1985 replacing broadleaves with conifers is unlikely to be proposed for ancient woods. Other factors that have had impacts on the ground flora over this period include a substantial increase in deer numbers, increased pollution from nitrogen compounds with climate change and the emergence of new pests and diseases of both native and introduced trees.

Coppice might yet be revived on a big scale in places to supply wood-chip and firewood as part of a future low-carbon economy. However, the experience of the last 60 years is that lack of markets and a reliable supply chain for coppice products outweighs the exhortations and grant-aid to restore this traditional management. So high forest ground flora patterns may be what we should expect in future. Hambler and Speight (1995) argue that more emphasis should anyway be placed on species associated with high forest and closed canopy conditions, because these are more natural. The next two chapters look at how the ground vegetation responds to more natural, or at least unplanned, disturbances that are not part of the forestry management cycle.

OPPOSITE PAGE:
Devastated woodland post Second World War (top).

Replanting of broadleaved woods with conifers completely changed their character (below).

Unplanned forest disturbances

For the last 6,000 years our woods have been managed to produce the structure and composition that provide what humans want, whether this is game, firewood or flood control. Superimposed on the changes caused by direct human intervention have then been the more natural influences of the weather, fire, tree diseases and grazing, all of which have their own effects on the ground flora.

At this point, we could wander off into a deep philosophical discourse as to whether or not human actions are part of 'natural processes'. Clearly in one sense they are, because for most of the existence of *Homo sapiens* our role in the world has been just that of another great ape. Yet we have been responsible for directed, if not always deliberate, changes in aspects of our environment, the nature and scale of which are otherwise unprecedented. We contributed to the extinction of much of the mega-fauna, cleared large areas of trees for arable farming, instigated large-scale herding of grazing animals, promoted selected tree species within and well beyond their native range and have changed the proportions of gases in the atmosphere. These cannot all be included as part of 'nature' without the word losing any useful meaning.

I therefore use terms such as natural landscapes, or natural processes, for situations and actions where the impact of human intervention is relatively small, generally indirect, or happened in the distant past. The contrast is with 'cultural' landscapes where there is a very much closer direct link between human management decisions and how the landscape looks and works. In practice, in Great Britain, all our landscapes are cultural, but with some natural elements.

OPPOSITE PAGE:
Natural gap creation through windblow.

In this chapter my focus is on the effects on the ground flora of disturbances from pests and diseases, floods and fire in Great Britain, through to the critical and often large-scale role for wind as a cause of gaps in woodland. The role of large herbivores in shaping the structure and composition of woods and forests is covered in the next chapter.

Pests and diseases

In the 1980s there were several years when British oakwoods were completely bare of leaves in mid-summer. I walked through them under a steady rain of frass, while scores of caterpillars on silk threads abseiled on to my cagoule. Such defoliation of oaks by Winter Moth was the subject of classic studies in Wytham Woods into the relationships between the various factors which control insect densities (Hambler *et al.* 2010). The growth of the trees is slowed but generally they recover from such one-off defoliation episodes. This extreme leaf loss has been less common in recent decades (for no obvious reason), but a variety of other pests has hit British trees. The Oak Processionary Moth for example is now in woods in west London, and other species currently present on the Continent could find their way here in the near future.

Some tree defoliation, if it does not lead to tree death, can be beneficial for the ground flora. There is more light available, because the canopy is more open, but also the frass can provide extra nitrogen, phosphorus and potassium to the ground flora (Kallio & Lehtonen 1975).

Winter Moth caterpillar on a Hazel leaf.

The 1970s saw 20–25 million trees (about 80% of the mature Elm population) killed by Dutch Elm Disease, a fungal disease spread by a bark beetle. While there has often been regrowth from the roots, this rarely gets above 4–5m high before it is hit by the disease again. Death of the main canopy stems created gaps, often accompanied by a pulse of nutrients in the soil that were no longer being taken up by the trees. Dense thickets of Bramble, Thistle, Cleavers and Nettle formed that might persist as open glades for several years, depending on how quickly the Elm regrew or whether there was invasion by other tree species.

At Hayley Wood, the ground flora response where the Elm died was initially rather like that after a coppice cut: Oxlip did well and buried-seed plants such as Ragged-Robin and Remote Sedge emerged. Deer were attracted to this area and grasses (Tufted Hair-grass, Rough Meadow-grass and Creeping Bent) became abundant (Rackham 2003). By 2018 the gaps had mostly closed over but could still be distinguished as patches of young Ash over low Bramble, Tufted Hair-grass, False Brome, Nettle and Meadowsweet.

In the north and west of Great Britain, Wych Elm was more common than English Elm. It is less susceptible to Dutch Elm Disease and is usually only a component of mixed woodland along streams and other base-rich sites rather than forming large single-species patches. The canopy gaps created where Wych Elm dies are usually smaller and more quickly filled by other tree species such as Ash and Sycamore. The disease has therefore had less effect on the ground flora. Losses of Elm-specific mosses, lichens and invertebrates, such as the White-letter Hairstreak, have however occurred.

These elm stems grew following the 1970s outbreak of Dutch Elm Disease but have since themselves died from the disease.

Since 2000 there has been a spate of new diseases affecting virtually all our major broadleaved trees, but Ash Dieback and Acute Oak Decline are the most notable. The Elm experience provides some useful pointers as to what might happen to the ground flora. Where Ash is a minor component of the canopy, even complete kill by Ash Dieback may lead to only small changes in the ground flora: the gaps should be quickly filled in by expansion of adjacent tree crowns, as with Dutch Elm Disease in north-western woods. Where Ash is the main tree species the increased openness of the canopy will stimulate growth of light-demanding and competitive elements of the ground flora. This is starting to happen in woods in eastern England where Ash Dieback first took hold. Now that Ash Dieback has reached Wytham Woods, we will be following how long it takes the vegetation to respond, which species prosper and which decline.

The tree species that are likely to replace Ash, for example Sycamore or Beech, are different in terms of the shade that they cast and the way their litter breaks down. This will influence the longer-term abundance, if not occurrence, of different ground flora species (Mitchell *et al.* 2014, 2016). Less work has been done on the ecological consequences of Acute Oak Decline, but where this becomes widespread, there will be parallels with the Elm and Ash situations.

Drought and fire

Droughts such as that in 1976 can be another source of gaps in the canopy by killing trees or slowing their growth, sometimes across large areas (Peterken & Mountford 1996). Drought also has direct effects on the ground flora, being implicated for example in the declines in Oxlip at Hayley Wood (Rackham 2003). The impacts are likely to be most serious where there are only small populations of a species, which might be lost completely in a bad year. With more abundant species there is a chance that small-scale soil variations allow some of the population to survive.

Droughts increase the risk of forest fires which annually damage large areas of forests across the world. In our Atlantic climate the chances of fires starting naturally, for example by lightning strike, are relatively low, and Oliver Rackham considered that British broadleaved woods burned like wet asbestos, that is hardly at all. The

OPPOSITE PAGE:
Ash groves at Hayley Wood developed where Elm patches died off (top).

Dying Ash at Lower Ashwellthorpe, Norfolk (below).

idea that our ancestors used fire extensively to clear the wildwood needs to be treated with caution. However, fires can spread through broadleaved woodland, where the canopy is relatively open with much dry grass or Bracken. There used to be occasional reports in the West Essex Gazette of fires in Epping Forest caused by human carelessness, and veteran oaks were killed by a fire at Ashstead Common in Surrey around 2000.

In the 1980s, at Sheephouse Wood, Buckinghamshire, there was an accidental fire in a newly-planted area dominated by tall Tufted Hair-grass and Wood Small-reed *Calamagrostis epigejos*. The plastic spiral rabbit-guards and tree shelters around the young trees also caught fire or melted, adding to the damage. Rosebay Willowherb came back in abundance in the year or two after the fire,

ABOVE:
Dog's Mercury in Wytham Woods showing severe wilting during the 2018 heatwave.

BELOW:
Fire-killed oaks in 2016 at Ashstead Common more than 10 years after the fire.

but the Tufted Hair-grass, Creeping Soft-grass and Wood Small-reed rapidly resumed their dominance. Part of Wytham Woods has burnt, not once, but twice in a similar way. Both fires occurred in late spring, with tall dry grass and Bracken carrying the flame. Fire scars are still visible on some of the oaks but there is little indication of any long-term effect on the ground flora.

Conifer woods are generally more flammable than broadleaved ones, because of the resin in their bark, the dry dead branches on their lower trunks and the dry needles on the ground below them. Fires started by people have been an important factor in the history of the Scottish pinewoods and controlled burns have been suggested as a way of reducing the ground vegetation and dense litter layer, to allow more opportunities for regeneration. It is possible that climate change may cause more fires, posing an increasing threat to productive plantations (chapter 16). A large area of pine burned in 2011 at Swinley Forest, near Windsor, Surrey. Many trees were killed and blackening on lower trunks of the trees left standing indicates how extensive the fire and its effects were. What was impressive, though, was the extent of Scots Pine and Birch regeneration that took place subsequently. The ground flora of Bracken, Bilberry and Heather, with Purple Moor-grass in the wetter areas, also came back well.

Recovery of Bilberry and Bracken after fire at Swinley Forest, Berkshire.

OPPOSITE PAGE:
Flooded birch and
alder woodland in the
Cairngorms (top).

A wild river at Rhiddoroch,
Wester Ross, with shingle
bars and trees being
washed downstream
(below).

Floods

Flooding shapes woodland ground flora communities firstly because some species, for example Marsh marigold, are more tolerant of submersion or periodic waterlogging of the soil than others, as indicated by their Ellenberg scores for soil moisture, and discussed in chapter 2. In wet alderwoods, less tolerant species, for example Wood-sorrel, can sometimes be found on the raised, drier mounds around the base of the trees. Secondly, seeds and vegetative fragments get caught up in floods and may be deposited downstream, which can facilitate the spread of invasive species such as the Japanese Knotweed *Fallopia japonica* seen growing in strips along some South Wales rivers. Thirdly, flooding can erode banks, and create shingle bars and bare mud banks which may provide opportunities for species that need bare soil for their seeds to germinate. Plants that might benefit from more exposed bare soil or the deposition of silt include the weedy or high light-demanding elements of our woodland flora, such as Nettle, Cleavers and Rough Meadow-grass.

Flood disturbance to woodland is not well described in Great Britain, where most of our major floodplains have long been cleared of woods and major channels deepened, straightened or embanked. River channel restoration projects are under way in various parts of the country, putting back meanders, for example, that may increase opportunities for riverine woodland habitat development, as may the re-introduction of beavers.

Marsh marigold
established amongst
dead reed litter, a species
tolerant of periodic
waterlogging.

Touch-me-not and Himalayan Balsam

These two species of balsam are often associated with riversides and flood disturbance in Great Britain. The first, Touch-me-not balsam *Impatiens noli-me-tangere*, is also found widely across Europe. In Białowieza Forest in Poland it forms large patches that are the preferred feeding areas for Deer and Wild Boar, or possibly the disturbance and nitrogen enrichment from the animals make such areas preferred sites for the Balsam (Falinski 1986). In Great Britain, in medieval times, the monks at Fountains Abbey in Yorkshire grew the plant to make into medicines used as diuretics and emetics. It was recorded in 1632 from the banks of the River Camlad in Shropshire and apparently is still there.

Elsewhere in Great Britain there are introduced populations scattered round the country, but it is considered native only in the Lake District, particularly around Coniston Water, and in parts of North Wales and the Welsh Borders (Hatcher 2003). It usually occurs in damp woods, at the edges of rivers and streams. Bare mud left by flooding provides the fertile but open conditions favourable for its growth, since it is not able to cope well with competition from other plants. Cattle will graze it, but their trampling also creates the bare gaps in which it can establish.

It produces intense yellow flowers in late summer. Nectar is secreted into the spur of the flower, which can then only be accessed by long-tongued bees. Other insects may bite holes in the spur to rob the nectar, bypassing the pollination mechanism. However, especially under shaded conditions, small flowers are produced that are self-fertilised at an early stage of development and do not open at all. The seed pods explode when touched, scattering the seeds to a distance of about 1–2 metres; the seeds may also be dispersed by water.

As well as being of interest as a rare plant, Touch-me-not is the sole host for one of our rarest moths – the Netted Carpet. A problem for the moth is that the populations of the Balsam fluctuate widely from year to year, and in a bad year the moth might go locally extinct because there are no food plants around. When the Balsam populations subsequently recover, the sites may be too isolated for the moth to spread back from another colony. Conservation management aims to build up a network of Touch-me-not populations to reduce the risk that the moth will be lost completely from a region. Re-introductions of the moth have also been considered, although this has had only variable success to date.

Touch-me-not's introduced cousin, Himalayan Balsam *Impatiens glandulifera*, is more of a problem because of its success in spreading (Beerling & Perrins 1993). The species was introduced to Europe in the early 19th century and is now present throughout most of England, Wales and lowland Scotland. Further extension of its range may depend on climate change because it may be damaged by hard frost.

Netted Carpet moth.

The invasive Himalayan Balsam with its explosive seed pods.

Himalayan Balsam is commonly seen on waste ground, particularly along waterways, because it needs moist bare soil, such as flood banks, for the seed to germinate. From these bridgeheads it may invade adjacent open woodland and grassland, except on the most acid sites. When fully grown it overtops nettles. The flowers are dramatic, giving rise to a common name of Policeman's Helmet. They are pollinated by bumble bees and may be an under-rated source of nectar and pollen in this respect. The exploding pods can send the seeds up to 6 metres, but water transport and humans are the main means of long-distance spread.

I first came across the plant along a roadside ditch, as a teenager out on a run during one games' afternoon. Intrigued by the exploding pods, and not knowing better, I took some seed home and threw them on the garden. The next year we were excited by this exotic plant that had suddenly appeared; two or three years later we were not so pleased by its spread! In 2017, I went back to where we had lived and as far as I could see the new owners had managed to wipe it out.

Few species can grow among dense patches of Himalayan Balsam. In a trial in north-east England, clearing the Balsam led to an increase in the cover and richness of native species, including False Brome, Moschatel, Foxglove, Wood Avens, Wood Speedwell *Veronica montana* and Wood-sorrel (Maule *et al.* 2000). It is now illegal to plant or allow it to grow in the wild and councils may seek to get major stands of it controlled. Small local infestations can be eliminated reasonably easily, but if the seed source is not tackled then re-invasion may rapidly occur. Complete eradication is difficult. Pulling up or severely trampling down the stems keeps it in check, but efforts at control need to take place early in the year to avoid spreading seeds. Some plants usually manage to escape destruction and the seeds may persist for up to two years in the soil, so the control measures may be needed for several years. The plant can be killed by herbicides, although stands by rivers and streams can be difficult to treat because the herbicide may get into the water, creating problems for aquatic life.

When the wind blows

Disturbance from flooding is rather restricted, but wind can affect almost any wood in Great Britain. Researchers for the Forestry Commission have put much effort into understanding the factors that make conifer plantations vulnerable to windthrow and into how to reduce that risk (Gardiner & Quine 2000). Generally, however, wind disturbance was not seen as a major issue for broadleaved and native pine woodland compared to the threat to upland spruce stands. The occasional tree or small group might go down but worked coppice and the pollards in wood-pasture tend to have short stems with small crowns compared to the size of their root systems, so are usually not very vulnerable to wind damage.

This sense of complacency came to an abrupt end with the arrival of the Great Storm on 15 October 1987. Overnight, millions of trees were uprooted or had the tops snapped out across south-east England. The trees were particularly vulnerable because they were still in leaf and the storm happened after a period of heavy rain that had loosened the roots. Some woods were more or less completely flattened, others had big holes punched in them; many semi-natural woods just had little pockets blown out (Kirby & Buckley 1994, Peterken 1996, Rackham 2003). The 1987 Great Storm stamped its mark, not only on the woods of south-east England, but on the thinking of the ecologists, foresters, planners, owners and managers of woods who had to deal with the consequences.

The initial focus was on the human cost (18 people died), and how the storm affected people (five million were without electricity) and property (houses with damaged roofs and roads blocked). Newspaper reports did though soon start to reflect the damage to woods and parks from the loss of trees. 'Foresters at Cowdray

Park are picking up the pieces from last week's environmental and emotional tragedy' (*The Daily Telegraph* 24/10/87) and 'damage to the country's forests and woodlands is more than double that of any previous gale in living memory' (*The Times* 17/11/87). Many of the blown-over or snapped-off trees remained alive, but with their crowns now much closer to the ground. The same thing was seen in Harvard Forest, USA, where they simulated a hurricane for

Storm damage in Kent, photo taken soon after the event, in October 1987.

research purposes by pulling down a part of the forest (Cooper-Ellis *et al.* 1999).

In south-east England, prior to the storm, broadleaved woodland had been becoming darker as neglected coppice woods grew up into high forests. The storm opened up many of these woods, giving opportunities for light-loving woodland plants. One or two commentators suggested that the extra light reaching the ground would lead to 'a massive increase in woodland flowers such as Primrose, Bluebells, Wood Anemones and Wood-sorrel' (*The Observer* 22/10/87), and a few years later it was clear this was what was happening: 'wild species from Bluebells to butterflies, deer to Dormice, Primroses to pipits all flourished in the wake of the storm' (*The Observer* 22/10/92). Woods in the track of the 1987 storm maintained or increased their ground flora richness over the period 1971–2001, whereas undisturbed woods elsewhere in the country lost species (Smart *et al.* 2014).

In some Hampshire sites, the response was similar to that after a coppice cut. Species such as Wood Spurge, Dandelion, Selfheal, Wood Avens and Creeping Thistle *Cirsium arvense* took advantage of increased openness, but then declined; Ivy increased, but other shade-tolerant species such as Dog's Mercury declined from the start (Kirby & Buckley 1994). Rampant vegetation growth, in the storm gaps, was perceived by foresters as a potential problem because there was concern that 'growth of surface vegetation [would] smother the prospects of new generations of trees' (*The Sunday Telegraph* 10/10/88). Toy's Hill, Kent, provided a test of these concerns.

Toy's Hill had been a mature Beech and Oak woodland, but the Storm blew over many of the trees on the top of the hill. Parts were cleared of fallen timber and stumps, creating large areas of bare and compacted ground that were replanted with Oak and Beech. Other areas were left to nature. Bramble thickets did indeed grow rampant in some gaps in both cleared and uncleared areas; Rosebay Willowherb favoured areas where the soil had been disturbed; Heather spread on the more acidic soils, emerging from buried seed.

Thirty years on, most of the Toy's Hill storm-damage area is again densely wooded. In 2017 differences between the planted and naturally-regenerated areas were not particularly obvious. Birch and Holly are abundant in both, but with some young Oak and Beech scattered through, as well as the odd survivor from the former woodland cover. Bramble, Bracken and Bilberry remained common in the ground flora, but often only as scattered individuals amongst expanses of leaf litter. Heather and Rosebay Willowherb, which need more light, were seen only occasionally along the edges of open paths. In the 'left to nature' areas the remains of the fallen logs and root plates from the fallen trees could be traced.

Plants of pit and mound

The plants of 'pit and mound' – the different microhabitats created by an uprooted tree – have long been a topic of research in North American woods (Beatty 1984). In Great Britain the same effect can be seen in upland spruce plantations. Pockets of ferns, grasses and rushes, perhaps the odd Foxglove, spring up where trees have blown. In ancient woodland in the lowlands of Great Britain, blowdowns had generally been rare, so had never attracted much attention. After the 1987 storm we had pit and mounds a-plenty and many plants benefited.

The root plates pulled out of the ground, particularly those of Beech on shallow soils, could be two to three metres high. Their crests provided space for herbs to grow free from the competition of existing vegetation and often in better light conditions as they were raised up towards the canopy gap. In the woods above Wye, in Kent,

Dense young growth, mainly Birch over Bracken and Bramble, at Toy's Hill in 2017.

A mop of Creeping Soft-grass on an old root plate, with regrowth of stems from the old trunk base.

we found Wild Mignonette *Reseda lutea*, Ragwort *Senecio jacobaea*, Annual Meadow-grass and Field Speedwell *Veronica arvensis* in such situations; at the Blean Woods north of Canterbury, Heather seed germinated on the disturbed root-plate surfaces.

The face of the plate that had come out of the ground was generally not very hospitable for plant growth, because it gradually shed soil and created a mound of loose material below it in the shallow depression created where it was ripped out of the ground. This loose soil gave short-lived opportunities for willowherbs and thistles to thrive, but soon these were overtaken by scrambling Bramble and Old-Man's Beard. The root pits were often damper than the surrounding woodland floor (sometimes temporarily water-filled), favouring the establishment of ferns and rushes.

Thirty years later, the canopy gaps created in the woods of south-east England have largely closed over, but the remains of the mounds are still visible. Their raised height means that litter does not accumulate on them and they may stand out as islands of moss, with the odd fern. At Norsey Wood in Essex the tops of the root plates have a mop of Creeping Soft-grass; in Stour Wood, also in Essex, wood anemones grow out from the now near-vertical soil surface of more recent windthrows.

The fallen trunks and major branches from the storm, where not cleared away, have been gradually mouldering into the woodland floor. Medieval woodmen called such windblown debris 'cablish'. North American studies of old-growth forests often mention the role that 'nurse logs' play in regeneration: tree seedlings establish in the damp rotting wood of decaying fallen tree trunks where they avoid some of the competition from plants of the forest floor and may escape browsing by deer. A short line of young trees may get away, giving the impression that they have been planted. Ground flora plants in this country also take advantage of the rotting wood, with ferns, Wood-sorrel, Dog's Mercury, Herb-Robert and Nettle all commonly occurring on logs.

A wider influence

Since 1987 the gaps created by the storm have gradually filled up by natural regeneration or by planting. Direct memories of the storm are fading; it was over 30 years ago, and most of the current generation of conservationists did not experience it. Yet its legacy can still be seen in many woods – blown-down trees, the tip-up mounds where the roots were pulled out of the ground – and in its general effect on the richness of the ground flora. Another legacy is in how foresters and ecologists have reacted to subsequent major storms. The 1987 storm was estimated to be a one-in-two-hundred-year event for southern Great Britain, but another strong blow occurred in 1990 through South Wales and southern England. Other storms have since hit northern England and Scotland.

We appreciate much more now how disturbance events – a storm, a disease outbreak, a fire and so forth – shape the structure of the woods and the wildlife found in them. There is far less of a rush to clear up damaged areas, much more willingness to accept that 'these things happen' and let the woods recover by themselves. This puts us in a better position to consider some of the changes we might expect in future under climate change projections, where it is expected that great storms and other types of extreme weather events will become more frequent.

This, more relaxed, less controlling attitude towards conservation is also reflected in changing attitudes to the place and effect of large herbivores in woodland (chapter 11).

A rare rediscovery

It was not just common species such as Rosebay Willowherb that benefited from the 1987 storm. The Starved Wood-sedge *Carex depauperata* is endangered across north-west Europe and very rare in Great Britain. It usually occurs in dry deciduous woodland, often associated with tracks, because it needs periodic soil disturbance to reduce competition from more vigorous species and to stimulate germination of its buried seed. Nonetheless it had in the past been fairly plentiful in woods that had just been felled or coppiced in Surrey, and the Fielding-Druce Herbarium in Oxford contains 15 different specimens from the Godalming area, collected between 1840 and 1940. With the decline of coppice as a common management practice, the sedge's fortunes sank.

In Surrey, Lousley (1976) had seen the sedge below Charterhouse in 1938, but it disappeared in the war. At another site, it steadily declined from five large plants in 1949 and still present in 1961, to one only seen in 1967. This was watched annually getting smaller and ceasing to flower until in 1973 it could not be found. Lousley thought it was lost from Surrey but hoped that 'it might yet be found in a wood on chalk, probably on a steep slope.' It survived in Somerset, but at one stage the sole English colony in the wild may have consisted of just one plant (Rich & Birkinshaw 2001).

Surrey's woods were in the eye of the 1987 storm, with many trees and large branches brought down in the Godalming area. Searches were organised to see if the gaps and disturbance might have encouraged buried seed of Starved Wood-sedge to germinate. These were initially unsuccessful, but in 1992 a single plant was found where it had been seen prior to 1970. It was directly under a gap formed by a large branch breaking off in the storm. The plant was in at least its third year with the remains of the previous year's flowering branches, consistent with a storm-related origin. In 1994 a few more plants were found, which had probably grown up from buried seed. Since storms cannot be relied on to create further gaps just where and when you need them, English Nature then funded a small project run by the charity Plantlife to open up the canopy, disturb the soil a bit more, and report on its recovery. This work has been continued by the Species Recovery Trust.

In 2017, I visited the Surrey site to see how the plant was doing, 30 years after the storm. My first visit was a failure. I found a Lime tree and a canopy gap in roughly the right place, but the sedges by the path turned out to be just the Prickly Sedge! Armed with a sketch map from someone who had recorded the plant in 2015, I had another go. This time I found the Starved Wood-sedge in flower with a scatter of younger plants around it.

As part of the Species Recovery Project, fruits were collected that could be grown on for possible restocking at nearby sites. Getting them to germinate proved difficult, so 25 plants (from splitting up of clumps previously grown in gardens) were reintroduced in 2009 to the grounds of Charterhouse School, where it had occurred in the 1900s. The reintroduced patches were reported in good condition in 2015 and 2018, although one patch was lost to rampant Bramble. Another reintroduction has been carried out at Cranborne Chase, where the plant became locally extinct in about 1905. In addition, there has been an increase in plant

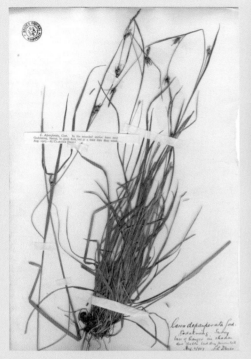

Starved Wood sedge – a specimen from the herbarium from when it was fairly common (left), and the small patch rediscovered in Surrey after the 1987 storm (right).

numbers at the site in Somerset. It is difficult to see this plant ever becoming as common as it clearly was in the past, but we may be able to build up a sufficient number of sites and populations so that they do not require quite so much 'gardening' to survive.

The need for more sites is emphasised by the risks to the storm-site. The patch is vulnerable to competition from more vigorous plants. A few *Crocosmia* have established and these or the trailing stems of Bramble might overwhelm the sedge, particularly if the patch were to become less shady. The patch is next to a track used by walkers, riders and mountain bikers. If one of them decided to go up the bank a bit to avoid the mud the young plants could easily be destroyed. The site may also be threatened by a housing development proposal. If that were to go ahead all the plants might end up having to be moved!

The effects of grazing animals

The woodland flora lies at the heart of a complex web of relationships. Many of these benefit the plant, as for example when insects pollinate flowers, birds distribute berries, or mycorrhizal fungi make mineral nutrients more available. However, there seems to be no obvious advantage to the plants when their leaves are eaten by deer and cows, or by tiny caterpillars that mine their way through the tissues of a leaf. Some plants have defences against grazing in the form of prickles and stinging hairs on their stems (roses, nettles), deposits of silica on and in their leaves (grasses and sedges), or poisonous chemicals, stored in cells (Bracken). These are only partly successful, and the investment in defence structures takes up resources that the plant might have used to produce more seeds. Defence efforts may be reduced when there is less of a threat: for example, the upper leaves of Holly, out of reach of large herbivores, lack prickles; conversely, brambles may respond to increased browsing by becoming thornier (Bazely *et al.* 1991).

Some plants, such as Bracken, are eaten by only a few species of insects, others by a lot; even in Tolkien's Mordor, the hobbits, Sam and Frodo, found that the brambles had 'maggot-ridden buds'. Invertebrate attacks may be specific to individual species or groups of species, and to individual organs on those plants. The Strawberry Tortrix moth feeds and form webs on the leaves of Water Avens, which are mined by sawfly larvae (*Metallus lanceolatus*), while small midges (*Contarina geicola*) form galls on the buds of flowers or leaves. Only rarely do the invertebrate impacts cause significant conservation concern for woodland ground flora plants. Usually this is where they feed on seeds and reduce the reproductive potential

OPPOSITE PAGE:
Longhorn cow in woodland.

A leaf eaten from within by a leaf-mining caterpillar: the width of the damaged leaf area (visible as a white line) increases as the caterpillar grows.

of rare plants. The annual appearance of the Lady's-slipper orchid has, on occasion, been cut short by a slug. More is also probably happening below ground; experiments in old fields have shown that the composition of the plant community does change when the soil is treated with insecticide.

However, the most obvious effects on woodland plants are the above-ground attacks by mammals. The larger herbivores, from rabbits and hares upward, alter the vegetation patterns in woods dramatically, and both the impacts, and the herbivores themselves, may once have been bigger.

Large herbivores lost and gained

Several hundred thousand years ago, giant elephants roamed Great Britain, pushing over trees and crashing through scrub, while spreading nutrients and seeds about the landscape in their dung. During the last Ice Age, large numbers of Mammoth and Woolly Rhinoceros lived in a steppe-like vegetation south of the major ice-sheets (Yalden 1999). Sadly, this mega-fauna has disappeared from the world, partly through the efforts of our ancestors (Stuart 2005). In Siberia there is, however, an inspirational project to see if the impact of Mammoth and Woolly Rhinoceros can be mimicked by Bison, Musk Ox and cattle, to switch the current tundra and low-productivity forest vegetation back to open, productive grassland (Zimov 2005).

Mammoths in the Ice Age, imagined by the artist William Kuhnert, 1900.

In Great Britain, the remains of mega-beasts have been found, but they have left no direct legacy in our current vegetation. Less mega, but still large, herbivores such as Bison and Wild Horse roamed the Continent in the immediate post-glacial period but did not survive in Great Britain for long. There were though Wild Ox, Elk, Red Deer and Roe Deer (Yalden 1999). Wild Boar were present, and although these are omnivores, their impact on woodland vegetation is considered here, alongside those of wild cattle and deer.

Wild animals, such as deer, were hunted for food by early humans, but with the introduction of farming, they might also be killed because they competed with domesticated animals for grazing and fed on crops planted for human consumption. From the Neolithic period onward, medium to large wild herbivores declined over most of the country until the last century. The Wild Ox was probably extinct in Great Britain by about 3,500 years ago. Deer survived where they were given special protection, perhaps in prehistoric times by taboos on hunting them; then in the medieval period through the provisions of Forest Law, which was concerned primarily with protecting resources such as deer for the Crown; and later in the parks and stalking grounds of wealthy landowners. Elsewhere they were largely hunted out as the Wild Ox had been before.

Meanwhile, the numbers and biomass of domestic livestock increased to dwarf those of all wild mammals put together (Yalden 1999). New plant-eating species have been added, accidentally or deliberately, to the countryside, notably grey squirrels, rabbits, Fallow Deer, Muntjac and Sika.

The evolution of wood-pastures

A Neolithic farming village of about 30 people might have needed a clearing of about 13 hectares for their crops, but 250 hectares of surrounding land for the grazing/rootling of their cattle, sheep and pigs (Gregg 1988). The composition of early Neolithic pig bones indicates that they were foraging in woodland more then, than later during the Iron Age (Hamilton *et al.* 2009).

Long-term grazing and rootling gradually open up woodland by slowing down regeneration. This effect might spread out from pre-existing glades, increasing the light reaching the ground and favouring the development of more grass-rich vegetation, with more potential food for stock. The animals would tend to prefer glades where there was more food available, and where there was better protection from predators such as wolves. In this situation, more young livestock would be born, the herds and flocks could increase and there would be further opening-up of the landscape. Grazing animals could use lands where arable production might be marginal or where there was more land than the community could, or needed to, cultivate for crops. The animals produced valuable products such as meat, milk, wool and hides, and were probably (as in similar societies today) a measure of wealth and status in themselves.

The practice of combining grazing livestock and wood production in generally rather open woodland is now known as wood-pasture (Hartel & Pleininger 2014). Iconic forest landscapes in Great Britain, such as the New Forest, Sherwood Forest and the major native pinewoods, are a product of wood-pasture management. Often, these sites are on relatively infertile soils, because the more fertile ground was generally favoured for crops, including hay. Stock grazed on the wood-pastures might be kept elsewhere at night, or over the winter, and slaughtered in a different place for food. Nutrients in their dung and bodies would gradually be transferred out of the forest. Over centuries this could lead to further reductions in soil fertility, as indicated by remnants of richer soils preserved under prehistoric

OPPOSITE PAGE:
Open oak wood-pasture in the New Forest (top).

Open pine wood-pasture (below).

burial mounds. The ground flora structure and composition changed, to favour generally low-growing or unpalatable plants and those that can tolerate low-nutrient soils.

Across Europe, wood-pasture is now in decline (Hartel & Pleininger 2014). Farming systems have changed and extensive grazing, perhaps guided by a herdsman, has often been abandoned. Increasingly, areas are either used just for grazing and arable, or for wood production. Large areas of traditional wood-pastures survive in central and eastern Europe, but even these systems are under threat. Forestry regulations may make it illegal to graze livestock in woodland. The wave of agricultural and forest management improvements that swept through western Europe in the post-war period is catching up with these landscapes, to the detriment of their conservation interests, as we have found in Great Britain. Here wood-pastures were grubbed up or ploughed in areas where the land went down the farming route after the Second World War. Where the foresters took control, the open spaces were planted with trees or filled up with natural regeneration (Kirby *et al.* 1995).

The flora of wood-pastures in Great Britain

The conservation priorities in most wood-pastures today tend to be associated with the veteran trees and the species that live on or in them – the lichens that encrust their trunks and the deadwood beetles and flies that inhabit the rot in the middle of the trees (Harding & Rose 1986, Rose 1993). In between the trees, there may be rough grassland or heath as in the New Forest, but often the land has been improved (in agricultural terms) through ploughing or reseeding.

Epping Forest on the edge of London illustrates some of these trends. The Forest was the subject of a major conservation campaign to stop it being cleared in the late 19th century, meaning it still survives as a mixture of open and closed habitats. However, it is now more closed than it was because pollarding of the branches of the old trees for charcoal at a height above the reach of cattle largely stopped in the late 19th century. The branches have got bigger since and carry more foliage. The Forest was still regularly grazed by cattle when I was young, but by the mid-1970s none of the remaining commoners were willing to put stock on to the Forest. Glades filled with young trees. Thorns and Oak spread out on to the grassy plains. Some open semi-natural grass/grass-heath and

wetland areas disappeared. Uncommon species such as Lousewort *Pedicularis palustris* declined even where the glades stayed open, because the grass growth became too tall and dense for it. More recently, the Corporation of London has restored grazing to parts of the Forest to reverse these trends (Dennis 2014).

Cattle grazing restored to Epping Forest.

Superficially, the flora of many wood-pastures can look rather uniform – a mixture of rough grasses, such as Sweet Vernal-grass, Common Bent, Creeping Soft-grass, or Wavy Hair-grass. Herbaceous species, such as Sheep's Sorrel and Tormentil, may be mixed in, but very bitten back. Species richness is encouraged, even under high grazing pressure, if there are variations in the landscape, because of irregular topography or soil conditions. A diversity of structure in the tree and shrub layer also helps. Woodland plants that are sensitive to grazing may survive and flower, for example, at the edge of thorn bushes.

The range of woodland plant species in working wood-pastures such as the New Forest can be as high as in neighbouring coppices (Chatters & Sanderson 1994). However, the New Forest is a special case: its size, and variety of soil nutrient and drainage conditions, are unparalleled in the south of England. Its location means that southern Continental species such as the Wild Gladiolus can establish a toehold in Great Britain. The relatively high average humidity

Under dense Holly shade in The Thicks section of Staverton Park.

permits Atlantic species such as the Hay-scented Fern to occur further east than might be expected from the general pattern of their distribution.

In both the New Forest and Epping Forest, one of the winners from reduced grazing has been Holly. Birds disperse its seeds in their droppings and young hollies often turn up at the base of old Oaks. Holly seedlings can establish and grow under deep shade, although they remain vulnerable to grazing until they have reached a couple of metres or more. They may then form dense thickets that are virtually impenetrable. This can be seen at Hainault Forest in Essex, at Sutton Park, on the edge of Birmingham, and at Ebernoe Common in Sussex.

Staverton Park in Suffolk indicates what holly-invaded sites can become. In the southern part of the site, The Thicks, there are ancient hollies that share the canopy with the great Oaks. Some gaps allow light down to ground level, but the vegetation cover is very sparse compared to the northern half where Holly is largely absent. Holly was probably always present in the Park and may have been cut for winter browse for the deer. The exceptional growth in The Thicks seems to have arisen from a spell of regeneration in the early 19th century when this area was not as heavily grazed as in the north (Peterken 1969).

Stock grazing in other woods

As the tree cover in Great Britain declined from the Neolithic period onward, those trees that were left became more valuable as a source of wood. Where tree cover was limited, it was often more efficient and effective to separate the grazing from the wood-growing places. Many of the latter came to be managed as coppices (Buckley & Mills 2015a, 2015b). Coppice woods and other forms of closed canopy woodland accumulated plant species tolerant of shade and/ or relatively intolerant of grazing (Rackham 2003).

Animals were sometimes let into the later stages of coppice, as at Hatfield Forest in Essex (Rackham 1989), although there is little fodder under the shade of a well-stocked, mature coppice. In addition, if the animals damaged the coppice stems by eating the bark this reduced the value of the coppice to a degree that might outweigh any benefits from the grazing. At Hatfield Forest there are reports from 1612 that the underwood was patchy because of the grazing pressure. Grazing could also take place in open areas such as rides and glades. Up until the 1970s a couple used to still let two cows graze in Whitecross Green Wood in Oxfordshire and the couple also made hay from the grass on the rides.

The incentive to keep livestock out of the woods became less as the value of the coppice products declined. Sheep came to be a regular

Under the coppice at Hatfield there is virtually no fodder for the animals – the Dog's Mercury is only at the ride edge.

feature of the western oakwoods for example, the animals benefiting from the shelter of the trees in bad weather, as well as whatever grazing was available. As a result, whereas in wood-pastures we have seen changes to the flora because animals have been removed from sites previously grazed, in other woods the changes occur where heavy grazing has been introduced to woods that had long been largely ungrazed. Both processes can be studied using fenced exclosures.

The difference a fence makes

In the New Forest, in 1963, 11 hectares were fenced and split into an ungrazed exclosure and a plot grazed by deer. The vegetation was recorded in 1969, 1978 and 1985 (Putman *et al.* 1989). Initially the amount of above-ground vegetation in the fenced area increased, compared to the adjacent grazed plot. Trees and shrubs grew up from 'seedlings' that had established some time before but had been grazed back whenever they got above the height of the grass. As trees became denser, some ground flora species were shaded out in the ungrazed paddock and the overall cover and species richness declined. Palatable species such as Heather and Gorse, which had initially grown well in the ungrazed plot, died out as the shade increased. By 1985 there were similar numbers of species in both plots but less ground flora cover in the ungrazed than in the grazed plot. Ivy, Bramble and Honeysuckle were still noticeably more abundant in the ungrazed plot, whereas Bent and Tufted Hair-grass were still common in the grazed area. Unfortunately, fences are difficult and costly to maintain, the experiment has now been abandoned, and deer now roam through both paddocks.

In an alderwood at Coedydd Aber in North Wales, a shift from open grassy vegetation to more woodland species was seen after 20 years of excluding sheep from a five-hectare block (Latham & Blackstock 1998). Honeysuckle, Bramble and Ivy increased in cover, along with Broad Buckler-fern, Wild Angelica and Smooth-stalked Sedge. The nearby site of Coed Gorswen, a mixed Oak–Ash wood, was mostly fenced to keep out sheep and cattle in 1960 (Linhart & Whelan 1980). By 2009, as at other sites, Bramble, Honeysuckle, Ivy and Bilberry were doing better in the ungrazed sections, which were shadier because of more tree and shrub regeneration. Many ground flora species recorded in 1964 were less frequent, particularly light-demanding species. In the long term, species richness might decline, as in the New Forest study, or this decline might be reversed if natural disturbances start to open up the canopy, for example through windthrow of trees or through Ash Dieback.

Many fenced plots have been set up in western oakwoods because of concerns about the lack of Oak regeneration, for example in the RSPB's Nagshead reserve in the Forest of Dean and at Wistman's Wood, high up on Dartmoor. A detailed record is available for an Oak stand at Yarncliff Wood, south-west of Sheffield, which was partly fenced off in 1955 by the National Trust. At that time, the ground flora was close-grazed Wavy Hair-grass, with sparse Bilberry, some Cowberry on the tops of rocks and small fronds of Bracken. After the fence was put up, the Wavy Hair-grass grew taller and there was recovery of the Bilberry shoots. By 1981 the Bilberry had overgrown much of the Cowberry and an unusual hybrid between the two species had disappeared. Bramble, Hairy Wood-rush and Climbing Corydalis *Ceratocapnos claviculata* increased and the regeneration of Oak, Birch and Rowan was able to get away (Pigott 1983). By 2018 sheep had been fenced out of most of the rest of the wood. Regeneration of Oak and Rowan is now widespread throughout, with tall Bilberry and patches of Bramble, Great Wood-rush and Broad Buckler-fern. The original exclosure area can be found from the remnants of the original fencing and there was still a clear difference with the small

Climbing Corydalis – one of the species benefiting from the fencing at Padley Gorge, Wharncliffe Wood.

Fenceline effects at Padley Gorge, Derbyshire, in 2018.

area of grazed woodland to the north and open moor to the west and south, with the tall Bilberry more or less stopping at the fenceline.

At Roudsea Wood in Cumbria an oakwood exclosure established in 1976 shows more luxuriant Honeysuckle, Bilberry and Wavy Hair-grass, while a second exclosure on limestone has abundant Bramble contrasting with the False Brome of the surrounding areas. Another limestone example comes from Rassal Ashwood (Wester Ross), which has large open-grown Ash that probably started their lives about 200 years ago. These trees grow mainly on rock outcrops and stone piles, perhaps because the better soils in between were cultivated in the past. In the wooded meadows of Estonia, the trees and shrubs similarly occupy the stonier patches and the grass between is mown for hay.

In 1975 two hectares of the open Ash–Hazel wood at Rassal were fenced to exclude sheep and deer. By 1985, within the fence, regeneration of Hazel, Rowan, Goat Willow and some Ash had reduced the cover of grasses, although some clearings remained. Tall herbs such as Meadowsweet and Hogweed flourished, and, under the Hazel, shade-tolerant herbs such as Upland Enchanter's-nightshade, Bluebell, Wild Strawberry, Herb-Robert, Wall Lettuce and Primrose were common (Peterken 1986). Alison Averis noted that the exclosure was 'a magnificent spectacle' with tall flowering Lady's-mantle, Melancholy

Thistle, Water Avens and bluebells amongst a rich matrix of grasses. By 2001 this rich flora had declined. The fenced areas were a dense Hazel thicket over a few grasses with scattered plants of Meadowsweet and Water Avens dotted here and there. Ivy formed tight mats over the rocks through a blanket of moss (Averis 2002). The whole wood had been fenced in 1990, so even outside the original exclosure the formerly-short turf vegetation grew taller and small species such as the elegant Fairy Flax *Linum catharticum* were shaded out.

By 2018, cattle grazing had been reinstated in the main reserve block, to judge from a faded notice warning of cows, calves and a bull! The young Ash and Rowan were being browsed. The vegetation was probably still too rank for Fairy Flax, but there was a good mix of the grasses and tall herbs recorded previously. Around the base of the big Ash were woodland species such as primroses, Upland Enchanter's-nightshade, Herb-Robert and Wood Willowherb. The original exclosure was still stockproof, although there were signs of deer within it. The canopy was of the tall Hazel and Ash that regenerated shortly after the fence was put up in the 1970s. The woodland flora included much Bluebell, Wood-sorrel, Primrose, Barren Strawberry as well as grasses and ferns. Bracken was less abundant than in the open grazed sections.

Mixture of grassland and woodland floras in the grazed areas at Rassal Ashwood.

The species that flourished in the early years after fencing, as at Rassal Ashwood, and in the birchwoods of Creagh Meaghaid National Nature Reserve in the central Highlands following a reduction in deer numbers, can also be found in places that sheep and deer cannot easily reach, such as small islands and steep stream-sides. Derek Ratcliffe (1977) listed 12 species characteristic of the tall herb community found on cliff ledges in the Highlands. One, Tufted Hair-grass, is a regular feature of rough pasture, but the other 11 show signs of sensitivity to grazing (Melancholy Thistle, Marsh Hawk's-beard, Meadowsweet, Water Avens, Angelica, Great Wood-rush, Red Campion, Common Valerian, Wood Crane's-bill, Stone Bramble and Globeflower). The ledges do appear to be acting as grazing refugia.

Fencing large herbivores out of the woods clearly benefits some species, at least initially, but there may then be declines in species richness and cover where the trees and shrubs increase their shade, or one of the more competitive ground flora species becomes dominant. Trying to reduce the numbers of animals using a wood might be a better solution for the flora overall than simply fencing them out.

The deer problem

Red Deer have long been an issue in Scottish woodland management because they have been encouraged for stalking since Victorian times. Much of the year the deer feed on the open hill, but in the winter, they move to lower ground, where many of the remnant broadleaved and native pinewoods occur. Because of this, many woods are relatively open, with little regeneration, little shrub layer, few of the palatable trees such as Aspen or Sallow, and a generally bitten-back ground flora.

By contrast, during the 19th and early 20th centuries in England and Wales deer were quite scarce. Roe Deer disappeared from large areas; Red Deer survived in south-west England because of hunting interests, and for their ornamental appearance in parks such as at Windsor. Fallow Deer were mainly confined to parks, although a distinctive dark-coloured herd roamed Epping Forest.

Since the Second World War, deer numbers have built up through most of Great Britain (Ward 2005). Hunting has declined, and, thanks to the mechanisation of farming, there are now far fewer people out in the fields, day in, day out, to disturb the animals. Milder

Great Wood-rush – interesting in small quantities

Despite its robust appearance, Great Wood-rush *Luzula sylvatica* is grazing-sensitive and in many upland woods it is largely confined to rock ledges. In ungrazed situations, Great Wood-rush may spread to the virtual exclusion of other species, as in parts of Wistmans Wood on Dartmoor and in the Great Wood of Cawdor near Nairn, perhaps the finest oakwood in north-east Scotland. Its competitiveness means that it can be grown en masse in gardens to suppress weeds.

Great Wood-rush is widespread in Europe, and through northern and western Great Britain. It is also quite common in south-east England, south of the Thames. It grows up to 80cm, with clumps of glossy, bright green leaves. It tends to be common on damp acid soils, for example along streamsides. A study in Belgium suggested that it prefers cool soil temperatures and high humidity (Godefroid

Great Wood-rush flowers.

et al. 2006). This may explain its scarcity in central and eastern England, particularly when many of the ancient woods were being managed for coppice, and why in the Highlands it can grow well outside woods.

There are reports that the leaves, which remain greenish for most of the winter, are picked by Golden Eagles to line their eyries, but I have never been close enough to an eyrie to check!

Great Wood-rush dominance at Cawdor Wood, near Nairn.

Red Deer stag at Windsor Great Park.

winters, and the availability of more food, in the form of green crops in the fields over the winter, have reduced the number that die in bad weather. Roe Deer have recolonised most of England, while Red Deer have shown local spread plus deliberate reintroduction to some areas. The Fallow Deer expansion is partly linked to park escapes during and following the Second World War. Two other species, Sika and Chinese Water Deer, were introduced in the late 19th and early 20th centuries and have built up significant populations in a few areas. A third new arrival, the Muntjac, has spread rapidly across much of England. For a long while, deer were scarce in Wales, but numbers are now rising across the Principality.

Wytham illustrates the trend: a few fallow deer were kept in the park prior to the Second World War and subsequently colonised the Woods. In 1959 there were thought to be about six adult deer in the whole 400ha. In the hard winter of 1962–3 a herd of 13 were tracked in the snow as they crossed the frozen Thames and back. Fallow were joined in 1967 by another species, as Charles Elton noted in his diary. 'There is excitement at the arrival… of 4 muntjac deer'. By the mid-1970s obvious impacts on the vegetation had begun to appear; the numbers of Fallow were estimated to be up to 60 in 1979, plus a few Muntjac (probably quite a lot!). By 1987, the numbers were considered unacceptably high – 200 or so Fallow and perhaps 300 Muntjac – but numbers continued to rise until the mid-1990s. Roe Deer recolonised the Woods.

Foresters were well aware of the damage that deer did to young trees, but for a long while they were not seen as a conservation problem. Tansley (1939) says of Fallow Deer that 'it is commonly kept in parks, often escapes and temporarily establishes itself in the more extensive woods till it becomes a nuisance and is exterminated'. Peterken (1993) considered deer in relation to wood-pasture management and woodland structure, but references to effects on the ground flora were few. Rodwell (1991) gives more detail on how grazing affects the ground flora, but deer impacts were not noted as particularly significant.

Rackham signalled a warning in his 1975 account of Hayley Wood, where he outlined the effect of deer on the growth and flowering of oxlips. Then, from about 1985, more and more examples were reported of direct deer impacts on the ground flora and of indirect effects on other species through deer changing the woodland structure, affecting nutrient cycling or promoting the growth of more grazing-tolerant species. The first signs of deer damage to the flora tended to be on palatable species, for example bitten-off stems of Bramble or Bilberry (Kirby 2001). Grazing of leaves and stems of Bluebell and Dog's Mercury reduces the resources that they can put into growth and flowering, leading to smaller plants. Flowers may be directly grazed off, leaving just the lower stem, for example, of a Lords-and-Ladies spike. Trampling by the deer creates bare paths, and in Brigsteer Park in the Lake District, Wild Daffodil bulbs were damaged by the hoof-scraping of Roe Deer (Barkham 1980).

Grasses, rushes and sedges commonly increase in grazed woods. Grasses grow from the base of the leaf rather than the tip, which means that they can recover better after being grazed. Many grasses also contain high levels of silica, which discourages animals from eating too much of them. However, even some woodland grasses are sensitive to damage and so are more common in ungrazed or only lightly-grazed situations. Wood Fescue, for example, is mainly found in sheltered gorges and on rock ledges in western Great Britain, rarely spreading out across the slopes.

Plants that benefit from having grazers around include weedy species such as Nipplewort *Lapsana communis*, Docks and Oxtongue *Picris hieracioides* that can take advantage of the disturbed ground. Similarly, if a tall competitor species is eaten more than a smaller plant, then the old adage that 'my enemy's enemy is my friend' applies. In Wytham Woods, tall plants such as Wild Angelica, Hogweed

False Brome carpet developed under high deer pressure.

and Bramble became less abundant as the deer increased, but low-growing species such as Germander Speedwell and Wavy Bitter-cress increased. There was little change in overall species richness in the ground flora, but quite a change in the appearance of the Woods. Between 1974 and 1999 Bramble went from covering nearly a third of the woodland floor to just 5% cover; from thickets commonly over a metre high, to most plants measuring less than 30cm. As deer numbers have been reduced, so the Bramble cover has started to come back at Wytham. The grasses that had spread under heavy grazing are no longer so common. The recovering Bramble thickets provide good cover, feeding and nesting sites for many small birds and mammals. Not everyone, though, is happy with the Bramble resurgence; there are fewer earthworms for the badgers to feed on under Bramble, and the thickets are little easier for them to push through than they are for those researching the badgers!

If deer are changing the vegetation in undesirable ways, then their numbers need to be reduced. However, estimating deer densities is notoriously difficult. Structured night-time surveys, using heat-sensitive night vision, have become the preferred method although the equipment is expensive: the animals are easy to see against the cooler vegetation.

False Brome – a winner under high deer regimes

False Brome is a grass typical of basic to neutral soils, widespread across Europe and in Great Britain, except in parts of the Highlands. It occurs predominantly in woodland, although flowering is reduced in deep shade. In full sunlight it can suffer from photobleaching, which may restrict its ability to spread outside woods. Greater water loss may also be an issue in the open. There are two forms, a hairy-edged and a non-hairy-edged type. The hairy form loses less water when growing in the open compared to the non-hairy form but does not survive as well under shade (Davies & Long 1991).

In the National Vegetation Classification False Brome helped to distinguish the rather open, dry ashwoods of the Peak District and other northern limestones, from the less free-draining, but still nutrient-rich ashwoods further south and east. In the latter, the grass was generally not very abundant if present at all (Rodwell 1991). Since the 1980s, False Brome, along with Tufted Hair-grass and Pendulous Sedge, has increased with the rise in deer pressure in these southern woods. At Wytham it went from being present in 64 of the 163 vegetation plots in 1974, to present in 146 of them by 2011. The main reason for its spread may be the indirect benefit of the deer reducing the Bramble cover. Deer may also help spread the seeds, which catch easily on to their fur. Its cover is now declining again as the Bramble recovers.

Dense stands of False Brome can be quite species-poor, both here in Great Britain and in North America where it was introduced and, like several other European woodland species, has become invasive.

False Brome flowers.

The deer fence has been effective, as indicated by the Bramble growth inside, but fences collapse when branches fall across them.

Other techniques that have been tried include walking systematically through a wood and counting the deer seen; counting the piles of deer dung found in a given area; and looking for indirect signs such as deer tracks or lying-up places. A method developed by Arnold Cooke from his studies at Monks Wood National Nature Reserve in Cambridgeshire (Cooke 2006) involved sticking groups of short Ivy sprigs into the ground one metre apart. These sprigs were inspected after 24 hours, three days and seven days, to assess the number of stems partly eaten and the number defoliated completely. The length of time taken for the sprigs to be grazed gave a measure of the likely impact on the woodland.

Knowing how many deer there are, or what impact they are having, gives an indication of what sorts of effort might be needed to manage their population, but there are no easy solutions. Fencing deer out of woods or blocks of woodland is difficult and costly. If fences are not maintained regularly then the deer quickly get back in. Effective population control through the use of contraceptives has not so far proved possible. Shooting deer to control their numbers can be effective but takes a lot of effort to bring the population down and becomes increasingly difficult as the deer density declines. The hunters must spend more and more time in the field for each deer killed. Deer management has to be done across a landscape or the animals simply find refuge in the areas where no control is taking place, and there may be public objections to shooting deer.

In hindsight, it would have been better on many sites, such as in Wytham Woods, if we had started to tackle deer numbers before they had caused large-scale changes to the vegetation. We have, perhaps, the chance to apply this lesson across the country with reintroduced Wild Boar.

The boaring bit

Boar were probably wiped out in the wild in Great Britain by the end of the 13th century though they may have survived later in parks. Various attempts were made to reintroduce them for hunting through to the 17th century, and they stayed in our memories in place-names such as Wildboarclough, heraldry (the badge of Richard III), and the odd folksong. During the 1980s increasing numbers were kept in farms for their meat, sometimes crossed with domestic pigs. Inevitably some escaped. Most were recaptured or shot, but in 1998 a government report concluded that there were populations of free-ranging Wild Boar living in Kent, East Sussex and Dorset (Wilson 2003). Later, a population established in the Forest of Dean and this has grown rapidly. Forestry England have a cull programme, although, even with the cull, the population is spreading out from the Forest. Wild boar or feral pigs (whichever you prefer) are back and seem likely to be here to stay.

Wild Boar in the Forest of Dean.

Wild Boar churn up the ground to expose bare soil.

The diet of Wild Boar includes acorns, seeds, roots, rhizomes, carrion, insects and live plants. These last are less important than for deer, but a wide range of species may be eaten. In Białowieza Forest in Poland, boar eat Nettle, Marsh-marigold, Herb-Robert, Yellow Archangel, Touch-me-not Balsam, Dandelion, Dock, Rushes, sedges and grasses (Falinski 1986). They rootle around, disturbing the soil surface, in their search for bulbs, roots, insects, according to the season, and create wallows. Quite large areas of ground may be churned up in this way, both under the trees and in open areas in the woods and adjacent fields. The long-term effects of this are unknown, but in the Polish studies, much of the damaged vegetation was not eaten and the plants might recover. The disturbance aerated the soil and speeded up release of nutrients to the benefit of Nettle, Raspberry and Lesser Celandine. Similar activity can be seen in and around the Forest of Dean.

A study in south-east England looked more closely at boar impact on bluebells. In early spring Wild Boar did eat the bulbs, which led to less cover and density of bluebells, and fewer flowers (Sims *et al*. 2014). If given some protection, the Bluebell stands recovered quickly, and even without protection there were more seeds germinating in the disturbed ground. Provided the Boar do not come back to the same patch every year, Boar and Bluebell might thus be able to thrive in the same wood. Their soil disturbance looks unsightly, but it does break through the mats of grass and bracken rhizomes that form in some woods. Wild Boar have even been trialled as a possible way of stimulating woodland regeneration in Scotland by creating gaps in heather moorland (Sandom *et al.* 2013). The disturbed soil may create opportunities for smaller plant species to establish, some of which may come from seed carried to the site on the boar's fur.

The Wild Boar story raises some interesting conservation issues: the releases were illegal, but the species was formerly native. The animals showed evidence of cross-breeding with domestic pigs, but were close enough to the wild type to justify them being considered a reintroduction. Now that they are re-established, do we accept their impact on the ground flora (and other aspects of the woodland system), even if they are damaging features that we currently value, such as Bluebell carpets? Do we try to maintain some woods in a boar-free state?

We have much less experience in Great Britain of dealing with Boar compared to deer and have had only limited success with deer management! In practice, any conservation case for Wild Boar management is likely to come second to concerns about them cross-breeding with outdoor pig herds, spreading swine diseases, causing public safety issues, or damaging people's gardens. The potential for vegetation recovery in disturbed woodland areas is heartening but little consolation to a farmer whose improved grass has become more thistly where the Boar have been, or for the children whose school playing field has been ripped up.

Other, smaller, mammalian herbivores

It is hard now to imagine the densities of rabbits that existed in the 1940s and the impact that they had, not just on semi-natural vegetation, but on crops as well. Post-war tree plantings generally had to be rabbit-fenced as a matter of course; small stems of shrubs and trees were at risk from ring-barking. Coppice regrowth could be stunted, delaying canopy closure and allowing Bramble to grow up into dense thickets, as E.J. Salisbury described in his Hertfordshire Oak–Hornbeam woods. The disturbed, and nutrient-enriched, ground around warrens favoured unpalatable species such as Elder, Ground-ivy and Nettle. Old warrens in the woods may still be marked by patches of these species.

A Rabbit in a woodland clearing.

Then, in the 1950s, myxomatosis arrived, a disease that caused such catastrophic rabbit deaths that they ceased to be a significant ecological factor over much of the country for many years. There had been hundreds of rabbits killed each year on the Wytham Estate, but when Mick Southern went out in the snow in 1955 he found not a single track. The rabbit decline was followed by a burst of tree regeneration as seedlings and saplings, previously held in check, were finally able to get away in the decade or so before deer numbers built up. Rabbit numbers have recovered somewhat but they still have nothing like the influence that they once had.

Smaller mammals such as mice and voles are generally more influenced by the vegetation structure, rather than vice versa. High populations of small mammals developed in many of the first-generation afforestation sites in the uplands as the grasses, Bilberry and Heather grew luxuriant after the stands were fenced and sheep excluded. The boom was relatively short-lived because once the trees had closed canopy, tall grasses and herbs were largely confined to the rides and occasional gaps where the planted trees had not grown well.

In the New Forest exclosure study, Wood Mouse, Bank Vole and Common Shrew were all regularly recorded in the taller, denser, vegetation of the ungrazed plot, but only the Wood Mouse was found, and at lower densities, in the grazed plot (Putman *et al.* 1989). In Wytham Woods, Bank Vole numbers declined during the period when the deer took out the Bramble and other low cover. Where the Bramble remained vigorous in small deer-fenced exclosures the voles had approximately five times the density inside as outside the fence. The wood mice did not show such sharp differences. Bank voles rely heavily on vegetation cover to protect them from predators; wood mice are more agile and may depend less on cover and more on early detection of their predators to allow them to escape (Buesching *et al.* 2010).

Where to now?

Large herbivores are part of natural woodland systems. Deer have a positive role in spreading seeds through a wood and from one wood to another. Red and Roe Deer are undisputed native species; Fallow have been with us for about 1,000 years, so might be classed as honorary natives. The pigs in the Forest of Dean may not be pure Wild Boar but they are genetically not very different from Wild Boar in France. Even cattle in woods could be considered as analogues for the lost

Wild Ox. Should we regard the return of these animals to our woods, after centuries of absence in some cases, as a conservation success?

Grazed or ungrazed: how much of each type of woodland do we want?

At the same time there is no doubt that large herbivores cause major changes in the abundance of other valued species, not just amongst the plants. The loss of low vegetation cover in woodland, as a result of grazing, has contributed to reductions in woodland breeding birds and in Dormouse populations. Locally, changes have occurred in woodland butterflies and moths because of effects on host plants and nectar sources (Fuller & Gill 2001). Colin Tubbs, the Nature Conservancy Council's representative in the New Forest, noted that the 19th-century Inclosures, which were ungrazed when first established, had once been renowned amongst butterfly and moth collectors. However, their interest declined from about the 1950s onward, partly because livestock were allowed into them (Tubbs 1986).

Many of the species assemblages and features we value have developed as part of cultural landscapes where the numbers of animals in woodland were controlled, but those control systems (whether through fences, herding or hunting) have broken down. If we had big enough areas, with fluctuations in numbers of animals and their impacts over time, then perhaps analogous assemblages and features could be maintained with unregulated numbers of grazing animals. Was this what the landscape looked like when wild herbivores predominated, in the time before farming?

The nature of the wildwood

Knowing what the landscape was like in the distant past helps us judge how humans have subsequently changed it. What species have we lost, which ones have been brought in? Where did species live before most of the countryside was converted to farmland? It also helps us to suggest what might happen if we now let land go wild. This chapter explores the evidence for how tree cover in Great Britain developed after the last Ice Age from the open landscapes left as the glaciers retreated.

A blank canvas?

Some 20,000 years ago much of northern Europe was covered by ice. The amount of water locked up in the glaciers lowered the general sea level to such a degree that Great Britain was connected to the Continent by land bridges across the Channel and parts of the North Sea (Doggerland). Parts of the Continental shelf to the south-west of Great Britain were also dry ground – a real Atlantis!

In Great Britain the ice reached down to about the Midlands; south of this would have been some sort of tundra. Further south, across Europe, this graded into open steppe-grassland that supported big populations of large mammals, such as Musk Ox, Bison, Mammoth and Woolly Rhinoceros. Trees, and the other plants and animals that we associate with woodland, mainly survived further south, in Spain, the Balkans or Italian peninsula where the climate was still warm, but not all forest species may have been pushed back quite so far. In the Qinngua Valley in Greenland there is today a small forest of Birch, Willow and Greenland Mountain Ash, with trees up to 8m tall. There were probably similar small pockets of woodland north of the Alps, including on the land now under the sea, south-west of

OPPOSITE PAGE:
As the ice retreated, what would become Great Britain was a largely open landscape, not unlike this valley at Graechen in Valais, Switzerland.

225

Great Britain. Such pocket woodland refugia could help explain the early reappearance in northern Europe of some forest species as the climate warmed again.

The landscape gradually turned into a mosaic of open and closed patches as the trees spread. This recolonisation was not like the March of the Ents in *Lord of the Rings*, or Shakespeare's Birnam Wood coming to Dunsinane: there was no blanket of forest moving northward steadily metre by metre, year by year. Species arrived independently in each region and spread at different rates; Oak spread north much more rapidly than Beech, for example. Sometimes colonisation would be rapid when conditions were particularly favourable; at other times there would be little change (Huntley & Birks 1983, Birks 1989). The same sorts of processes and patterns can be seen today in North America where the treeline is still moving north.

Exploring the landscapes of the past

The hero of Robert Holdstock's novel *Mythago Wood* goes further back in time as he moves deeper into the wood to end up in the primeval forest at its heart. Ecologists, more prosaically, do the same thing by looking at what can be found at different levels in peat soils.

To the south side of Wytham Hill lies Marley Fen, an open area of tall Reed, Great Horsetail and sedges. This fen lies where water percolating down through the limestone and sandy layers on the top of the hill meets the impermeable Oxford Clay. Over the centuries the fen plants have grown, died and been transformed into peat. Trapped within the peat are grains of pollen from whatever plants were growing around the fen at any one time. Pollen from the depths is older than that near the top, and absolute ages can be assigned to different depths in a peat column (with varying degrees of accuracy) using radio-carbon dating. The amount of pollen in the Wytham peat is rather low, but enough to suggest the changes in the surrounding woodland over the last few thousand years (Hone *et al.* 2001). A clearer picture comes from another fen near Oxford, at Sydlings Copse (Day 1993).

About 10,000 years ago the Sydlings Copse area appears to have been mainly open grassland with some Birch, Scots Pine and Willow. Hazel then increased, perhaps forming closed stands, with some Oak and Elm, which could explain a sharp drop in the herb and grass pollen, as these were shaded out. About 7,000 years ago Alder and Lime became more common. Around 5,000 years ago the levels

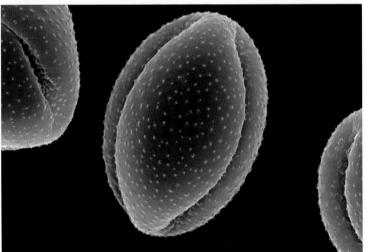

of Elm pollen declined. The Elm decline is seen in many places across Europe and its precise cause is debated: an early outbreak of Dutch Elm Disease or the impact of early farmers lopping the trees?

At Sydlings Copse, Lime also declined, which, with an increase in Hazel and some increase in herb and grass pollen and fern spores, suggests a period when the landscape was again more open. Subsequently both Elm and Lime recovered, but around 4,000 years ago there were further tree pollen declines accompanied by an increase in herb and grass pollen, fern spores and cereal pollen. Farming had arrived in the area and by about 1,700 years ago most of the woodland had probably been cleared from around the fen hollow. From about 1,000 years ago there was recovery of Oak and Hazel, species that, with Field Maple and Ash, now make up most of the ancient woodland. From this last period there is also pollen of Dog's Mercury and Wood Anemone, which are still common in the ground flora (Day 1993).

Elsewhere, other remains, such as twigs, leaves and flowers, animal bones, charcoal, beetle wing-cases and snail shells, can be extracted from peat or soil deposits. These help to fill in gaps and ambiguities in the pollen record (Allen 2017, Greig 1982, Whitehouse & Smith 2010), though each set of data has its own biases. Trees are better represented in pollen records than ground flora plants; beetle remains are preserved better than those of flies. We only see what has survived in a particular sample: we cannot know what was originally present but by chance was not preserved. The remains may represent only whatever was living immediately around the collection site, or might include inputs from a much wider regional landscape. These problems can be addressed by looking at how the pollen collected varies in modern landscapes with distance from its source, for example a wood or grassy field. Other insights come from combining and comparing different pollen records from the same region, for example Fyfe *et al.* (2013). Less work of this sort has been done for beetle and snail remains.

Remains of a 5,000-year-old forest exposed at Pett Level, Sussex.

Wild oxen, perhaps 2m high, once roamed the British wildwood – this skeleton is in the National Museum of Denmark, Copenhagen.

Our view of the past is incomplete: it is like trying to judge what a jigsaw might look like from just 5–10% of the pieces, and there is always a risk that we interpret the results to fit with our existing ideas. However, until we invent a time-machine these are the only records we have of the times before humans started drawing or writing landscape descriptions.

The rise of the trees

We have a good understanding of what tree species were present at different times. The Sydlings Copse pollen record is fairly typical for lowland Great Britain. Early colonisation was by Birch and Hazel after the ice retreated. Scots Pine became abundant in the Hampshire Basin, but subsequently died out. Oak and Elm increased, followed by increases in Small-leaved Lime and Alder, before declining tree pollen levels suggest the spread of farming and woodland clearance from the Neolithic period onward. Beech seems to have been amongst the slowest of the trees to spread back across Europe (Godwin 1975, Huntley & Birks 1983). It may have been present in Great Britain about 9,000 years ago, but it started to become abundant only from about 3,000 years ago. Beech pollen has been found in northern England, but if it was present in the woods there, it soon died out.

Some of the same elements are present in the uplands of Wales. At Bryn y Castell, Snowdonia, an open post-glacial landscape of grasses,

Small-leaved lime was formerly widespread through lowland Great Britain but is now quite limited.

with herbs such as Dock or Sorrel and Meadowsweet, was gradually replaced by open woodland of Birch, Hazel and Willow from about 9,000 years ago (Mighall & Chambers 1995). The grass and herb component declined, with increased Pine, Oak and Elm until about 7,000 years ago, after which there are increasing amounts of Alder. From about 2,000–3,000 years ago traces of cereal pollen suggest that people were farming in the area, and from then on the proportion of tree pollen in the record declines. Sphagnum, Heather and Bilberry increase, which may represent the development of the largely open landscape of grassland and mires found there today. The change to an open landscape was probably a combination of human activity and the shift to a cooler, wetter climate that favoured peat development.

In the Highlands of Scotland, at the eastern end of Glen Affric, Juniper scrub developed, followed by increasing levels of Birch and Hazel between 11,000 and 8,000 years ago (Froyd & Bennett 2006). Scots Pine then increased and remained abundant for about the next 6,000 years. Birch was present, probably in a patchy mosaic with the Pine. By contrast, Oak and Alder might have occupied more fertile areas in the bottom of the glens, as at Talladale in Wester Ross today.

The broadleaves declined in the pollen record from about 2,000 years ago, alongside evidence for blanket peat development, but the Pine pollen remained high. In eastern Glen Affric, the Scots Pine really might be directly descended from the original forests, although Pine stands further west in the glen do not show such a strong continuity of woodland cover.

Pollen records may show the shift to open landscapes such as heather moorland (here in Northumberland).

Throughout the country different tree species would have occurred according to the local soils and topography. Preserved twigs, flowers and charcoal fragments indicate that Small-leaved Lime rather than Oak was at least locally dominant through much of southern England (Greig 1982). Early colonists such as Scots Pine might have hung on in small amounts in some places, long after they had been lost from the landscape more generally. John Evelyn, writing in the 17th century, referred to accounts of pines ('hundreds of great fir trees' in the original text) on the lowland bogs of Hatfield Chase in Yorkshire/ Lincolnshire. Perhaps scattered Pine also survived on some poor sandy soils such as in the Breckland of Norfolk, or at high altitude in Northumberland, as at Williams Cleugh in Kielder Forest (Manning *et al.* 2010). The fragments of Hazel woodland that survive in the coastal zone of western Scotland, such as at Ballachuan in Argyll, might include descendants of the early post-glacial hazelwoods.

Colonisation by tree species is still going on across Europe and not all plants have reached their climatic limits (Svenning & Skov 2004, Svenning *et al.* 2008). Beech has expanded through southern Scandinavia over the last few thousand years (Bradshaw & Lindbladh 2005), so it might have spread naturally to Scotland by now, even if humans had not helped it along by planting.

A variably tree-covered countryside

In the early post-glacial period (about 11,500–8,000 years ago) there is good evidence that the landscapes in Great Britain were quite open. In the later Mesolithic (8,000–6,000 years ago) the fossil beetle record and pollen evidence seem to suggest a denser forest structure (Sandom *et al.* 2014). Great Britain had more trees 6,000–8,000 years ago than in the last thousand years; even Orkney, Shetland and the Isle of Lewis in the Hebrides developed some sort of shrubby cover, with a mixture of tall herbs and ferns in the ground flora. However, the remains of dung beetles from this period point to the landscape being open enough in places to support sufficient grass for large herbivores to feed on (Whitehouse & Smith 2010). Some beetle species found from the past are now only recorded from veteran trees. Such old trees are unlikely to have been in dense woodland because they would have been overgrown by younger trees (Ranius & Jansson 2000). Thus, there were probably some open areas with oaks, with large spreading crowns, such as can still be seen in Woodstock Park, near Oxford (Farjon 2017), or Dalkeith Old Park near Edinburgh.

Dung beetle remains point to the presence of dung and hence large mammals.

There were also places where the trees grew up densely together, with tall straight trunks and few low branches. The trunks of such trees have been dug out of the fens; others survive in the form of dug-out canoes and the Bronze Age Dover Boat. This last was made from massive Oak trees that had perhaps 9m of clear trunk before the first major limbs (Clark 2004).

ABOVE:
Beetles found now only on veteran trees such as these at Dalkeith Old Park suggest areas of open grown trees in the wildwood.

RIGHT:
Trees lacking low branches found deep in bogs and surviving as dugout canoes indicate that there were areas of dense tree cover.

What about the ground flora?

Our picture for the return of the ground flora after the last Ice Age is less complete than for the trees because there are fewer records and some of these can only be put into broad classes, such as *Poa*-type grasses. Not all species thought to be native have yet been detected in the pollen record from the time before Great Britain was cut off from the Continent. However, the spread of the ground flora back into Great Britain did not necessarily end with the formation of the English Channel and the inundation of Doggerland. Even quite big seeds could have been blown across the Channel if there were a storm such as that of October 1987. Plants of wet woodland might be spread in mud on the feet of waterbirds or carried in their gut to be voided at some new site. The big rivers flowing into the North Sea would have brought down floating mats of logs and vegetation that might subsequently be washed up on our beaches. The chance of a successful invasion by a new species by any one of these mechanisms is low, but over millennia such successes mount up; plants have spread to very remote oceanic islands elsewhere in the world.

Plants now found in rides or disturbed areas in woods, such as Common Valerian, Devil's bit Scabious, Common Cow-wheat and Hemp-nettle, were present in the early post-glacial period before there was much tree cover. Species such as Honeysuckle, Bluebell and Wood Anemone tend to appear later in the pollen record when

Woodland plants such as Common Valerian, a tall plant with divided leaves, could have colonised Great Britain before there was much woodland.

there was a higher level of tree cover in the landscape. As the trees spread, the ground flora would have started to separate out, with light-demanding species dominating where there were gaps, shade-tolerant species under the trees.

As nowadays, gaps would appear from time to time, through different types of disturbance. High winds can knock holes in closed woodland, uproot freestanding trees or flatten whole stands (chapter 10). Oak and Alder stumps and fallen trees preserved in peat in the Bristol Channel, dated to between 6,000 and 2,500 years ago, appear to be from such a major storm (Allen 1992). Trees might be killed by disease. As we have seen, the widespread decline in the amount of Elm in the pollen record about 6,000 years ago might reflect an outbreak of Dutch Elm Disease (Parker *et al.* 2002). In the valley bottoms the effects of floods and the activities of beavers would have periodically reshaped the structure and abundance of the tree cover, creating open marsh and meadows. The Wild Ox might have been attracted by the better grazing in the valley bottoms (chapter 11) and helped to keep such meadows open (Van Vuure 2005). However, some ecologists have suggested that large mammals played a much more important role in shaping the whole post-glacial landscape.

More a crocheted bedspread than a blanket of trees?

One model of the landscape of Great Britain about 7,000 years ago is of a dense forest such as can be seen today at Białowieza in Poland (Falinski 1986, Peterken 1996), with tall trees, closed canopy and much of the forest floor in shade. Recently there has developed an alternative view that the landscape of north-west Europe was a shifting mosaic of open grassland and heath interspersed with scattered trees, patches of woodland and occasional larger continuous blocks of woodland (Rackham 1998, Vera 2000) more like the New Forest than Białowieza.

The Dutch ecologist, Frans Vera (2000), argues that the landscape must have been relatively open because large amounts of Hazel pollen have been found, and Hazel does not flower well under shade. The abundance of Oak pollen also suggests an open landscape because young oaks do not grow well under an oak canopy and are poor competitors in woodland against shade-bearing trees such as Small-leaved Lime and Beech. Vera proposed that large grazing animals created open grassy areas; here, trees such as Oak could establish and grow up through association with thorny shrubs such as Hawthorn and Blackthorn, following in the footsteps of the poet William Wordsworth. In the latter's *Guide to the Lakes* (1835) he notes: 'the seedling or sucker if not cropped by animals (Nature is often careful to prevent by fencing it about with brambles and other prickly shrubs) thrives and the tree grows sometimes single, taking its own shape without constraint, but for the most part compelled to conform itself to some law imposed upon it by its neighbours.'

A representation of Vera's shifting mosaic cycle

I have attempted to model what this sort of landscape might look like, using what seem realistic assumptions for how long each stage in the cycle might last (Open, Scrub dominant, Closed canopy, Canopy collapse) (Kirby 2004). Several different scenarios were considered but generally the outcomes were that much of the landscape is occupied by trees or scrub.

Scrub dominant 15%; developing scrub limits animal movement; but oaks gradually overtop the thorns and start to shade them out.

Open landscape 25%; grass/heath type flora in which thorns and oak regenerate; developing thorny patches help protect the oak from grazing animals.

Closed canopy (grove) 50%; as the thorns are shaded out, the animals can get under the trees again and eat any regeneration, preventing direct replacement of the mature trees.

Canopy collapse 10%; as the mature trees die, the canopy starts to open out; light-demanding grasses or heather that are tolerant of grazing start to spread.

Young Oak growing up amongst thorns.

Under Vera's hypothesis the trees, once established, would eventually overtop and shade out the thorns. The grazing animals could then get back under the canopy and would stop any further regeneration at that point. Only after the trees had died back and the grove had become open grassland again was there enough light for thorns to start to seed in and restart the cycle. The landscape of the pre-Neolithic period would thus have been a mixture of open and closed conditions, scattered trees and closed woodland.

Frans Vera's hypothesis and the 'closed forest' model differ in whether the landscape was substantially open with scattered patches of trees (singly or in more extensive groves), or predominantly wooded with scattered gaps. Recent research has increased our estimates of landscape openness prior to the spread of farming (Fyfe *et al.* 2013, Allen 2017). However, there seems to be no direct evidence yet for places undergoing shifts from open to tree-covered, then back to open again as implied by Vera's model, without human intervention. Open landscapes are for example indicated by grassland snail remains in the Cranborne Chase area and around Stonehenge (Wiltshire), but in this part of England there was a lot of human activity; on similar soils in parts of the South Downs, where evidence for humans is much less, the snail record contains more woodland species (Allen 2017).

A second difference between the two models is whether or not the large herbivores, which were certainly present, did create and maintain a half-open shifting mosaic across large swathes of Europe. The vegetation record from the Continent, where large herbivores remained abundant, does not differ much from that in Great Britain and Ireland where the number and range of large herbivores were more limited (Mitchell 2005). A half-open mosaic landscape is also potentially unstable. The grazing pressure must be sufficient to stop most, but not quite all, tree regeneration. If grazing levels are higher, so little regeneration occurs that the landscape would be largely open, as the Scottish Highlands are today. Such large-scale openness does not seem to be reflected in the pollen and insect records for the pre-farming period.

If grazing levels dropped, then the tree regeneration would outpace the herbivores and most open areas would close over. It only needs about one sapling per hectare each year to escape the teeth of the Wild Ox before, after a few decades, there is a fairly closed woodland. With the spread of tree cover the more productive ground flora species would be shaded out, resulting in less food for the animals, and further declines in their numbers, leading to more tree regeneration. Dung beetle records do seem to dip during the period of maximum tree cover (Sandom *et al.* 2014), which would be consistent with lower herbivore populations.

The role of predators such as Lynx and wolves in influencing prey numbers and behaviour remains disputed.

Large predators, such as Wolf, Lynx and Bear, would also have affected the herbivore populations. Where carnivores have been reintroduced (for example, wolves in Yellowstone Park, USA) or have spread back naturally (wolves in various European countries), there have sometimes been changes in the behaviour and abundance of their prey species such as Deer, bursts of tree regeneration and lusher vegetation growth (Ripple *et al.* 2014). Other researchers are less convinced that these effects are all due to the reintroduction of predators (Kauffman *et al.* 2010), so their role in past landscapes remains debatable.

Frans Vera's hypothesis is difficult to test because much of the evidence is incomplete or ambiguous. Nevertheless, his ideas have generated lively debates over the last two decades and made us reassess past assumptions. At the moment, I feel the arguments still come down in favour of the predominantly wooded landscape model, although the landscape of Great Britain before our ancestors started farming was much more variable and complicated than we thought even just 30 years ago.

The human element

Humans in Great Britain have affected where and how trees grew across the landscape since the ice retreated. Mesolithic people probably burned areas to encourage game animals, to make them easier to hunt (Innes & Blackford 2003). Neolithic people cut down trees in abundance for firewood, canoes and houses, for trackways across marshes and bogs, and for the many wooden henges that predate the better-known stone circles (Noble 2017). Lopping of elms for fodder may have contributed to the Elm decline by making the trees more susceptible to disease.

The natural landscape of Great Britain, whatever it was like, was transformed into open countryside with scattered wooded areas. Field systems of varying complexity and extent have been identified from the Neolithic through to the Iron Age (Taylor 1975). Heathlands were created from woodland in the Bronze Age. The written descriptions of Great Britain in Roman accounts imply a country already well settled with extensive farmland. There is more detail for much of England a thousand years later in the Domesday accounts (Rackham 1986). Our ancestors separated out different land uses, with arable land here, haymaking there; pigs here, cattle there; trees and grazing here, trees without grazing there. Plant distributions had to change in response to the creation of this patchwork quilt.

Some species thrived. Heather would have been part of temporary openings in woodland on acid soils but became a widespread permanent vegetation cover on heathlands. Bluebells and Wood Anemone would always have grown well under dense shade, but their ability to form dense carpets increased as the numbers of Wild Boar declined. Species that were grazing-sensitive found sanctuary behind the wood-banks created to keep stock out of coppices. The short cutting-cycles used in coppice woods provided regular opportunities for light-demanding species that formed well-developed soil seed banks.

A last remnant of the wildwood? A prehistoric forest exposed on the beach near Borth, Ceredigion.

As more woods were cleared, the remaining patches became increasingly isolated. The opportunities for long-distance movement of seeds and exchange of pollen were reduced. Species once spread by Wild Boar or Wild Ox lost their natural dispersal agents and were less able to colonise new sites. Differences developed between long-established woodland patches and those that grew up on abandoned farmland, and we have now formalised these as Ancient and Recent woodland respectively.

In the 1980s we might have suggested that some ancient woods and their flora were direct descendants of the prehistoric closed

wildwood, but that now seems less likely to be true. The nature of the wildwood is itself a matter for debate, and archaeological remains of earlier open landscapes turn up regularly in ancient woods here and on the Continent as well. The deep history of our woods and their flora makes it clear that they have always been part of wider cross-European patterns, as discussed in the next chapter. The similarities to, and differences from, woods on the Continent help to put our conservation activity into a wider context and indicate how our woods could develop in the light of future climate change.

Woodland plants across the channels

Great Britain and Ireland were connected to each other and the main mass of Europe for thousands of years, allowing free movement of species whenever conditions were suitable. Rising sea levels separated Great Britain and Ireland about 11,000 years ago. Then, about 7,000–8,000 years ago, the final land bridges between Great Britain and the Continent were lost. Doggerland disappeared under the North Sea and the chalk between Dover and Calais was cut through to form the English Channel. However, our woods still remain outposts of those that spread across the Continent, our flora and fauna a subset of that for Europe as a whole. The differences in our woodland flora arise from the peculiarities of our climate and soils, and in the history of land use in Great Britain and Ireland compared to that on the Continent.

Virtually all our woodland plants can be found somewhere else in Europe. Some species, such as the Oxlip and Italian Lords-and-Ladies, are almost accidental parts of our flora, occurring in only a few places and at the limits of their range. Other species, such as Bluebell, Welsh Poppy, Primrose and Stinking Iris, are more widespread in Great Britain than generally across the Continent and should command more attention in conservation debates. I remember the glee on the local foresters' faces in Poland and again in Estonia, when they promised to take us to see a 'rare plant' that turned out to be Ivy! In Great Britain it is of course common, but it gets scarcer and more confined to ground-creeping, the further east you go. The plant we saw in Poland only grew about 30cm up a tree and then it stopped – any further and it risked being above the snow cover in winter and the buds would have been killed by frost.

OPPOSITE PAGE:
A wood in the Pas de Calais, France, but it could be in the Weald of Sussex.

European distribution patterns

Europe can be divided into a series of broad regions that reflect the major differences in its vegetation. The distribution of individual plant species does not correspond precisely to these areas, but the degree to which a plant's range overlaps different regions may provide clues as to what is limiting their occurrence (Dahl 1998). For example, Wild Madder shows a southerly and westerly distribution (southern Atlantic and Mediterranean regions), Oak Fern *Gymnocarpium dryopteris* more of northerly (Boreal) and Central European distribution, and Mistletoe an Atlantic and Central European distribution.

Great Britain lies in the Atlantic Zone, which is characterised by low temperature variations between summer and winter. Rainfall occurs in every season, which means that there is usually ample soil moisture for active plant growth through spring and summer. Atlantic species may be limited by winter temperatures further east and north. The distributions of Black Bryony, Bluebell and Gorse, for example, correspond very roughly to a mean temperature for the coldest winter month of +2°C or warmer. Species such as Scaly Male-fern and

Stinking Iris, more common in Great Britain than on the Continent.

Great Wood-rush spread further east and north, corresponding roughly to the -4°C line. Hardier plants such as Wild Garlic and Hard-fern can be found within the zone defined by the -8°C line, thus spreading well into the Boreal Zone.

Wood-sedge, a species with central and southern European affinities.

Some species with their centre of distribution in the Boreal and Central European zones occur in Great Britain, for example Beech Fern, Wood Crane's-bill, Chickweed-wintergreen, Common Cow-wheat and Mountain Melick. Their seed may depend on a period of more intense winter cold before it will germinate; or they may be vulnerable in mild winters, because they rely on snow cover to protect the plant or seeds from extremes of cold and frost, as with the Ivy in Poland.

Coming in from central and southern Europe, and more dependent on high summer warmth, are Southern Wood-rush, Narrow-leaved Helleborine, and the less-demanding Meadowsweet, Toothwort, False Brome and Wood-sedge. Least well represented in our woodland flora are plants from the Mediterranean zone; for example, the Wild Gladiolus now occurs only in the New Forest.

Assemblages

Most of the woodland communities found in Great Britain are linked to those on the Continent (Rodwell & Dring 2001). Our beechwoods are the western end of a vast complex of mixed beechwoods found across Europe, with for example a beechwood over Box in the Cevennes looking not unlike one on the North Downs. Heinz Ellenberg listed the plants in samples taken from a beechwood on fertile soils in the Jura Mountains on the French–Swiss border (Ellenberg 1988). There were of course no bluebells, but the main species – Dog's Mercury, Bugle and Wood Anemone – are common in British woods. Eleven others, including Ivy, Early Dog-violet, Yellow Archangel and Herb-Paris, would not look out of place in a Chilterns beechwood. Five species in his list occur in Great Britain but are generally rare – Spiked Rampion, Martagon Lily *Lilium martagon*, Lesser Hairy-brome *Bromopsis benekenii*, Fingered Sedge *Carex digitata* and Wood Fescue. This last occurs mainly on ledges in gorges in western Great Britain, but in the Wye Valley it spreads out over the forest floor, mirroring its behaviour in Ellenberg's Jura sample. Four species from his samples are not native to Great Britain, but two of these, Asarabacca *Asarum europaeum* and Spring Pea *Lathyrus vernus*, sometimes escape into woods from gardens. Our acid beechwoods show similar overlaps with the flora of Continental woods: we lack the White Wood-rush *Luzula luzuloides* as a native species (although it has naturalised in some places, on acid soils, often by streams) but we have a greater abundance of more Atlantic species such as Hard-fern, Butcher's-broom and Slender St John's-wort.

Another of Ellenberg's lists, from Oak–Hornbeam woods in the Hartz Mountains in Germany, includes Wood Anemone, Yellow Archangel, Wood Meadow-grass, Greater Stitchwort and Dog-violet as the common species. Of the 50 species named, 40 are native to Great Britain and not uncommon in our lowland mixed woods. A further four are British rarities (Martagon Lily, Spiked Rampion, May Lily and Unspotted Lungwort). The Continental additions are then Ground Elder and Lesser Periwinkle *Vinca minor*, both commonly naturalised in our woods; some less common garden escapes – Liverleaf, Asarabacca and Spring Pea; leaving just a bedstraw that does not occur in Great Britain at all.

The oakwoods of western Great Britain beyond the native range of Hornbeam are distinctive and of international importance because of the richness of their mosses and liverworts, which are favoured

ABOVE:
Beech over Box in the
Cevennes, but it could be
the North Downs.

RIGHT:
Asarabacca is native on
the Continent, but not
in Great Britain – here
growing in the Botanic
Garden in Oxford.

Young Hornbeam among Oak in Poland, but it could be Hertfordshire.

by our mild, moist climate. These conditions also encourage an abundance of ferns such as Hard-fern, the Shield-ferns (*Polystichum aculeatum, P. setiferum*), Male-fern and Broad Buckler-fern, with in places the more frost-sensitive Hay-scented Fern and Filmy ferns (*Hymenophyllum wilsonii, H. tunbrigense*), none of which are so common on the Continent. However, other species making up the ground flora of our oakwoods (Wavy Hair-grass, Bilberry, Heath Bedstraw and Heather) are the same as those found in acid oakwoods in the foothills of central Europe and around the Baltic.

Ashwoods are more prominent in Great Britain, because in central and southern Europe similar fertile woodland soils are usually dominated by Beech, Sycamore, Norway Maple or limes. Nonetheless where ashwoods do occur on the Continent they have many ground flora species that we would recognise. A grove of Narrow-leaved Ash (a close relative of our Ash) from the northern coastal region of Spain, for instance, boasted Wood Spurge, Bugle, Primrose, Betony *Betonica officinalis*, False Brome, Remote Sedge, Thin-spiked Wood-sedge and Lady Fern (Polunin & Walters 1985).

Other similarities between our ashwoods and the woods of Scandinavian river valleys are indicated by northern montane

species such as Stone Bramble, Globeflower, Melancholy Thistle and Wood Geranium. This rich flora is also closely related to that found in traditional northern meadows (Peterken 2013). In northern Europe the wood-meadow was a distinctive part of local culture. Fine examples still survive in Estonia where 'grassland' and 'woodland' plants form colourful mixtures: Herb-Paris and Lily-of-the-valley hobnob with Cowslip *Primula veris* and Viper's-grass *Scorzonera humilis*. Wood-meadows do not seem to have been widespread in Great Britain. Perhaps, because woodland was less extensive, it was easier to keep the hay meadows and the coppice woods separate.

Polunin & Walters (1985) list 21 species from herb-rich birchwood flora from Iceland including Alpine Bistort *Polygonum viviparum*, Alpine Meadow Rue *Thalictrum alpinum*, Stone Bramble, Water Avens, Wood Crane's-bill, Heather and Bilberry. All occur in Great Britain and there are similarities to the assemblages found in the ungrazed birchwoods of base-rich soils in Great Britain, such as Morrone Birkwood near Braemar.

The ground flora of Scandinavian Pine and Spruce woods described by Polunin & Walters (1985) with Wood-sorrel, Bilberry, Northern Buckler-fern *Dryopteris expansa*, Chickweed-wintergreen,

Oak coppice in the Czech Republic, but it could be Norfolk.

Hairy Wood-rush and Wavy Hair-grass could be from a native pinewood in Scotland. To find May Lily in a Scottish pinewood would be a surprise, but Scots Pine on the Continent occurs across a wider range of conditions as native woodland than in Great Britain. However, in some cases we may have recent planted equivalents. The natural pinewoods on long-established dunes on the Continent find an echo in the older plantations on dunes at Ainsdale, near Liverpool, or Culbin Sands in north-east Scotland. The stunted pines on some Northumberland bogs derived from 17th/18th-century plantations are similar to the pines found naturally on mire systems on the Continent. Some mature spruce stands can have a similar appearance to semi-natural spruce stands in Sweden.

Yew is more abundant in Great Britain than on the Continent, where it now occurs primarily in the understorey of beechwoods. There are few deep groves of pure Yew such as occur on the chalk and limestone in Great Britain. Holly, a southern Atlantic species, also does particularly well with us. However, the understorey of these two heavy shading evergreens is distinctive only in being very poor.

Other similarities and differences

The greater clearance and fragmentation of British woodland cover in the past compared to much of the Continent means that there are few large-scale landscapes where woodland types grade into one another in combination with other habitats. This does happen, though, on a small scale at Roudsea Wood in Cumbria, where the flora of acid and basic, free-draining and waterlogged woodland soils can be seen side by side, along with transitions to lowland raised bog and tidal estuary.

Our biggest rivers are quite small on a European scale. Any surviving strips of alder and willow alongside them are usually hemmed in by arable fields or intensive pastures. The water courses tend to be fixed, preventing the joyous meandering of the main channel that would once have taken down mature trees and exposed new ground to potential tree and herb colonisation. This process can be seen in the few large examples of braided channels that survive, as along the River Spey, or on a smaller scale at Urquhart Bay on the shores of Loch Ness. We have only fragmentary areas of wooded backwaters and swampy scrub, but perhaps more will develop in future in the areas where beavers have

OPPOSITE PAGE:
Estonian ash wood-meadows with a right old mixture of species (top).

Stone Bramble – a plant found in Icelandic birchwoods, but also at sites such as Morrone Birkwoods near Braemar (below).

been reintroduced. On the Continent, wet woodland also often grades into tall, highly productive, mixed forests of Ash, Elm and poplars. This exists in fragmentary form in the New Forest, but more usually our native Black Poplar and Aspen (as a riverside tree) occur as scattered individuals, such that they are hardly thought of as woodland trees at all.

There are few places in Great Britain where you can see the altitudinal gradients in forest types that are common on the Continent, but at Talladale on Loch Maree a walk can take you from Oak by the lochside up through Birch to Pine at the upper levels. There is a change in the ground flora too, related to changing soil conditions, from Creeping Soft-grass and Bracken under the Oak with Tormentil, Bluebells and Wood-sorrel, to a flora with more Heather, Bilberry and Purple Moor-grass higher up. At Craig Fhiaclach in the Cairngorms there is a clear change in structure of the pinewood with increasing altitude, ranging from tall, little-branched trees, to the low twisted pines found at high altitude, but these are not accompanied by any major change in the ground flora.

A comparison with Irish woodland

Ireland has only about 70% of the vascular plant species considered native to Great Britain (Webb 1952, Preston *et al.* 2002), and this applies to its woodland flora as well. A surprise to me was the scarcity of Dog's Mercury, although it is considered possibly native (Parnell *et al.* 2012). Other scarce or missing species include Herb-Paris, the two Bryony species, Spurge-laurel and Wood Spurge. There may be a temperature factor involved, as these plants have a southerly distribution generally in Europe, reach their north-westerly climatic limits in south-eastern Great Britain, and are largely absent from the West Country, Wales and western Scotland. Some of the species meeting their south-westerly limits in Great Britain, such as Melancholy Thistle, Wood Crane's-bill and Globeflower (this last occurs in Ireland but in only a few places), might also be excluded by climatic factors. The absence of pinewood specialists such as Chickweed-wintergreen, Twinflower and Creeping Lady's-tresses is not surprising, as until recently there were thought to be no native pinewoods surviving in Ireland (Roche *et al.* 2018).

Some species may simply not have spread back fast enough from southern Europe to reach Ireland before the split with Great Britain.

RIGHT:
Spurge-laurel, widespread in southern England, but absent as a native plant from Ireland.

BELOW:
Irish Spurge *Euphorbia hyberna*, a rare plant in Great Britain.

They do not appear to be climate-limited because they grow well where they have been introduced. Wild Hop, an occasional relic of cultivation, is long-established in some locations; Old Man's Beard is common, widely naturalised and may be spreading; Wall Lettuce is definitely introduced and now fairly common on limestone pavement, walls and in woodland.

On the plus side, the higher rainfall, and particularly its even spread through the year, increases the richness of the mosses and liverworts in Irish oakwoods. Hard, Hay-scented, Soft Shield and Hart's-tongue ferns are more common in Ireland than in Great Britain, as is the eponymous Irish Spurge, which in Great Britain is limited to a few locations in Devon and Cornwall. Other ground flora plants that in Great Britain are more often found in woods, grow freely in open country in Ireland, for example Dog-violet, Primrose and Wild Strawberry.

We are part of Europe

It is possible to visit Continental woods and find a ground flora that is quite different from anything that occurs in British woods. Polunin and Walters provide an example of Austrian Black Pine forest vegetation made up of Buckler Mustard *Biscutella laevigata*, Shrubby Milkwort *Polygaloides chamaebuxus*, Garland Flower *Daphne cneorum*, Spring Heath *Erica carnea*, Matted Globularia *Globularia cordifolia* and Blue Moor-grass *Sesleria caerulea*; only the last of which is native to Great Britain. However, as long as you do not go too far, the differences are more in the quantity of familiar species, or the replacement of a well-known one by a sister species, Oxlip for Primrose for example, with just a handful or two of totally new species to learn.

Our woods are part of the wide sweep of variation across Europe. These similarities and differences between our woods and those on the Continent have been important in developing conservation priorities (Rodwell & Dring 2001), particularly under the European Habitats and Species Directive. Our beechwoods and pinewoods are significant as some of the most westerly examples of their type, even though we only hold a small proportion of the total European extent. Our ravine and rocky slope ashwoods are floristically rich: they generally lack some of the tree species, such as Large-leaved Lime, that are widespread on the Continent, but they have more of the Atlantic fern species. Great Britain and Ireland have most of Europe's moss and liverwort-rich oakwoods; we have in our wood-pastures an amazing survival of ancient trees, particularly oaks (Farjon 2017); and in the spring displays of bluebells are a world-class plant spectacle.

Looking across the Channel should give us hope that as the climate shifts more towards that currently experienced in southern and eastern Europe, many of our species may still be able to find a space in the changed woodland communities that develop. We might though reconsider our attitude to species found in European woods that are not native here, but sometimes escape from gardens into the wild. These might be the next stage in the continued development of our post-glacial flora. Often such escapes first appear along hedges or tracks through woodland, illustrating the role that these features play in linking woods into the surrounding landscape at a local scale.

Lines and links in the landscape

Ordnance Survey maps may encourage us to think of British landscapes as Green (wooded) and White (non-wooded) land, but many trees and shrubs occur outside woods, in hedges around rock outcrops, in field corners, along roadsides and by streams. Small streams provide a part-shaded, moist microclimate where woodland plants may survive in landscapes largely cleared of woodland, as George Peterken noted in his Lincolnshire study. Streamsides in the uplands may have more fertile soils than the adjacent open hill, allowing greater species richness, and can act as a refuge from grazing animals. Rock outcrops can similarly provide some shelter and more favourable conditions for woodland plants. An extreme example of this is the woodland plants in the deep cracks in the rocks on limestone pavement, such as Hart's-tongue Fern, Green Spleenwort *Asplenium viride* and Herb-Robert, and rarer species such as the Dark-Red Helleborine *Epipactis atrorubens*.

The most obvious of these non-woodland habitats for woodland plants are hedges, estimated to stretch to about half a million kilometres (over 300,000 miles) in Great Britain. Open tracks and paths through woods (often called rides) fulfil an analogous, but reverse, function, allowing shade-intolerant plants to move into and survive within an otherwise largely closed habitat. Rides and hedges form complementary sets of lines through the landscape.

Hedges as habitats for woodland plants

In poorly-wooded counties such as Cambridgeshire the extent of non-woodland trees may be several times that of the woods. Even in well-wooded Hampshire the non-woodland tree cover is

OPPOSITE PAGE:
Woodland flowers along a hedge.

the equivalent of half the wooded area (Brown & Fisher 2009). A hedge may be all that remains of a wood that has been cleared: these are sometimes known as 'ghost hedges'. Some hedges mark field boundaries that may go back to the Iron Age, whereas others were only planted in the last few decades as part of agri-environment schemes (Pollard *et al.* 1974, Watt & Buckley 1994). Their composition reflects differences in soil types and climate, but also the history of local landscapes (Rackham 1986). Parts of the country are characterised by small, irregularly shaped fields, with very mixed hedges; in other areas large, more regular, field patterns were formed from the parcelling-up of the farmland under parliamentary enclosure acts in the last couple of centuries.

The wildlife potential of hedges has long been recognised, and the oldest hedges tend to be the richest. The number of trees and shrub species in a 27.5m length very roughly corresponds to the age of the hedge in centuries, although the calculation could be out by 200 years either side! The rule is also invalidated where several species were deliberately planted to establish a mixed hedge. On the Isle of Man, the number of Bramble species present has been linked to hedge age, though the problems of identifying the different Bramble micro-species mean that this approach to aging hedges has not been widely used.

Dog-rose, also known as Hedge-speaks, in Gloucestershire.

The association of woodland plants with hedges is reflected in the local names collected by Grigson (1975), for example Hedge Garlic and Hedge Poppy (Foxglove). Greater Bindweed is also known as Hedge Bells and Hedge Lily (Somerset), and Old-Man's Beard as Hedge Feathers (Yorkshire). White Bryony might be called Hedge Grape (Worcestershire), but, as the berries are poisonous, do not use it to make wine. There are Hedge Lovers (Herb-Robert), Hedge Violet (Common Dog-violet, Devon), Hedge Maids (Ground-ivy, East Anglia) and Hedge Pink (Soapwort *Saponaria officinalis*, Hants). The Dog-rose might be Hedge-speaks in Gloucestershire but Hedgy-pedgies over the border in Wiltshire.

Woodland plants that occur in hedges are often tall-growing species that can tolerate high levels of light and moderately rich

nutrient soils, such as Nettle, Hogweed, Cow Parsley, Ivy, Bramble and Cleavers. They need to compete alongside the coarse grasses often found in field margins such as Yorkshire-fog, Cock's-foot and False Oat Grass. Smaller woodland specialist plants may though occur: even in dry Norfolk, Barren Strawberry, Bluebell and Wood Anemone can be found (Barnes & Williamson 2006), while in wet Wales, Primrose and Hart's-tongue Fern are common along hedge-banks. The presence of a ditch may allow opportunities for some wet woodland plants such as Meadowsweet and Bittersweet.

The abundance of coarse grasses and nettles suggests enrichment of the soil along this hedge.

If hedges start to thin out at the base through neglect, over-cutting or clearance of the trees and shrubs, the specialist woodland plants may decline but they are not always lost completely. The remnants of Dog's Mercury, Bluebell or Lords-and-Ladies along a bank may indicate where a hedge used to be. A spreading hedge can equally be a threat, however, since few plants survive beneath the shade of very dense Blackthorn or Hawthorn.

Plants within the hedge may be afforded some protection from grazing by domestic stock, depending on the width of the hedge and whether it has been supplemented by a wire fence. However, rabbits and Muntjac also use hedgerows as the sites for burrows, or

as convenient cover for their tracks, making plants in the hedge more vulnerable to being eaten.

Grassy strips along the edges of woods provide some buffering against the drift of herbicides applied to adjacent fields or overspill of fertilisers, as well as adding another element of habitat diversity. Fertiliser and pesticide placement have become more precise in recent years, but there may still be indirect effects where these re-volatilise and are then scavenged by the trees and shrubs in the hedge (chapter 16).

Hedges that are the remnants of old woods may have a rich woodland flora because the plants have just stayed where they were when the rest of the wood was cleared. With new hedges, generally the species have colonised after the hedge was created. Ernie Pollard and Max Hooper, then of the Nature Conservancy, showed in the 1970s that both legacy effects and colonisation could be important. The medieval section of a hedge that had once formed the boundary of Monks Wood in Cambridgeshire contained Dog's Mercury, Wood Anemone and Bluebell, whereas these species were far less common in a newer, though still 150-year-old, adjacent hedge section. Resurveys of the same hedge in 1998, led by Tim Sparks, one of their successors at the Monks Wood Experimental Station, found all three species had declined in the old sections. By 2011 there had been some recovery in Dog's Mercury and Bluebell (Mountford *et al.* 2012) and

Wood Anemone was seen again in 2016. These three species seem to be behaving as survivors from an earlier woodland phase. However, other woodland plants such as False Brome, Black Bryony, Ground-ivy and Germander Speedwell had spread into the new section.

Dog's Mercury amongst the grass in the foreground, showing where once there was a hedge.

In another hedge study in Northamptonshire from the early 1970s Dog's Mercury was considered to have spread along two old enclosure hedges attached to an ancient wood at about a metre a year (Pollard *et al.* 1974). Dog's Mercury was still there in 2017 and appeared to have spread a bit further away from the wood in the intervening 40 years. However, the hedges had expanded out from the original line, creating a dense Blackthorn thicket, five or six metres wide, with little beneath the bushes. The surviving Mercury patches were not very vigorous, just scattered clumps. There was a clear animal path down the centre of the hedge, so seeds may be being carried along on the coat of a Muntjac. This was probably also the source of a small Bluebell clump established some way from the wood-edge. In another two hedges the Dog's Mercury was more vigorous and still had a more or less

Germander Speedwell, a species that spreads quite quickly into new hedges.

continuous presence along the hedgerow. These were narrow hedges, regularly trimmed, and mainly Hawthorn rather than Blackthorn.

Hedges can therefore be important habitats for woodland plants, particularly woodland generalists, provided they are managed sympathetically. In addition, colonisation of new woods by plants may be quicker and seeds moved further if carried by animals along hedges. However, this role for hedges should not be overstated as there is not much evidence that hedges are critical for the spread of woodland plants from one site to another (Davies & Pullin 2007).

Clearance and recovery

The hedges behind my childhood house in Essex dated from the early to mid-19th century. They had been created to divide up riverside grazing and meadows into separate paddocks, only for the hedges to be taken out again in the late 1970s to make one huge wheatfield. Clearance of hedges, alongside the piping of streams and ditches to create larger fields, was one of the most visible and contentious changes seen in the countryside in the post-war period (Peterken & Allison 1989, Norton *et al.* 2012).

Hedge removal may not have had major effects on the overall distribution of woodland plants because those in hedges tended to be the commoner ones anyway. However, it thinned their distribution through the countryside and reduced the nectar and pollen available to invertebrates from species such as Hogweed, Cow Parsley, Bramble and Ivy. In recent decades hedge clearance has slowed and new (in some cases replacement) hedges have been established under agri-environment schemes. It will take some decades before these acquire the same value for wildlife as those that were lost, although combining the hedge with sowing a flower-rich field margin will speed things along.

The 19th-century poet John Clare lamented the enclosure of common land, often through the creation of hedges as a tragedy, yet now clearance of those hedges is seen as undesirable from a conservation and a cultural perspective. So much of the general countryside has been impoverished, that small features such as verges, green lanes and hedges have become local hotspots for wildlife and protected by law. In a similar way, glades, rides and roadsides are hotspots for plants within a wood.

Rides

Nearly half the plant species in a wood may be found in rides and glades, even though they may occupy only 5–15% of the ground. The term 'ride' for the grassy tracks that separate the different blocks of woodland presumably arose because you could ride a horse down them, as opposed to the older, narrower paths where the canopy might meet just above a walker's head. Many rides originate in the 18th or 19th centuries and were created to allow shots at game or views of a hunt. They are still important in woods managed for shooting today, but also to provide access to the timber crop.

Species often commoner in rides than under the tree canopy include Hedge Woundwort, Bitter-vetch *Lathyrus linifolius*, Common Figwort, Wood Speedwell and Wood Small-reed. More strictly confined to rides and wood edges are Wood Vetch *Vicia sylvatica*, Narrow-leaved Everlasting Pea *Lathyrus sylvestris* and Greater Burnet-saxifrage *Pimpinella major*. Ride and wood margins are also some of the best remaining sites for the rare Crested Cow-wheat in East Anglia. The woodland ride flora includes species also associated with ancient grassland such as Betony, Bloody Crane's-bill *Geranium sanguineum*, Wood Crane's-bill, Water Avens, Slender St John's-wort, Adder's-tongue Fern, Tormentil, Saw-wort *Serratula tinctoria*, Devil's-bit Scabious, Ragged-Robin and Globeflower. In Suffolk, Lineage Wood was actually notified as a Site of Special Scientific Interest in 1971 in part because of the rich unimproved neutral grassland in its rides. The rides have become narrower, and the grassland more rank since, but there are still many species typical of the False Oat–Yorkshire-fog grassland type. In other parts of the wood, glades created by the removal of conifers planted during the 1950s and 1960s now include Bee and Pyramidal orchids (*Orchis apifera, Anacamptis pyramidalis*).

Wide rides where at least part of the vegetation receives direct sunlight at some time during the day are usually richer in plants and insects than narrow ones where the tree canopies meet overhead. Rides running east–west receive more sunlight for a given width and so again tend to hold more species than those running north–south. Rides need to be kept open and the vegetation cut regularly, preferably with the cuttings removed to avoid the build-up of nutrients that favour tall competitive species at the expense of the smaller grassland and woodland herbs. Detailed prescriptions

ABOVE:
Different vegetation zones across a ride.

RIGHT:
Betony, a plant of woodland rides and grassland.

have been developed for cutting the different zones along a ride (Warren & Fuller 1993).

The centre of the ride should be kept quite short with patches of bare ground by means of annual or biannual mowing. This gives opportunities for low-growing annuals such as Field Pansy, Corn Mint *Mentha arvensis* and Field Forget-me-not. Outside this may be a zone, cut perhaps every other year, of taller grasses (Cock's-foot, False Oat and Yorkshire-fog) and herbs such as Marsh Thistle, Hemp-agrimony and Meadowsweet. This tall, rather scruffy vegetation is referred to on the Continent by the much more interesting titles of Mantle or Saum vegetation. Giving it a proper name helps emphasise this zone's importance as a source of food and shelter for a wide variety of species, from bees on the Knapweed *Centaurea nigra* to leafhoppers sheltering in the grassy tussocks. Between the Mantle and the main tree-crop may be a zone of shrubs and Bramble cut every three to four years.

Peter Buckley and colleagues at Wye College in Kent studied how these different zones developed when previously narrow rides were widened (Buckley *et al.* 1997). There was an initial increase in plant species richness, often with double the number recorded in new ride-side quadrats compared to those taken under the shade. The additional species, such as Rosebay Willowherb, were mostly associated with disturbed ground. Over the course of a few years, species richness declined as perennial grasses became more dominant, along with tall herbs and scramblers such as Nettle and Bramble. Deer grazing promoted the increase in grass cover in some woods. More shade-tolerant woodland species such as Bluebell, Dog's Mercury and Yellow Archangel survived where the shrubs were cut and allowed to regrow as a sort of coppice.

Ditches along the edges of rides help to keep them passable to forestry traffic, but also add to the variety of conditions and plants present. In Bourne Woods in Lincolnshire the ditches have Ragged-Robin, Great Horsetail, Yellow Loosestrife and Square-stemmed St Johns-wort. Deep ruts in rides formed by heavy vehicles can subsequently fill with water, forming temporary pools with Duckweed *Lemna* spp., Water-starwort *Callitriche stagnalis* and patches of Water-pepper *Polygonum hydropiper*. If they last long enough, they may provide breeding sites for frogs and attract dragonflies. We could view such ruts as a modern analogue of wallows created by Wild Boar, Red Deer or Wild Ox.

Ditches alongside rides allow in wet woodland plants such as Yellow Loosestrife.

Unsightly ruts or the modern analogue of a Wild Boar wallow?

Maintaining the different cutting regimes across a ride can be difficult even on National Nature Reserves. Other priorities or budget cuts mean that the mowing is not done some years. Heavy deer browsing may frustrate efforts to develop the gradation of vegetation heights from the centre of the ride out to the tree zone. Spread of competitive grasses, such as Wood Small-reed, can reduce the abundance of flowering herbs.

Wood Small-reed *Calamagrostis epigejos* – a clay forester's nightmare

This tall grass, with leaves up to 2cm wide and 1m long, occurs in Great Britain mainly south-east of a line running roughly from the mouth of the Humber to the Severn, on a wide range of soils, being tolerant of both waterlogging and drought. It is present through most of the rest of Europe but becomes more scattered in the north, on a range of habitats from sand-dunes, meadows and open ground in heavy-clay woods (Jefferson 2006, Rebele & Lehmann 2001). The grass can also tolerate various forms of pollution and has been used on the Continent in land reclamation projects.

Wood Small-reed spreads by underground stems. In clear-fells and ride verges it can form dense stands up to about 1m tall. The feathery flowering heads are quite attractive en masse and it is the food plant for two rare Wainscot moths and a range of flies and bugs. However, dense stands can cover several hectares and are quite species-poor. Young trees, whether planted or naturally regenerated, struggle to grow amongst it. Fortunately, it is not very tolerant of shade, so that once the young tree or coppice growth does start to close canopy the Small-reed declines.

Wood Small-reed may have become more widespread since the 1960s. It is favoured by increasing levels of nitrogen deposition from atmospheric pollution and there are more reports of it invading dry heathland and acid grassland. In semi-natural grassland across the Continent its increase has been linked to reduced levels of stock grazing. Wild Boar eat the underground stems, disrupting dense stands, but as they are not yet in the Midlands Clay Belt of England where Small-reed is most abundant, we cannot say whether they would be effective in its control there.

Wood Small-reed developing at the ride edge.

Rides and invertebrates

During the 1970s and early 1980s conservationists found themselves in a quandary. We were trying to stop ancient broadleaved woodland being felled and replanted with conifers (with some success). However, some of the best sites for butterflies and other sun-loving insects were precisely those sites that had suffered the most drastic forestry treatments, such as Bernwood Forest east of Oxford. The felling and restocking had created lots of open flowery rides, rich in butterfly food plants and sources of nectar (Sparks *et al.* 1996). Not without some soul-searching, Bernwood Forest was designated a Site of Special Scientific Interest, conifers and all.

Many insect species that were formerly common in coppice colonised the rides of replanted woods, because these provided a similar range of open scrubby conditions rich in flowers. On some sites, as the planted trees grew, the rides became too shaded for the plants to flower and the insect richness declined. However, at Bernwood, a change in forestry policy meant that the conifers are being removed to leave an Oak crop, and a stated priority for the Forestry Commission is to encourage butterfly food plants throughout the forest.

A study of butterflies using woodland rides in the Wyre Forest found they particularly liked feeding on thistles and yellow dandelion-like flowers; Bramble, Bugle, Heather, Self-heal and buttercups also came out well (Tudor *et al.* 2004). Some insects fed across the range of available species; others focused on just one or two. Some less-favoured plant species overall were nonetheless important as food for

Lady's Smock – one of the food plants of the Orange-tip butterfly.

Orange-tip butterfly.

particular butterfly species; for example, Lady's Smock was used by only 12 butterfly species compared to 42 using brambles, but Lady's Smock was critical as a food plant for the Orange-tip butterfly.

The association of woodland butterflies with rides has proved convenient when it comes to monitoring their abundance in woodland. A standard method developed in the 1970s involves the surveyor walking along a fixed route and counting how many individuals of different species were seen (Pollard & Yates 1993). A similar methodology has recently been adapted for studying bee populations, often in association with setting up bee hotels (collections of small tubes of different sizes bundled together) to attract solitary bees and wasps.

Hedges, rides and new woodland

Hedges and rides take on another role when considered in relation to the development of new woods, which form the topic for the next chapter. Hedges can provide a local source of woodland plants for adjacent plantings. Conversely, rides may preserve remnants of the former vegetation. Breckland plants such as Candytuft *Iberis amara* and Wild Mignonette occur amongst the disturbed ground along the rides in Thetford Forest. In the big upland plantations of Sitka Spruce, rides and road edges contain a higher cover and diversity of species than the stands themselves; a similar result was found in more recent studies of Irish plantations (Hill 1979, Smith *et al.* 2007).

New woods and their flora

Woodland cover in Great Britain has expanded from about 4–5% of the land surface around 1900 to about 13–14% today. A century ago woodland cover was predominantly broadleaved and concentrated in southern England, whereas now conifers predominate in many areas and our largest forests are in northern England, Wales and Scotland. This expansion has been the result of Government policies to reduce our dependence on imports of wood and wood products, although we remain the second- or third-largest importer of such materials in the world. However, even our most ancient woods were new once. Any direct descendants of the wildwood (if they exist) are on land that was covered by ice or tundra some 15,000 years ago. Other ancient woods are underlain by Bronze or Iron Age field systems, Roman and medieval farms. So how long does it take for the ground flora to move into new woodland, and where do the plants come from?

As a teenager, I helped my maths master, Bill Dawkins, weed and dig up Christmas trees that he had planted in a field behind his house. Intermediate rows of mixed hardwoods and conifers were to be left to grow into a wood. Fifty years later I went back to see what had happened to this wood. I found myself looking up into the canopy of trees that I remembered as barely overtopping me. The ground flora was mostly of Bramble and Nettle, but there were also daffodils (cultivated), bluebells (native), Pendulous Sedge, Soft Shield-fern, Common Figwort, Lesser Celandine and Primrose. The daffodils, and perhaps the bluebells, were planted in; the primroses had spread from remnants of an orchard that had been in one corner of the field and the other species had come in from hedges and gardens around the new wood. While nowhere near as rich as nearby ancient woods, the formerly grassy inter-rows are turning into a proper woodland ground flora.

OPPOSITE PAGE:
Carrifran, Scotland
– a landscape being
transformed.

The wood at Cox Green, Essex, 45 years on from my Christmas tree weeding.

Afforestation blight or habitat restoration

During the 20th century large-scale conifer plantations were created on lowland heaths, upland moors and bogs (Gambles 2019, Tsouvalis 2000). There was extensive spread of broadleaved woodland through natural regeneration on the downs of southern England following the sharp decline in rabbits from myxomatosis in the 1950s. Oak, Ash and Thorn sprang up on commons as livestock grazing became uneconomic or too risky because of traffic collisions on nearby roads. Replacing steam trains by diesel meant fewer line-side fires, and railway embankments became lines of trees, exacerbating the annual problem of 'leaves on the line'. Miles of new woodland have been planted or grown up naturally along motorways and other major trunk roads. Abandoned land in or on the edges of towns and cities has turned into scrub. Thousands of small broadleaved woods have been planted under various farm woodland schemes. Some estates in Scotland have promoted large-scale natural regeneration of Birch and Scots Pine where they have fenced deer out of wide areas or increased the levels of deer control.

Conservationists have been ambivalent about this forest expansion. There were objections from the 1930s onwards to large-scale conifer afforestation because of its effects on the landscape and the restrictions

ABOVE:
Spruce plantations
at Kielder Forest,
Northumberland.

RIGHT:
Scrub reclaiming the
remains of a bungalow on
the Dunton plotlands, near
Basildon in Essex.

on where people could walk (Symonds 1936). In the 1970s and 1980s major campaigns were organised against the planting up of lowland heaths, bogs and upland moors because of the losses to breeding bird populations and to moorland and bog vegetation (NCC 1986, Warren 2000). Conservation organisations regularly seek to remove or suppress developing native woodland on grassland and heath reserves through the judicious use of cutting and grazing. Small-scale farm planting on improved pasture has been dismissed as a waste of time because such woods may not support woodland specialist species in our lifetimes. Some previous colleagues even formed a group called Conservationists against Tree Planting or CAT-P (say it!).

At the same time, we applaud woodland restoration projects such as that at Carrifran Woods, which aims to 're-create an extensive tract of mainly forested wilderness' in the Southern Uplands (Ashmole & Ashmole 2009). In the Highlands, the charity Trees for Life seeks to link up ancient native pinewoods through establishing islands of 'healthy young forest scattered throughout the barren, deforested glens. As these new trees reach seed-bearing age, they are expected to form the nuclei for expanded natural regeneration in the surrounding area'. Another charity, the Woodland Trust, has been creating thousands of hectares of new woodland across Great Britain, both on its own land, and through helping others to plant trees and

Woodland Trust planting on their Smithhills Estate near Bolton.

new woods for a wide range of benefits. The spread of scrub on the rewilded Knepp Estate in Sussex has been associated with increases in local populations of nightingales, Purple Emperor butterflies and turtle doves (Tree 2018).

New woodland can contribute to the targets for woodland expansion in the Biodiversity Action Plans (reflecting international commitments under the Convention for Biological Diversity) by helping to improve conditions for threatened woodland species and communities. Woodland expansion fits with the recommendations for more, bigger, and more joined up, conservation areas proposed in the *Making space for nature* report to Defra (Lawton 2010), and also with climate change adaptation strategies (chapter 16). The increase in overall woodland cover may be part of the reason that woodland plants have shown fewer declines and more increases compared to species associated with unimproved grassland or arable weeds (Preston *et al.* 2002). We need, therefore, to look at how the flora in new woods develops.

New woods in the lowlands

Many new woods in the south and east of Great Britain are small, and planted on former arable or pasture. Before the canopy closes, the nutrient-rich ex-farmland soils that often underlie such woods favour competitive grasses and weeds, rather than shade-tolerant species. As the trees grow, their shade reduces the cover of the open ground plants, but the soil fungi content may still not be suitable for the establishment of woodland species. There are seldom any woodland species already present on site and the seed bank is usually of non-woodland plants, although there may be woodland species in nearby hedges that can colonise the new woodland.

A major programme of such lowland woodland planting was stimulated in the early 1990s by the then Countryside Agency through the Community Forests programme. This sought to encourage environmental and social regeneration through creating woods around towns, and more than 10,000 hectares of new woodland were planted (Mell 2011). One of the younger examples is Thames Chase, on the floodplain close to the Dartford–Thurrock River Crossing in south Essex. The Chase was formerly farmland, but even in the early days, when it was just rows of trees with rough grass in between, people came to walk in it. Some of the plantings have now closed canopy and a woodland flora is just starting to appear: the odd bit of Bramble, Ivy and Lords-and-Ladies. Compared to the bleak fields there previously, it is a considerable improvement.

The National Forest was a parallel initiative to the Community Forest programme, but on a bigger scale. Spread across 500 square kilometres, it covers parts of Derbyshire, Leicestershire and Staffordshire. Since 1995, its woodland cover has increased from about 6% to just over 20% in 2016 (Cloke *et al.* 1996). The trees are in the ground, but again the ground flora has taken its time to arrive. At Battram Wood near Ibstock in Leicestershire 20-year-old Oak plantations have mainly Bramble in the ground flora, the odd clump of Male and Broad Buckler-fern and occasional plants of Wood Avens. Remnants of the early open vegetation phase hang on in places – Rosebay Willowherb, dandelions and grasses such as Cock's-foot, Common Bent and Red Fescue. There are also large areas of bare leaf litter with no plants growing at all. The same sort of pattern has been reported from woods created in the Central Belt of lowland Scotland.

Nevertheless, over a longer time-scale more interesting species do appear. Thirty-three small farm woods (0.1–31ha) planted on fields in the first half of the 20th century in the Vale of York were surveyed for their ground flora in 1990 (Usher *et al.* 1992). The surveyors found 115 species in total. Bramble, Nettles, Yorkshire-fog,

Male-fern – a common species in new woodland.

Rosebay, Male and Broad Buckler-fern were widespread, but amongst the other species recorded were Wood Avens, Enchanter's-nightshade, and specialists such as Common Dog-violet, Dog's Mercury, Sanicle and Primrose. Nearly half the species were found in fewer than four woods, but Wood Speedwell and Wood-sorrel were in nine woods each and Bluebell in 24 out of the 33.

Primrose and Dog's Mercury were found in a survey of new farm woods in Yorkshire.

Herb-Robert, one of the faster colonising woodland plants in Geescroft Wilderness, Hertfordshire.

In 1918, the Reverend Adrian Woodruffe-Peacock described the species found in Poolthorn Covert, North Lincolnshire (Woodruffe-Peacock 1918), which was planted in 1797 on a rough pasture of Tufted Hair-grass. The Reverend noted various species that came and went, including Male-fern, Lesser Burdock, Common Hemp-nettle, Water Figwort *Scrophularia auriculata*, Marsh Thistle, Rosebay and Great Willowherbs. He thought that the Wood Anemone came in on shooters' clothes, while Spurge-laurel and Honeysuckle were probably brought in by blackbirds. Bluebell might have come in with starlings: it first appeared under 'fetid blackthorn bushes' used as their roost. Unfortunately, that wood is no longer there to allow us to follow up his work, but the fortunes of plants in other new woods can be observed.

At Rothamsted Experimental Station in Hertfordshire (Harmer *et al.* 2001) there are two small self-sown woods which developed from arable fields abandoned in the 1880s. There was an initial increase in the species richness of the ground flora but many of these early colonists were light-demanding species that disappeared as the trees and shrubs grew up. By 1915, one of the woods, Broadbalk Wilderness (0.13ha), had Ivy throughout with Lords-and-Ladies, Sanicle and Dog-violet. Dog's Mercury with traces of False Brome were present, mainly towards the woodland margins, along with Hogweed, False Oat-grass, Hedge Woundwort and Nettle (Brenchley & Adam 1915).

By 1998 the flora included Bluebell, Black Bryony and Lesser Celandine, species that might be found in long-established mixed woodland in the Midlands. Other species were still only at the woodland edges – Ground-ivy, Wood Avens, White Bryony. The somewhat larger Geescroft Wilderness (1ha) had more woodland species. Bluebell and Lesser Celandine dominated the ground flora and formed dense patches throughout the wood, although again other woodland species were mainly confined to the margins.

The flora in these two small woods is limited by their size, closed canopy and lack of open space, hence the many species found mainly at the margins. Under the canopy, competition from ground-growing Ivy may also be a limiting factor, and in Geescroft the spread of Holly in the understorey will slow further expansion of the woodland flora. The various surveys include some species that established for a while but had died out again by 1998, including False Brome, Pignut, Sanicle and Bittersweet in Broadbalk, and Wood-sedge, Giant Fescue, Sanicle and Sweet Violet at Geescroft.

Presumably these could colonise again if conditions within the wood became more suitable for their growth; their current absence is not because they cannot reach the woods.

Another study of woodland development is under way at Monks Wood National Nature Reserve in Cambridgeshire. A four-hectare field next to the wood has been left to colonise naturally since the 1960s with Oak, Ash, Blackthorn, Hawthorn and Dogwood. After 38 years Kevin Walker and Tim Sparks recorded 89 ground flora species in it, including both woodland generalist and specialist species. Some were largely confined to the edges (Bugle, Dog's Mercury, Wood Avens, Three-veined Sandwort), but others had spread through most of the area (Ground-ivy, False Brome, Lords-and-Ladies) (Walker & Sparks 2000).

Oxlip, bluebells and Dog's Mercury have spread into the self-sown triangular field (believed to have developed as woodland since the 1920s) next to Hayley Wood in Cambridgeshire (see also chapter 4). In 2017, I also saw False Brome, Wood-sedge, Spurge-laurel, Wild Strawberry, Wood Avens, Honeysuckle, Sanicle, Black Bryony and Common Dog-violet, which is not a bad plant list for a small piece of young closed-canopy woodland! Bird's-nest Orchid has also been recorded there.

Bird's-nest Orchid, here shown in a beechwood, has spread into the Hayley Wood Triangle in less than a century.

These studies show that a surprising number of species may make it even into small woods. They allow woodland plants such as Enchanter's-nightshade to occur in landscapes where they would otherwise be rare. Moreover, compared to the improved fields and arable crops that they generally replace, small woods provide opportunities for common species such as Bramble and Nettle to spread, so increasing the potential food plants for a wide range of invertebrates.

Enchanter's-nightshade

Despite its common name, Enchanter's-nightshade *Circaea lutetiana* is not related to the other (poisonous) nightshades but is in fact part of the same family as Evening Primrose and Fuchsia. It is found throughout Great Britain, except in parts of northern Scotland, as well as occurring across much of the rest of Europe. It favours fertile, disturbed soils, including shaded gardens (Grime *et al.* 2007).

Enchanter's-nightshade is one of the later plants to emerge in the spring, and its small white flowers provide some summer variety for the woodland flora. It has rather thin, weak leaves compared to Dog's Mercury, with which it often grows, but is more able than the Mercury to colonise new woodland sites. The rounded fruits are covered by hooked bristles – miniature burdocks – that are easily picked up on the fur of passing animals or surveyors' socks, giving the potential for long-distance spread. Once established, creeping above-ground stems allow the plant to fill its immediate surroundings. Its tolerance of shade means that it can form dense stands under conditions that exclude more vigorous, taller-growing species such as Rosebay Willowherb.

Enchanter's nightshade, a fast-colonising woodland species.

The vegetation of a planted conifer forest

After the First World War, the Forestry Commission was looking for areas to plant up and the Breckland, a large sandy area on the Suffolk/Norfolk border, was identified as being of little value for farming. Its heaths and acid grassland were known for their unusual flora, the closest perhaps we have in Great Britain to central European steppe-type grass-heath (Dolman *et al.* 2012). However, this did not stop large areas being planted with Scots and Corsican Pine to become what is now Thetford Forest.

Fortuitously, we have a detailed account of the vegetation development for one area. West Tofts on the eastern side of the Forest had been divided into small blocks, each of which was planted with a different tree species. In the 1950s, some 20 years after the trees had been established, John Ovington, a researcher with the fledgling Nature Conservancy, recorded what was growing under the trees (Ovington 1955). The unplanted plot was the richest, with over 43 vascular plant species recorded and 99% ground flora cover. Deciduous plots (Birch, Alder and European Larch) were generally similar to each other in richness and cover of the ground flora (17–21 species; 64–77% ground flora cover), with grasses (Common Bent, Sheep's-fescue, Yorkshire-fog) being the most frequent species. Nettles were common in the Alder plot, probably reflecting higher soil nutrient levels as a result of the nitrogen-fixing nodules on Alder roots. The Corsican Pine and Douglas Fir plots had only six and two vascular plant species recorded respectively, and less than 3% cover. There was little Bracken.

In the early 1970s Mark Anderson of Forest Research resurveyed this area. The stands were still fairly grassy, but Bracken had increased under the Larch and Douglas Fir. The two stands that had been species-poor in 1952 (Corsican Pine and Douglas Fir) had been thinned and gained species, whilst the Larch and Alder plots had lost species, probably because they had become more shaded (Anderson 1979). Anderson concluded that the vegetation under different tree species tended to converge around a dozen common species, although this pattern was less clear at West Tofts than in his other two sites (Bedgebury in Kent, Abbotswood in the Forest of Dean).

When I visited West Tofts in 2017 some stands in the original trial had been felled and replanted and others had opened up through windthrow. Most of the plots consisted of tall Bracken with Raspberry, grasses and a little Nettle, almost exclusively woodland generalists.

The unplanted plot in the original Ovington study had become a young pine stand over Bracken.

With relatively uniform site conditions (flat topography, free-draining soils) and a predominance of one type of trees (pines) in the crop, the woodland flora that developed in Thetford Forest was always likely to be uniform. Large areas are dominated by Bracken as in the West Tofts section, some areas by Bramble, with a scatter of Wood Sage, Heath Bedstraw, Bent Grasses and Sweet Vernal-grass. Where denser canopied conifers, such as Spruce, have been planted, or in the young pine stands, there is very little flora. Beech stands, often planted as strips along the forest roads, show a slightly different development with small patches of False Brome and Enchanter's-nightshade – perhaps heralding the start of a richer woodland flora in future.

The creation of Thetford Forest certainly destroyed large areas of the Breckland flora. However, the Breckland flora has also been lost from much of the unplanted surrounding landscape because of agricultural improvements since the Second World War. At least in the forest some of the commoner open ground species remain along the rides and timber stacking areas or reappear after disturbances such as felling. Of the 43 species that Ovington recorded from the unplanted area in 1955 I saw about half, for example Lady's Bedstraw and Wild Mignonette, along a track leading up to Ovington's study area in 2017.

Rosebay Willowherb – a plant of young plantations and other disturbed ground

Rosebay Willowherb *Chamerion angustifolium* was once considered rather rare, although familiar enough to be mentioned in Gerard's herbal. The last century then saw a major expansion of this species. It spread dramatically in London after the Blitz, on the mass of rough ground, broken walls and roofs. This affinity with burnt or disturbed sites such as along railway lines is reflected in its common American name of Fireweed.

It is generally common in the early stages of new woodland, although by 1955 in Thetford it survived mainly in the unplanted areas (Ovington 1955, Grime *et al.* 2007). In new woodland, or after felling in established woods, it takes over bare ground to create dense stands over a metre tall. Below ground Rosebay has long, horizontally-spreading, roots and in America these can help to stabilise areas of bare ground after fires or logging that would otherwise be subject to soil erosion. In British woods it may also help reduce loss of nutrients and soil on disturbed ground.

Rosebay's reign may be brief, because it does not survive long under shade. In the Thetford study, it was hardly recorded where the planted stands had closed canopy. Similarly, in Wytham it was found in 38 (nearly a quarter) of the permanent plots in 1974, when many stands had only just closed over following a period of post-war planting. By 1991, 17 more years of shade and little disturbance reduced Rosebay to 13 plots, and it was completely absent from the 1999 records. It has since turned up occasionally in one or two plots, usually where there has been thinning or windthrow. These disturbances provide the right conditions of bare ground and lots of light that allow the Rosebay to bounce back again from wind-blown seeds, whose drifting white plumes are a common sight in autumn.

Rosebay's abundance and association with derelict ground mean that it is sometimes dismissed as just another weedy species by botanists, but that is to overlook the brilliance of its massed flowers. Londoners voted it as their County Flower in Plantlife's 2002 competition.

Though often thought of as a weedy species, Rosebay is attractive en masse.

New woods in the uplands

There are fewer differences in the vascular plants found in recent versus ancient broadleaved woods in the uplands of Great Britain. Upland woods often have many gaps in the canopy, making them quite open, and may be heavily grazed like the adjacent hill-land. Woodland boundaries may be less fixed, with periods of woodland expansion and contraction in response to changes in grazing pressures. There are also more places in the uplands where woodland ground flora species can survive outside woods, such as along stream-sides and under Bracken.

Carrifran, in the Southern Uplands, was typical of many valleys and glens in having very little tree cover in the late 1990s, but, as mentioned earlier, a fantastic new woodland is now developing (Ashmole & Ashmole 2009). Bracken, Bilberry and Wavy Hair-grass were widespread on the open moor prior to planting, and a range of other woodland species, including Wood-sorrel, Common Dog-violet, Primrose, Sanicle and Opposite-leaved Golden-saxifrage, were scattered through the valley. On a visit in 2014, I also saw Wood Anemone, Bluebell, Early-purple Orchid, Globeflower and Water Avens. As the trees grow, there will be the potential for these woodland species to spread.

Pre-existing woodland flora at Carrifran including primroses and Great Wood-rush.

Birch, one of the main trees planted at Carrifran, is also common in naturally-developing woods in the uplands, such as in the strips along railway lines that were fenced against stock. Very dense young Birch stands may have just litter below, but usually there is more of a ground flora in new birchwoods than under many new lowland woods. This flora may be mainly Bilberry, Wavy Hair-grass and Bracken, with Purple Moor-grass where conditions are wetter, or Bramble if the soils are a bit richer.

The changes in the vegetation under a developing birchwood were studied in north-east Scotland in a series of woods that had been growing on moorland for 20 to over 60 years. Heather initially increased, because the grazing was reduced, then declined with increasing canopy closure because Heather is not very shade-tolerant (Hester *et al.* 1991, Mitchell *et al.* 2007). Common Bent and Wavy Hair-grass spread as the woodland matured and opened out. The changes in the vegetation were mainly driven by the changing light regime under the trees. However, some soil nutrients were also more available under old Birch than on moorland. Where the woods continued to be grazed Bilberry was reduced, giving the less palatable but slower-growing Cowberry more of a chance.

A pioneering exercise in woodland creation under extreme conditions was carried out in the 1960s to extend the native woodland on the National Nature Reserve of the Island of Rum in the Inner Hebrides. Some areas were ploughed, and Lodgepole Pine used as nurse crops that were eventually to be removed. Peter Wormell, the warden, was involved from the outset and some of the first trees were hand-planted by his wife in 1959. In 1994 he wrote enthusiastically of the thousands of trees established, their growth, and the variety of structures developing in this new woodland (Wormell 1994).

There were woodland ground flora species already on the island of Rum, in isolated fragments of woodland on crags and in gulleys, and in places these spread. In the Kilmory Fank plot Peter described bluebells bursting with seeds under the planted trees; in the Kilmory North Plot Wood Sage, Wood-sorrel and Bilberry were spreading below the trees, Golden-scaled Male-fern and Hard-fern more in evidence and natural regeneration of Honeysuckle abundant. Underneath young alders, Marsh-marigold, Primrose and Meadowsweet were extending along a streamside. A later report on the Rum plantings was more circumspect (Stiven & Smith 2005); while a significant area of woodland had been established, tree growth was slow with little

sign that the trees were regenerating outside the original plantings. Nevertheless, a gradual development of woodland plant communities was taking place.

When I visited Rum in 2018, I could see how both sets of conclusions might be drawn. There are some mature 19th-century mixed plantings established in sheltered sites on relatively fertile soils. These have well-developed carpets of Bluebell, Primrose, Pignut, Wood-sorrel and Honeysuckle. On an undercliff on the east coast there is a strip of Birch and Rowan, with occasional Alder and willows, which has a flora of Bluebell, Creeping Soft-grass, Bracken and Wood-sorrel. It looks largely semi-natural but runs into a patch of young Oak that was clearly part of the conservation plantings and has a similar ground vegetation. Some of the patches of Alder and Birch, established in the 1960s along stream gullies, have mainly Purple Moor-grass, but with Bramble, Lady Fern, Broad Buckler-fern, Hard-fern, Tormentil, Self-heal and Soft Rush. Other 1960s pine stands have just Purple Moor-grass beneath them, with the old plough lines still visible. However, Purple Moor-grass is the major component of some western native pinewoods, such as at Sheildaig Forest in Wester Ross on the mainland, so perhaps even these species-poor stands on Rum are in one sense developing the 'expected' woodland ground flora.

OPPOSITE PAGE:
New plantings from the 1960s on Rum (top).

Coastal Oak plantation on Rum, over Bluebell (below).

Conifer plantations in the uplands

There are, in Great Britain, about 126,000ha of Larch and 665,000ha of Sitka Spruce, making the latter now our commonest forest tree. Many were established, both by the Forestry Commission and private owners, in the 20th century, in regions and on soils where semi-natural woodland was scarce. In the first few years after planting there was often increased vegetation growth because the rabbits, sheep and deer were fenced out (Hill 1979, Coote et al. 2012). However, once the trees got away and closed canopy, vascular plants were more or less eliminated over large areas under crops of Hemlock *Tsuga* sp., firs and the ubiquitous Sitka Spruce. In a study at Kielder Forest, 17% of stands had no ground vegetation, while in a further 40% of stands the vegetation was too sparse to assign to any specific vegetation type (Wallace & Good 1995). The plantations were often managed on short rotations (30–50 years), generally under 'no-thin' regimes to reduce the risk of windthrow.

Spot the ground flora under thicket stands of spruce.

This gave little opportunity for the flora to reappear in older stands before they were clear-felled.

Where a ground flora does develop under conifers, the commonest species tend to be Broad Buckler-fern, Wavy Hair-grass and Bilberry; less frequent species include Heather, Rosebay Willowherb, Heath Bedstraw and Purple Moor-grass. Mosses and liverworts can be abundant (though limited in species richness). Thicker patches of grasses and sedges often pick out small gaps in the canopy. More extensive vegetation cover is generally found under mature Larch and Pine, with Bramble and Bracken on fertile sites. In Ireland, a grass-dominated community has been described under mature Larch with Common Bent, Sweet Vernal-grass, Sheep's-fescue, Wavy Hair-grass (French *et al.* 2008) that is similar to some of the grassy stands in lowland pinewoods in Great Britain.

After the trees are felled, the ground flora spreads back, mainly from species in the soil seed bank, for example Heather, various sedges and rushes, Heath Bedstraw and Foxglove. Incoming wind-dispersed species such as Rosebay Willowherb can be important. Woodland species that were already present in the stand benefit from the increased light after felling, but these are usually just a small range of grasses and Bramble. At Kielder, Purple Moor-grass tends

Broad Buckler-fern

If a species is to become common in upland conifer plantations it needs to be able to tolerate generally acid soils, heavy shade and have an efficient system for dispersing across the landscape. Broad Buckler-fern *Dryopteris dilatata* meets these criteria. It is one of our most common ferns, in all types of woodland, along with Male-fern and Bracken (Page 1988).

Its much-divided fronds emerge from the underground stem, often looking a little untidy or straggly compared to Male-fern. The clumps may be quite dispersed or locally abundant. On deep humus-rich soils the clumps can be massive, with fronds up to waist height. In wet alderwoods the fern may be clustered on the raised drier ground around the tree bases. Like some other ferns it contains toxins that reduce its palatability to herbivores, but it may be eaten none the less. In winter it dies back, the fronds being susceptible to hard frosts that leave them blackened.

In late summer, small round structures develop on the underside of the fronds which contain the spores. Millions of them may be produced from a single plant! These are wind-dispersed and can be found in the top few centimetres of many woodland soils. They germinate in response to light, but what is produced is not a new fern as we usually see it. Instead, a different type of plant grows that has only half the number of chromosomes. It is much more like a moss or liverwort and needs moist, humid conditions. Cross-fertilisation occurs during this stage and a sporeling with the more familiar fern structure then develops, often to be seen on old tree stumps.

Like many common woodland plants Broad Buckler-fern may be dismissed as not of much interest, but the tracery of its leaves is worth a second look.

Broad Buckler-fern with its finely dissected fronds.

to dominate the clear-fells at higher altitudes, Wavy Hair-grass on drier sites with shallower peat and Tufted Hair-grass at lower levels. Bracken may spread in from plants surviving along ride-sides. Where Heather re-establishes quickly and in abundance, the replanted area may for a short time show some similarities to the former moorland vegetation. As the second-rotation crop starts to grow, however, the species of open conditions are shaded out again.

The second and subsequent rotations of conifers in these new forests are likely to be more varied than the first. Foresters are moving away from very large clear-fells on many sites and are trying to use a wider range of tree species to reduce risks from climate change and outbreaks of pests and diseases. Where the trees can be thinned and allowed to grow on for longer, the vegetation underneath them starts to become more interesting, with carpets of mosses, Bilberry and Wood-sorrel. The occasional wind-thrown tree, with its associated pit-and-mound, adds to the diversity. There may be, over time, a gradual accumulation of woodland plant species (Quine 2015), such that stands start to resemble more natural Larch forests on the Continent or stands in the Pacific North-West of America where Sitka Spruce is native (Tittensor 2016). For the time being, though, their flora may remain limited, with mainly woodland generalists such as Broad Buckler-fern.

New elements of the cultural landscape

The National Vegetation Classification (NVC) has been used, and sometimes abused, as a model of how we might expect new woods of native trees to develop. Some of the Rum plantings, and pine plantations elsewhere, do show similarities to types described by Rodwell (1991) and may contain pinewood specialists such as Twinflower. Mature/over-mature stands of Sitka Spruce can show some overlaps with upland Oak type communities (W11, W17) (Ferris *et al.* 2000), partly because these Oak communities themselves are poor in vascular plants. We should not, however, expect the vegetation of new upland plantations to be a direct analogue of that in nearby broadleaved woodland (Wallace 2003). Conifer forests have a different structure and create a different type of microclimate for the ground flora. Conifer woods are generally darker, there are changes in the water regime and the rain of needle litter is different to the autumnal broadleaf leaf-fall.

People sometimes compare habitat conservation to the listing and conservation of buildings. If we pursue that analogy ancient woods can be likened to old houses and churches that should generally be protected. Some new woods clearly show potential to become treasured features of the future, while other commercial Sitka stands may be seen as equivalent to the 1960s 'brutalist' period of concrete architecture. However, just as old churches and thatched cottages do not make good office space compared to modern designed buildings, upland conifer plantations can fulfil different and still valued functions for society. When there were proposals to sell off the state forests in England around 2010, the big plantation forests of Kielder and Thetford had as passionate supporters as did the New Forest or the Forest of Dean.

New woods and plantations are part of the 20th century's additions to our landscapes. Our successors will have their views on what parts of this legacy they want to keep and which to discard. However, we should at least try to improve the quality of the new woodland we are leaving the next generation.

Improving the flora of new woods – site choice

If the only objective in creating a new wood is to produce timber, what matters is getting the trees into the ground and growing well. However, most woods also fulfil other functions, and many woodland owners are interested in wildlife: they may therefore want their new woods to have a rich flora. New woods created where there are already a lot of woodland plant species on or near the sites are likely to end up richer than those formed on species-poor and isolated locations.

Some of the species moving in to Geescroft and Broadbalk Wildernesses, described above, were probably already present in the adjacent hedge. In Lincolnshire, woods created next to old hedges or ancient woodland were more likely to have been colonised by woodland species (Peterken & Game 1984). In Sweden, oak plantations showed decreasing species richness with increasing distance from the new site to the nearest ancient woods (Brunet 2007). Similar results are also emerging from a major study of the new woods created in the Central Belt of Scotland and in the National Forest in central England (Watts et al. 2016).

New woods are also likely to end up richer in plant species if they grow where there are already some woodland/woodland edge species present. John Rodwell, primary author of the National Vegetation

Classification volumes, and Gordon Patterson from the Forestry Commission, identified the sorts of semi-natural open vegetation that would be best for developing different broad groupings of woodland communities (Rodwell & Patterson 1994). For example, to create (by planting or natural regeneration) a lowland Oak–Bramble–Bracken woodland the best sort of site might be one with rough grassland of False Oat-grass, Yorkshire-fog, Cock's-foot, Hogweed, Rosebay, Nettle and Thistle. For an upland Oak–Birch–Bilberry woodland we should look for moorland with Heather, Bilberry, Bell-heather, Wavy Hair-grass, Sheep's-fescue, Mat-grass, Common Bent, Sweet Vernal-grass, Heath Bedstraw and Tormentil.

The Reverend Woodruffe-Peacock's list of species that were probably in the rough pasture where Poolthorn Covert was planted is quite long, as is the list for what was on Broadbalk Wilderness before the trees started to grow. Species such as Tufted Hair-grass and Marsh Thistle can carry over from grassland to the woodland edge/ride component of a new woodland; Wavy Hair-grass and Bilberry do the same over the moorland/woodland transition.

In Allt Gleann a'Chlachain in the central Highlands of Scotland a new woodland was planted with the intention that this would provide shelter for sheep and improve the farming productivity. John Holland from Scotland's Rural College looked at how the vegetation changed after the sheep were fenced out. There was extensive growth of Heather,

New planting is generally pushed towards former arable or improved pasture.

Bilberry and Purple Moor-grass. Tall herbs emerged and flowered, including Meadowsweet, Wood Crane's-bill, Lady's Mantle, Angelica, Melancholy Thistle, Common Valerian, Northern Bedstraw *Galium boreale* and Goldenrod. Large patches of Wood Anemone developed across the well-drained slopes. There was also an increase in butterflies such as Scotch Argus and Small Pearl-bordered Fritillary.

Rodwell and Patterson, however, stress that 'existing vegetation may have great conservation and amenity value in its own right'. Often the decision is made that we should not sacrifice the existing open vegetation character and value for the sake of any potential increase in value of the new woodland cover. Woodland development then goes on to other land where the vegetation is not so rich, but this means that conditions may not be so suitable for developing woodland plant communities. No wonder new woods are often initially rather dull botanically!

High soil fertility in ex-farmland soils often limits the spread of species into and through new woods. Woodland specialists may grow better under high nutrient conditions in greenhouse experiments (Hipps *et al.* 2005), but in the field they are likely to be outcompeted by tall species, such as Nettle, False Oat-grass and Cow Parsley, that are better able to thrive in enriched soils. While it is easy to add nutrients through fertilisers, it is not so easy to reduce fertility levels. An approach trialled by the charity Landlife was to use a machine like a deep plough that turns the soil over, effectively burying the topsoil. The new surface layer consists of the less fertile subsoil and does not have as many buried weed seeds as the original upper layers. The vegetation that then grows up is less competitive for the trees and more attractive for visitors to the site, because it contains more flowers. The technique has been used to produce rich woodland edge communities amongst new tree plantings.

Ground flora introductions: the Milton Keynes experience and beyond

The Reverend Woodruffe-Peacock concluded 'that in time most, if not all, woodland species adapted to any particular soil or soils gradually arrive, by chance means, at a covert ... as isolated as Poolthorn.' However, 'in time' may mean a century or more. There is a case for giving some species a helping hand, because 'It is better to light a candle than to curse the darkness' (William Watkinson 1907).

The principles around introducing wildflowers to new sites as a nature conservation practice were developed in the 1980s for creating species-rich grassland (Wells *et al.* 1981). There are now a wide variety of grassland wildflower mixes available from commercial seed firms. It has taken longer for woodland ground flora introductions to be accepted as a conservation technique in new woodland (Blakesley & Buckley 2010). It may still feel too much like gardening for some, but in 2008 the charity Flora Locale noted in one of its leaflets 'On farms, in forests, city parks, suburban gardens, quarries and on roadsides – British wildflowers, trees and shrubs are being sown and planted on an unprecedented scale'.

People had long been introducing species for aesthetic reasons: there are clumps of daffodils and snowdrops on the top of Wytham Hill for example. Other species, such as Pendulous Sedge, might be introduced as potential food for pheasants. Then in the 1980s Laurie Boorman of the Institute of Terrestrial Ecology, whose colleagues were working on creating flower-rich grassland, set up a small-scale trial of woodland ground flora introductions for conservation purposes in Milton Keynes. Milton Keynes was chosen because there was a great deal of planting of native trees and shrubs along roadsides and amongst the houses. The initial work involved both the sowing of seeds and planting of young plants into six young plantations. Establishment was good: all, but one, species were found a couple of years later.

The work was then followed up by Joanna Francis as part of her PhD from the University of London (Francis & Morton 2001). Over the next ten years, regular visits confirmed that the introduced species were surviving and in 2000 a more detailed re-survey was carried out. Foxglove was no longer found, but it needs open woodland and the plantations had probably just become too dark for it. The other species were still in most of the woods where they had been introduced, although the spread to new areas was slow. Wood Avens had done well, as had Red Campion and Hedge Garlic where conditions were suitable. Bluebell spread was perhaps enhanced where the plantations were on embankments: the seeds could just roll downslope.

Since the initial trials, more than 100 hectares at Milton Keynes have had woodland species introduced to them, including specialists such as Wild Garlic, Primrose, Pignut and Sweet Woodruff. The species used were, with a few exceptions, all locally native plants. As Francis and Morton (2001) put it 'A visit to these plantations in spring

ABOVE:
Daffodils and snowdrops introduced to new woodland for aesthetic purposes.

RIGHT:
Primroses introduced to Milton Keynes roadside plantings.

may surprise the majority of woodland managers. Those expecting rank "weed" species to dominate … will find instead a wealth of woodland field layer species growing vigorously beneath the trees'.

In April 2019 I was shown examples of the Milton Keynes roadside belts and their developing flora. Unthinned areas were typically densely shaded with little ground flora, or, where there was a bit more light, a ground-covering carpet of Ivy. Where the ground flora had been introduced, primroses were blooming in abundance; bluebells were less advanced, but other woodland species seen included Pendulous Sedge, Wood Avens, Greater Stitchwort, Wild Garlic and Red Campion.

The Highways Agency have taken an interest in further development of this work, because extensive tree planting and natural regeneration happens regularly alongside major roads. The Highways Agency (2005) guidance is that the plants should be put into relatively open ground conditions with extensive leaf litter, and only a low cover of competitive species such as Bramble, Bracken, Ivy and tussocky grasses. The sites must not be too shaded, or the plants will not grow, nor too open as competitive species will dominate the introductions. Moderately fertile soils are best – if conditions are too rich there will be lots of nettles. Various mixtures of species have been designed, comparable to the different grassland mixtures, and experience gained on which species may be best introduced as seed, and which as small plants. Generally, the aim is to establish 'islands' of woodland flora that can subsequently spread on their own.

About the same time as Boorman was starting his experiments in Milton Keynes, woodland flora introductions were being trialled on Rum (Stiven & Smith 2005). The 1984 proposals were for species to be introduced to the oldest planted plots, in isolated situations where possible confusion with any natural immigration or spread from the pre-existing flora would be limited. Red Campion, Wood Anemone, Dog's Mercury and Hairy Wood-rush were used. The plants apparently established well, but unfortunately there is little information on how these trials did subsequently.

Recently there has been renewed interest in Scotland in introducing woodland ground flora to the many plantings that have taken place through the Central Belt and which are often overrun by just nettles, Hogweed or Rosebay Willowherb. Trials are being established to demonstrate cost-effective ways of integrating the introduction of the ground flora with other aspects of the woodland creation process.

The idea is that the introduced plants should act as sources for further natural colonisation of the woodland (Worrell *et al.* 2016).

As happened with grassland wildflower introduction, the initial research sowings have progressed to the point where commercial woodland seed mixes are now available. A wide range of woodland plants may be included, ranging from woodland specialists such as Wild Garlic, Pignut and Nettle-leaved Bellflower, through generalists such as Foxglove, Hedge Garlic and Wood Sage, to non-woodland species such as Yarrow and Agrimony (Blakesley & Buckley 2010). If a species is to be included in the mixes it is helpful if it produces lots of seed on a regular basis. This is better for the nurseries who need it to bulk it up, and also for the subsequent spread of the plant in the sites to which it is introduced. One obvious species in this respect is Red Campion, which may have several thousand seeds per individual.

Did the earth move for you, Primrose?

If woodland plants struggle to establish well in new woods because the soils are not suitable, could this problem be partly overcome by bringing in ancient woodland topsoil with its array of micro-organisms as well as buried seeds, bulbs and rhizomes? There are now instances where this has been done, usually associated with the granting of planning permission to destroy a patch of ancient woodland. Soil collected from the threatened site has been taken to a new location; there the existing topsoil is removed and the material from the ancient woodland spread in its place.

An early case involved Biggins Wood in Kent, a small ancient wood that had the misfortune to lie where the Folkestone terminal for the Channel Tunnel rail-link is now. In 1988, some topsoil from this coppice was moved to a nearby hillslope; the area was then planted up. In the new wood there was an initial increase in the abundance of open-ground species, mostly from the soil seed bank, but many shade-tolerant species survived and spread, including Wood-sedge, Primrose, Stinking Iris and Wood Speedwell (Buckley *et al.* 2017). Some woodland specialists such as Remote Sedge and Narrow-spiked Wood-sedge did not transfer well and were limited to small seepage areas on the new site, which was generally drier than the original wood. The trees planted on the new site created a rather uniform canopy, and a more variable light climate might have allowed a wider range of ground flora to develop.

Red Campion

Red Campion *Silene dioica* is a tall, opposite-leaved herb, commonly found in woods and hedgerows where it can provide a summer nectar source for bees and butterflies (Comba *et al.* 1999). It generally grows on damp fertile soils in lightly shaded situations. There is little risk of it being planted outside its native range because it is present through much of Great Britain, except the central and northern Highlands and south-west of the Wash. In Cambridgeshire and Huntingdonshire it has been described as rare in the past, possibly as these are low rainfall areas and the plant is not very tolerant of drought, but also because these counties have few woods!

Campion can survive in deep shade as non-flowering rosettes of leaves, but then flower profusely after coppicing, or along woodland edges (Grime *et al.* 2007), further characteristics that make it a good species for woodland introductions. There are separate male and female plants which have rather different behaviours. Male plants tend to be more common and to produce more flowers and leaves than female plants; female plants make up more of those flowering in June. Later in the summer males and females flower equally. However, it is unlikely that any sowing would be made up of just male or just female plants, so the separation of the sexes is not likely to be a problem. A final point in its favour for planting mixes is that it has attractive flowers.

Red Campion, a favoured species for woodland introductions.

A second example involved a five-hectare outlier of the Blean Woods north of Canterbury that was to be quarried. The soil was stripped off the old site and loose-tipped on to the prepared new site. Weedy species, such as Sowthistles *Sonchus* spp. and Redshanks *Polygonum persicaria*, quickly colonised the open, disturbed soil surface, although they soon declined as competitive species such as False Oat-grass, Soft Rush and Creeping Soft-grass increased. There were still differences from the pre-translocation state after ten years, but the development of the woodland vegetation was faster than if the new woodland had been left to be colonised naturally from surrounding areas. Some of the woodland specialists, such as Wood Anemone and Yellow Archangel, were less common than in the donor area, although no species was lost completely (Craig *et al.* 2015). Others, such as Bluebell, were more resilient and became dominant with Bramble over large areas. Autumn translocation of the soil was better for the woodland ground flora than moving the soil in spring, particularly in the early years, possibly because in autumn more of the plant material was dormant when the soil was moved and so less likely to be damaged.

A third example from Kent is where the A21 was widened past Tunbridge Wells in 2015–2017. Nine hectares of ancient woodland, mainly Sweet Chestnut, were destroyed in the process. The mitigation involved work to improve 27 hectares of existing woodland and the creation of 18 hectares of new woodland. Live stools of Sweet

Remote Sedge translocation in soil to New Biggin Wood was only partially successful.

New planting, with and without accompanying translocated soil, on the Tunbridge Wells bypass.

Chestnut and Hazel stools were transplanted into the new sites along with other stumps and logs so that the new woodland would start with a substantial legacy of dead wood. The top 20 centimetres of soil from the ancient woodland were spread on some of the new woodland areas.

Not all the Sweet Chestnut and Hazel survived the move, but enough did in the short term to give the new areas a very different structure from a standard plantation. The initial response from the soil translocation was also promising. Bramble and grasses, such as Sweet Vernal, dominated large areas, as they would in a clear fell or coppice, but when I was shown the site, I saw other woodland species such as Bluebell, Primrose, Pendulous Sedge and Wood Anemone amongst them. There was a clear contrast to the weedy flora found where no topsoil had been spread. None of these woodland species would have been on the site, a rather nondescript grass field, beforehand. I also saw more butterflies flitting amongst the soil translocation areas than elsewhere.

Soil translocation is a controversial, expensive and uncertain procedure, so has only been considered with major infrastructure projects such as new roads or airports. It may, for example, also become part of a package of mitigation measures applied where ancient woodland is destroyed along the route of the new HS2 London–Birmingham rail link.

A licence to trash, or the way of the future?

Planting woodland ground flora and moving woodland soils may lead to claims that ancient woodland communities can be recreated in this way, weakening the need to protect such sites from development. This is not true. At best, only some of the relevant species, even among the vascular plants, are transferred and the translocated soil and its micro-organisms are much disturbed in the process. It should only be considered when all other options for avoiding the destruction of ancient woodland have been exhausted.

We are not 'recreating ancient woodland' but are (hopefully) speeding up the development of more interesting and richer woodland ground flora communities in these new woods. The experience gained may be relevant to situations where we might want to assist the spread of species beyond their current native range as part of adaptation to climate change, considered in the next chapter.

A changing atmosphere

In the 1960s Bob Dylan sang about 'changing times', and this certainly applies to our woods. Previous chapters have considered how differences in woodland management and the increases in deer pressure are affecting the ground flora. This chapter looks at another set of changes, the effects of pollutants in the form of sulphur and nitrogen compounds added to the atmosphere, the fertilisers that may be spreading into our woods from adjacent fields, and the potentially all-pervading effects of climate change.

The scavenging trees

Trees are better than shorter growing vegetation such as Heather or grasses at capturing gases and particles in the atmosphere – a process known as 'scavenging'. This is beneficial when trees along roads in towns scavenge the pollutants coming from cars and lorries and improve the air quality in nearby houses and schools. Shelter belts around intensive livestock units on farms help capture some of the ammonium compounds that are produced by the units, stopping them spreading any further.

However, pollutants from the atmosphere collected on the foliage may wash down the trunks and into the soil. There they contribute to the release of hydrogen ions, which acidify the soil and streams or lakes into which they are subsequently washed (Ormerod *et al.* 1989). In very acid conditions aluminium ions are released, which can be toxic to plants. On the Continent, researchers compared records of plants growing in the woods from the 1920s and 1940s with 1980s surveys from the same areas. They showed that there were links between changes in soil acidity and which species had increased or

OPPOSITE PAGE:
Ferns such as Common Polypody growing on trees may be particularly sensitive to pollution and to climate change, especially hotter drier summers.

Wavy Hair-grass is a species likely to have benefited from acidification.

decreased over this period (Falkengren-Grerup 1995, Brunet *et al.* 1996). Studies in British woods suggested some similar trends (Ling 2003, Kirby *et al.* 2005).

Since the 1980s, atmospheric sulphur emissions have been reduced and woodland soils in Great Britain are generally becoming less acid. There are now regulations to control pollution, such as The National Emissions Ceiling Directive, which sets commitments for EU member states, including for nitrogen and sulphur compounds. (These commitments are likely to remain now that Britain has left the European Union).

Concentrations of nitrogen oxides in the atmosphere have declined, but there has been little change in the emissions of ammonium compounds (RoTAP 2012). The net result is that the total deposition of nitrogen has changed little since the 1980s. Over much of Great Britain, the levels are still above those at which significant adverse effects on pollution-sensitive species may occur (Matejko *et al.* 2009). An eminent scientist at the Centre for Ecology and Hydrology once calculated that an annual deposition of nitrogen about 20kg/ha/yr was the equivalent of that found in 2,000 standard-sized cowpats! The excess nitrogen deposition from past emissions has led to changes to the diversity and composition of open habitats such as grassland, heaths, moors and dunes (Field *et al.* 2014), but the evidence for changes in the woodland flora has been less clear-cut until recently.

In experiments in greenhouses and gardens, woodland plants grow better with more nutrients, which may help them survive better under dense shade. With extra nitrogen the plants can produce larger leaves and capture more sunlight. In the field, however, a greater availability of nutrients can be a disadvantage for the woodland flora. The plants may be lusher and more attractive to herbivores. Additional nutrients may favour tall, more competitive species that outgrow smaller, stress-tolerant woodland specialists. Extra nutrients may change the nature of the below-ground relationships between fungi and plant roots.

Continental researchers found a link between the nitrogen oxides and ammonium compounds taken up by the trees, greater growth and increased carbon storage in the forests – a good thing in relation to climate change. However, as the levels of nitrogen compounds scavenged by the trees increased, so more of the nitrogen accumulated in the soils and, at the highest levels, started to be washed into streams (de Vries *et al.* 2009, Dise & Wright 1995). In Swedish Oak forests the extra nitrogen in regions with high pollution encouraged species such as Broad Buckler-fern, Rosebay Willowherb, Raspberry, Nettle and Wavy Hair-grass (Brunet *et al.* 1998).

In 2008, Sally Keith from Bournemouth University revisited woods in Dorset that had first been recorded by Professor Ronald Good, a local botanist, in the 1930s when nitrogen pollution levels were lower. The mean number of species in each wood was much the same, but there were fewer differences between sites. Species typical of fertile soils were more common in 2008 than in the 1930s (Keith *et al.* 2009). Katy Ling at the University of the West of England

The decrease in Sanicle found in a study of Cotswold beechwoods between the 1960s and 1990s may be linked to changes in atmospheric deposition.

compared records from the 1960s for beechwoods in the Cotswolds with what she found in the 1990s, and again nitrogen-loving species tended to have increased, whereas stress-tolerating species such as Sanicle decreased (Ling 2003). The Countryside Survey 2007, which covers the whole of Great Britain, found an increase in competitive species, which are favoured by high nitrogen, in woodland compared to the 1990s survey results (Norton *et al.* 2012).

Other studies looking at change across Europe over the last 20–40 years have not shown such clear evidence of a nitrogen impact (Verheyen *et al.* 2012). In some of these studies the baseline for the comparison was after 1970, so the main changes in plant species caused by increased nitrogen might already have happened. Elsewhere the nitrogen levels may still be building up in the soil, but the effects on the vegetation have not yet come through because the plant growth is still more limited by light than by nutrients. This raises the risk that the nitrogen time-bomb may be triggered when woods are opened up by coppicing or thinning, which allows more light to reach the ground.

Spillovers from farmland

In addition to the general effects of atmospheric pollution, woodland edges are particularly affected by nitrogen coming off farmland. This can lead to increases in 'weedy' species at woodland edges, sometimes well into the woodland interior. For example, there is a dairy farm on one side of Wytham Woods, and if the wind is in the right direction I get a strong whiff of slurry and dung. Hedge Garlic and Cow Parsley are now common where the wood-edge abuts the farmland.

Elsewhere in Great Britain the impacts of ammonia compounds on woodland downwind of more intensive livestock units can be very marked, leading to fewer species overall as well as increases to some high-nutrient species. In one study, Carole Pitcairn and co-workers found more Yorkshire-fog, Raspberry and nettles close to livestock units (Pitcairn *et al.* 2002). Other species that increase where nitrogen levels are raised include Rosebay and other willowherbs, Lady and Broad Buckler-fern, Three-nerved Sandwort and Common Hemp-nettle. Pesticides may also drift off arable crops and into the woodland, leading to reductions in the abundance of woodland specialists such as Primrose, Dog's Mercury and Wood Dog-violet in the outer ten metres of the wood (Gove *et al.* 2007).

Hedge Garlic, for better or worse?

Hedge Garlic *Alliaria petiolata* is common in hedges and wood-edges on moist, relatively fertile soils, where there is some disturbance. People who collect wild plants for food value its leaves, which do taste of garlic when crushed. In America it has been reported that the leaves can have a higher concentration of vitamin C than oranges, and higher levels of vitamin A than spinach (Cavers *et al.* 1979).

Hedge Garlic is widespread through Great Britain and much of the temperate zone in Europe. It grows from an overwintering rosette of leaves up to about a metre high the following summer, with small white flowers (Grime *et al.* 2007). In Great Britain, Green-veined White butterfly caterpillars feed on the leaves of Hedge Garlic, and it is also one of the food plants for the Orange-tip butterfly, which feeds mainly on the flowers and developing seed-pods. Another food plant for the Orange-tip is Lady's Smock. In the early 1990s a study of the butterfly at Monks Wood in Cambridgeshire commented that Lady's Smock was then the only food plant present in the wood. By 2016 Hedge Garlic was also common towards the edges of the wood as at Wytham, presumably because of increased nitrogen coming off the adjacent fields.

Hedge Garlic is one of several woodland plants (Purple-loosestrife and False Brome are others) that have become invasive in woodland in parts of the mid-western and north-eastern United States and Canada, displacing the indigenous ground flora. Once established, Hedge Garlic becomes a permanent part of the community, slowly increasing and taking advantage of any disturbance that happens. When railing against introductions to Great Britain such as Himalayan Balsam or Japanese Knotweed it is easy to forget that our woodland plants can be just as troublesome elsewhere.

Hedge Garlic and nettles are species that benefit from nutrient enrichment at wood-edges.

A changing climate and the need to change our thinking?

Over long timescales the climate has changed dramatically: Ice Ages and warmer interglacial periods have come and gone. In this interglacial there have been shorter-term fluctuations in some regions. There was a warm period in early medieval times in Europe followed by the Little Ice Age that lasted from the 16th to mid-19th century. Since then, mean temperatures have been rising and have gone above that of the medieval warm period. Records for the warmest days, months and years ever recorded are regularly being broken (Beebee 2018). Human-generated emissions of greenhouse gases are the main cause of this current rising trend in temperatures, and most projections suggest that temperatures will continue to rise for much of this century.

All areas of the UK are likely to get warmer, more so in summer than in winter, with the greatest increase in summer mean temperatures in southern England. This should lead to longer growing seasons, but also to an increased risk of heatwaves, so the woodland flora may suffer from more frequent droughts. Oxlips, weakened by deer grazing, died following the hot dry summers of 1976, 1990 and 1995 in Hayley Wood (Rackham 2003). Dog's Mercury showed severe wilting by the end of the hot summers of 1995, 2003 and 2018 in Wytham Woods. The vegetation subsequently recovered, but this recovery may be less complete if droughts become more common (Morecroft & Taylor 2010).

Total annual rainfall may not change very much, but average winter rainfall is likely to increase, particularly in western Great Britain, while summer rainfall is likely to decrease. Rainfall may be more intense when storms do occur, increasing the risks of severe flooding.

In 1991 Plantlife published a booklet called *Death knell for the Bluebells*, a first attempt to suggest what the implications of climate change might be for this most-loved flower. With hindsight the analysis was perhaps somewhat naïve, and a more recent report noted that the fate of the native Bluebell in a warmer climate remains uncertain (Plantlife 2004). However, it set the scene for further studies ranging from analyses of which species are potentially at most risk, to ideas on adapting the management of habitats and landscapes to cope with the expected future conditions (Natural England & RSPB 2014, Morecroft & Speakman 2015, Pearce-Higgins *et al.* 2017).

These studies suggest that by the end of the 21st century, and earlier in some cases, temperatures and rainfall levels in some areas of Great Britain may no longer be suitable for certain species currently growing there. Other places that are currently not climatically suitable may become so. Recent decades have seen marked northerly expansions in the ranges of some butterflies and birds, for example the Speckled Wood butterfly and Nuthatch (Beebee 2018). Conversely some northern mountain butterflies are showing a decline.

There is so far little evidence that woodland plant distributions are changing. However, this may be because the microclimate changes within woodland have not been as great as outside the woods. Many woodland plants are also long-lived, with stored reserves that allow them to cope with several unfavourable years, and those reserves have not yet been exhausted (Carey 2015). Change will also be slow for the many woodland plants that only disperse over a short distance in any one year, meaning that it may take decades for distribution changes to be detected. We may however see signs of change happening by comparing what we find in woods today with what was recorded in the same spots 30, 40 and 50 years ago (De Frenne *et al.* 2013, Kirby *et al.* 2005).

As individual species grow faster or slower, spread to new sites or die out from old localities, the composition of the ground flora

More intense rainfall may lead to greater flooding.

communities will gradually change. Over the longer term, we expect that some plants currently limited to southern Great Britain might spread further north, while more plants from southern climates that are currently grown in gardens may escape into nearby woodland. Scattered plants of Honey Garlic *Nectaroscordum siculum*, a native of southern Europe with showy clusters of bell-shaped blossoms, have started to appear in Wytham Woods several hundred metres away from where it had been planted in a garden.

When will plants flower in the future?

While plants may be slow to move to new areas to escape climate change, they can adapt to new conditions through varying the time of year when they flower, fruit, or lose their leaves. Tim Sparks showed in 1994 that Oak trees were coming into leaf significantly earlier than in the past, helping to make phenology – the study of the timing of natural events – respectable science again. Nature's Calendar, a recording scheme managed by the Woodland Trust, allows anyone to record the times of first flowering of Bluebell, Lesser Celandine, Lady's Smock, Hedge Garlic and Ivy, or the first sightings of ripe blackberries. You can follow the records from the south-west peninsula up to north Scotland.

Another champion of phenology was the naturalist Richard Fitter. He and his son Alastair, Professor in the Department of Biology at the University of York, showed that the average first flowering dates for 385 British species since 1990 were 4.5 days earlier than in the previous four decades (Fitter & Fitter 2002, Fitter *et al.* 1995). There were differences between species: White Dead-nettle used to flower in winter only occasionally, but now does so regularly; the flowering of Lady's Smock advanced by over a week, but Wood Spurge hardly advanced its flowering at all. Some plants only flower after they have experienced cold periods in winter; warmer autumns could interfere with this process, which means early flowering species, such as Green Hellebore *Helleborus viride* and Moschatel, may flower later under a warming climate. The order of spring events might thus change (Roberts *et al.* 2015).

Warmer spring temperatures mean earlier starts to leaf growth. Early emergence of leaves – provided they are not blighted by frosts – should give plants a longer growing season, enabling the plants to produce more seed or bigger bulbs. Species such as Wood Anemone,

Herbarium specimens show that Moschatel was flowering in April in 1953. In future it may be later.

Lady's Smock and Cock's-foot seem able to track these temperature patterns well (Tansey *et al.* 2017). The flowers that bloom in the spring, however, might not enjoy a longer season. Oak, and other trees and shrubs, have also started to come into leaf earlier. If the advance of tree canopy green-up is more than the advance in growth of the spring flowers, then the period of high light availability, and therefore high growth, for the ground flora plants will be reduced by climate warming.

What else can we expect?

In future the flora may change faster, as the tree and shrub layers respond to climatic variations. Extreme droughts are a threat to shallow rooting trees (Peterken and Mountford 1996, Cavin *et al.* 2013); many Beech in Lady Park Wood on the Gloucestershire/ Monmouthshire border, and in the New Forest, died after the 1976 drought. More frequent storms and the spread of new pests and diseases may create more canopy gaps. Alternatively, dense-canopied trees such as Sweet Chestnut and Small-leaved Lime with more of a southerly distribution in Europe may do better under a warmer climate and replace Oak or Ash, creating more shade and cooler conditions at ground level.

Partly because of these uncertainties, woodland has generally been classed as at medium to low risk from climate change from a conservation perspective (Natural England & RSPB 2014). Climate change effects on woodland plants are currently small compared to other factors such as deer browsing or emerging tree diseases. However, while the impacts on the woodland flora may be delayed, they cannot be avoided altogether: what then for the banks of sweet primroses?

Models have been developed to suggest how species will cope with future climates, based on the temperature and rainfall patterns where a species currently occurs across Europe. Projections of climate change across Great Britain are then used to see where suitable conditions might occur in future (Pearce-Higgins *et al.* 2015). Woodland generalists are less likely to be at risk than woodland specialists; northern species are more at risk than those with a southerly distribution. The results are not precise predictions of where Primrose, Bluebell or Twinflower will grow in future, but help us to think about what future changes to look for. The models may also help in identifying ways we might offset some of the more undesirable changes.

The outputs from the models raise challenges for conservation policy and practice. If there are suitable conditions beyond the current range of a species and the chances of natural colonisation are small, should we assist their migration? Which species currently in woods on the near Continent, not native to Great Britain but grown in gardens, might be accepted as part of our woodland flora under future climatic conditions?

Coping with environmental change

It is to be hoped that further pollution controls will eventually lead to falls in the overall emissions of nitrogen compounds. At the wood level it may be possible to offset some of the potential effects of increased nitrogen entering the system by avoiding opening up the tree canopy through large fellings. This may allow the more shade-tolerant woodland flora species to maintain themselves alongside more light-demanding, competitive species, that are favoured by high nitrogen levels. Developing grassy strips between woods and arable fields can help to reduce the spread of nitrogen from agricultural fertilisers into the wood and also allows for a more

A future native for our woods?

Liverleaf *Hepatica nobilis*, gets its name from the shape of the three-lobed leaf which was thought to resemble a liver, and is one of the plants I look out for on visits to Continental woods. It is a member of the buttercup family but with (usually) blue flowers that grow from a basal rosette of leaves, and is found in a wide range of conditions from deeply shaded beechwoods to more open grassy places, often associated with limestone but sometimes on sandy and clay-rich soils. In a Swedish study, individual plants of Liverleaf and Sanicle were followed over the course of several decades with little mortality, suggesting that these herbs may live as long as some of the trees and shrubs above them (Inghe & Tamm 1985).

The seeds are ant-dispersed and the plant is often associated with ancient woodland on the Continent. Another Swedish study looked at the colonisation of new woodland next to an ancient wood and found a pattern not dissimilar to that shown by Rackham (2003) for Oxlip at Hayley Wood: Liverleaf declined in abundance with increasing distance from the ancient woodland boundary, with scattered outliers well ahead of the main invasion front (Brunet & Von Oheimb 1998).

Liverleaf is rather intolerant of frost, which may explain why it did not establish in Great Britain or western France naturally. However, it is now grown in gardens and has naturalised in scattered places across Great Britain. It is an attractive little plant that seems unlikely to prove too competitive for other members of our woodland flora.

Liverleaf *Hepatica nobilis* – a possible future addition to our flora?

scrubby, flowery wood-edge vegetation to develop. This will buffer the woodland edge, keeping it cooler and more humid.

Our projections of the real impact of long-term climate change on the woodland flora remain somewhat sketchy, and ideas as to what we might do about them are necessarily generalised. Woodland management recommendations for conservation might need to be altered. Reducing the size of gaps created by felling, as well as possibly helping with the nitrogen problem mentioned above, should also help maintain a cooler microclimate for the ground flora. We may need to give higher conservation priority to woods where the topography allows potentially vulnerable species to survive for longer, for example on north-facing slopes or areas close to the water table (Suggitt *et al.* 2018).

We must reduce other pressures on our woodland flora, because individuals and populations that are growing well are more likely to be able to cope with whatever the future climate holds. Climate change then becomes another reason for managing deer, for example, because there is little hope for plants to spread if the deer are eating the flowers and so stopping seed production. Maintaining and restoring mixed landscapes with trees and hedges between woods may increase the potential for species to spread out through the landscape.

Almost inevitably, there will be unexpected side effects for the woodland flora, with climate change altering the range or severity of pest and disease impacts on our forest trees. The way that land is managed, and the balance between farm and forest, may also alter. Some of these effects could be positive. A substantial increase in woodland cover could form part of the nation's climate change adaptation and mitigation strategies (Read *et al.* 2009), meaning more potential habitat for woodland plants, provided the plants can get to this new woodland.

Above all, it means agreeing what sorts of woodland we want in future and what we want it to provide, not just from the point of view of wood production or wildlife conservation, but also for the enjoyment that people get from visiting woods (chapter 17). This is now seen as an increasingly valuable service that woodland provides.

Osmunda regalis

Fun and games in the woods

W oodland is one of the most visited habitats in the UK, not just to collect flowers or meet a lover, as in the ballad of *Tam Lin* (see p.325), but because it offers people something very different from their daily routine (unless you are a forester!). In 2011, one survey reported over 500 million visits to forests across Great Britain. Woods absorb people, so that you can feel alone even though there may be others close by. They are often less crowded than the coast, and, being mostly inland, can be the most accessible local green areas; more prosaically, they are often equipped with toilets and car parks. There is shelter and shade from the wind and sun. On a visit to Newborough Forest on Anglesey one changeable April day, there were many more people in the pine plantations than out on the open dune.

In Japan, a form of therapy has developed known as Shinrin-yoku, which means 'taking in the forest atmosphere' or 'forest bathing'. Being in a wood helps with mental and physical well-being; visiting a wood and walking in a relaxed way, a person becomes calmer and feels better. Perhaps this is part of what William Blake meant by seeing 'heaven in a wild flower'.

People do sometimes worry about getting physically lost in woods. This is not helped by tales of Robin Hood and his men hiding for years in Sherwood Forest, when actually that was a landscape of open heath and scattered trees where the outlaws would have stood out a mile away. There may be a fear of wild animals, reflected in some current writings about the spread of wolves in Europe, although in reality the risks are very low. Wild men, unfortunately, can be a real concern, particularly in urban woods, but the journey to a wood in a car is likely to be riskier than anything you'll experience once there.

OPPOSITE PAGE:
Finding unusual plants such as this Royal Fern can be one of the fun things in visiting woods, but over-collecting them can be a problem.

317

Now where is Little Red Riding Hood?

We need to help people become more familiar with woods as they really are. The Forest Schools initiative does this by taking children of all ages to visit local woods on a regular basis and in all weathers (O'Brien & Murray 2007). They have a chance to learn about the natural environment, how to handle risks, to use their own initiative and cooperate with others to solve problems. My own early expeditions to woods were not so organised, or even botanical: we just rushed about, picking up sticks and bashing nettles. The common factor is that woods should be places that are fun to be in and to explore, for people of all ages.

Entertainment has always been one of the reasons why woods have been kept: as places for the grand hunts enjoyed by kings and queens of the medieval period, or the organised pheasant drives of the modern era; as sites for individual nature walks, or for pop concerts. When the returns from harvesting the timber were negligible, the wood might still be kept because of the opportunities for a weekend shoot or because it improved the look of the local countryside. The effects of these different activities on the flora, past and present, need to be considered alongside the impact of timber production, because recreation in woods is both part of their history and a new *raison d'être* (Marzano & Dandy 2012).

The path taken

When people visit a wood, they create paths. Initially, these may be just a line of bruised vegetation, then a definite strip where the vegetation and litter have been worn away (Thomas *et al.* 1994). Woodland plants are generally not very resistant to trampling: they tend to have large leaves to catch the limited light under the canopy and thinner cell walls because the more humid conditions make water loss less of an issue. Plant communities of wet ground, with species such as Opposite-leaved Golden Saxifrage, Marsh-marigold and Marsh Fern, are more vulnerable to damage than those of drier ground, because there tends to be more disturbance to the soil in wet places. Species with underground shoots or bulbs may recover quicker, if trampling is stopped, than those that rely on recolonisation from seed.

King John on a stag hunt, from a 14th-century manuscript.

In 1969, the Surrey Naturalists' Trust organised a week-long nature trail at a reserve near Dorking. An ecologist was on hand to look at the impact, over the course of a week, of the more than 7,000 people who went along it (Burden & Randerson 1972). The path got wider, while the centre became worn and lost all its vegetation. Dog's Mercury and Hairy Violet disappeared quickly. Ivy in a beechwood section was greatly reduced, largely through the loss of leaves; the stems were more resistant. Three weeks later, after no further use, Bracken and Yorkshire-fog shoots were starting to reappear as well as some regrowth of the violets and Mercury.

The effects of trampling have also been tested by setting up experimental 'trampling lanes' through different vegetation types with from zero to 500 tramples. Low-growing species such as Bluebell were relatively resistant to low levels of trampling, but more vulnerable in the longer term because they did not recover as quickly as more robust plants such as Bramble and Bracken (Littlemore & Barker 2001). Studies in Belgium found that herb-rich vegetation was more sensitive to the initial trampling than that in acid, heathy woods with Bilberry and Wavy Hair-grass, but recovery was faster in the herb-rich site. After six years of path closure there was more or less full recovery, with no substantial differences between the centre of the path and adjacent undisturbed vegetation (Roovers *et al.* 2004, 2005).

Opposite-leaved Golden-saxifrage, a plant of wet soils and so particularly vulnerable to trampling.

Much of the trampling damage is done during the initial use of a path: once a path has started to form it is generally better to encourage people to stick to that route, rather than to spread them out over a wider area of woodland. Dense path-side vegetation, such as Bramble, may dissuade people from straying into new areas. Vegetation more than 50cm high, particularly if prickly or irritating, may be enough to form an effective natural deterrent (Roovers *et al.* 2006).

Paths, once formed, broaden the more they are used, particularly as people walk round muddy places. The centre of the path may be largely bare. Weedy species, such as Annual Meadow-grass, take advantage of the open ground, while Water-starwort and Water-pepper establish in the deeper puddles. The less trampled path margins may contain species not common in the undisturbed areas of the wood, but these additions may not be welcome. People bring in seeds of invasive plants on their boots, such as the Slender Rush *Juncus tenuis* which has spread widely on the tracks at Epping Forest, or the Small Balsam that occurs at various points along the rides in Wytham. Spores of *Phytophthora* species that are the cause of various tree diseases can be moved about in this same way.

Cutting back the trees and shrubs above the path to help dry the ground out a bit and to make it sunnier and attractive for those walking along it, encourages people to stay on the route and can also enrich the wood (chapter 14). The extra light allows a wider range of both woodland and grassland plants such as Ragwort and Fleabane to spread, along with butterflies, hoverflies and beetles attracted to their nectar and pollen (Warren & Fuller 1993).

If more people start to use the wood and walk within the stands, as well as along the paths, large areas lose their vegetation cover and become just bare, compacted soil. Concerns about safety in urban areas may lead to clearing out the understorey so that people can see what is ahead and behind them. The edges of woods may be used as official or unofficial car parks and become dumping grounds for litter. The woodland flora disappears. In the end, it can be difficult to defend such woods against further damage, or clearance.

Extreme litter dumping in a Scottish wood, but the flora around it is relatively undisturbed.

A boardwalk created to reduce the pressure on a small urban wood.

Urban woods, however, if properly managed, can be more loved and enjoyed than rural ones, despite the pressures. Wykery Copse, a rich but small ancient wood, has over the last three decades become surrounded by houses and roads as Bracknell has expanded. English Nature and its successors argued for a buffer zone of about 15 metres around the Copse, to prevent building right up to the edge and to reduce the disturbance to the wood. This zone has developed into a mixture of rough grass and scrub. Initial suggestions from the developers for a picnic site and BBQ area in a clearing in the Copse were rejected, and instead a boardwalk was installed that provides easy access through the wood but leaves most of the site untrampled. On a visit in the 2018 heatwave it was a cool delight. In the 1980s there was a proposal to clear part of Oxleas Wood in south-east London for a new Thames crossing; I suspect the campaigns by local groups to save it were more influential than the official Nature Conservancy Council protests.

Pressure on the woodland from public access comes not just from people but also from their dogs. The occasional dog running through a wood is not likely to cause many problems and can help to disperse the seeds of woodland plants. Deer may avoid areas around car parks because of these surrogate wolves, so that there is less browsing and more regeneration in well-walked areas. The regeneration in a little Beech wood above Kendal was so dense in 2003 that I had to push hard to get through the saplings. However, where there are many dogs being walked, all too often there is an accumulation of their faeces on the ground, or, worse, in plastic bags hung in the bushes. These are unpleasant, contribute excess nitrogen to the soil, and are a disease risk to humans and livestock. Dogs may regularly go into the water of shallow ponds, stirring up the mud, with the result that most water plants are lost. In Epping Forest, Water Violet has disappeared from two ponds, probably from this cause. In Bernwood Forest, Buckinghamshire, extra ponds have had to be created next to the popular dog-walking route to reduce the pressure on ponds created elsewhere for amphibians. Dog walkers need to recognise that their pets and their behaviour can be a threat to wild places and to take their responsibilities seriously.

Dogs free-ranging through the undergrowth, disturbing ground and low shrub-nesting birds and small mammals, would in the past have included the hunt. There is now a ban on chasing animals with packs of dogs, but leisure riding in general has increased. In

Surfacing paths to reduce conflicts between users may attract more usage.

woods the horses can cut up the paths. This may not in itself cause significant long-term damage to the vegetation, and the disturbed bare soil may allow seeds to germinate, but the broken ground does make it more awkward for walkers using these same tracks. Other riders, on mountain bikes zipping through the woods at high speed or building unofficial tracks and obstacles, can cause localised damage and disturbance to the flora and to other wood-users.

Different groups need to work together with each other and with forest managers to reduce the potential conflicts (Littlemore & Rotherham 2008). Creating hard surfaces and separating different users of the trails and paths can work, provided it does not damage rich grassland communities on rides. However, in popular spots such as Epping Forest, the surfaced paths, created initially for horse riders, are now used by others as well and may have attracted more people into the Forest.

Organised events

In the mid-1980s paintball games emerged, where you rush round and shoot your friends with sticky paint pellets. One of my nephews arranged a paintball session as part of his stag party. As it was in a 40-year-old conifer plantation on former improved farmland, I felt I could take part with a reasonably clear conscience. Paintball games in ancient woodland are, however, more damaging. Most paintballs, even if biodegradable, leave unsightly marks on the trees. There can be heavy trampling of sensitive vegetation and a gradual accumulation of infrastructure on the edge of, or often within, the wood itself including car-parking and toilets. Shelters and dug-outs may be built in the wood. After an initial outburst of interest in the 1990s the situation seems to have stabilised and there are fewer new sites being proposed. Measures that can be taken to reduce the pressure on the vegetation include limiting the frequency of events and numbers of people involved and fencing off sensitive areas such as marshy patches, or areas with uncommon species.

Other types of mass event, such as orienteering trials, cause conservation concerns from time to time. Where these happen only infrequently, they can be scheduled to avoid sensitive times of year, such as the bird breeding season or when the bluebells are in full bloom. Orienteers are used to working with detailed vegetation structure maps, which means that it is relatively easy to integrate no-go areas for the participants. The ground flora is also more likely to have time to recover from occasional disturbances.

Increasingly, woods are also being used as venues for other types of cultural event, from pop-up opera in Wytham Woods to pop concerts as at Thetford, although it is uncertain how many of those attending appreciate the woodland setting as such. The sorts of sites used for large events often have generally fairly robust floras (Bramble or Bracken-dominated, grasses or bare litter), so effects on the vegetation tend not to be an issue.

Opera Anywhere singers performing in Wytham Woods.

People need to get out into woods, if we want them to value and love them. A degree of damage to the ground flora from time to time, and in some places, may then be a small price to pay for this love. However, what happens when people also want to take some of the wood home with them by picking flowers?

Picking flowers

In the traditional border ballad, *Tam Lin*, 'Fair Margaret ran in the merry greenwood, she pulled a flower but one; when at her side stood young Tam Lin, said "Margaret leave it alone"'. Picking a flower leads to Margaret having to face down the Elfin Queen to save her lover. Gathering flowers is not usually so fraught with danger and many of us have done it at some time or other, a wilting clutch of blossoms presented to parents when we were toddlers, or a more earnest collection pressed into a notebook as we tried to learn species names. Neither does flower picking pose a real threat to most plant populations, but there have been, and sometimes still are, exceptions.

The Victorians developed a craze for ferns, for which the author Charles Kingsley coined the term Pteridomania (Kingsley 1873). Nona Bellairs was one such Pteridomaniac. In her book *Hardy Ferns: how I collected and cultivated them* (Bellairs 1865) she describes a visit to the Devil's Punchbowl near Chepstow. She crushed every fern to smell

Pteridomania: 'Gathering Ferns', a drawing by Helen Allingham published in *The Illustrated London News*, July 1871.

Lemon-scented Fern
really does smell
of lemons.

OPPOSITE PAGE:
No longer so secret orchids
– a Victorian specimen and
modern sign (top).

Lady's-slipper Orchid
reintroduced to Gait
Barrows National Nature
Reserve (below).

it, till she found the Lemon-scented Fern that was her goal. At Kirkstone Pass in Cumbria she found so much Parsley Fern *Cryptogramma crispa* that she packed up a large hamper full and sent it off home. No wonder she noted that 'we who boast ourselves lovers of nature are often at best only destroyers'.

The Royal Fern was a particular target. This magnificent plant, with coarsely-divided fronds that may be over a metre high, is long-lived, and clumps have survived in gardens for over a hundred years. Some of the more massive plants in the wild may be several centuries old (Page 1982). The fern is found in a wide range of wet but always acidic places, mainly in western parts of Great Britain. Nona Bellairs found it in an old forsaken orchard near Exmouth 'where one took each step, in danger of being swamped'. The Victorians collected it on a commercial scale, sometimes by the wagonload (making Nona Bellairs' hampers seem restrained) to use as a medium for the culturing of orchids, another prize group for the plant hunters.

In the Fielding-Druce herbarium in Oxford there are 14 sheets of Lady's-slipper Orchid collected between 1799 and 1928, from at least six sites. This fabulously showy species was found scattered through the limestone woods of northern England. The notes with one specimen state that it was not uncommon in Castle Eden Dene, near Durham, but flowered only in the more open places. It is no longer there. Over-collecting reduced the known populations to a single plant in the wild, whose location was a closely guarded secret. Well, not entirely secret, and every year some student or the like would be recruited to spend the flowering season keeping watch on it, making sure it was not collected, or eaten by a wandering sheep. After some years of effort, staff at the Royal Botanic Gardens, Kew, managed to cross the wild British plant with another that had been growing for a long time in a garden but was of British origin. Young plants have been reintroduced to sites where it occurred in the past, and although it will be some years before we can tell whether the reintroduced plants can maintain themselves and produce offspring, there are indications that they are picking up the right fungal associates on their roots. If you visit Gait Barrows Reserve (Lancashire) in May, you may find a sign directing you along the orchid trail.

A lot of resources were expended on the preservation and propagation of one plant, and although the Lady's-slipper is uncommon, it is quite widely distributed across the Continent. We had no difficulty finding it on a visit to Estonia to look at wooded meadows in 2011. Species can be brought back from the brink in this way, but it would be better if they did not reach that dire strait in the first place. It is now generally illegal to uproot plants without the landowner's permission, and some plants, such as the Lady's-slipper, Red Helleborine and Whorled Solomon's-seal *Polygonatum verticillatum*, must not be picked under any circumstances. The various botanical societies have codes of conduct to ensure that botanists themselves act responsibly even with common species (no hamper-packing please). Plantlife have moreover produced a list of common species that it should not be a problem to pick in moderation, including Primrose, Common Dog-violet, Greater Stitchwort, Cow Parsley, Red Campion and Meadowsweet. Otherwise the key advice is to take flowers and foliage only from large patches of the plant, and pick in moderation so that plenty are left for others to enjoy; for example, only take one if there are twenty left behind (BSBI 2017). Increasingly, a digital photograph may replace the need to collect a plant at all, since the image can be checked against identification pages on the internet. Picking flowers must though be seen in perspective: for every species that has suffered from collection, many more have been lost locally from habitat loss and damage.

Hog, forage, avoid

The bulk of our food comes from farmers' fields, but woodland plants were at least a minor part of the diet of rural communities until the early 20th century. Rosehips were collected as a source of Vitamin C during the Second World War, as were medicinal herbs such as Foxglove, Deadly Nightshade, Dandelion and Common Valerian. An attenuated tradition survived after the war in the collection of blackberries, elderflowers and sloe-berries. The 1970s saw a revival of interest in eating wild plants, as part of ideas around greater self-sufficiency, encouraged by books such as *Food for Free* (Mabey & Blamey 1972). The revival has continued, leading to foraging courses, books, blogs, the occasional article on Radio 4's Farming programme, and television programmes on wild survival skills. Such foraging should be only for personal use and with the permission of the landowner.

The leaves of Common Chickweed, Dandelion, Nettle and young Cleavers can be used as salads, garnishes, or in soups. Other flowers and young leaves (Meadowsweet, Bramble, Rose, Honeysuckle) are recommended for infusing teas, flavouring wines and cordials. Stems and roots (Wild Angelica, Burdock) provide a bit more bulk. Blackberries and bilberries add a touch of sweetness. When we help ourselves to some little wild strawberries or raspberries, we are aligning ourselves with other woodland mammals such as badgers, foxes and pine martens.

You must though know what you are about to eat, to avoid damaging rare or unusual plants and, more importantly, to avoid poisoning yourself or your family. Cooper and Johnson's (1984) book on British poisonous plants documents the severe illness, even fatalities, caused because people (usually children) mistook the berries of Deadly Nightshade and Herb-Paris for bilberries; Mezereon and Spurge-laurel for currants; Hemlock for Parsley; Monk's-hood root for Horse-radish (although deliberate Monk's-hood poisoning did feature in an episode of *Midsomer Murders*); and Meadow Saffron or daffodils for onions. Symptoms may appear in a few hours, as after eating Foxglove, Hemlock, Monk's-hood or Meadow Saffron; or, in

One to avoid – Monk's-hood in a Welsh wood.

the case of some other species, may become apparent only weeks or months after the first consumption. The toxins may remain even if the material is cooked: Bracken fiddleheads are regularly eaten in Japan, but they contain high concentrations of carcinogens, so are not to be recommended.

Even plants that do not kill may still cause strange effects. A man who drank tea made from Foxglove leaves noticed yellow haloes around objects. Some have speculated whether digitalis-based medication from foxgloves contributed to the haloes and yellows in Van Gogh's later works. Unfortunately, there is only circumstantial evidence for the artist's use of this drug (Lee 1981).

Plants may generate poisons to reduce the likelihood that they will be eaten, the chemical equivalent of developing thorny stems. This makes evolutionary sense when the poison is in the leaves, roots or stem, but seems less advantageous when the poison is in the berries that are generally designed to be eaten and the seeds they contain dispersed. The toxins may be degraded during the ripening process, so that they only discourage premature consumption, as with Bittersweet. However, poisoning has still been reported from ripe fruits, so the change in berry colour as they mature cannot be relied on.

Many poisonous plants have an unpleasant smell or acrid taste which limits how much is eaten. An undergraduate on a field course who decided to try a berry of Lords-and-Ladies, against strict instructions, quickly spat it out! Nevertheless, animals may develop a craving for poisonous plants; they may eat the plants unknowingly, as when livestock eat horsetails mixed into a hay crop; or eat it simply because the only greenery available is poisonous. Dog's Mercury can break down blood cells, leading to haemoglulinuria, but Muntjac grazed it to near oblivion in parts of Monks Wood. Muntjac also eat bluebells, despite them containing glycosides similar in structure to those produced by foxgloves. Some animals may be able to detoxify the poison; for example, some rabbits produce an enzyme that breaks down atropine, one of the key alkaloids in Deadly Nightshade. Where poisonous plants are abundant there might be local selection in the herbivore populations for genes that code for these breakdown enzymes. Humans should not however try this approach.

Private pursuits

Picking flowers, or foraging for plants such as Wild Garlic, relies on people having access to woods in the first place. In Scotland there is a right to roam over most of the countryside, but this does not apply over most of England and Wales, with the exception of common land registered with the local council, and areas designated as 'open access' or 'access land'. There may be public footpaths, through or more often along the edges of a wood, but many more woods are isolated, a field or two away from any right of way. There is usually a muddy field edge to traipse, a ditch to jump and a fence to tear your jeans on, even if you have permission to visit the site.

Many woods are closed to the public (as a boy I was ordered out of a few for trespassing). Landowners from the 19th century onward often enforced this privacy, because it allowed them to build up stocks of pheasants out of reach of the common people. Woods kept for shooting often have glades cut to provide sunny spots for the pheasants to scratch about in, or for the guns to shoot from, which benefits other wildlife. Shooting and hunting interests have led to new woods being planted that could be colonised by woodland plants, such as that described by the Reverend Woodruffe-Peacock (chapter 15).

Managing woods for Pheasant shooting can have both positive and negative effects on the ground flora.

Game management also has a darker side – the past slaughter by gamekeepers of anything that was perceived to be a threat to their birds; and the planting of thickets of Rhododendron that now shade out the ground flora. Some of the worst practices have for the most part ceased: it is a long while since I saw a Stoat-hung gibbet. However, there are increasing questions about the effects of pheasants on the woodland system (Draycott *et al.* 2008, Neumann *et al.* 2015), particularly as the scale of the industry has increased, with tens of millions of birds now released each year (Park *et al.* 2008).

By some estimates up to one in twelve woods may contain a release pen where the birds are first introduced to the wood. Within these pens the woodland flora is often pecked almost clear and there is a build-up of nutrients in the soil from the bird droppings. Such plants as are present tend to be weedy, high-nutrient demanding species such as Broad-leaved Dock, Annual Meadow-grass and Common Chickweed. The effects may be largely limited to the pens themselves, with relatively little impact 15m or more from the pen (Sage *et al.* 2005), but pens are regularly moved around to reduce the risks of bird diseases building up in the soil. This increases the woodland area affected because the vegetation in the abandoned pen area takes longer to recover than for the initial damage to show.

Other people value the privacy of their own bit of woodland, not to kill the wildlife but to enjoy it, as somewhere to relax, or somewhere to try to develop a different sort of lifestyle. A market has developed to satisfy this demand whereby woods are divided up into small parcels of a few hectares each and sold off separately. In Kent, in the early 2000s, the Forestry Commission identified 44 woods covering, in total, more than 1,500 hectares that had been split up in this way. Such 'wood-lotting' has received a mixed reception from conservation proponents. It can lead to a proliferation of fire-sites, sheds and fences and to *ad hoc* cutting of trees and shrubs. Weedy species and bare ground may increase. Getting coherent management over the whole of a large wood becomes more difficult because the various owners all want different things. On the other hand, should it be only rich people who can afford to own woodland? Wood-lotting is a way of getting more people involved with woodland, a modern form of commoning and communing with nature. The woods being sold in this way rarely have active management plans (or they would probably not be being sold), so a bit of management here and there might be better than continuing with no management at all. At least one of the owners might be interested in creating glades where primroses can flower, buried seed plants emerge and a more varied structure develop. Richard Fortey in *The wood for the trees* describes eloquently the pleasure he has experienced from being able to acquire a small bit of a Chiltern beechwood in this way.

Family woodland picnics may be fun when the children are young, but once they become teenagers their interests usually lie elsewhere. Wood-lots may gradually sink into neglect, as did many of the Essex plotlands from the 1930s. Future woodland archaeologists may note the tell-tale shapes of old hut foundations, traces of charcoal from barbecues, and the odd garden plant left over from this phase in a wood's history.

Close encounters with woodland and its flora

Even with wood-lotting only a few people in any community are ever likely to be woodland owners, but many more people own a garden. In 2018, Wild Garlic suddenly appeared in my back yard alongside the Lesser Celandine, Sweet Woodruff and Marsh Thistle. I was quite excited by this example of long-distance seed dispersal by a woodland specialist plant, until my partner told me she had bought it in the local garden centre. Nevertheless, the fact that she could buy it there reflects an increased interest in wild gardens and the use of native species.

Crocosmia growing on the roadside edge of a wood.

Other species introduced to gardens jump the fence of their own accord. Soft Shield-fern was recorded for the first time from Wytham Woods in 2018. This is not common in the region and the spores probably come from a nearby garden. I will treat it as a native to the Woods from now on, but would the same principle apply to an introduced species, or if the species had spread from garden rubbish dumped over the fence or out of the boot of the car? Might we draw a line at *Crocosmia*, but accept snowdrops or Lesser Periwinkle?

Beyond their gardens, some people seek a chance to work in woods through volunteering. There are national volunteer

Getting involved with
woodland management.

schemes and programmes organised by the Woodland Trust,
RSPB, the National Trust and the Conservation Volunteers
(formerly British Trust for Conservation Volunteers, BTCV).
Together these run thousands of volunteer days a year. There are
smaller bodies such as Trees for Life, working in Scotland to restore
the ancient Caledonian pine forest. This runs conservation weeks
where volunteers can help with planting trees, removing non-native
species, putting up fences, collecting seeds and berries, and growing
trees in a nursery. In their Project Wolf volunteers walk through
the woodland at dawn and dusk to disturb deer and so reduce the
number of seedlings and saplings eaten.

Quite often, the urge to create a wild garden, get out into woods
as a volunteer or just go for a walk in a wood can be traced back to
a book, a poem or a television programme. A gift of a countryside
anthology in the early 1960s introduced me to writers about woods
and places I might not otherwise have encountered. One extract was
from *Lady Chatterley's Lover*: a field sports magazine noted that the
book contained many passages on pheasant rearing and the duties of
a professional gamekeeper, which is not how most people remember

that work! Books and magazines have been joined by the numerous blogs, tweets and websites, covering everything from foraging to forestry, which woods to visit and images of what you might see when you get there. They inspire people to get involved in conservation through campaigns and petitions. At its simplest, they encourage people to join a conservation body. At the time of writing, for example, the membership of just one of these, the Woodland Trust, stood at over half a million.

Woods are more than just open-air wood-production factories, they are places for people and nature as well. There can be conflicts between managing for wildlife and the needs and desires of different interest groups. The excesses of Victorian plant collectors may have been curbed but the increasing footfall in some woods can cause much damage. Game management brings in an income for sites with little other economic potential but can be at the expense of specialist woodland plants and other wildlife.

There is clear evidence that people care about woods in a general sense; they appreciate their flora whether as visitors or volunteers, and in a recent survey wildlife conservation was identified as a prime objective by many woodland owners. Yet, despite this tremendous interest, the future for our woodland remains uncertain (chapter 18). In recent years many different groups of woodland species (birds, butterflies, lichens, vascular plants) have been in decline. We need to move to a position where more people care *for* woods as well as *about* them (chapter 19).

Seven ages of conservation

There was a suggestion in 1762 that stealing of 'curious plants' might be made punishable by transportation, which seems a little extreme. In the 19th century more widespread concerns about threats to plants and animals began to emerge in Great Britain. Interest in, and support for, woodland conservation increased through the 20th century and into the early years of this century. Perhaps we have now hit, even passed, 'peak conservation', although I hope not. We face the uncertainties of our exit from the European Union (at the time of writing), climate change and the impacts of imported pests and diseases. This evolution of woodland conservation ideas over the last 200 years can perhaps be compared to Shakespeare's 'seven ages of man' as propounded by Jacques in *As You Like It*.

1820–1900 Mewlings: all is not well with nature

At first, the infant,
Mewling and puking in the nurse's arms.

Many habitats and species were still widespread in the 19th century, but they were coming under threat. The Industrial Revolution was in full swing. Landscape transformation was happening on an unprecedented scale through the unregulated expansion of towns, factories, mines, quarries, canals and railways, accompanied by extensive air and water pollution. People started to see that the legacy of wildlife and wild places was not inexhaustible, whereas previously such concerns might have been largely confined to clergymen such as Gilbert White of Selborne, or poets such as William Wordsworth. More people became aware of, and were able to document, what was happening because of improved education, correspondence groups

OPPOSITE PAGE:
A view from the Forest of Arden; a 1913 illustration for Shakespeare's *As You Like It* by Hugh Thomson.

337

and the facility of cheap printing. In her novel *Mary Barton* (first published 1848), Elizabeth Gaskell says of the Lancashire handloom weavers that 'there are botanists amongst them, equally familiar with either the Linnaean or the Natural system, who know the name and habitat of every plant within a day's walk from their dwellings'.

Some of this enthusiasm went too far. In 1842, 300 specimens of Sickle-leaved Hare's-ear *Bupleurum falcatum* were collected from its sole British locality (Allen 1987). There are 18 sheets of it in the Fielding-Druce Herbarium ranging from 1835 (just four years after it was first found) to 1912. In 1864 the *Botanists' Chronicle* thought that 'Its exact situation may be definitely described without danger to the plant's existence there; for its plenty is so great as to exclude all risks of extermination' (Anon. 1864). The hedge-bank is not far from where I was brought up in Essex, but I never saw the plant; the last record from the site was in 1962. Fortunately, it has long been used in Chinese medicine and is grown in gardens such that its status as ever being a native plant is now under question.

The tide, though, was turning against excessive collections. When the Horticultural Society proposed a competition for the three best herbarium collections per county the *Botanists' Chronicle*

A Victorian day out in Epping Forest; engraving published in *The Graphic*, 1871.

was critical. This 'amounts to offering two or three hundred prizes for the extirpation of all the rare plants in the British Islands; it will let loose all the idle dilettanti to search out and pillage all the localities of rare plants giving them moreover a direct interest in taking or destroying every specimen they can find, that what they do not themselves want may be made inaccessible to their competitors' (Anon 1864). The comment struck home, and the competition was changed. Even that rampant collector of ferns, Nona Bellairs (chapter 17), considered that 'we must have fern laws and preserve them like game'. The ferns and other plants had a long wait for such a law, which finally arrived with the 1975 Conservation of Wild Creatures and Wild Plants Act.

Meanwhile, opposition to the proposed break-up of Epping Forest led to the 1878 Act that placed it in the hands of the Corporation of London. The National Trust for Places of Historic Interest or Natural Beauty was founded in 1895. Campaigns against the extravagant use of feathers in ladies' hats led to the foundation of the Royal Society for the Protection of Birds in 1904 (Sheail 1998). The first steps were being taken towards the modern conservation movement.

1901–1948 Early learning: lists of sites and types of vegetation

And then the whining schoolboy, with his satchel
And shining morning face, creeping like snail
Unwillingly to school.

A future director of the Royal Botanic Gardens at Kew, W. T. Thiselton-Dyer, had written in 1873 that it would be 'well worth the attention of an intelligent government … to preserve spots of primitive land-surface of which the vegetation is especially interesting'; in effect, to create nature reserves (Allen 1987). However, where was this interesting vegetation in Great Britain to be found? Pioneering mapping studies of the variation in fields and woods were undertaken in Yorkshire by W. G. Smith of Leeds College, and in 1904 he and Arthur Tansley set up the British Vegetation Committee. This was subsumed into the British Ecological Society, founded in 1913 (Sheail 1998). Descriptions of sites and vegetation types appeared in the early volumes of the *Journal of Ecology* and were brought together in *The British Islands and their Vegetation* (Tansley 1939).

In another development, Charles Rothschild, a scion of the great banking family, organised, between 1912 and 1915, a list of several hundred potential reserves (Rothschild & Marren 1997). Woods were not strongly represented on the list compared to grassland and heath; perhaps they were thought less likely to come under immediate threat. Some prime sites were left out apparently because they were already de facto reserves. Burnham Beeches, an open access Corporation of London site, was not listed, but the adjacent Dorney Wood was. In the 1970s George Peterken considered Bedford Purlieus in Cambridgeshire to be the richest site known for vascular plants, but it was not on the Rothschild list, perhaps because it was not as well known as other nearby woods for its butterflies and moths.

The list of sites produced by Charles Rothschild and colleagues had a strong influence on subsequent catalogues of important conservation sites. Some subsequently became National Nature Reserves or jewels in the voluntary sector's portfolio of reserves. A few sites still exist but are no longer seen as so special. A damp Ash copse which contained the naturalised herb Asarabacca was part of the reason for listing Weston Turville Reservoir: this would not now justify special protection for a wood. Others on that first Rothschild

A 'Rothschild' site that did not survive: Oakleigh Purlieus in Northamptonshire.

list did not survive: Oakleigh Purlieus in Northamptonshire was judged more important than Monks Wood in Cambridgeshire. The Purlieus was clear-felled in the Second World War and then quarried for ironstone. Neglect and lack of management were a major cause of loss and damage to the interests in other cases. The woods generally became shadier, exacerbated where broadleaved crops were replaced by conifers (Rothschild & Marren 1997).

During the inter-war years there was a separate, sometimes complementary, sometimes competing, movement to establish National Parks in Great Britain. Much of this was focused on maintaining the landscape of, and access to, open heaths and moors, as epitomised by the Mass Trespass on Kinder Scout in 1932. There were the first rumblings of concerns about large-scale upland afforestation, brought to a head in the Lake District when the Forestry Commission proposed to plant the upper end of the Duddon Valley (Symonds 1936). However, despite a strong start, nature conservation on the ground rather stagnated.

1949–1980 A passion for conservation may not stop major losses

And then the lover,
Sighing like furnace, with a woeful ballad
Made to his mistress' eyebrow.

During the height of the Second World War there were discussions within government and more widely about post-war conservation policies. These led to the 1949 National Parks and Access to the Countryside Act and an equivalent act for Scotland (Sheail 1998) that brought into being both the National Parks in England and Wales and the first GB-wide conservation service – the Nature Conservancy. Sites on the lists of potential reserves that had been accumulating since 1915 were acquired as National Nature Reserves, including Beinn Eighe, Monks Wood in Cambridgeshire (Oakleigh Purlieus no longer being available) and Roudsea Wood in Cumbria.

The legislation setting up the Nature Conservancy introduced a new form of designation, Sites of Special Scientific Interest (SSSI). The Conservancy depended largely on the goodwill of the owners to ensure that their interest was not damaged, because the sites remained under their existing, mostly private, ownership. Some

The pinewoods at Beinn Eighe, one of the first National Nature Reserves.

people looked on having an SSSI wood positively, but others saw it as an unreasonable restriction on their freedom to manage their land. With government policy seeking to build new towns, increase food and timber production from our own resources, even SSSI woodland might be destroyed for houses, converted to arable fields, or planted with non-native conifers.

SSSIs were selected, and their descriptions written, with an emphasis on specific features or species: this site was important for this orchid here, or to maintain that woodland type there. Efforts were made to assess the overall woodland resource, to put the selected sites into a wider perspective and to make such selections and descriptions more robust. In the mid-1960s a national woodland survey produced over 2,000 records for woods, including details of their ground flora. This work fed into the Nature Conservation Review, which listed the most important sites across Great Britain, including some 234 woodland sites, and generated the basis for my woodland plant list (Ratcliffe 1977).

During the 1970s ideas around ancient woodland and its importance for the woodland flora came to the fore (chapter 3), but also the degree to which such woodland was under threat (Peterken 1974, 1977b). The ancient woodland inventory project (initiated in 1981) established that about 7% of the ancient woods present in the 1930s had, like Oakleigh Purlieus, been completely cleared by the mid-1980s, and about 38% survived only as plantations on ancient woodland sites (Roberts *et al.* 1992, Spencer & Kirby 1992). Such losses to our richest and culturally most significant woods had been masked because, overall, the total extent of broadleaved woodland was maintained, and even increased, in many areas. New woods were springing up as grazing by livestock and by rabbits declined (chapter 15). Unfortunately, this new woodland was as much of a problem for grassland or heathland conservation as the more obvious conifer afforestation.

The conservation sector became more aware of the degree to which woods had been managed in the past (chapter 9) and that the species and features we valued often depended on that management continuing (Peterken 1977a). Restoration of traditional management was promoted, with suggestions that there should be a large-scale expansion of coppicing (Steele & Peterken 1982). There were, though, still just a few studies that provided good evidence on what effect such management actually had on the flora. To visiting ecologists from North America, this interventionist approach looked very like the British obsession with gardening transferred into the wider countryside.

Despite the passion and enthusiasm of their staff, the Nature Conservancy and its successor, the Nature Conservancy Council (NCC), were limited in what they could achieve. When I joined NCC in 1979 there were still only about 350 people in the whole GB organisation. We benefited, however, from the support of a vibrant voluntary sector. The voluntary conservation movement had found its feet, with more and more county naturalists' trusts being formed (most now called Wildlife Trusts). Specialist conservation societies emerged, such as the Woodland Trust, founded in 1972. Membership of these organisations blossomed, and many sites were acquired as reserves. The voluntary bodies became increasingly vocal about the state of the countryside and the need to protect habitats and species. The 1981 Wildlife and Countryside Act was part of the Government's response to these concerns.

1980–1990 Conservation militant: moving out from the protected sites

Then a soldier,
Full of strange oaths and bearded like the pard,
Jealous in honour, sudden and quick in quarrel,
Seeking the bubble reputation
Even in the cannon's mouth.

The 1981 Wildlife and Countryside Act started as an administrative necessity to enable the Government to implement the Birds' Directive to which we had signed up through being in the European Economic Community. Through the lobbying efforts of the voluntary conservation sector and the Nature Conservancy Council, the Act became a step-change in the protection that it gave to Sites of Special Scientific Interest (SSSIs). Farming and forestry operations threatening to damage SSSIs were brought under a system of prior notification alongside planned developments such as housing (Sheail 1998).

The Nature Conservancy Council was required under this Act to re-notify all SSSIs, to consider how they were being managed and whether the species for which they were deemed important were thriving. However, despite increased awareness of and protection for SSSIs, by themselves the protected sites were not enough. Many species were in serious decline, including in well-studied groups such as birds, butterflies and flowering plants. Large-scale removal of hedges, small woods, ditches and streams from their surroundings, had left the protected sites increasingly isolated in a matrix of improved grassland and arable fields (NCC 1984).

The emergence of landscape ecology as a distinct discipline during the 1980s provided a theoretical framework for demonstrating the reasons as to why protecting reserves and SSSIs on their own was not enough (Forman & Godron 1986): there was exchange of species and individuals between protected sites and other habitat patches in the wider countryside. If species were lost by chance from a protected patch, there might be recolonisation from other sites nearby, but this was only possible if the non-protected sites survived. Small patches of woodland, even individual trees, in between the larger sites might be important for long-term population survival. Sir John Lawton would later sum up the general problem with the English SSSI system, in noting that there needed to be more sites, that were bigger, better-managed and more joined-up (Lawton 2010).

It was one thing to recognise that the wider countryside around protected sites was important, but in the 1980s the Nature Conservancy Council's powers and scope for funding were already stretched by the special sites, which covered only about 8% of the land surface. Changes in the policies and financial support for land use administered by the Ministry of Agriculture/Department of Environment and the Forestry Commission were needed. A first step was a new forestry policy in 1985 (Forestry Commission 1985). Rather than promoting the conversion of stands of Birch, Ash and Oak to more productive conifer crops, broadleaved woodland was in future expected to remain broadleaved. The accompanying management guidelines leaflet emphasised the need to maintain the special character of ancient semi-natural woodland.

The lists of ancient woods produced by the Nature Conservancy Council started to be used by local authorities in their development planning decisions. The Forestry Commission gave more attention to the wildlife of broadleaved woodland (Niemann 2016). Coniferous plantations began to be converted back to native broadleaves, and not just because the conifer crops were failing anyway (as had happened in the 1970s). New conservation training programmes were brought in for Commission staff; management advice booklets for private

In 1986 the Forestry Commission started to restore the conifer-dominated areas of Dalavich Oakwood, Lochaweside. By 2014, when this photograph was taken, the Bilberry had re-established across the whole wood.

landowners, grants and other support mechanisms were rejigged in line with this new approach (Forestry Commission 2010). The woodland flora assumed a higher profile in foresters' considerations as an important indicator of whether sites were ancient or not, and as a measure of their condition.

In the second half of the 1980s agri-environment schemes emerged. These were partly an instrument to control agricultural over-production, but evolved into mechanisms for improving the farmland environment, including through the management of non-woodland trees and hedges and the creation of new farm woods. Overall, the scope and extent of woodland conservation work increased, there were increased funds to back up our efforts, and more regulations, although with them came increasing conservation bureaucracy.

The conservation vision largely remained the same, however: this was to conserve the species, the sorts of woods and landscapes that had thrived in the late 19th and early 20th centuries. We just needed to do what we had been trying to do on the reserves and special sites since 1949 more widely across the countryside. For many, the Habitats and Species' Directive that came into force in 1992 was the apogee of this approach, with its emphasis on fixed vegetation types and targets for habitats and species to be maintained at a favourable conservation status (European Commission 1992).

1990–2000 Judicious rethinking: can we actually conserve what we thought we valued?

And then the justice,
In fair round belly with good capon lined,
With eyes severe and beard of formal cut,
Full of wise saws and modern instances;
And so he plays his part.

Hayley Wood, Cambridgeshire, and the Bradfield Woods in Suffolk are noted for their relative stability of management over the last 500–1,000 years (Rackham 2003) and we might therefore suppose that their flora has similarly been relatively constant, within the dynamic pattern of the coppice system (chapter 9). However, other studies showed that this stability was not true for all ancient woods. The land now covered by trees at Wytham was in the 18th century a series of scattered ancient woods, common grazings and small-scale quarries. Coed y Rhygen in North Wales, now a closed canopy oakwood, noted for its rare mosses and liverworts, probably had an open park-like structure in the late-medieval period, whilst parts were coppiced about 40 years ago (Edwards 1986). Some of the Glen Affric pinewoods have been dominated by Scots Pine for several thousand years, but with more broadleaved trees than now (chapter 6); elsewhere the stands derive from expansion on to open ground just a few hundred years ago (Shaw & Tipping 2006). Such changes in management and extent have left legacies in the ground flora patterns at these sites, so why try to 'fix' the wood at the point when these sites first became known to the conservation movement?

During the 1990s it also became clear that climate change was affecting species' phenology and distribution (chapter 16) and questions started to be asked in conservation circles as to whether what we had inherited was really what we could and should seek to conserve (Jarman 1995). Extreme events, such as droughts, floods and storms, reinforced the message that the patterns of habitats and species were going to be different. Early climate models, for example, suggested that Beech was not going to grow very well in south-east England under the expected climate regime of 2080. If correct, could we meet our commitments under the Habitats Directive to

An important oakwood for bryophytes in Wales, but the trees are almost certainly planted.

maintain favourable conservation status for beechwoods in southern Great Britain? Should we accept the spread of Beech in northern England and Scotland (chapter 7) as replacements for stands that might be lost in the south-east? The ground flora would not be exactly the same as under southern beechwoods, but neither would it stay the same in southern beechwoods where other trees would gradually replace Beech as the canopy dominant under future climates. Subsequent models indicated that the risk of losing Beech completely was overstated, but the questions raised about how we deal with the changing distribution of species remain relevant.

Our choice of conservation baselines, and the targets for future management, are thrown open for debate by these different woodland states in the past – we might choose the 19th-century pattern rather than that of the 11th century, but others might make a different choice. Nor can we fall back on the generalised vision of the post-glacial natural landscape as dense forest as a fixed model for future conservation. This vision has been challenged by Frans Vera's ideas of a grazed landscape (Peterken 1996, Vera 2000) (chapter 12) and increasing recognition that human influences extended into the deep past.

2000–2020 Conservation in transition

The sixth age shifts
Into the lean and slippered pantaloon,
With spectacles on nose and pouch on side;
His youthful hose, well saved, a world too wide
For his shrunk shank; and his big manly voice,
Turning again toward childish treble, pipes
And whistles in his sound.

Modern research points to humans as at least contributing to the elimination of mega-fauna such as Mammoth and Woolly Rhinoceros. We continued with the extinction of the Aurochs, and extirpation, in Great Britain, of Bear, Elk, Lynx, Wolf, Beaver and Wild Boar (chapter 12). We know we have lost some invertebrate species, but there will be others we never knew we had (Hambler *et al.* 2011). We have introduced to Great Britain other species, for example Rabbit, Fallow Deer, Grey Squirrel and Muntjac. These gains and losses, particularly amongst the medium to large herbivores, have had profound influences on our woods and their flora (chapter 11). Through

Muntjac – a recent addition to our woodland fauna.

labelling bits of the landscape 'woodland' we have concentrated trees in these areas, while stripping them from the heaths and meadows elsewhere. This parcelling up of the landscape has limited the ability of some species to spread through it and exacerbated the differences in the ground flora of old and new woods (chapters 3, 15). The gases we have added to the atmosphere mean that the future environment will be different from anything that our woods and their flora have experienced in the last 1,000 years (chapter 16).

We inherited patterns of habitats and species fitted to the past social and economic conditions. The conservation movement has tried (and frequently failed) to maintain these landscapes under the very different conditions that have emerged since the Second World War. For example, we value the open woods created by particular types of past management such as coppicing and promote the idea that a rich flora will develop in the first few years after a coppice cut (chapter 9). However, we have not succeeded in reinstating coppice on the large, industrial scale that would allow species such as the Pearl-bordered Fritillary butterfly to recover their former abundance. And would conservationists really be happy with that degree of activity in woods today (Hambler & Speight 1995)? Conservation has made progress over the last 200 years, but often it has been only to slow the rates of species decline.

2020 Onward, second (perhaps final) chance

Last scene of all,
That ends this strange eventful history,
Is second childishness and mere oblivion,
Sans teeth, sans eyes, sans taste, sans everything.

The international Convention on Biological Diversity refers to conserving the variability among living organisms from all sources including, *inter alia*, terrestrial, marine and other aquatic ecosystems and the ecological complexes of which they are part; this includes diversity within species, between species, and of ecosystems. It does not specify what varieties of species and ecosystems should take priority. So which bits of past, present and potential future biodiversity should we be conserving, and where, in Great Britain? Rather than trying to recreate (in the face of climate change) the range of habitats with the similar mix of species that existed in the past, should modern conservation be more about creating the type of countryside that will be rich in species capable of coping with the environmental conditions (including new pests and diseases) expected by 2100?

One way of moving to a future-orientated conservation lies with the current interest in rewilding and the restoration of ecological processes (Monbiot 2013, Lorimer *et al.* 2015). However, there still remains a need to make decisions as to what sort of wildness we want. For example, consider a proposal for rewilding a very large British woodland including an appropriate range of mammal species. Would the model for this rewilded area be the species mix that existed 200 years ago: more wild cats, pine martens, polecats; only Fallow, Red and Roe deer with fewer rabbits and no Grey Squirrel? Taking 1,000 years or so ago as the baseline would require us to add in Beaver, Wild Boar and Wolf, possibly Lynx, but take out rabbits and Fallow Deer. A 7,000 years ago baseline would add in Lynx (definitely), Wild Ox, Bear and Elk (chapter 12).

On the plant side, we are now more likely to accept the introduced tree Sycamore in our woods, as studies suggest its invasiveness and impact on the ground flora are not as great as once thought (Taylor 1995, Natural England 2009). We remain concerned about the impact of the spread of Rhododendron, since not only does little grow beneath it but even after it is cleared ground flora recovery may take decades (Maclean *et al.* 2017). Moreover, we have little choice but to accept the changes in the vegetation that follow from the impact of introduced pests and pathogens, such as Ash Dieback in both managed and rewilded woods (chapter 9).

Different baselines, and future visions against which conservation efforts can be measured, will be appropriate in some areas but not in others. Our actions will also need to take account of the cultural and historic associations of different landscapes, which Oliver Rackham called the 'meaning' of the countryside. The development of dense swathes of Wood Anemone may be in part a consequence of the eradication of Wild Boar from our woods (chapters 7, 10), but if we value such displays as part of our heritage we may decide to try to curb the spread of Wild Boar in some woods. We will continue to face tensions between the emphasis placed on increasing woodland cover versus the conservation of open habitats and their associated species that may be threatened by woodland expansion (chapter 15). Similarly, actions that might benefit conservation at home, for example restricting the use of conifers in broadleaved woodland because of their impact on the ground flora (chapter 9), may increase our need to import timber with potentially more serious biodiversity impacts on forests overseas. The outcomes for our landscapes cannot avoid being the product of the interaction of human culture and the environment, with elements reflecting past conditions, but incorporating novel aspects, 'recombinant ecology' (Rotherham 2017).

The shape of this Beech tree comes from its cultural, not natural, history and would eventually be lost under rewilding.

Future-natural woodland: holding the line/going with the flow

O ur lives are generally much richer and easier than they were 100 years ago, and we should not expect people to have to go back to living as they did then. However, if we do not alter our lifestyles, we cannot avoid continued losses of habitats and species.

Recent reports from the International Panel on Climate Change are clear that we are not doing enough to head off major damaging impacts from increasing global temperatures, changed rainfall patterns and rising sea levels. We, in Great Britain, should play a greater role in reducing global emissions of greenhouse gases, since we often claim to have started the Industrial Revolution, which kicked off the current rises. Reducing emissions substantially will mean changes in how we get our energy, farm the land and seas, manage water supplies, move about Great Britain (road, rail, bicycle, foot) and the world (the number of flights we take). We need to bring our consumption down and manage our waste better.

Changing how land is managed over the next few decades is a critical part of that process and is likely to involve a substantial increase in tree cover. There are places, such as peatlands, where it is not appropriate to plant trees or even encourage natural woodland regeneration. However, if we are to make any progress with the recommendations of the Climate Change Committee (up to 1.5 million hectares of new woodland by 2050, increasing woodland cover from 13% to 19%), increased woodland creation

OPPOSITE PAGE:
Looking to the
future – a monument
commemorating the
Women's Timber Corps.

rates are needed. Woodland expansion, for commercial, environmental and social reasons, has been part of successive Government strategies for forestry across Great Britain, but finding the right incentives and locations to make it happen have proved difficult. However, if recent calls for a shift to a more plant-based diet lead to large-scale reductions in livestock farming, there may be much more space potentially available for new trees and woods, and fundamental changes in our landscapes are probably unavoidable (Committee on Climate Change 2018).

How this expansion of tree cover happens, and how we manage both this new resource and our existing woods, will determine which, and how many, of our woodland species will be thriving in the landscapes of the 2050s. We must, in the short term, maintain and improve the woodland that we have through traditional management techniques such as coppicing as well as new approaches such as ground flora introductions (chapters 9, 15). At the same time, we must develop a more dynamic, expanded approach to conservation for the medium to longer term, which may involve both more and fewer interventions according to the mix of objectives that we seek to achieve in any one landscape.

Securing and expanding the legacies we inherited

Nature reserves and ancient woods will be affected by the changing environment (chapter 16) just as much as their surroundings, so need our protection and nurturing more than ever. Within them will develop the communities and assemblages best suited to future conditions. They can also be the sources from which species spread to new woods, particularly if these are developed next to an existing woodland.

Small woods (less than 5ha) are particularly vulnerable to clearance, or to the loss of tree and shrub cover over the whole site through disease, pests, exceptional droughts or storms. They generally contain fewer species than large woods and the populations of the species they do contain are limited by the size of the woodland. Making small woods bigger allows more species to survive in a patch and there can be more individuals of each species. There is also more space to include a sheltered glade or ride with the additional benefits to the flora and fauna that come from creating this new habitat in the wood (chapter 14).

Adding 2 hectares to a 2-hectare wood obviously doubles its size; adding 2 hectares to a 20-hectare wood, however, adds only an additional 10%. With increasing woodland size, each hectare added makes less difference to the number of species that the wood can contain and how big their populations can be. So, for medium-size woods (say 6–30ha) the most useful way of adding to their extent is to focus on new strips of woodland and scrub (between 20m and 100m wide) as buffers around the edges of the wood. Using the new woodland allowance in this way reduces potential nitrogen enrichment from adjacent farmland and the drying out of the ancient woodland edge (chapter 16). This new edge strip can be rapidly colonised by woodland species because all of it is in contact with the existing wood. Even slow-moving specialists stand a chance of spreading into the new area once soil and light conditions become suitable.

For very small woods such as this, just increasing its size would improve its potential for woodland plant diversity.

The relative benefits from creating buffer strips round woods decline as the wood size increases, because most of the woodland is already some distance away from the external edge. The priority for new woodland and trees is then in creating more connections and stepping stones through the countryside, in effect re-creating the sorts of treescapes that existed before the ravages of Dutch Elm Disease and farming improvements removed small woods and hedges from

355

many landscapes. New small patches of woodland by themselves are of only limited importance as habitat for woodland specialist plants, although a surprising array of species can turn up even in small woods (chapter 15). However, small patches do benefit the 'common' woodland generalists, not all of which are now common in intensively farmed landscapes, and should also increase the ease with which woodland species can move through the landscape.

Old and new forms of woodland management

Most of our woods have been managed in the past (chapter 9), but a large amount (perhaps between a third and a half) of broadleaved woodland does not appear to be actively worked at present. Encouraging more woodland management, alongside forest expansion, has also been an aim in successive woodland strategies for England, Scotland and Wales, but with only limited success. The recent rise in the price of firewood has provided an incentive for some owners to fell trees again, reversing a trend towards increasing shadiness. However, if felling is not done carefully, the woodland specialist flora may be damaged, while only weedy or competitive species benefit. We need to monitor whether practices such as coppicing continue to produce the expected carpets of spring flowers now there are more deer, more nitrogen in the soils, a warming climate and more extreme weather. If not, what are the alternatives?

Most woods have been clear-felled (or coppiced) in patches from about half a hectare up to many tens of hectares, but there is increasing interest in what is termed 'Continuous Cover Forestry'. Under this system, only individual trees or small groups are ever felled at any one time, so that there is always some canopy left to maintain shade and higher humidity at ground level. There is less disturbance to the soil surface and slower breakdown of litter after felling, and more opportunities to develop mixed age and mixed species stands. Preliminary indications from the woods in Cranborne Chase are that much of the typical woodland flora survives well under this form of management, although some of the more light-demanding species may not benefit as much as under a larger fell. Grey Squirrel control will also need to be addressed if we want woods to produce quality broadleaved timber as well as biodiversity. New woodland surveys will be needed to determine whether the initial promise of Continuous Cover Forestry is

maintained as far as the woodland soils, plants and animals are concerned (chapter 2).

Thinning of Oak as part of Continuous Cover Forestry conversion in Cranborne Chase – Bramble certainly benefits.

Continuous Cover Forestry approaches will also have a place in the restoration of the ancient woods that existed in the 1930s, and which were, by the 1980s, plantations mainly dominated by coniferous species (Spencer & Kirby 1992) as a result of previous forestry policies (chapter 18). The woodland ground flora under such crops was often reduced to a thin scatter of woebegone-looking plants. However, much of the flora can be, and is being, restored in places. When, in 2014, I visited a restoration scheme carried out in the late 1980s at Dalavich Wood in Argyll (Kirby & May 1989), it was not at all obvious which areas had been under conifer plantations in the early 80s and which not. In Salcey Forest in Northamptonshire, and Bernwood in Buckinghamshire, areas of Oak from which the Spruce nurse crop has been removed, or which were felled and replanted with broadleaves, now have similar richness to the mature Oak stands that were left alone (Kirby *et al.* 2017). There are still questions about the best ways to carry out restoration: when and where is it appropriate to clear-fell the conifer element all at once, or better to open out the canopy gradually by thinning (Brown *et al.* 2015)? The likelihood of getting a good response from the ground flora also depends on how much has managed to survive under the planted crop. However,

Restoration of
broadleaved woodland
following conifer removal
at Bernwood Forest.

in most circumstances any action is likely to be better than none,
provided that the deer are sufficiently managed that any regeneration
or sensitive ground flora will not just get immediately eaten.

Managing deer

In the woods around Orielton in Pembrokeshire, deer are scarce.
On my annual visit to these woods I am struck each year by the
abundance of ground-creeping Ivy, herbs and ferns, and lack of
grasses compared to similar woods in eastern England where deer
are common (chapter 11). Similarly, on the Isle of Wight, which
remained largely deer-free until recently, coppice grows rapidly in
the first year after cutting without the need for fencing; herbs rather
than grasses predominate in the ground flora, and most woods have
a well-developed understorey.

Kate Holl, a woodland ecologist with Scottish Natural Heritage,
looked at ungrazed or only lightly-grazed woods from the French
Pyrenees to western Norway and Iceland to get a feel for what
might be missing in the heavily-grazed woods that she deals with in
Scotland. Her conclusions were that Scottish woods largely lacked
a 'filling': the tall flowering herbs actually in flower, climbing and

scrambling species such as Ivy and Honeysuckle, berry-bearing shrubs, and tree regeneration. She concluded that many woods in Great Britain would benefit from a grazing-free period to allow them to recover that 'filling' (Holl 2017).

Deer management is not easy. The two main approaches, fencing and shooting, may be opposed by people who object to killing animals or limiting their movements. Where control is successful in bringing numbers down there are still likely to be fluctuations in the vegetation cover. For example, Bramble cover tends to increase as deer are controlled, but this makes the deer harder to shoot, so numbers build up again. Variability in vegetation structure across sites, and over time, allows for greater diversity overall at the landscape level but should not be used as an excuse for not trying to keep deer numbers down. If deer control is not acceptable or possible everywhere, some woods will continue to have a high-deer, grazed composition and structure in the future. The flora will be mainly grasses, Bracken and moss, with fewer herbs such as Dog's Mercury and dwarf shrubs such as Bilberry. Tree regeneration is likely to be very limited, unless the deer numbers crash periodically, for example through starvation in very bad winters or as a result of a disease outbreak. Such events become more likely the larger the area being considered.

Ungrazed ferns and Ivy in the Orielton Estate woods.

Scaling-up conservation areas/scaling down intervention

To some extent much conservation management, sometimes called conservation 'gardening', is only necessary because we are dealing with very small reserves. The current population of Starved Wood-sedge at Godalming, Surrey (chapter 10), is spread across about 6 square metres and so has to be managed at the microscale – the gap in the canopy immediately above it needs to be kept open; a gap 20m away is no use. If woods in the vicinity, on the right soils, were all managed as coppice then it would be possible to re-establish a series of local populations of the sedge that would come and go with the open coppice phase; micro-management of conditions around each sedge clump would no longer be necessary. If even more of the south-east were under woodland, it might not be necessary to have to coppice to create gaps for the Starved Wood-sedge because there would always be disturbed open patches, formed following wind-storms or tree deaths from disease, somewhere on suitable soils. Large-scale conservation may therefore mean that less intervention/management is needed.

Reduced intervention is being trialled in various rewilding schemes. These seek to reduce direct management, preferably in a planned way, so that natural environmental processes have more scope to shape the composition and structure of the landscape. The result should be a more resilient and sustainable form of land use that is also richer in wildlife. It is not an all-or-nothing approach, but a gradation of actions. At one extreme it could be trying to have a reserve large enough that populations of large carnivores might be reintroduced, and all human management removed from that reserve (a hypothetical case!). At the other it is letting the park grass grow up as a hay crop rather than being regularly shaved to a few centimetres high (this can be done almost anywhere).

We are starting to see what happens with rewilding in practice, if we put fewer restrictions on where animals can graze by removing fences, or allow rivers to move their channels rather than constraining them via embankments. Well-publicised projects across the country include the Knepp Estate in Sussex, Ennerdale in Cumbria and at Alladale in Sutherland. A recently established project in mid-Wales seeks to rewild an area from 'Summit to Sea', while a proposal to rewild native pinewoods in the Cairngorms has also received funding.

Promoters of rewilding in Great Britain generally see an increase in tree cover and woodland regeneration as one of the beneficial

outcomes. The assumption is that once woodland cover has been restored there is expected to develop some sort of dynamic equilibrium between the ongoing effects of grazing and tree growth, although this might be apparent only at a large scale and over long timescales. However, James Fenton, a Scottish ecologist, argues that the open, largely treeless landscape of the Highlands maintained by deer *is* the natural state and that the assumption that there *should* be a lot more trees and woodland in the Highlands is wrong. Putting in exclosures and heavy deer culling to re-establish trees is then the antithesis of rewilding because it is managing towards a target vegetation type (woodland), rather than accepting whatever develops (open moor).

Fenton may or may not be right about upland vegetation, but in the lowlands, the prospects for tree and woodland spread in rewilded areas are much better. Trees grow faster, and there are more thorny species to give protection to saplings, allowing a cohort of regeneration to get away if there is a temporary downturn in grazing levels. This should provide opportunities for woodland plants to benefit, provided they can spread into the area and are not disrupted by cattle grazing or the rootling of pigs. The vegetation communities that develop in these new lowland wildwoods may be more like the flora of wood-pastures, grassier and with fewer massed displays of vernal flowers. This is not a 'bad thing', just a change in the nature of the cultural landscapes in which we live.

Woodland plants may be sheltered by developing scrub under rewilding.

How wild will our wildflowers be in future?

As a teenager, I was a member of a traditional folk music club. We attached a special virtue to songs that had come through the 'oral tradition' and imagined ourselves as the inheritors of that tradition. With the naivety of youth, we roared out songs about fox-hunting, whaling, the glories of war, in the pub in the evening, while being heartily opposed to such practices during the day. In a similar way the conservation sector promotes what we call traditional management, but we cut the coppice with chainsaws, and unwanted tops are burnt or left in habitat piles for invertebrates. There is little scavenging of twigs for kindling or leaves for animal bedding. More of the nutrients in the stems stay in the wood than in the past, leading to soil enrichment (chapter 9).

We tend towards a simplified, often romantic, view of the past. We often say that there was little woodland planting before 1600, making ancient woods more 'authentic' than 17th- or 18th-century plantations. Yet in 1458, James II's Scottish parliament passed a law exhorting landowners to get their tenants to plant trees and Broom. Presumably the law was not very effective, because in 1535 a somewhat stronger version was promulgated, and again in 1607 and 1661. Planting may have been more widespread before 1600, with a greater influence on the composition of our woods, than we appreciate.

Today, Wildlife Trusts cut back competing vegetation to allow orchids to flower more freely, and fence out medium to large native herbivores. Little cages may be placed over rare plants to protect them, and they are artificially pollinated to increase seed production (Marren 2005). Do such practices detract from the experience of seeing the plant, because it is less wild? I did feel something similar when I came across planted Hazel cuttings in Berriedale Wood on the Orkney island of Hoy. However, where we draw the line on what is acceptable changes over time. In the 1970s sowing wildflowers was anathema to much of the conservation movement: there is now increasing support for introducing ground flora species to new plantations. This becomes part of the 'meaning' of these woods in the same way that past coppice management is often part of the meaning of many ancient woods.

At present, conservation priorities often sharply distinguish native from introduced species, but that distinction is not wholly clear-cut (chapter 4) and will become more confused as climate change takes hold. Our woods are part of a broader European pattern (chapter 13),

Where does conservation become wild gardening? Here fencing is used to protect a small orchid patch.

and species from further south on the Continent may find our climate in 2050 or 2080 perfectly suitable for their growth. Should we trial how these behave in combination with our existing flora in some new woodland plantings, just as foresters trial new crop trees? Conversely, if some native species start to decline, primarily as a consequence of climate change, should we shift our conservation efforts to palliative care only or explore their assisted migration to more suitable locations? We may not be at this point yet, but we need a wider discussion on how far we manage future species distributions, with decisions based on what species do, rather than on just when and how they arrived in Great Britain.

Given the extent of past woodland management, does the degree of future intervention in itself ultimately matter, provided it achieves the desired result? Concern for the 'authentic folk voice' did not prevent our club stalwarts enthusiastically joining in modern songs by Tom Paxton and Ewan McColl. Anyway, we may find that the traditional conservation sector no longer calls the tune.

Who will decide what conservation is about in future?

In the 1970s, a relatively small group of scientists developed the philosophy and priorities in the Nature Conservation Review which would shape much of the next 30 years of nature conservation (Ratcliffe 1977). The relevant expertise outside the Nature Conservancy/Nature Conservancy Council was generally with individuals who were in close touch with the NC/NCC specialists.

For the next few decades woodland conservation benefited from both a strong voluntary sector and state agencies (the Forestry Commission, NCC and its current manifestations Natural England, Natural Resources Wales, Scottish Natural Heritage). Meanwhile expertise burgeoned in the private consultancy sector. Relevant legislation expanded immensely, both through domestic efforts and also through the transposition of European regulations. Conservation initiatives became linked to a wide range of other activities including controlling pollution, water quality, people's health and renewable energy amongst others.

It seems to me that the future for conservation may now be shifting back to local and individual activity. The efforts of the government agencies have become more diluted as their remits have broadened without concomitant staff increases (in some cases rather substantial staff reductions). Increased regulation and legislation have brought increased scrutiny and potential for legal challenge, which can put

Will conservation priorities and actions still be determined by the conservation professionals or by Twitter?

more conservation decisions into the hands of judges and inquiry inspectors. At the time of writing there is also much uncertainty about the consequences of the United Kingdom leaving the European Union, for the economy, trade relationships, environmental regulation and funding. Social media have become a major means of influencing policy and practice. Defining what the countryside in 2050 might be like could be determined in part by popular demand (for example, Twitter-feed) and legal precedent.

Final thoughts

No-one predicted a storm as severe as that of 1987, and the impacts it would have on woodland in south-east England, but severe storms, periods of heavy rainfall and droughts are likely to become more common. We should expect further new tree pests and diseases, perhaps more forest fires, as well as the consequences of the changes in land use that are likely over the next 30 years. We need to increase the longer-term resilience of our woodland: that is, its ability to cope with major sudden disturbances as well as ongoing, more gradual, changes in conditions, but we must accept that there will always be much that is outside our control.

We can perhaps take heart that woods that seemed to have lost most of their interest under a conifer needle mat now show green and are becoming flower-rich. Heavily-grazed areas regrow if they are fenced. Rare species have been brought back from the brink of local extinction. We understand better now the opportunities and limitations involved in introducing woodland species to existing woods and hedges. There are exciting and ambitious countryside restoration schemes in progress.

Ideally, we should be moving towards a state where special conservation measures to sustain rich woodland ground floras are not needed because general land-use practices (including rewilding) do this as a matter of course. The conservation agencies' role, and that of the voluntary sector, could be scaled down because they were no longer needed. We are, of course, a long way off this point!

The celandines and Lords-and-Ladies in the back garden of my childhood home disappeared in the garden makeover that happened after we left. However, each spring I am still excited to see their leaves pushing through in other hedges and woods as I jog by. Compared to the fate of flowers on farmland, woodland plants have fared reasonably well over the last 60 years and the new planting that has taken place should eventually produce more opportunities for them to spread. I am cautiously optimistic that we could reach the mid-point of this century with something like the variety of woodland plants we had 70 years ago. I look to a world where kids (of all ages) can enjoy the spectacle of a Bluebell swathe or Primrose bank, and if someone wants to pick a few, we do not need to feel concerned. The wood beneath the trees should and will continue to thrive, if we give it a chance and a hand.

As I walked out, one fine summer's morning, for to view the fields and
to take the air,
Down by the banks of the sweet primroses, there I beheld a most
wondrous fair.

(Traditional ballad)

A bank of
sweet primroses.

Appendices

Appendix 1: A woodland-plant list

1a: Ordered by English Names – Specialists

English Name	Scientific Name	English Name	Scientific Name
Adder's-tongue	Ophioglossum vulgatum	False Brome	Brachypodium sylvaticum
Allseed	Radiola linoides	Field-rose	Rosa arvensis
Alternate-leaved Golden-saxifrage	Chrysosplenium alternifolium	Fingered Sedge	Carex digitata
		Fly Orchid	Ophrys insectifera
Angular Solomon's-seal	Polygonatum odoratum	Giant Bellflower	Campanula latifolia
Barren Strawberry	Potentilla sterilis	Giant Fescue	Schedonorus giganteus
Bastard Balm	Melittis melissophyllum	Globeflower	Trollius europaeus
Bearded Couch	Elymus caninus	Goldenrod	Solidago virgaurea
Beech Fern	Phegopteris connectilis	Golden-scaled Male-fern	Dryopteris affinis
Betony	Betonica officinalis	Goldilocks Buttercup	Ranunculus auricomus
Bilberry/Blaeberry	Vaccinium myrtillus	Great Horsetail	Equisetum telmateia
Birds-nest Orchid	Neottia nidus-avis	Great Woodrush	Luzula sylvatica
Bitter-vetch	Lathyrus linifolius	Greater Burnet-saxifrage	Pimpinella major
Black Bryony	Tamus communis	Greater Butterfly-orchid	Platanthera chlorantha
Black Currant	Ribes nigrum	Greater Chickweed	Stellaria neglecta
Bloody Crane's-bill	Geranium sanguineum	Greater Stitchwort	Stellaria holostea
Bluebell	Hyacinthoides non-scripta	Greater Tussock-sedge	Carex paniculata
Broad-leaved Helleborine	Epipactis helleborine	Green Hellebore	Helleborus viridis
Bush Vetch	Vicia sepium	Green-flowered Helleborine	Epipactis phyllanthes
Butcher's-Broom	Ruscus aculeatus		
Climbing Corydalis	Ceratocapnos claviculata	Hairy Lady's-mantle	Alchemilla filicaulis
Columbine	Aquilegia vulgaris	Hairy St John's-wort	Hypericum hirsutum
Common Cow-wheat	Melampyrum pratense	Hairy Wood-rush	Luzula pilosa
Common Dog-violet	Viola riviniana	Hairy-brome	Bromopsis ramosa
Common Figwort	Scrophularia nodosa	Hard Shield-fern	Polystichum aculeatum
Common Gromwell	Lithospermum officinale	Hard-Fern	Blechnum spicant
Common Polypody	Polypodium vulgare	Hart's-tongue	Asplenium scolopendrium
Common Twayblade	Neottia ovata	Hay-scented Buckler-fern	Dryopteris aemula
Common Valerian	Valeriana officinalis	Heath Cudweed	Gnaphalium sylvaticum
Common Wintergreen	Pyrola minor	Hedge Woundwort	Stachys sylvatica
Coralroot	Cardamine bulbifera	Herb-Paris	Paris quadrifolia
Cornish Moneywort	Sibthorpia europaea	Herb-Robert	Geranium robertianum
Creeping Soft-grass	Holcus mollis	Honeysuckle	Lonicera periclymenum
Cuckoo-pint	Arum maculatum	Ivy Broomrape	Orobanche hederae
Dewberry	Rubus caesius	Ivy-leaved Bellflower	Wahlenbergia hederacea
Dog's Mercury	Mercurialis perennis	Lady Orchid	Orchis purpurea
Downy Currant	Ribes spicatum	Lady-Fern	Athyrium filix-femina
Early Dog-violet	Viola reichenbachiana	Large Bitter-cress	Cardamine amara
Early-purple Orchid	Orchis mascula	Lemon-scented Fern	Oreopteris limbosperma
Elongated Sedge	Carex elongata	Lesser Hairy-brome	Bromopsis benekenii

English Name	Scientific Name	English Name	Scientific Name
Lesser Pond-sedge	Carex acutiformis	Spreading Bellflower	Campanula patula
Lesser Skullcap	Scutellaria minor	Spurge-laurel	Daphne laureola
Lily-of-the-valley	Convallaria majalis	Square-stemmed St John's-wort	Hypericum tetrapterum
Lords-and-Ladies	Arum maculatum		
Marsh Valerian	Valeriana dioica	Stinking Hellebore	Helleborus foetidus
Marsh Violet	Viola palustris	Stinking Iris	Iris foetidissima
May Lily	Maianthemum bifolium	Stone Bramble	Rubus saxatilis
Meadow Saffron	Colchicum autumnale	Sweet Violet	Viola odorata
Melancholy Thistle	Cirsium heterophyllum	Sweet Woodruff	Galium odoratum
Mezereon	Daphne mezereum	Thin-spiked Wood-sedge	Carex strigosa
Monk's-hood	Aconitum napellus	Three-nerved Sandwort	Moehringia trinervia
Moschatel	Adoxa moschatellina	Toothwort	Lathraea squamaria
Mountain Melick	Melica nutans	Townhall Clock	Adoxa moschatellina
Narrow Buckler-fern	Dryopteris carthusiana	Tunbridge Filmy-fern	Hymenophyllum tunbrigense
Narrow-leaved Bitter-cress	Cardamine impatiens	Tutsan	Hypericum androsaemum
Narrow-leaved Everlasting-pea	Lathyrus sylvestris	Upland Enchanter's-Nightshade	Circaea x intermedia
Narrow-leaved Helleborine	Cephalanthera longifolia	Violet Helleborine	Epipactis purpurata
Narrow-leaved Lungwort	Pulmonaria longifolia	Water Avens	Geum rivale
Narrow-lipped Helleborine	Epipactis leptochila	Water-purslane	Lythrum portula
Nettle-leaved Bellflower	Campanula trachelium	White Helleborine	Cephalanthera damasonium
Oak Fern	Gymnocarpium dryopteris	Wild Daffodil	Narcissus pseudonarcissus
Opposite-leaved Golden-saxifrage	Chrysosplenium oppositifolium	Wild Garlic/Ramsons	Allium ursinum
		Wild Strawberry	Fragaria vesca
Orpine	Sedum telephium	Wilson's Filmy-fern	Hymenophyllum wilsonii
Oxlip	Primula elatior	Wood Anemone	Anemone nemorosa
Pale Lady's-mantle	Alchemilla xanthochlora	Wood Barley	Hordelymus europaeus
Pale Sedge	Carex pallescens	Wood Club-rush	Scirpus sylvaticus
Pendulous Sedge	Carex pendula	Wood Crane's-bill	Geranium sylvaticum
Pignut	Conopodium majus	Wood Fescue	Festuca altissima
Primrose	Primula vulgaris	Wood Forget-me-not	Myosotis sylvatica
Purple Small-reed	Calamagrostis canescens	Wood Horsetail	Equisetum sylvaticum
Ramsons	Allium ursinum	Wood Meadow-grass	Poa nemoralis
Red Campion	Silene dioica	Wood Melick	Melica uniflora
Red Currant	Ribes rubrum	Wood Millet	Milium effusum
Remote Sedge	Carex remota	Wood Small-reed	Calamagrostis epigejos
Rough Horsetail	Equisetum hyemale	Wood Speedwell	Veronica montana
Sanicle	Sanicula europaea	Wood Spurge	Euphorbia amygdaloides
Saw-wort	Serratula tinctoria	Wood Stitchwort	Stellaria nemorum
Slender St John's-wort	Hypericum pulchrum	Wood Vetch	Vicia sylvatica
Small Cow-wheat	Melampyrum sylvaticum	Wood-sedge	Carex sylvatica
Small Teasel	Dipsacus pilosus	Wood-sorrel	Oxalis acetosella
Smooth-stalked Sedge	Carex laevigata	Yellow Archangel	Lamiastrum galeobdolon
Snowdrop	Galanthus nivalis	Yellow Bird's-nest	Hypopitys monotropa
Soft Shield-fern	Polystichum setiferum	Yellow Loosestrife	Lysimachia vulgaris
Soft-leaved Sedge	Carex montana	Yellow Pimpernel	Lysimachia nemorum
Solomon's-seal	Polygonatum multiflorum	Yellow Star-of-Bethlehem	Gagea lutea
Southern Wood-rush	Luzula forsteri		

Ia: Ordered by English Names – Generalists

English Name	Scientific Name	English Name	Scientific Name
Alpine Enchanter's-nightshade	Circaea alpina	Creeping Cinquefoil	Potentilla reptans
		Creeping Lady's-tresses	Goodyera repens
Annual Meadow-grass	Poa annua	Crested Cow-wheat	Melampyrum cristatum
Asarabacca	Asarum europaeum	Cuckooflower	Cardamine pratensis
Baneberry	Actaea spicata	Cyperus Sedge	Carex pseudocyperus
Bath Asparagus	Ornithogalum pyrenaicum	Dandelion	Taraxacum officinale agg.
Bee Orchid	Ophrys apifera	Dark-red Helleborine	Epipactis atrorubens
Bithynian Vetch	Vicia bithynica	Deadly Nightshade	Atropa belladonna
Bittersweet	Solanum dulcamara	Devil's-bit Scabious	Succisa pratensis
Black Bent	Agrostis gigantea	Dog-rose	Rosa canina
Black Spleenwort	Asplenium adiantum-nigrum	Enchanter's-nightshade	Circaea lutetiana
Bog Stitchwort	Stellaria alsine	False Oat-grass	Arrhenatherum elatius
Bog-myrtle	Myrica gale	Field Forget-me-not	Myosotis arvensis
Bracken	Pteridium aquilinum	Field Pansy	Viola arvensis
Bramble/Blackberry	Rubus fruticosus	Foxglove	Digitalis purpurea
Brittle Bladder-fern	Cystopteris fragilis	Garlic Mustard	Alliaria petiolata
Broad Buckler-fern	Dryopteris dilatata	Germander Speedwell	Veronica chamaedrys
Broad-leaved Dock	Rumex obtusifolius	Gooseberry	Ribes uva-crispa
Broad-leaved Meadow-grass	Poa chaixii	Goosegrass/Cleavers	Galium aparine
		Gorse	Ulex europaeus
Broadleaved Willowherb	Epilobium montanum	Goutweed/Ground-elder	Aegopodium podagraria
Broom	Cytisus scoparius	Great Willowherb	Epilobium hirsutum
Brown Bent	Agrostis vinealis	Greater Burdock	Arctium lappa
Bugle	Ajuga reptans	Greater Pond Sedge	Carex riparia
Butterbur	Petasites hybridus	Green Figwort	Scrophularia umbrosa
Caper Spurge	Euphorbia lathyris	Green Spleenwort	Asplenium viride
Chickweed-wintergreen	Trientalis europaea	Green-ribbed Sedge	Carex binervis
Clustered Dock	Rumex conglomeratus	Ground-elder	Aegopodium podagraria
Cock's-foot	Dactylis glomerata	Ground-ivy	Glechoma hederacea
Common Bent	Agrostis capillaris	Gypsywort	Lycopus europaeus
Common Chickweed	Stellaria media	Hair Sedge	Carex capillaris
Common Hemp-nettle	Galeopsis tetrahit	Hairy Sedge	Carex hirta
Common Marsh-bedstraw	Galium palustre	Hairy Violet	Viola hirta
Common Nettle	Urtica dioica	Harebell (Bluebell in Scotland)	Campanula rotundifolia
Common Sorrel	Rumex acetosa		
Common Spotted-orchid	Dactylorhiza fuchsii	Heath Bedstraw	Galium saxatile
Common St John's-wort	Hypericum perforatum	Heath Ragwort	Senecio sylvaticus
Compact Rush	Juncus conglomeratus	Heath Speedwell	Veronica officinalis
Copse-bindweed	Fallopia dumetorum	Heath Wood-rush	Luzula multiflora
Coralroot Orchid	Corallorhiza trifida	Heather	Calluna vulgaris
Corn Mint	Mentha arvensis	Hedge Bindweed	Calystegia sepium
Cow Parsley	Anthriscus sylvestris	Hedge Garlic	Alliaria petiolata
Cowberry	Vaccinium vitis-idaea	Hemlock	Conium maculatum
Cowslip	Primula veris	Hemp-agrimony	Eupatorium cannabinum
Creeping Bent	Agrostis stolonifera	Hogweed	Heracleum sphondylium
Creeping Buttercup	Ranunculus repens	Imperforate St John's-wort	Hypericum maculatum

English Name	Scientific Name
Intermediate Polypody	Polypodium interjectum
Intermediate Wintergreen	Pyrola media
Italian Lords-and-Ladies	Arum italicum
Ivy	Hedera helix
Ivy-leaved Speedwell	Veronica hederifolia
Lady's Smock/ Cuckooflower	Cardamine pratensis
Lesser Burdock	Arctium minus
Lesser Butterfly-orchid	Platanthera bifolia
Lesser Celandine	Ficaria verna
Lesser Meadow-rue	Thalictrum minus
Lesser Periwinkle	Vinca minor
Lesser Spearwort	Ranunculus flammula
Lesser Stitchwort	Stellaria graminea
Lesser Tussock-sedge	Carex diandra
Lesser Twayblade	Neottia cordata
Limestone Fern	Gymnocarpium robertianum
Maidenhair Spleenwort	Asplenium trichomanes
Male-fern	Dryopteris filix-mas
Marsh Fern	Thelypteris palustris
Marsh Hawk's-beard	Crepis paludosa
Marsh Horsetail	Equisetum palustre
Marsh Thistle	Cirsium palustre
Marsh Woundwort	Stachys palustris
Marsh-marigold	Caltha palustris
Martagon Lily	Lilium martagon
Meadowsweet	Filipendula ulmaria
Mountain Currant	Ribes alpinum
Nipplewort	Lapsana communis
Old-man's Beard/ Traveller's-joy	Clematis vitalba
One-flowered Wintergreen	Moneses uniflora
Pale St John's-wort	Hypericum montanum
Pale Willowherb	Epilobium roseum
Pink Purslane	Claytonia sibirica
Ploughman's-spikenard	Inula conyzae
Purple Moor-grass	Molinia caerulea
Purple-loosestrife	Lythrum salicaria
Ragged-Robin	Silene flos-cuculi
Raspberry	Rubus idaeus
Red Fescue	Festuca rubra
Rock Stonecrop	Sedum forsterianum
Rosebay Willowherb	Chamerion angustifolium
Rough Meadow-grass	Poa trivialis
Round-leaved Wintergreen	Pyrola rotundifolia
Royal Fern	Osmunda regalis
Selfheal	Prunella vulgaris

English Name	Scientific Name
Serrated Wintergreen	Orthilia secunda
Sharp-flowered Rush	Juncus acutiflorus
Sheep's Sorrel	Rumex acetosella
Sheep's-Fescue	Festuca ovina
Sherard's Downy-rose	Rosa sherardii
Shining Crane's-bill	Geranium lucidum
Short-fruited Willowherb	Epilobium obscurum
Short-styled Field-rose	Rosa stylosa
Silverweed	Potentilla anserina
Small-flowered Sweet-briar	Rosa micrantha
Smooth Lady's-mantle	Alchemilla glabra
Soapwort	Saponaria officinalis
Soft Downy-rose	Rosa mollis
Soft Rush	Juncus effusus
Southern Polypody	Polypodium australe
Spear Thistle	Cirsium vulgare
Square-stalked Willowherb	Epilobium tetragonum
Suffolk Lungwort	Pulmonaria obscura
Sweet Vernal-grass	Anthoxanthum odoratum
Sweet-briar	Rosa rubiginosa
Tormentil	Potentilla erecta
Touch-me-not Balsam	Impatiens noli-tangere
Trailing St John's-wort	Hypericum humifusum
Trailing Tormentil	Potentilla anglica
Traveller's-joy	Clematis vitalba
Tufted Hair-grass	Deschampsia cespitosa
Twinflower	Linnaea borealis
Upright Hedge Parsley	Torilis japonica
Wall Lettuce	Mycelis muralis
Water Chickweed	Myosoton aquaticum
Water Figwort	Scrophularia auriculata
Water Mint	Mentha aquatica
Wavy Bitter-cress	Cardamine flexuosa
Wavy Hair-grass	Deschampsia flexuosa
Welsh Poppy	Meconopsis cambrica
Welted Thistle	Carduus crispus
White Bryony	Bryonia dioica
White Dead-nettle	Lamium album
White Wood-rush	Luzula luzuloides
Wild Angelica	Angelica sylvestris
Wild Hop	Humulus lupulus
Wild Madder	Rubia peregrina
Wood Avens	Geum urbanum
Wood Bitter-Vetch	Vicia orobus
Wood Dock	Rumex sanguineus
Wood Sage	Teucrium scorodonia
Yellow Iris	Iris pseudacorus
Yorkshire-fog	Holcus lanatus

Appendix 1: A woodland-plant list

1b: Ordered by Scientific Names – Specialists

Scientific Name	English Name
Aconitum napellus	Monk's-hood
Adoxa moschatellina	Moschatel/Townhall Clock
Alchemilla filicaulis	Hairy Lady's-mantle
Alchemilla xanthochlora	Pale Lady's-mantle
Allium ursinum	Wild Garlic/Ramsons
Anemone nemorosa	Wood Anemone
Aquilegia vulgaris	Columbine
Arum maculatum	Lords-and-Ladies/Cuckoo-pint
Asplenium scolopendrium	Hart's-tongue
Athyrium filix-femina	Lady-Fern
Betonica officinalis	Betony
Blechnum spicant	Hard-Fern
Brachypodium sylvaticum	False Brome
Bromopsis benekenii	Lesser Hairy-brome
Bromopsis ramosa	Hairy-brome
Calamagrostis canescens	Purple Small-reed
Calamagrostis epigejos	Wood Small-reed
Campanula latifolia	Giant Bellflower
Campanula patula	Spreading Bellflower
Campanula trachelium	Nettle-leaved Bellflower
Cardamine amara	Large Bitter-cress
Cardamine bulbifera	Coralroot Bitter-cress
Cardamine impatiens	Narrow-leaved Bitter-cress
Carex acutiformis	Lesser Pond-sedge
Carex digitata	Fingered Sedge
Carex elongata	Elongated Sedge
Carex laevigata	Smooth-stalked Sedge
Carex montana	Soft-leaved Sedge
Carex pallescens	Pale Sedge
Carex paniculata	Greater Tussock-sedge
Carex pendula	Pendulous Sedge
Carex remota	Remote Sedge
Carex strigosa	Thin-spiked Wood-sedge
Carex sylvatica	Wood-sedge
Cephalanthera damasonium	White Helleborine
Cephalanthera longifolia	Narrow-leaved Helleborine
Ceratocapnos claviculata	Climbing Corydalis
Chrysosplenium alternifolium	Alternate-leaved Golden-saxifrage
Chrysosplenium oppositifolium	Opposite-leaved Golden-saxifrage

Scientific Name	English Name
Circaea x intermedia	Upland Enchanter's-nightshade
Cirsium heterophyllum	Melancholy Thistle
Colchicum autumnale	Meadow Saffron
Conopodium majus	Pignut
Convallaria majalis	Lily-of-the-valley
Daphne laureola	Spurge-laurel
Daphne mezereum	Mezereon
Dipsacus pilosus	Small Teasel
Dryopteris aemula	Hay-scented Buckler-fern
Dryopteris affinis	Golden-scaled Male-fern
Dryopteris carthusiana	Narrow Buckler-fern
Elymus caninus	Bearded Couch
Epipactis helleborine	Broad-leaved Helleborine
Epipactis leptochila	Narrow-lipped Helleborine
Epipactis phyllanthes	Green-flowered Helleborine
Epipactis purpurata	Violet Helleborine
Equisetum hyemale	Rough Horsetail
Equisetum sylvaticum	Wood Horsetail
Equisetum telmateia	Great Horsetail
Euphorbia amygdaloides	Wood Spurge
Festuca altissima	Wood Fescue
Fragaria vesca	Wild Strawberry
Gagea lutea	Yellow Star-of-Bethlehem
Galanthus nivalis	Snowdrop
Galium odoratum	Sweet Woodruff
Geranium robertianum	Herb-Robert
Geranium sanguineum	Bloody Crane's-bill
Geranium sylvaticum	Wood Crane's-bill
Geum rivale	Water Avens
Gnaphalium sylvaticum	Heath Cudweed
Gymnocarpium dryopteris	Oak Fern
Helleborus foetidus	Stinking Hellebore
Helleborus viridis	Green Hellebore
Holcus mollis	Creeping Soft-grass
Hordelymus europaeus	Wood Barley
Hyacinthoides non-scripta	Bluebell
Hymenophyllum tunbrigense	Tunbridge Filmy-fern
Hymenophyllum wilsonii	Wilson's Filmy-fern
Hypericum androsaemum	Tutsan
Hypericum hirsutum	Hairy St John's-wort
Hypericum pulchrum	Slender St John's-wort

Scientific Name	English Name
Hypericum tetrapterum	Square-Stemmed St John's-wort
Hypopitys monotropa	Yellow Bird's-nest
Iris foetidissima	Stinking Iris
Lamiastrum galeobdolon	Yellow Archangel
Lathraea squamaria	Toothwort
Lathyrus linifolius	Bitter-vetch
Lathyrus sylvestris	Narrow-leaved Everlasting-pea
Lithospermum officinale	Common Gromwell
Lonicera periclymenum	Honeysuckle
Luzula forsteri	Southern Wood-rush
Luzula pilosa	Hairy Wood-rush
Luzula sylvatica	Great Woodrush
Lysimachia nemorum	Yellow Pimpernel
Lysimachia vulgaris	Yellow Loosestrife
Lythrum portula	Water-purslane
Maianthemum bifolium	May Lily
Melampyrum pratense	Common Cow-wheat
Melampyrum sylvaticum	Small Cow-wheat
Melica nutans	Mountain Melick
Melica uniflora	Wood Melick
Melittis melissophyllum	Bastard Balm
Mercurialis perennis	Dog's Mercury
Milium effusum	Wood Millet
Moehringia trinervia	Three-nerved Sandwort
Myosotis sylvatica	Wood Forget-me-not
Narcissus pseudonarcissus	Wild Daffodil
Neottia nidus-avis	Birds-nest Orchid
Neottia ovata	Common Twayblade
Ophioglossum vulgatum	Adder's-tongue
Ophrys insectifera	Fly Orchid
Orchis mascula	Early-purple Orchid
Orchis purpurea	Lady Orchid
Oreopteris limbosperma	Lemon-scented Fern
Orobanche hederae	Ivy Broomrape
Oxalis acetosella	Wood-sorrel
Paris quadrifolia	Herb-Paris
Phegopteris connectilis	Beech Fern
Pimpinella major	Greater Burnet-saxifrage
Platanthera chlorantha	Greater Butterfly -orchid
Poa nemoralis	Wood Meadow-grass
Polygonatum multiflorum	Solomon's-seal
Polygonatum odoratum	Angular Solomon's-seal

Scientific Name	English Name
Polypodium vulgare	Common Polypody
Polystichum aculeatum	Hard Shield-fern
Polystichum setiferum	Soft Shield-fern
Potentilla sterilis	Barren Strawberry
Primula elatior	Oxlip
Primula vulgaris	Primrose
Pulmonaria longifolia	Narrow-leaved Lungwort
Pyrola minor	Common Wintergreen
Radiola linoides	Allseed
Ranunculus auricomus	Goldilocks Buttercup
Ribes nigrum	Black Currant
Ribes rubrum	Red Currant
Ribes spicatum	Downy Currant
Rosa arvensis	Field-rose
Rubus caesius	Dewberry
Rubus saxatilis	Stone Bramble
Ruscus aculeatus	Butcher's-Broom
Sanicula europaea	Sanicle
Schedonorus giganteus	Giant Fescue
Scirpus sylvaticus	Wood Club-rush
Scrophularia nodosa	Common Figwort
Scutellaria minor	Lesser Skullcap
Sedum telephium	Orpine
Serratula tinctoria	Saw-wort
Sibthorpia europaea	Cornish Moneywort
Silene dioica	Red Campion
Solidago virgaurea	Goldenrod
Stachys sylvatica	Hedge Woundwort
Stellaria holostea	Greater Stitchwort
Stellaria neglecta	Greater Chickweed
Stellaria nemorum	Wood Stitchwort
Tamus communis	Black Bryony
Trollius europaeus	Globeflower
Vaccinium myrtillus	Bilberry/Blaeberry
Valeriana dioica	Marsh Valerian
Valeriana officinalis	Common Valerian
Veronica montana	Wood Speedwell
Vicia sepium	Bush Vetch
Vicia sylvatica	Wood Vetch
Viola odorata	Sweet Violet
Viola palustris	Marsh Violet
Viola reichenbachiana	Early Dog-violet
Viola riviniana	Common Dog-violet
Wahlenbergia hederacea	Ivy-leaved Bellflower

1b: Ordered by Scientific Names – Generalists

Scientific Name	English Name	Scientific Name	English Name
Actaea spicata	Baneberry	Clematis vitalba	Old-man's Beard/ Traveller's-joy
Aegopodium podagraria	Goutweed/Ground-elder	Conium maculatum	Hemlock
Agrostis capillaris	Common Bent	Corallorhiza trifida	Coralroot Orchid
Agrostis gigantea	Black Bent	Crepis paludosa	Marsh Hawk's-beard
Agrostis stolonifera	Creeping Bent	Cystopteris fragilis	Brittle Bladder-fern
Agrostis vinealis	Brown Bent	Cytisus scoparius	Broom
Ajuga reptans	Bugle	Dactylis glomerata	Cock's-foot
Alchemilla glabra	Smooth Lady's-mantle	Dactylorhiza fuchsii	Common Spotted-orchid
Alliaria petiolata	Garlic Mustard/Hedge Garlic	Deschampsia cespitosa	Tufted Hair-grass
Angelica sylvestris	Wild Angelica	Deschampsia flexuosa	Wavy Hair-grass
Anthoxanthum odoratum	Sweet Vernal-grass	Digitalis purpurea	Foxglove
Anthriscus sylvestris	Cow Parsley	Dryopteris dilatata	Broad Buckler-fern
Arctium lappa	Greater Burdock	Dryopteris filix-mas	Male-fern
Arctium minus	Lesser Burdock	Epilobium hirsutum	Great Willowherb
Arrhenatherum elatius	False Oat-grass	Epilobium montanum	Broadleaved Willowherb
Arum italicum	Italian Lords-and-Ladies	Epilobium obscurum	Short-fruited Willowherb
Asarum europaeum	Asarabacca	Epilobium roseum	Pale Willowherb
Asplenium adiantum-nigrum	Black Spleenwort	Epilobium tetragonum	Square-stalked Willowherb
Asplenium trichomanes	Maidenhair Spleenwort	Epipactis atrorubens	Dark-red Helleborine
Asplenium viride	Green Spleenwort	Equisetum palustre	Marsh Horsetail
Atropa belladonna	Deadly Nightshade	Eupatorium cannabinum	Hemp-agrimony
Bryonia dioica	White Bryony	Euphorbia lathyris	Caper Spurge
Calluna vulgaris	Heather	Fallopia dumetorum	Copse-bindweed
Caltha palustris	Marsh-marigold	Festuca ovina	Sheep's-Fescue
Calystegia sepium	Hedge Bindweed	Festuca rubra	Red Fescue
Campanula rotundifolia	Harebell (Bluebell in Scotland)	Ficaria verna	Lesser Celandine
		Filipendula ulmaria	Meadowsweet
Cardamine flexuosa	Wavy Bitter-cress	Galeopsis tetrahit	Common Hemp-nettle
Cardamine pratensis	Lady's Smock/ Cuckooflower	Galium aparine	Goosegrass/Cleavers
		Galium palustre	Common Marsh-bedstraw
Carduus crispus	Welted Thistle	Galium saxatile	Heath Bedstraw
Carex binervis	Green-ribbed Sedge	Geranium lucidum	Shining Crane's-bill
Carex capillaris	Hair Sedge	Geum urbanum	Wood Avens
Carex diandra	Lesser Tussock-sedge	Glechoma hederacea	Ground-ivy
Carex hirta	Hairy Sedge	Goodyera repens	Creeping Lady's-tresses
Carex pseudocyperus	Cyperus Sedge	Gymnocarpium robertianum	Limestone Fern
Carex riparia	Greater Pond Sedge	Hedera helix	Ivy
Chamerion angustifolium	Rosebay Willowherb	Heracleum sphondylium	Hogweed
Circaea alpina	Alpine Enchanter's-nightshade	Holcus lanatus	Yorkshire-fog
		Humulus lupulus	Wild Hop
Circaea lutetiana	Enchanter's-nightshade	Hypericum humifusum	Trailing St John's-wort
Cirsium palustre	Marsh Thistle	Hypericum maculatum	Imperforate St John's-wort
Cirsium vulgare	Spear Thistle	Hypericum montanum	Pale St John's-wort
Claytonia sibirica	Pink Purslane	Hypericum perforatum	Common St John's-wort
		Impatiens noli-tangere	Touch-me-not Balsam

Scientific Name	English Name
Inula conyzae	Ploughman's-spikenard
Iris pseudacorus	Yellow Iris
Juncus acutiflorus	Sharp-flowered Rush
Juncus conglomeratus	Compact Rush
Juncus effusus	Soft Rush
Lamium album	White Dead-nettle
Lapsana communis	Nipplewort
Lilium martagon	Martagon Lily
Linnaea borealis	Twinflower
Luzula luzuloides	White Wood-rush
Luzula multiflora	Heath Wood-rush
Lycopus europaeus	Gypsywort
Lythrum salicaria	Purple-loosestrife
Meconopsis cambrica	Welsh Poppy
Melampyrum cristatum	Crested Cow-wheat
Mentha aquatica	Water Mint
Mentha arvensis	Corn Mint
Molinia caerulea	Purple Moor-grass
Moneses uniflora	One-flowered Wintergreen
Mycelis muralis	Wall Lettuce
Myosotis arvensis	Field Forget-me-not
Myosoton aquaticum	Water Chickweed
Myrica gale	Bog-myrtle
Neottia cordata	Lesser Twayblade
Ophrys apifera	Bee Orchid
Ornithogalum pyrenaicum	Bath Asparagus/Spiked Star-of-Bethlehem
Orthilia secunda	Serrated Wintergreen
Osmunda regalis	Royal Fern
Petasites hybridus	Butterbur
Platanthera bifolia	Lesser Butterfly-orchid
Poa annua	Annual Meadow-grass
Poa chaixii	Broad-leaved Meadow-grass
Poa trivialis	Rough Meadow-grass
Polypodium australe	Southern Polypody
Polypodium interjectum	Intermediate Polypody
Potentilla anglica	Trailing Tormentil
Potentilla anserina	Silverweed
Potentilla erecta	Tormentil
Potentilla reptans	Creeping Cinquefoil
Primula veris	Cowslip
Prunella vulgaris	Selfheal
Pteridium aquilinum	Bracken
Pulmonaria obscura	Suffolk Lungwort
Pyrola media	Intermediate Wintergreen
Pyrola rotundifolia	Round-leaved Wintergreen

Scientific Name	English Name
Ranunculus flammula	Lesser Spearwort
Ranunculus repens	Creeping Buttercup
Ribes alpinum	Mountain Currant
Ribes uva-crispa	Gooseberry
Rosa canina	Dog-rose
Rosa micrantha	Small-flowered Sweet-briar
Rosa mollis	Soft Downy-rose
Rosa rubiginosa	Sweet-briar
Rosa sherardii	Sherard's Downy-rose
Rosa stylosa	Short-styled Field-rose
Rubia peregrina	Wild Madder
Rubus fruticosus	Bramble or Blackberry
Rubus idaeus	Raspberry
Rumex acetosa	Common Sorrel
Rumex acetosella	Sheep's Sorrel
Rumex conglomeratus	Clustered Dock
Rumex obtusifolius	Broad-leaved Dock
Rumex sanguineus	Wood Dock
Saponaria officinalis	Soapwort
Scrophularia auriculata	Water Figwort
Scrophularia umbrosa	Green Figwort
Sedum forsterianum	Rock Stonecrop
Senecio sylvaticus	Heath Ragwort
Silene flos-cuculi	Ragged-Robin
Solanum dulcamara	Bittersweet
Stachys palustris	Marsh Woundwort
Stellaria alsine	Bog Stitchwort
Stellaria graminea	Lesser Stitchwort
Stellaria media	Common Chickweed
Succisa pratensis	Devil's-bit Scabious
Taraxacum officinale agg.	Dandelion
Teucrium scorodonia	Wood Sage
Thalictrum minus	Lesser Meadow-rue
Thelypteris palustris	Marsh Fern
Torilis japonica	Upright Hedge Parsley
Trientalis europaea	Chickweed-wintergreen
Ulex europaeus	Gorse
Urtica dioica	Common Nettle
Vaccinium vitis-idaea	Cowberry
Veronica chamaedrys	Germander Speedwell
Veronica hederifolia	Ivy-leaved Speedwell
Veronica officinalis	Heath Speedwell
Vicia bithynica	Bithynian Vetch
Vicia orobus	Wood Bitter-Vetch
Vinca minor	Lesser Periwinkle
Viola arvensis	Field Pansy
Viola hirta	Hairy Violet

Appendix 2: Other plants mentioned in the text

2a: Ordered by English Names

Rare woodland plants	
Ghost Orchid	*Epipogium aphyllum*
Irish Spurge	*Euphorbia hyberna*
Lady's-slipper Orchid	*Cypripedium calceolus*
Red Helleborine	*Cephalanthera rubra*
Spiked Rampion	*Phyteuma spicatum*
Starved Wood-sedge	*Carex depauperata*
Tintern Spurge	*Euphorbia serrulata*
Whorled Solomon's-seal	*Polygonatum verticillatum*
Wild Gladiolus	*Gladiolus illyricus*
Wood Calamint	*Clinopodium menthifolium*

Invasive ground flora	
Himalayan Balsam	*Impatiens glandulifera*
Honey Garlic	*Nectaroscordum siculum*
Hottentot fig	*Carpobrotus edulis*
Japanese Knotweed	*Fallopia japonica*
Slender Rush	*Juncus tenuis*
Small Balsam	*Impatiens parviflora*
Skunk-cabbage	*Lysichiton americanus*
Spanish Bluebell	*Hyacinthoides hispanica*

Plants of other habitats	
Alpine bistort	*Polygonum viviparum*
Alpine Lady's Mantle	*Alchemilla alpina*
Alpine Meadow-rue	*Thalictrum alpinum*
Annual Mercury	*Mercurialis annua*
Blue Moor-grass	*Sesleria caerulea*
Borage	*Borago officinalis*
Bottle Sedge	*Carex rostrata*
Bristly Oxtongue	*Picris echioides*
Candytuft	*Iberis amara*
Common Century	*Centaurium erythraea*
Common Reed	*Phragmites australis*
Creeping Thistle	*Cirsium arvense*
Cross-leaved Heath	*Erica tetralix*
Fairy Flax	*Linum catharticum*
Field Bindweed	*Convolvulus arvensis*
Field Speedwell	*Veronica arvensis*
Fleabane	*Pulicaria dysenterica*
Flote Grass	*Glyceria* spp.
Hare's-tail Cotton-grass	*Eriophorum vaginatum*
Hemlock Water-dropwort	*Oenanthe crocata*
Knapweed	*Centaurea nigra*
Marsh Lousewort	*Pedicularis palustris*
Meadow Buttercup	*Ranunculus acris*
Mistletoe	*Viscum album*
Mouse-eared Chickweed	*Cerastium fontanum*
Northern Buckler-fern	*Dryopteris expansa*
Parsley Fern	*Cryptogramma crispa*
Prickly Sedge	*Carex muricata*
Pyramidal Orchid	*Anacamptis pyramidalis*
Ragwort	*Senecio jacobaea*
Redshanks	*Polygonum persicaria*
Reed Canary-grass	*Phalaris arundinacea*
Viper's-grass	*Scorzonera humilis*
Water-pepper	*Polygonum hydropiper*
Water-starwort	*Callitriche stagnalis*
Wild Mignonette	*Reseda lutea*
Wild Teasel	*Dipsacus fullonum*

Native/naturalised trees and shrubs	
Ash	Fraxinus excelsior
Aspen	Populus tremula
Bay Willow	Salix pentandra
Beech	Fagus sylvatica
Black Poplar	Populus nigra
Blackthorn	Prunus spinosa
Box	Buxus sempervirens
Common Alder	Alnus glutinosa
Common Hawthorn	Crataegus monogyna
Crab apple	Malus sylvestris
Dogwood	Cornus sanguineus
Elder	Sambucus nigra
Elms	Ulmus spp.
Field Maple	Acer campestre
Goat Willow	Salix caprea
Grey Sallow	Salix cinerea
Hazel	Corylus avellana
Holly	Ilex aquifolium
Hornbeam	Carpinus betulus
Juniper	Juniperus communis
Privet	Ligustrum vulgare
Rowan	Sorbus aucuparia
Scots Pine	Pinus sylvestris
Sessile Oak	Quercus petraea
Silver Birch/Downy Birch	Betula pendula/pubescens
Small-leaved Lime	Tilia cordata
Spindle	Euonymus europaeus
Sweet Chestnut	Castanea sativa
Sycamore	Acer pseudoplatanus
Wayfaring Tree	Viburnum lantana
Whitebeam	Sorbus aria
Wild-service Tree	Sorbus torminalis
Yew	Taxus baccata

Commercial forestry species	
Corsican Pine	Pinus nigra
Douglas Fir	Pseudotsuga menziesii
Larches	Larix spp.
Lawson's Cypress	Chamaecyparis lawsonii
Lodgepole Pine	Pinus contorta
Norway Spruce	Picea abies
Silver Fir	Abies alba
Sitka Spruce	Picea sitchensis

Appendix 2: Other plants mentioned in the text

2b: Ordered by Scientific Names

Rare woodland plants	
Carex depauperata	Starved Wood-sedge
Cephalanthera rubra	Red Helleborine
Clinopodium menthifolium	Wood Calamint
Cypripedium calceolus	Lady's-slipper Orchid
Epipogium aphyllum	Ghost Orchid
Euphorbia hyberna	Irish Spurge
Euphorbia serrulata	Tintern Spurge
Gladiolus illyricus	Wild Gladiolus
Phyteuma spicatum	Spiked Rampion
Polygonatum verticillatum	Whorled Solomon's-seal

Invasive ground flora	
Carpobrotus edulis	Hottentot fig
Fallopia japonica	Japanese Knotweed
Hyacinthoides hispanica	Spanish Bluebell
Impatiens glandulifera	Himalayan Balsam
Impatiens parviflora	Small Balsam
Juncus tenuis	Slender Rush
Lysichiton americanus	Skunk-cabbage
Nectaroscordum siculum	Honey Garlic

Plants of other habitats	
Alchemilla alpina	Alpine Lady's Mantle
Anacamptis pyramidalis	Pyramidal Orchid
Borago officinalis	Borage
Callitriche stagnalis	Water-starwort
Carex muricata	Prickly Sedge
Carex rostrata	Bottle Sedge
Centaurea nigra	Knapweed
Centaurium erythraea	Common Century
Cerastium fontanum	Mouse-eared Chickweed
Cirsium arvense	Creeping Thistle
Convolvulus arvensis	Field Bindweed
Cryptogramma crispa	Parsley Fern
Dipsacus fullonum	Wild Teasel
Dryopteris expansa	Northern Buckler-fern
Erica tetralix	Cross-leaved Heath
Eriophorum vaginatum	Hare's-tail Cotton-grass
Galium boreale	Northern bedstraw
Glyceria spp.	Flote Grass
Iberis amara	Candytuft
Linum catharticum	Fairy Flax
Mercurialis annua	Annual Mercury
Oenanthe crocata	Hemlock Water-dropwort
Pedicularis palustris	Marsh Lousewort
Phalaris arundinacea	Reed Canary-grass
Phragmites australis	Common Reed
Polygonum hydropiper	Water-pepper
Polygonum persicaria	Redshanks
Polygonum viviparum	Alpine bistort
Pulicaria dysenterica	Fleabane
Ranunculus acris	Meadow Buttercup
Reseda lutea	Wild Mignonette
Scorzonera humilis	Viper's-grass
Senecio jacobaea	Ragwort
Sesleria caerulea	Blue Moor-grass
Thalictrum alpinum	Alpine Meadow-rue
Veronica arvensis	Field Speedwell
Viscum album	Mistletoe

Native/naturalised trees and shrubs	
Acer campestre	Field Maple
Acer pseudoplatanus	Sycamore
Alnus glutinosa	Common Alder
Betula pendula/pubescens	Silver Birch/Downy Birch
Buxus sempervirens	Box
Carpinus betulus	Hornbeam
Castanea sativa	Sweet Chestnut
Cornus sanguineus	Dogwood
Corylus avellana	Hazel
Crataegus monogyna	Common Hawthorn
Euonymus europaeus	Spindle
Fagus sylvatica	Beech
Fraxinus excelsior	Ash
Ilex aquifolium	Holly
Picris echioides	Bristly Oxtongue
Juniperus communis	Juniper
Ligustrum vulgare	Privet
Malus sylvestris	Crab apple
Pinus sylvestris	Scots Pine
Populus nigra	Black Poplar
Populus tremula	Aspen
Prunus spinosa	Blackthorn
Quercus petraea	Sessile Oak
Salix caprea	Goat Willow
Salix cinerea	Grey Sallow
Salix pentandra	Bay Willow
Sambucus nigra	Elder
Sorbus aria	Whitebeam
Sorbus aucuparia	Rowan
Sorbus torminalis	Wild-service Tree
Taxus baccata	Yew
Tilia cordata	Small-leaved Lime
Ulmus spp.	Elms
Viburnum lantana	Wayfaring Tree

Commercial forestry species	
Abies alba	Silver Fir
Chamaecyparis lawsonii	Lawson's Cypress
Larix spp.	Larches
Picea abies	Norway Spruce
Picea sitchensis	Sitka Spruce
Pinus contorta	Lodgepole Pine
Pinus nigra	Corsican Pine
Pseudotsuga menziesii	Douglas Fir

References

Abeywickrama, B.S. 1949. A study of the variation in the field layer vegetation of two Cambridgeshire woods. PhD thesis. Cambridge: University of Cambridge.

Adamson, R.S. 1912. "An Ecological Study of a Cambridgeshire Woodland." *Journal of the Linnean Society of London, Botany* 40: 339–387.

Allen, D.E. 1986. *The Botanists*. Winchester: St Paul's Bibliographies.

Allen, D.E. 1987. "Changing attitudes to nature conservation: the botanical perspective." *Biological Journal of the Linnean Society* 32: 203–212.

Allen, J.L. 1992. "Trees and their Response to Wind: Mid Flandrian Strong Winds, Severn Estuary and Inner Bristol Channel, Southwest Britain." *Philosophical Transactions: Biological Sciences* 338: 335–364.

Allen, M.J. 2017. "The southern English chalklands: molluscan evidence for the nature of the post-glacial woodland cover." In: Allen, M. J. (ed.) *Molluscs in Archaeology: Methods, Approaches and Applications*, edited by M.J. Allen: 144–164. Oxford: Oxbow books.

Anderson, M. 1979. "The development of plant habitats under exotic forest crops." In *Ecology and design in amenity land management*, edited by S. Wright: 87–108. Wye: Recreation Ecology Research Group.

Anon. 1864. "Notes on the locality, etc of two plants recently added to the British flora." *The Botanists' Chronicle* 12: 89–90.

Anon. 1864. "On the impending eradication of rare British plants." *The Botanists' Chronicle* 15: 33–34.

Anon. 1865. "The following rare British plants have been reported during the year 1864." *The Botanists' Chronicle* 15: 116–117.

Ash, J.E., and J.P. Barkham. 1976. "Changes and variability in the field layer of a coppiced woodland in Norfolk, England." *Journal of Ecology* 64: 697–712.

Ashmole, M., and P. Ashmole. 2009. *The Carrifran Wildwood story: ecological restoration from the grass roots*. Ancrum: Borders Forest Trust.

Averis, A.M. 2002. Vegetation survey and assessment: Rassal SSSI & cSAC, June 2001. Inverness: Scottish Natural Heritage.

Averis, B. 2013. *Plants and habitats: an introduction to common plants and their habitats in Britain and Ireland*. Norwich: Swallowtail Print Ltd.

Barkham, J.P. 1980. "Population dynamics of the wild daffodil (*Narcissus pseudonarcissus*): ii. changes in number of shoots and flowers, and the effect of bulb depth on growth and reproduction." *Journal of Ecology* 68: 635–664.

Barnes, G., and T. Williamson. 2006. *Hedgerow history: ecology, history and landscape character*. Macclesfield: Windgather Press.

Barnes, G., and T. Willliamson. 2015. *Rethinking ancient woodland: the archaeology and history of woods in Norfolk.*, Hatfield: University of Hertfordshire Press.

Bazely, D.R., J.H. Myers, and K.B. Da Silva. 1991. "The response of numbers of bramble prickles to herbivory and depressed resource availability." *Oikos* 61: 327–336.

Beatty, S.W. 1984. "Influence of microtopography and canopy species on spatial patterns of forest understory plants." *Ecology* 65: 1406–1419.

Beebee, T. 2018. *Climate change and British wildlife*. London: British Wildlife Collection.

Beerling, D.J., and J.M. Perrins. 1993. "*Impatiens glandulifera* Royle (Impatiens Roylei Walp.)." *Journal of Ecology* 81: 367–382.

Beevor, H. 1925. "Norfolk woodlands from the evidence of contemporary chronicles." *Quarterly Journal of Forestry* 19: 87–110.

Bellairs, N. 1865. *Hardy Ferns: how I collected and cultivated them*. London: Smith, Elder & co.

Bentham, G., J.D. Hooker, and A.B. Rendle. 1930. *Handbook of the British flora: a description of the flowering plants and ferns indigenous to, or naturalised in, the British Isles: for the use of beginners and amateurs*, Ashford: Reeve.

Birks, H.J.B. 1982. "Mid-Flandrian forest history of Roudsea Wood National Nature Reserve, Cumbria." *New Phytologist* 90: 339–354.

Birks, H.J.B. 1989. "Holocene isochrone maps and patterns of tree-spreading in the British Isles." *Journal of Biogeography* 16: 503–540.

Björkman, E. 1960. "*Monotropa hypopitys* L – an epiparasite on tree roots." *Physiologia Plantarum* 13: 308–327.

Blackman, G.E. and A.J. Rutter. 1954. "*Endymion non-scriptus* (L.) Garcke." *Journal of Ecology* 42: 629–638.

Blakesley, D., and G.P. Buckley. 2010. *Woodland creation for wildlife and people in a changing climate: principles and practice*. Newbury: Pisces.

Bohlen, P. J., S. Scheu, C.M. Hale, *et al.* 2004. "Non-native invasive earthworms as agents of change in northern temperate forests." *Frontiers in Ecology and the Environment* 2: 427–435.

Bradshaw, R.H.W., and M. Lindbladh. 2005. "Regional spread and stand-scale establishment of *Fagus sylvatica* and *Picea abies* in Scandinavia." *Ecology* 86: 1679–1686.

Brenchley, W.E., and H. Adam. 1915. "Recolonisation of cultivated land allowed to revert to natural conditions." *Journal of Ecology* 3: 193–210.

Brown, A.H.F., and S.J. Warr. 1992. "The effects of changing management on seed banks in ancient coppices." In *Ecology and management of coppice woodlands*, edited by G.P. Buckley: 147–166. London: Chapman and Hall.

Brown, N.D., T. Curtis, and E.C. Adams. 2015. "Effects of clear-felling versus gradual removal of conifer trees on the survival of understorey plants during the restoration of ancient woodlands." *Forest Ecology and Management* 348: 15–22.

Brown, N.D., and R. Fisher. 2009. Trees outside woods. Grantham: Woodland Trust.

Brunet, J.G. 2007. "Plant colonization in heterogeneous landscapes: an 80-year perspective on restoration of broadleaved forest vegetation." *Journal of Applied Ecology* 44: 563–572.

Brunet, J.G., M. Diekmann, and U. Falkengren-Grerup. 1998. "Effects of nitrogen deposition on field layer vegetation in south Swedish oak forests." *Environmental Pollution* 102: 35–40.

Brunet, J.G., U. Falkengren-Grerup, and G. Tyler. 1996." Herb layer vegetation of south Swedish beech and oak forests – effects of management and soil acidity during one decade." *Forest Ecology and Management* 88: 259–272.

Brunet, J.G., and G. von Oheimb. 1998. "Migration of vascular plants to secondary woodlands in southern Sweden." *Journal of Ecology* 86: 429–438.

BSBI. 2017. BSBI Code of Conduct for picking, collecting, photographing and enjoying wild plants. https://bsbi. org/wp-content/uploads/dlm_uploads/Code-of-Conduct-v5-final.pdf (Accessed 16/8/2019).

Buckley, G.P. 1992. *Ecology and management of coppiced woodland*. London: Chapman and Hall.

Buckley, G.P., R. Howell, T.A. Watt, R. Ferris-Kaan, and M. Anderson. 1997. "Vegetation succession following ride edge management in lowland plantations and woods. I. The influence of site factors and management practices". *Biological Conservation* 82: 289–304.

Buckley, G.P., and J. Mills. 2015a. "Coppice silviculture: from the mesolithic to 21st century." In *Europe's changing woods and forests: from wildwood to managed landscapes*, edited by K.J. Kirby and C. Watkins: 77–92. Wallingford: CABI.

Buckley, G.P. and J. Mills. 2015b. "The flora and fauna of coppice woods: winners and losers of active management or neglect." In *Europe's changing woods and forests: from wildwood to managed landscapes*, edited by K.J. Kirby and C. Watkins: 129–139. Wallingford: CABI.

Buckley, G.P., D.R. Helliwell., S. Milne, and R. Howell. 2017. "Twenty-five years on – vegetation succession on a translocated ancient woodland soil at Biggins Wood, Kent, UK." *Forestry* 90: 561–572.

Buesching, C.J. Clarke, S. Ellwood, C. King, C. Newman, and D. Macdonald. 2010. "The mammals of Wytham woods." In *Wytham Woods: Oxford's Ecological Laboratory*, edited by P.S. Savill, C. Perrins, K.J. Kirby and N. Fisher: 173–196. Oxford: Oxford University Press.

Bunce, R.G.H. 1982. *A field key for classifying British woodland vegetation*. Cambridge: Institute of Terrestrial Ecology.

Burden, R., and P. Randerson. 1972. "Quantitative studies of the effects of human trampling on vegetation as an aid to the management of semi-natural areas." *Journal of Applied Ecology*: 439–457.

Carey, P.D. 2015. Impacts of climate change on terrestrial habitats and vegetation. Biodiversity Report Card Paper 5. https://nerc.ukri.org/research/partnerships/ride/lwec/report-cards/biodiversity-source05/ (Accessed 16/8/2019).

Castle, G.J. Latham, and R. Mileto. 2008. "Identifying Ancient Woodland in Wales – The role of the Ancient Woodland Inventory, historical maps and indicator species." *Contract Science Report No. 819*. Bangor: Countryside Council for Wales.

Cavers, P. B., M. Heagy, and R.F. Kokron. 1979. "The biology of Canadian weeds: 35. *Alliaria petiolata* (M. Bieb.) Cavara and Grande." *Canadian Journal of Plant Science* 59: 217–229.

Cavin, L., E.P. Mountford, G.F. Peterken, and A.S. Jump. 2013. "Extreme drought alters competitive dominance within and between tree species in a mixed forest stand." *Functional Ecology* 27: 1424–1435.

Chatters, C., and N. Sanderson. 1994. "Grazing lowland-pasture woods." *British Wildlife* 6: 78–88.

Chlumský, J., P. Koutecký, V. Jílková, and M. Štech. 2013. "Roles of species-preferential seed dispersal by ants and endozoochory in *Melampyrum* (Orobanchaceae)." *Journal of Plant Ecology* 6: 232–239.

Christy, M. 1897. "*Primula elatior* in Britain: its distribution, peculiarities, hybrids, and allies." *Journal of the Linnean Society of London, Botany* 33: 172–201.

Church, A.H. 1922. *Introduction to the Plant-life of the Oxford District*. Oxford: Oxford University Press.

Clapham, A.R., T.G. Tutin, and E.F. Warburg. 1962. *Flora of the British Isles (2nd edition)*. Cambridge: Cambridge University Press.

Clark, P. 2004. *The Dover Bronze Age boat*. Swindon: English Heritage.

Cloke, P., P. Milbourne, and C. Thomas. 1996. "From wasteland to wonderland: opencast mining, regeneration and the English National Forest." *Geoforum* 27: 159–174.

Coley, M. 1932. *Wild flower preservation: a collector's guide*, London: Phillip Allan.

Comba, L., S.A. Corbet, L. Hunt, and B.E.N. Warren. 1999. "Flowers, nectar and insect visits: evaluating British plant species for pollinator-friendly gardens." *Annals of Botany* 83: 369–383.

Committee On Climate Change. 2018. *Land use: reducing emissions and preparing for climate change*. https://www.theccc.org.uk/publication/land-use-reducing-emissions-and-preparing-for-climate-change/ (Accessed 16/8/2019).

Cooke, A.S. 2006. *Monitoring Muntjac deer muntiacus reevesi and their impacts in Monks Wood National Nature Reserve*. Peterborough: English Nature.

Cooke, A. S., and L. Farrell. 2001. "Impact of muntjac deer (*Muntiacus reevesi*) at Monks Wood National Nature Reserve, Cambridgeshire, eastern England." *Forestry* 74: 241–250.

Cooper-Ellis, S., D.R. Foster, G. Carlton, and A. Lezberg. 1999. "Forest response to catastrophic wind: results from an experimental hurricane." *Ecology* 80: 2683–2696.

Cooper, M.R., and A. Johnson. 1984. *Poisonous plants in Britain and their effects on animals and man.* London: HMSO.

Coote, L., L.J. French, K.M. Moore, F.J.G. Mitchell, and D.L. Kelly. 2012. "Can plantation forests support plant species and communities of semi-natural woodland?" *Forest Ecology and Management* 283: 86–95.

Coppins, S., and B.J. Coppins. 2012. *Atlantic hazel: Scotland's special woodlands.* Edinburgh: Atlantic Hazel Action Group.

Craig, M., G.P. Buckley, and R. Howell. 2015. "Responses of an ancient woodland field layer to soil translocation: methods and timing." *Applied Vegetation Science* 18: 579–590.

Dahl, E. 1998. *The phytogeography of northern Europe.* Cambridge: Cambridge University Press.

David, R.W. 1978. "The distribution of *Carex elongata* L. in the British Isles." *Watsonia* 12: 158–160.

Davies, M.S., and G.L. Long. 1991. "Performance of two contrasting morphs of *Brachypodium sylvaticum* transplanted into shaded and unshaded sites." *Journal of Ecology,* 79: 505–517.

Davies, Z.G. and A.S. Pullin. 2007. "Are hedgerows effective corridors between fragments of woodland habitat? An evidence-based approach." *Landscape Ecology* 22: 333–351.

Day, S.P. 1993. "Woodland origin and 'ancient woodland indicators': a case-study from Sidlings Copse, Oxfordshire, UK." *The Holocene* 3: 45–53.

De Frenne, P., F. Rodríguez-Sánchez, D.A. Coomes, et al. 2013. "Microclimate moderates plant responses to macroclimate warming." *Proceedings of the National Academy of Sciences* 110: 18561–18565.

De Vries, W., S. Solberg, M. Dobbertin, et al. 2009. "The impact of nitrogen deposition on carbon sequestration by European forests and heathlands." *Forest Ecology and Management* 258: 1814–1823.

Dempsey, M.A., M.C. Fisk, J.B. Yavitt, T.J. Fahey, and T.C. Balser. 2013. "Exotic earthworms alter soil microbial community composition and function." *Soil Biology and Biochemistry* 67: 263–270.

Dennis, P. 2014. Grazing assessor's report on status of cattle grazing and associated habitat monitoring across Epping Forest. Report to the Conservators of Epping Forest, City of London. Aberystwyth: Aberystwyth University (Aber-Bangor Consultancy).

Dise, N.B., and R.F. Wright. 1995. "Nitrogen leaching from European forests in relation to nitrogen deposition." *Forest Ecology and Management* 71: 153–161.

Dolman, P.M., C.J. Panter, and H.L. Mossman. 2012. "The biodiversity audit approach challenges regional priorities and identifies a mismatch in conservation." *Journal of Applied Ecology* 49: 986–997.

Draycott, R.A., A.N. Hoodless, and R.B. Sage. 2008. "Effects of pheasant management on vegetation and birds in lowland woodlands." *Journal of Applied Ecology* 45: 334–341.

Dupouey, J.L., E. Dambrine, J.D. Laffite, and C. Moares. 2002. "Irreversible impact of past land use on forest soils and biodiversity." *Ecology* 83: 2978–2984.

Dzwonko, Z., and S. Gawroński. 2002. "Effect of litter removal on species richness and acidification of a mixed oak-pine woodland." *Biological Conservation* 106: 389–398.

Edwards, M.E. 1986. "Disturbance histories of four Snowdonian woodlands and their relation to Atlantic bryophyte distributions." *Biological Conservation* 37: 301–320.

Ehrlén, J., Z. Münzbergova, M. Diekmann, and O. Eriksson. 2006. "Long-term assessment of seed limitation in plants: results from an 11-year experiment." *Journal of Ecology* 94: 1224–1232.

Ellenberg, H. 1988. *The vegetation ecology of central Europe.* Cambridge: Cambridge University Press.

Elton, C.S. 1966. *The pattern of animal communities.* London: Chapman and Hall.

Ericson, L., and A. Wennstrom. 1997. "The effect of herbivory on the interaction between the clonal plant *Trientalis europaea* and its smut fungus *Urocystis trientalis.*" *Oikos* 80: 107–111.

Eriksson, O. 1992. "Population structure and dynamics of the clonal dwarf-shrub *Linnaea borealis.*" *Journal of Vegetation Science* 3: 61–68.

Eriksson, O. 1994. "Seedling recruitment in the perennial herb *Actaea spicata* L." *Flora* 189: 187–191.

Ernst, W.H.O. 1979. "Population biology of *Allium ursinum* in northern Germany." *Journal of Ecology* 67: 347–362.

European Commission. 1992. *Directive on the conservation of natural habitats and wild fauna and flora: the habitats directive, 92/43/EEC.* Brussels: European Commission.

Falinski, J.B. 1986. *Vegetation dynamics in temperate lowland primeval forests.* Dordrecht: W. Junk.

Falkengren-Grerup, U. 1995. "Long-term changes in flora and vegetation in deciduous forests of southern Sweden." *Ecological Bulletins* 45: 215–226.

Farjon, A. 2017. *Ancient oaks in the English landscape.* London: Kew.

Ferris, R., A.J. Peace, J.W. Humphrey, and A.C. Broome. 2000. "Relationships between vegetation, site type and stand structure in coniferous plantations in Britain." *Forest Ecology and Management* 136: 35–51.

Field, C.D., N.B. Dise, R.J. Payne, et al. 2014. "The role of nitrogen deposition in widespread plant community change across semi-natural habitats." *Ecosystems* 17: 864–877.

Fitter, A.H. and R.S.R. Fitter. "Rapid changes in flowering time in British plants." *Science* 296: 1689–1691.

Fitter, A.H., R.S.R. Fitter, I.T.B. Harris, and M.H. Williamson. 1995. "Relationships between first flowering date and temperature in the flora of a locality in central England." *Functional Ecology* 9: 55–60.

Ford, E.D., and P.J. Newbould. 1977. "The biomass and production of ground vegetation and its relation to tree cover through a deciduous woodland cycle." *Journal of Ecology* 65: 201–212.

Forestry Commission. 1985. *The policy for broadleaved woodland.* Edinburgh: Forestry Commission.

Forestry Commission. 2003. *National Inventory of woodland and trees.* Edinburgh: Forestry Commission.

Forestry Commission. 2010. *Managing ancient and native woodland in England.* Bristol: Forestry Commission England.

Forman, R.T.T., and M. Godron. 1986. *Landscape Ecology,* New York: Wiley.

Fortey, R. 2016. *The wood for the trees: the long view of nature from a small wood.* London: William Collins.

Francis, J.L., and A. Morton. 2001. "Enhancement of amenity woodland field layers in Milton Keynes." *British Wildlife* 12: 244–251.

French, L.J., G.F. Smith, D.L. Kelly, *et al.* 2008. "Ground flora communities in temperate oceanic plantation forests and the influence of silvicultural, geographic and edaphic factors." *Forest Ecology and Management* 255: 476–494.

Froyd, C.A., and K.D. Bennett. 2006. "Long-term ecology of native pinewood communities in East Glen Affric, Scotland." *Forestry* 79: 279–291.

Fuller, R.J., and R. Gill. 2001. "Ecological impacts of deer in British woodland." *Forestry* 74: 193–299.

Fuller, R.J., and M.S. Warren. 1993. *Coppiced woodlands: their value for wildlife.* Peterborough: Joint Nature Conservation Committee.

Fyfe, R.M., C. Twiddle, S. Sugita, *et al.* 2013. "The Holocene vegetation cover of Britain and Ireland: overcoming problems of scale and discerning patterns of openness." *Quaternary Science Reviews* 73: 132–148.

Gambles, I. 2019. *British forests: the Forestry Commission 1919–2019.* London: Profile Editions.

Gardiner, B.A., and C.P. Quine. 2000. "Management of forests to reduce the risk of abiotic damage – a review with particular reference to the effects of strong winds." *Forest Ecology and Management* 135: 261–277.

Glaves, P., C. Handley, J. Birbeck, I. Rotherham, and B. Wright. 2009. A survey of the coverage, use and application of ancient woodland indicator lists in the UK. Grantham: Woodland Trust.

Godefroid, S., S. Rucquoij, and N. Koedam. 2005. "To what extent do forest herbs recover after clearcutting in beech forest?" *Forest Ecology and Management* 210: 39–53.

Godefroid, S., S. Rucquoij, and N. Koedam. 2006. "Spatial variability of summer microclimates and plant species response along transects within clearcuts in a beech forest." *Plant Ecology* 185: 107–121.

Godwin, H. 1975. *The history of the British flora,* Cambridge: Cambridge University Press.

Goldberg, E.A. 2003. *National vegetation classification – ten years of experience of using the woodland section.* Peterborough: Joint Natural Conservation Committee (Research Report 335).

Goldberg, E.A., G.F. Peterken, and K.J. Kirby. 2011. "Origin and evolution of the Ancient Woodland Inventory." *British Wildlife* 23: 90–96.

Gove, B., S.A. Power, G.P. Buckley, and J. Ghazoul. 2007. "Effects of herbicide spray drift and fertiliser overspread on selected species of woodland ground flora: comparison between short-term and long-term impact assessments and field surveys." *Journal of Applied Ecology* 44: 374–384.

Grayson, A.J. and E.W. Jones. 1955. *Notes on the history of the Wytham Estate with special reference to the woodlands.* Oxford: Imperial Forestry Institute.

Gregg, S.A. 1988. *Foragers and farmers: population interactions and agricultural expansion in prehistoric Europe.* Chicago: University of Chicago Press.

Greig, J. 1982. "Past and present lime woods of Europe." In *Archaeological aspects of woodland ecology* (British Archaeological Report 146): 23–55.

Grigson, G. 1975. *The Englishman's flora.* St Albans: Paladin.

Grime, J.P., J.G. Hodgson, and R. Hunt. 2007. *Comparative plant ecology (revised edition).* Dalbeattie: Castlepoint Press.

Hall, J.E., K.J. Kirby, and A.M. Whitbread. 2001. *National Vegetation Classification field guide to woodland.* Peterborough: Joint Nature Conservation Committee.

Hambler, C., P. Henderson, and M.R. Speight. 2011. "Extinction rates, extinction-prone habitats, and indicator groups in Britain and at larger scales." *Biological Conservation* 144: 713–721.

Hambler, C.P. and M.R. Speight. 1995. "Biodiversity conservation in Britain: science replacing tradition." *British Wildlife* 6: 137–147.

Hambler, C.P., G.R.W. Wint and D.J. Rogers. 2010. "Invertebrates". In *Wytham Woods, Oxford's ecological laboratory,* edited by P.S. Savill, C.M. Perrins, K.J. Kirby and N. Fisher: 109–144. Oxford: Oxford University Press.

Hamilton, J., R.E. Hedges, and M. Robinson. 2009. "Rooting for pigfruit: pig feeding in Neolithic and Iron Age Britain compared." *Antiquity* 83: 998–1011.

Harding, P.T., and F. Rose. 1986. *Pasture-woodlands in Lowland Britain.* Huntingdon: Institute of Terrestrial Ecology.

Harley, J. L., and E. Harley. 1987. "A check-list of mycorrhiza in the British flora." *New Phytologist* 105: 1–102.

Harmer, R., G.F. Peterken, G. Kerr, and P. Poulton. 2001. "Vegetation changes during 100 years of development of two secondary woodlands on abandoned arable land." *Biological Conservation* 101: 291–304.

Hartel, T., and T. Pleininger. 2014. *European wood-pastures in transition: a socio-ecological approach.* Abingdon: Earthscan/Routledge.

Hatcher, P.E. 2003. "*Impatiens noli-tangere* L." *Journal of Ecology* 91: 147–167.

Heinken, T. 2000. "Dispersal of plants by a dog in a deciduous forest." *Botanische Jahrbücher für Systematik, Pflanzengeschichte und Pflanzengeographie* 122: 449–467.

Hermy, M., O. Honnay, L. Firbank, C. Grashof-Bokdam, and J.E. Lawesson. 1999. "An ecological comparison between ancient and other forest plant species of Europe, and the implications for forest conservation." *Biological Conservation* 91: 9–22.

Hester, A.J., J. Miles, and C.H. Gimingham. 1991. "Succession from Heather moorland to Birch woodland. I. Experimental alteration of specific environmental conditions in the field." *Journal of Ecology* 79: 303–315.

Highways Agency. 2005. The establishment of an herbaceous plant layer in roadside woodland. http://www.standardsforhighways.co.uk/ha/standards/dmrb/vol10/section3/ha11505.pdf (Accessed 16/8/2019).

Hiirsalmi, H. 1969. "*Trientalis europaea* L. A study of the reproductive biology, ecology and variation in Finland." *Annales Botanici Fennici* 6: 119–173.

Hill, A. 2003. Plant species as indicators of ancient woodland in the Malvern Hills and Teme Valley natural area. PhD Thesis. Coventry: Coventry University.

Hill, M.O. 1979. "The development of a flora in even-aged plantations." In *The ecology of even-aged forest plantations*, edited by E.D. Ford, D.C. Malcolm, and J. Atterson: 175–192. Cambridge: Institute of Terrestrial Ecology.

Hill, M.O., R.G.H. Bunce, and M.W. Shaw. 1975. "Indicator species analysis, a divisive polythetic method of classification, and its application to a survey of native pinewoods in Scotland." *Journal of Ecology* 63: 597–613.

Hill, M.O., C.D. Preston, and D.B. Roy. 2004. *PLANTATT: attributes of British and Irish plants.*, Cambridge: Biological Records Centre (NERC).

Hipps, N., M. Davies, P. Dodds, and G.P. Buckley. 2005. "The effects of phosphorus nutrition and soil pH on the growth of some ancient woodland indicator plants and their interaction with competitor species." *Plant and Soil* 271: 131–141.

HMSO. 1952. *Census of woodlands 1947–1949*. London: HMSO.

Holl, K. 2017. *Where have all the flowers gone?* London: Winston Churchill Memorial Trust.

Holmes, W., and A. Wheaten. 2002. *The Blean: the woodlands of a cathedral city*. Whitstable: The Blean Research Group.

Hone, R., D.E. Anderson, A.G. Parker, and M.D. Morecroft. 2001. "Holocene vegetation change at Wytham Woods, Oxfordshire." *Quaternary Newsletter* 94: 1–15.

Hort, A.F.T. 1916. *Theophrastus, enquiry into plants, volume I: books 1–5*. Cambridge, MA: Harvard University Press.

Huntley, B., and H.J.B. Birks. 1979. "The Past and Present Vegetation of the Morrone Birkwoods National Nature Reserve, Scotland: II. Woodland Vegetation and Soils." *Journal of Ecology* 67: 447–467.

Huntley, B., and H.J.B. Birks. 1983. *An atlas of past and present pollen maps for Europe: 0–13,000 years ago*. Cambridge: Cambridge University Press.

Hutchings, M.J., and A.C.P. Elizabeth. 1999. "*Glechoma hederacea* L. (*Nepeta glechoma* Benth., *N. hederacea* (L.) Trev.)." *Journal of Ecology* 87: 347–364.

Inghe, O., and C.O. Tamm. 1985. "Survival and flowering of perennial herbs. IV. The behaviour of *Hepatica nobilis* and *Sanicula europaea* on permanent plots during 1943–1981." *Oikos* 45: 400–420.

Innes, J.B., and J.J. Blackford. 2003. "The ecology of Late Mesolithic woodland disturbances: model testing with fungal spore assemblage data." *Journal of Archaeological Science* 30: 185–194.

Jacquemyn, H., R. Brys, O. Honnay, M. Hermy, and I. Roldán-Ruiz. 2006. "Sexual reproduction, clonal diversity and genetic differentiation in patchily distributed populations of the temperate forest herb *Paris quadrifolia* (Trilliaceae)." *Oecologia*, 147: 434–444.

Jacquemyn, H., R. Brys, and M.J. Hutchings. 2008. "Biological Flora of the British Isles: *Paris quadrifolia* L." *Journal of Ecology* 96: 833–844.

Jacquemyn, H., P. Endels, R. Brys, M. Hermy, and S.R.J. Woodell. 2009. "Biological Flora of the British Isles: *Primula vulgaris* Huds. (*P. acaulis* (L.) Hill)." *Journal of Ecology* 97: 812–833.

Jannink, M., and T. Rich. 2010. "Ghost orchid rediscovered in Britain after 23 years." *Journal of the Hardy Orchid Society* 7: 14–15.

Jarman, R.A. 1995. "Ecological restoration: the end of status quo-ism in the National Trust?" *Biological Journal of the Linnean Society* 56: 213–215.

Jefferson, R.J. 2006. "Wood Small-reed – a new conservation dilemma." *Conservation Land Management* Spring issue: 15–18.

Jefferson, R.J. 2008. "Biological Flora of the British Isles: *Mercurialis perennis* L." *Journal of Ecology* 96: 386–412.

Jefferson, R.J., and K.J. Kirby. 2018. "A scent of musk – the 'life and times' of Moschatel, the Good Friday flower." *British Wildlife* 30: 79–85.

Jefferson, R.J., and K.J. Kirby. 2011. "Boggarts, ants and poison: the shady natural history of Dog's mercury." *British Wildlife* 22: 241–245.

Kallio, P., and J. Lehtonen. 1975. "On the ecocatastrophe of birch forests caused by *Oporinia autumnata* (Bkh.) and the problem of reforestation." In *Fennoscandian Tundra Ecosystems: Part 2 Animals and Systems Analysis*, edited by F.E. Wielgolaski: 174–180. Berlin/Heidelberg: Springer.

Kauffman, M. J., J.F. Brodie, and E.S. Jules. 2010. "Are wolves saving Yellowstone's aspen? A landscape-level test of a behaviorally mediated trophic cascade." *Ecology* 91: 2742–2755.

Keble-Martin, W. 1965. *The concise British flora in colour*. London: Ebury Press.

Keith, S.A., A.C. Newton, M.D. Morecroft, C.E. Bealey, and J.M. Bullock. 2009. "Taxonomic homogenization of woodland plant communities over 70 years." *Proceedings of the Royal Society B: Biological Sciences* 276: 3539–3544.

Kennedy, F. 2002. *The identification of soils for forest management: field guide*. Edinburgh: Forestry Commission.

Kimberley, A., G.A. Blackburn, J.D. Whyatt, K.J. Kirby, and S.M. Smart. 2013. "Identifying the trait syndromes of conservation indicator species: how distinct are British ancient woodland indicator plants from other woodland species?" *Applied Vegetation Science* 16: 667–675.

Kingsley, C. 1873. *Glaucus, or the Wonders of the Shore*. London: MacMillan and Co.

Kirby, K.J. 1988. "Changes in the ground flora under plantations on ancient woodland sites." *Forestry* 61: 317–338.

Kirby, K.J. 2001. "The impact of deer on the ground flora of

British broadleaved woodland." *Forestry* 74: 219–229.

Kirby, K.J. 2004. "A model of a natural wooded landscape in Britain as influenced by large herbivore activity." *Forestry* 77: 405–420.

Kirby, K.J. 2016. "Charles Elton and Wytham Woods." *British Wildlife* 27: 256–263.

Kirby, K.J., and G.P. Buckley. 1994. *Ecological responses to the 1987 Great Storm in the woods of south-east England.* English Nature Science 23. Peterborough: English Nature.

Kirby, K.J., T. Bines, A. Burn, J.Mackintosh, P. Pitkin, and I. Smith. 1986. "Seasonal and observer differences in vascular plant records from British woodlands." *Journal of Ecology* 74: 123–131.

Kirby, K.J., E.A. Goldberg, and N. Orchard. 2017. "Long-term changes in the flora of oak forests and of oak:spruce mixtures following removal of conifers." *Forestry* 90: 136–147.

Kirby, K.J., and J.E. Hall. 2019. *Woodland survey handbook: collecting data for conservation in British woodland.* Exeter: Pelagic Publishing.

Kirby, K.J., and J. May. 1989. "The effects of enclosure, conifer planting and the subsequent removal of conifers in Dalavich oakwood (Argyll)." *Scottish Forestry* 43: 280–288.

Kirby, K.J., D.G. Pyatt, and J.S. Rodwell. 2012. "Characterization of the woodland flora and woodland communities in Britain using Ellenberg Values and Functional Analysis." In *Working and Walking in the Footsteps of Ghosts: volume 1: the wooded landscape,* edited by I. Rotherham, M. Jones, and C. Handley: 66–86. Sheffield: Wildtrack Publishing.

Kirby, K.J., S.M. Smart, H.J. Black, R.G.H. Bunce, P. Corney, and R.J. Smithers. 2005. *Long-term ecological changes in British woodland (1971–2001).* English Nature Research Report 653. Peterborough: English Nature.

Kirby, K.J., and R.C. Thomas. 2000. "Changes in the ground flora in Wytham Woods, southern England, from 1974 to 1991 – implications for nature conservation." *Journal of Vegetation Science.* 11: 871–880.

Kirby, K.J., R.C. Thomas, R.S. Key, I.F.G. Mclean, and N. Hodgetts. 1995. "Pasture woodland and its conservation in Britain." *Biological Journal of the Linnean Society* 56: 135–153.

Kirby, K.J., and C. Watkins. 2015. *Europe's changing woods and forests: from wildwood to managed landscapes.* Wallingford: CABI.

Knight, G.H. 1964. "Some Factors Affecting the Distribution of *Endymion non-scriptus* (L.) Garcke in Warwickshire Woods." *Journal of Ecology* 52: 405–421.

Kohn, D.D., P.E. Hulme, P.M. Hollingsworth, and A. Butler. 2009. "Are native bluebells (*Hyacinthoides non-scripta*) at risk from alien congenerics? Evidence from distributions and co-occurrence in Scotland." *Biological Conservation* 142: 61–74.

Latham, J., and T.H. Blackstock. 1998. "Effects of livestock exclusion on the ground flora and regeneration of an upland Alnus glutinosa woodland." *Forestry* 71: 191–197.

Lawton, J. (ed.) 2010. *Making space for nature: a review of England's wildlife sites and ecological network.* London: Defra.

Lee, T.C. 1981. "Van Gogh's vision: Digitalis intoxification?" *Journal of the American Medical Association* 245: 727–729.

Ling, K.A. 2003. "Using environmental and growth characteristics of plants to detect long-term changes in response to atmospheric pollution: some examples from British beechwoods." *Science of The Total Environment* 310: 203–210.

Linhart, Y.B., and R.J. Whelan. 1980. "Woodland regeneration in relation to grazing and fencing in Coed Gorswen, North Wales." *Journal of Applied Ecology* 17: 827–840.

Littlemore, J., and S. Barker. 2001. "The ecological response of forest ground flora and soils to experimental trampling in British urban woodlands." *Urban Ecosystems* 5: 257–276.

Littlemore, J., and I.D. Rotherham. 2008. "Trees, forests and public access: reconciling recreation and conservation." *World of Trees* 17: 8–11.

Lorimer, J., C. Sandom, P. Jepson, C. Doughty, M. Barua, and K.J. Kirby. 2015. "Rewilding: Science, Practice, and Politics." *Annual Review of Environment and Resources* 40: 39–62.

Lousley, J.E. 1976. *The flora of Surrey.* Newton Abbot: David and Charles.

Mabey, R. 1996. *Flora Britannica.* London: Sinclair-Stevenson.

Mabey, R., and M. Blamey. 1972. *Food for free.* London: Collins.

Maclean, J. E., R.J. Mitchell, D.F. Burslem, D. Genney, J. Hall, and R.J. Pakeman. 2017. "Understorey plant community composition reflects invasion history decades after invasive Rhododendron has been removed." *Journal of Applied Ecology* 55: 874–884.

Manning, A.D., J. Kesteven, J. Stein, A. Lunn, T. Xu, and B. Rayner. 2010. "Could native Scots pines (Pinus sylvestris) still persist in northern England and southern Scotland?" *Plant Ecology & Diversity* 3: 187–201.

Mark, S., and J.M. Olesen. 1996. "Importance of elaiosome size to removal of ant-dispersed seeds." *Oecologia* 107: 95–101.

Marren, P. 1992. *The wildwoods.* Newton Abbot: David and Charles.

Marren, P. 1999. *Britain's rare flowers.* London: Poyser.

Marzano, M., and N. Dandy. 2012. "Recreationist behaviour in forests and the disturbance of wildlife." *Biodiversity and Conservation* 21: 2967–2986.

Matejko, M., A.J. Dore, J. Hall, *et al.* 2009. "The influence of long term trends in pollutant emissions on deposition of sulphur and nitrogen and exceedance of critical loads in the United Kingdom." *Environmental Science & Policy* 12: 882–896.

Maule, H., M. Andrews, C. Watson, and A. Cherrill. 2000. "Distribution, biomass and effect on native species of *Impatiens glandulifera* in a deciduous woodland in northeast England." *Aspects of Applied Biology* 58: 31–38.

Mell, I.C. 2011. "The changing focus of England's Community Forest programme and its use of a green infrastructure approach to multi-functional landscape planning." *International Journal of Sustainable Society* 3:

431–450.

Merton, L.F.H. 1970. "The history and status of the woodlands of the Derbyshire limestone." *Journal of Ecology* 58: 723–744.

Metcalfe, D.J. 2005. "*Hedera helix* L." *Journal of Ecology* 93: 632–648.

Mighall, T.M., and F.M. Chambers. 1995. "Holocene vegetation history and human impact at Bryn y Castell, Snowdonia, north Wales." *New Phytologist* 130: 299–321.

Mitchell, F.J.G. 2005. "How open were European primeval forests? Hypothesis testing using palaeoecological data." *Journal of Ecology* 93: 168–177.

Mitchell, R.J., J.K. Beaton, P.E. Bellamy, *et al.* 2014. "Ash dieback in the UK: A review of the ecological and conservation implications and potential management options." *Biological Conservation* 175: 95–109.

Mitchell, R.J., C.D. Campbell, S.J. Chapman, *et al.* 2007. "The cascading effects of birch on heather moorland: a test for the top-down control of an ecosystem engineer." *Journal of Ecology* 95: 540–554.

Mitchell, R.J., R.L. Hewison, A.J. Hester, A. Broome, and K.J. Kirby. 2016. Potential impacts of the loss of *Fraxinus excelsior* (Oleaceae) due to ash dieback on woodland vegetation in Great Britain. *New Journal of Botany* 6: 2–15.

Monbiot, G. 2013. *Feral: searching for enchantment on the frontiers of rewilding*. London: Penguin.

Morecroft, M.D., and L. Speakman. 2015. *Biodiversity Climate Change Impacts Summary Report*. London: Living With Environmental Change.

Morecroft, M.D., and M.E. Taylor. 2010. "Wytham in a changing world." In *Wytham Woods: Oxford's ecological laboratory*, edited by P.S. Savill, C.M. Perrins, K.J. Kirby, and N. Fisher: 217–229. Oxford: Oxford University Press.

Mountford, J.O., T.H. Sparks and R.A. Garbutt. 2012. "Judith's Hedge: changes in the botanical diversity of a species-rich hedgerow over 40 years." In *Hedgerow Futures*, edited by J. Dover: 16–26. London: Tree Council.

Natural England. 2009. *Guidance on dealing with the changing distribution of tree species*. Technical Information Note TIN053. Peterborough: Natural England.

Natural England and RSPB. 2014. *Climate change adaptation manual*. Peterborough: Natural England.

NCC. 1984. *Nature conservation in Great Britain*. Peterborough: Nature Conservancy Council.

NCC. 1986. *Nature conservation and afforestation in Britain*. Peterborough: Nature Conservancy Council.

Neumann, J.L., G.J. Holloway, R.B. Sage, and A.N. Hoodless. 2015. "Releasing of pheasants for shooting in the UK alters woodland invertebrate communities." *Biological Conservation* 191: 50–59.

Niemann, D. 2016. *A tale of trees*. London: Short Books.

Noble, G. 2017. *Woodland in the Neolithic of Northern Europe*. Cambridge: Cambridge University Press.

Norton, L., L. Maskell, S. Smart, *et al.* 2012. "Measuring stock and change in the GB countryside for policy – key findings and developments from the Countryside Survey 2007 field survey." *Journal of environmental management* 113: 117–127.

O'Brien, L., and R. Murray. 2007. "Forest School and its impacts on young children: Case studies in Britain." *Urban Forestry & Urban Greening* 6: 249–265.

Ormerod, S. J., N. Allenson, D. Hudson, and S.J. Tyler. 1986. "The distribution of breeding dippers (*Cinclus cinclus* (L.); Aves) in relation to stream acidity in upland Wales." *Freshwater Biology* 16: 501–507.

Ormerod, S.J., A.P. Donald, and S.J. Brown. 1989. "The influence of plantation forestry on the pH and aluminium concentration of upland Welsh streams: A re-examination." *Environmental Pollution:* 62: 47–62.

Ovington, J.D. 1955. "Studies of the development of woodland conditions under different trees: III. The ground flora." *Journal of Ecology* 43: 1–21.

Page, C.N. 1982. *The ferns of Britain and Ireland*. Cambridge: Cambridge University Press.

Page, C.N. 1988. *A natural history of Britain's ferns*. London: Collins.

Park, K.J., K.E. Graham, J. Calladine, and C.W. Wernham. 2008. "Impacts of birds of prey on gamebirds in the UK: a review." *Ibis* 150: 9–26.

Parker, A.G., A.S. Goudie, D.E. Anderson, M.A. Robinson, and C. Bonsall. 2002. "A review of the mid-Holocene elm decline in the British Isles." *Progress in Physical Geography* 26: 1–45.

Parnell, J., T. Curtis, and E. Cullen. 2012. *Webb's An Irish Flora*. Cork: University Press.

Patch, D. 2004. "Ivy – boon or bane." *Arboricultural Practice Note* 10: 1–12. Farnham: Forest Research.

Pavord, A. 2005. *The naming of names: the search for order in the world of plants*. London: Bloomsbury.

Pearce-Higgins, J.W., M.A. Ausden, C.M. Beale, T.H. Oliver, and H.P.Q. Crick. 2015. *Research on the assessment of risks and opportunities for species in England as a result of climate change*. Peterborough: Natural England.

Pearce-Higgins, J.W., C.M. Beale, T.H. Oliver *et al.* 2017. "A national-scale assessment of climate change impacts on species: Assessing the balance of risks and opportunities for multiple taxa." *Biological Conservation* 213: 124–134.

Pearman, D.A. 2018. "The discovery of the native flora of Britain and Ireland." *British Wildlife* 29: 259–265.

Perring, F.H., and S.M. Walters. 1976. *Atlas of the British Flora (second edition)*. Wakefield: Botanical Society of the British Isles.

Peterken, G.F. 1969. "Development of vegetation in Staverton Park, Suffolk." *Field Studies* 3: 1–39.

Peterken, G.F. 1974. "A method for assessing woodland flora for conservation using indicator species." *Biological Conservation* 6: 239–245.

Peterken, G.F. 1977a. "General management principles for nature conservation in British woodlands. *Forestry* 50: 27–48.

Peterken, G.F. 1977b. Habitat conservation priorities in British and European woodlands. *Biological Conservation* 11: 223–236.

Peterken, G.F. 1986. "The status of native woods in the Scottish uplands." In *Trees and Wildlife in the Scottish Uplands*, edited by D. Jenkins: 14–19. Banchory: Institute of Terrestrial Ecology.

Peterken, G.F. 1993. *Woodland conservation and management (second edition)*. London: Chapman and Hall.

Peterken, G.F. 1996. *Natural woodland: ecology and conservation in northern temperate regions*. Cambridge: Cambridge University Press.

Peterken, G.F. 2000. "Identifying ancient woodland using vascular plant indicators." *British Wildlife* 11: 153–158.

Peterken, G.F. 2013. *Meadows*. Gillingham: British Wildlife Publishing.

Peterken, G.F., and H. Allison. 1989. *Woods, trees and hedges: a review of changes in the British countryside*. Peterborough: Nature Conservancy Council.

Peterken, G.F., and M. Game. 1981. "Historical factors affecting the distribution of *Mercurialis perennis* in central Lincolnshire." *Journal of Ecology* 69: 781–796.

Peterken, G.F., and M. Game. 1984. "Historical factors affecting the number and distribution of vascular plant species in the woodlands of central Lincolnshire." *Journal of Ecology* 72: 155–182.

Peterken, G.F., and E.P. Mountford. 1996. "Effects of drought on beech in Lady Park Wood, an unmanaged mixed decidous woodland." *Forestry* 69: 125–136.

Peterken, G.F., and E.P. Mountford. 2017. *Woodland development: a long-term study of Lady Park Wood*. Wallingford: CABI.

Phillips, R. 1977. *Wild flowers of Britain*. London: Pan Books.

Pigott, C.D. 1982. "The Experimental Study of Vegetation." *New Phytologist* 90: 389–404.

Pigott, C.D. 1983. "Regeneration of oak-birch woodland following exclusion of sheep." *Journal of Ecology* 71: 629–646.

Pitcairn, C.E.R., U.M. Skiba, M.A. Sutton, D. Fowler, R. Munro, and V. Kennedy. 2002. "Defining the spatial impacts of poultry farm ammonia emissions on species composition of adjacent woodland ground flora using Ellenberg Nitrogen Index, nitrous oxide and nitric oxide emissions and foliar nitrogen as marker variables." *Environmental Pollution* 119: 9–21.

Plantlife. 2004. *Bluebells for Britain: a report on the 2003 Bluebells for Britain survey*. Salisbury: Plantlife.

Plue, J., M. Hermy, K. Verheyen, P. Thuillier, R. Saguez, and G. Decocq. 2008. "Persistent changes in forest vegetation and seed bank 1,600 years after human occupation." *Landscape Ecology*, 23: 673–688.

Poland, J., E.J. Clement, R. Bucknall, *et al.* 2009. *The vegetative key to the British Flora*. London: Botanical Society of the British Isles.

Pollard, E., M.D. Hooper, and N.W. Moore. 1974. *Hedges*. London: Collins.

Pollard, E., and T.J. Yates. 1993. *Monitoring butterflies for ecology and conservation*. London: Chapman and Hall.

Polunin, O., and M. Walters. 1985. *A guide to the vegetation of Europe*. Oxford: Oxford University Press.

Prentice, H.C., and I.C. Prentice. 1975. "The hill vegetation of North Hoy, Orkney." *New Phytologist* 75: 313–367.

Preston, C.D., and P.H. Oswald. 2012. "Britain's first county flora: John Ray's Cambridge catalogue of 1660." *British Wildlife* 23: 159–165.

Preston, C.D., D.A. Pearman, and T.D. Dines. 2002. *New atlas of the British and Irish flora*. Oxford: Oxford University Press.

Preston, C.D., F.J. Valtueña, and J.W. Kadereit. 2012. "The intriguing case of the Welsh poppy *Meconopsis cambrica*." *British Wildlife* 24: 16–20.

Proctor, M. 2013. *Vegetation of Britain and Ireland*. London: Collins.

Proctor, M., and P. Yeo. 1973. *The pollination of flowers*. London: Collins.

Putman, R. J., P.J. Edwards, J.C.E. Mann, R.C. How, and S.D. Hill. 1989. "Vegetational and faunal changes in an area of heavily grazed woodland following relief of grazing." *Biological Conservation* 47: 13–32.

Quine, C.P. 2015. "The curious case of the even-aged plantation: wretched, funereal or misunderstood?" In *Europe's changing woods and forests*, edited by K.J. Kirby and C. Watkins: 207–223. Wallingford: CABI.

Rackham, O. 1975. *Hayley wood*. Cambridge: Cambridgeshire and Isle of Ely Naturalists' Trust.

Rackham, O. 1986. *The history of the countryside*. London: Dent.

Rackham, O. 1989. *The Last Forest: the story of Hatfield Forest*. London: Dent.

Rackham, O. 1990. *Trees and woodland in the British landscape (revised edition)*. London: Dent.

Rackham, O. 1998. "Savanna in Europe." In *The ecological history of European forests*, edited by K.J. Kirby, and C. Watkins: 1–24. Wallingford: CABI.

Rackham, O. 2003. *Ancient woodland: its history, vegetation and uses in England (revised edition)*. Dalbeattie: Castlepoint Press.

Ranius, T., and N. Jansson. 2000. "The influence of forest regrowth, original canopy cover and tree size on saproxylic beetles associated with old oaks." *Biological Conservation* 95: 85–94.

Ratcliffe, D.A. 1969. "An ecological account of Atlantic bryophytes in the British Isles." *New Phytologist* 67: 365–439.

Ratcliffe, D.A. 1977. *A nature conservation review*. Cambridge: Cambridge University Press.

Read, D.J., P. Freer-Smith, J. Morison, N. Hanley, C. West, and P. Snowdon. 2009. *Combating climate change: a role for UK forests. An assessment of the potential of the UK's trees and woodlands to mitigate and adapt to climate change*. London: The Stationery Office.

Rebele, F., and C. Lehmann. 2001. "Biological Flora of Central Europe: *Calamagrostis epigejos* (L.) Roth." *Flora* 196: 325–344.

Rich, T., and C. Birkinshaw. 2001. "Conservation of Britain's biodiversity: *Carex depauperata* with (Cyperaceae), Starved Wood-Sedge." *Watsonia* 23: 401–412.

Ripple, W.J., J.A. Estes, R.L. Beschta, *et al.* 2014. "Status and ecological effects of the world's largest carnivores." *Science*, 343. DOI: 10.1126/science.1241484

Roberts, A.J., C. Russell, G.J. Walker, and K.J. Kirby. 1992. "Regional variation in the origin, extent and composition of Scottish woodland." *Botanical Journal of Scotland* 46: 167–189.

Roberts, A.M. I., C. Tansey, R.J. Smithers, and A.B. Phillimore.

2015. "Predicting a change in the order of spring phenology in temperate forests." *Global Change Biology* 21: 2603–2611.

Roche, J., F.J. Mitchell, S. Waldren, and B. Stefanini. 2018. "Palaeoecological evidence for survival of Scots Pine through the Late Holocene in Western Ireland: implications for ecological management." *Forests* 9: 350.

Rodwell, J. 2005. "Woodlands at the edge: A European perspective on the Atlantic oakwood plant communities". *Botanical Journal of Scotland* 57: 121–133.

Rodwell, J.S. 1991. *British plant communities: 1 woodlands and scrub.* Cambridge: Cambridge University Press.

Rodwell, J.S., and J. Dring. 2001. *European significance of British woodland types.* English Nature Research Report 460. Peterborough: English Nature.

Rodwell, J.S., and G. Patterson. 1994. *Creating new native woodland.* Forestry Commission Bulletin 112. Edinburgh: Forestry Commission.

Roovers, P., B. Bossuyt, H. Gulinck, and M. Hermy. 2005. "Vegetation recovery on closed paths in temperate deciduous forests." *Journal of Environmental Management* 74: 273–281.

Roovers, P., B. Dumont, H. Gulinck, and M. Hermy. 2006. "Recreationists' perceived obstruction of field and shrub layer vegetation." *Urban Forestry & Urban Greening* 4: 47–53.

Roovers, P., K. Verheyen, M. Hermy, and H. Gulinck. 2004. "Experimental trampling and vegetation recovery in some forest and heathland communities." *Applied Vegetation Science* 7: 111–118.

Rose, F. 1981. *The Wildflower Key: British Isles and Northern Europe.* London: Warne.

Rose, F. 1993. "Ancient British woodlands and their epiphytes." *British Wildlife* 5: 83–93.

Rose, F. 1999. "Indicators of ancient woodland." *British Wildlife* 10: 241–251.

Rose, F.C. and C. O'Reilly. 2006. *The wild flower key (revised edition).* London: Warne.

ROTAP. 2012. *Review of transboundary air pollution (RoTAP): acidification, eutrophications, ground level ozone and heavy metals in the UK.* Penicuik: Department for Environment, Food and Rural Affairs and Centre for Ecology and Hydrology.

Rotherham, I.D. 2017a *Recombinant Ecology – A Hybrid Future?* SpringerBriefs in Ecology DOI 10.1007/978-3-319-49797-6_1.

Rotherham, I.D. 2017b. "Searching for 'shadows' and 'ghosts' in the landscape." *Arboricultural Journal* 39: 39–47.

Rothschild, M., and P. Marren. 1997. *Rothschild's reserves: time and fragile nature.* Colchester: Harley Books.

Sage, R.B., C. Ludorf, and P.A. Robertson. 2005. "The ground flora of ancient semi-natural woodlands in pheasant release pens in England." *Biological Conservation* 122: 243–252.

Salisbury, E.J. 1916. "The Oak-Hornbeam woods of Hertfordshire parts I and II." *Journal of Ecology* 4: 83–117.

Salisbury, E.J. 1918. "The Oak-Hornbeam woods of Hertfordshire Parts III and IV." *Journal of Ecology* 6: 14–52.

Sandom, C.J., R. Ejrnæs, M.D.D. Hansen, and J-C. Svenning. 2014. "High herbivore density associated with vegetation diversity in interglacial ecosystems." *Proceedings of the National Academy of Sciences* 111: 4162–4167.

Sandom, C.J., J. Hughes, and D.W. Macdonald. 2013. "Rooting for rewilding: quantifying Wild Boar's *Sus scrofa* rooting rate in the Scottish Highlands." *Restoration Ecology* 21: 329–335.

Sarker, F. 2014. "Hirta, St Kilda (v.c.110), a remote island of flowers." *BSBI News* 126: 17–19.

Schmidt, M., K. Sommer, W-U. Kriebitzsch, H. Ellenberg, and G. von Oheimb. 2004. "Dispersal of vascular plants by game in northern Germany. Part I: Roe deer (*Capreolus capreolus*) and wild boar (*Sus scrofa*)." *European Journal of Forest Research* 123: 167–176.

Schmidt, W. 1989. "Plant dispersal by motor cars." *Plant Ecology* 80: 147–152.

Scobie, A., and C. Wilcock. 2009. "Limited mate availability decreases reproductive success of fragmented populations of *Linnaea borealis*, a rare, clonal self-incompatible plant." *Annals of Botany* 103: 835–846.

Scott, M. 2016. *Mountain Flowers.* London: Bloomsbury.

Shaw, H., and R. Tipping. 2006. "Recent pine woodland dynamics in east Glen Affric, northern Scotland, from highly resolved palaeoecological analyses." *Forestry* 79: 331–340.

Sheail, J. 1998. *Nature conservation in Britain – the formative years.* London: The Stationery Office.

Shirreffs, D.A. 1985. "*Anemone nemorosa* L." *Journal of Ecology* 73: 1005–1020.

Sims, N. K., E.A. John, and A.J.A. Stewart. 2014. "Short-term response and recovery of bluebells (*Hyacinthoides non-scripta*) after rooting by wild boar (*Sus scrofa*)." *Plant Ecology* 215: 1409–1416.

Smart, S.M., A.M. Ellison, R.G.H. Bunce, *et al.* 2014. "Quantifying the impact of an extreme climate event on species diversity in fragmented temperate forests: the effect of the October 1987 storm on British broadleaved woodlands." *Journal of Ecology* 102: 1273–1287.

Smith, G.F., S. Iremonger, D.L. Kelly, S. O'Donoghue, and F.J. Mitchell. 2007. "Enhancing vegetation diversity in glades, rides and roads in plantation forests." *Biological Conservation* 136: 283–294.

Snow, B., and D. Snow. 1988. *Birds and berries.* London: Poyser.

Southall, E., M. Dale, and M. Kent. 2003. "Floristic variation and willow carr development within a southwest England wetland." *Applied Vegetation Science* 6: 63–72.

Sparks, T.H., J.N. Greatorex-Davies, J.O. Mountford, M.L.Hall, and R.H. Marrs. 1996. "The effects of shade on the plant communities of rides in plantation woodland and implications for butterfly conservation." *Forest Ecology and Management* 80: 197–207.

Spencer, J.W., and K.J. Kirby. 1992. "An inventory of ancient woodland for England and Wales." *Biological Conservation* 62: 77–93.

Stace, C. 2010. *New Flora of the British Isles (third edition).* Cambridge: Cambridge University Press.

Steele, R.C., and G.F. Peterken, 1982. "Management

objectives for broadleaved woodland: conservation." In *Broadleaves in Britain: future management and research,* edited by D.C. Malcolm, J. Evans, and P.N. Edwards: 91–103. Edinburgh: Institute of Chartered Foresters.

Steele, R.C., and R.C. Welch. 1973. *Monks Wood: a nature reserve record.* Cambridge: Nature Conservancy/ Natural Environment Research Council.

Sternberg, T., H. Viles, and A. Cathersides. 2011. "Evaluating the role of ivy (*Hedera helix*) in moderating wall surface microclimates and contributing to the bioprotection of historic buildings." *Building and Environment* 46: 293–297.

Sternberg, T., H. Viles, A. Cathersides, and M. Edwards. 2010. "Dust particulate absorption by ivy (*Hedera helix* L) on historic walls in urban environments." *Science of The Total Environment* 409: 162–168.

Steven, H.M., and A. Carlisle. 1959. *The native pinewoods of Scotland.* Edinburgh: Oliver and Boyd.

Stiven, R., and M. Smith. 2005. *Lessons learned from tree planting on Rum National Nature Reserve 1957–2004.* Edinburgh: Scottish Natural Heritage (commission research report).

Stuart, A.J. 2005. "The extinction of woolly mammoth (*Mammuthus primigenius*) and straight-tusked elephant (*Palaeoloxodon antiquus*) in Europe." *Quaternary International* 126–128: 171–177.

Suggitt, A.J., R.J. Wilson, N.J.B. Isaac, *et al.* 2018. "Extinction risk from climate change is reduced by microclimatic buffering." *Nature Climate Change* 8: 713–717.

Summers, R.W. 2018. *Abernethy Forest: the history and ecology of an old Scottish pinewood.* Sandy: RSPB.

Summers, R.W., R. Proctor, M. Thorton, and G. Avey. 2004. "Habitat selection and diet of the Capercaillie *Tetrao urogallus* in Abernethy Forest, Strathspey, Scotland." *Bird Study* 51: 58–68.

Svenning, J-C., S. Normand, and F. Skov. 2008. "Postglacial dispersal limitation of widespread forest plant species in nemoral Europe." *Ecography* 31: 316–326.

Svenning, J-C., and F. Skov. 2004. "Limited filling of the potential range in European tree species." *Ecology Letters* 7: 565–573.

Symonds, H.H. 1936. *Afforestation in the Lake District.* London: Dent.

Tansey, C.J., J.D. Hadfield, and A.B. Phillimore. 2017. "Estimating the ability of plants to plastically track temperature-mediated shifts in the spring phenological optimum." *Global Change Biology.* http://dx.doi.org/10.1111/gcb.13624.

Tansley, A.G. 1939. *The British islands and their vegetation.* Cambridge: Cambridge University Press.

Taylor, C. 1975. *Fields in the English landscape.* London: Dent.

Taylor, K. 2009. "Biological Flora of the British Isles: *Urtica dioica* L." *Journal of Ecology* 97: 1436–1458.

Taylor, K., D.C. Havill, J. Pearson, and J. Woodall. 2002. "*Trientalis europaea* L." *Journal of Ecology* 90: 404–418.

Taylor, K., and S.R.J. Woodell. 2008. "Biological Flora of the British Isles: *Primula elatior* (L.) Hill." *Journal of Ecology* 96: 1098–1116.

Taylor, N.W. 1995. The sycamore *Acer pseudoplatanus*

in Britain – its natural history and value to wildlife. Discussion papers in conservation 42. London: University College.

Thomas, P.A., and T.A. Mukassabi. 2014. "Biological Flora of the British Isles: *Ruscus aculeatus.*" *Journal of Ecology* 102: 1083–1100.

Thomas, R., P. Anderson, and E. Radford. 1994. "The ecological effects of woodland recreation." *Quarterly Journal of Forestry* 88: 225–231.

Tittensor, R. 2016. *Shades of green: an environmental and cultural history of Sitka spruce.* Oxford: Oxbow Books.

Tittensor, R.M., and R.C. Steele. 1971. "Plant communities of the Loch Lomond oakwoods." *Journal of Ecology* 59: 561–582.

Tree, I. 2018. *Wilding: The return of nature to a British farm.* London: Pan Macmillan.

Tsouvalis, J. 2000. *A critical geography of Britain's state forests.* Oxford: Oxford University Press.

Tubbs, C.R. 1986. *The New Forest: a natural history.* London: Collins.

Tudor, O., R.L.H. Dennis, J.N. Greatorex-Davies, and T.H. Sparks. 2004. "Flower preferences of woodland butterflies in the UK: nectaring specialists are species of conservation concern." *Biological Conservation* 119: 397–403.

Türke, M., K. Andreas, M. Gossner, *et al.* 2012. "Are Gastropods, rather than ants, important dispersers of seeds of myrmecochorous forest herbs?" *The American Naturalist* 179: 124–131.

Usher, M.B., A.C. Brown, and S.E. Bedford. 1992. "Plant species richness in farm woodlands." *Forestry* 65: 1–13.

Van Der Veken, S., J. Rogister, K. Verheyen, M. Hermy, and R.A.N. Nathan. 2007. "Over the (range) edge: a 45-year transplant experiment with the perennial forest herb *Hyacinthoides non-scripta.*" *Journal of Ecology* 95: 343–351.

Van Vuure, C. 2005. *Retracing the Aurochs.* Sofia-Moscow: Pensoft.

Vera, F.W.M. 2000. *Grazing ecology and forest history.* Wallingford: CABI.

Verheyen, K., L. Baeten, P. De Frenne, *et al.* 2012. "Driving factors behind the eutrophication signal in understorey plant communities of deciduous temperate forests." *Journal of Ecology* 100: 352–365.

Von Oheimb, G., M. Schmidt, W-U. Kriebitzsch, and H. Ellenberg. 2005. "Dispersal of vascular plants by game in northern Germany. Part II: Red deer (*Cervus elaphus*)." *European Journal of Forest Research* 124: 55–65.

Walker, K., and T.H. Sparks. 2000. "The colonisation of ground flora species within a 38 year old self-sown woodland." In *Long term studies in British woodland,* edited by K.J. Kirby and M.D. Morecroft: 48–50. Peterborough: English Nature.

Wallace, H. 2003. "Vegetation of plantation Sitka spruce – development of new 'forest noda'." In *National Vegetation Classification – ten years experience of using the woodland section,* edited by E.A. Goldberg: 36–50. Peterborough: Joint Nature Conservation Committee.

Wallace, H.L., and J.E.G. Good. 1995. "Effects of afforestation on upland plant communities and implications for vegetation management." *Forest Ecology and Management* 79: 29–46.

Ward, A.I. 2005. "Expanding ranges of wild and feral deer in Great Britain." *Mammal Review* 35: 165–173.

Warren, C. 2000. "'Birds, bogs and forestry' revisited: The significance of the flow country controversy." *Scottish Geographical Journal* 116: 315–337.

Warren, M.S. 1991. "The successful conservation of an endangered species, the heath fritillary butterfly *Mellicta athalia*, in Britain." *Biological Conservation* 55: 37–56.

Warren, M.S., and R.J. Fuller. 1993. *Woodland rides and glades: their management for wildlife.* Peterborough: Joint Nature Conservation Committee.

Warren, M.S., and J.A. Thomas. 1992. Butterfly responses to coppicing. In *Ecology and management of coppice woodlands*, edited by G.P. Buckley: 249–270. London: Chapman and Hall.

Watt, T.A., and G.P. Buckley. 1994. *Hedgerow management and nature conservation.* Wye: Wye College Press.

Watts, K., E. Fuentes-Montemayor, N.A. Macgregor, et al. 2016. "Using historical woodland creation to construct a long-term, large-scale natural experiment: the WrEN project." *Ecology and Evolution* 6: 3012–3025.

Webb, D.A. 1952. "The flora and vegetation of Ireland." In *Die Pflanzenwelt Irlands* edited by W.E. Ludi: 48–78. Bern: Hans Huber.

Welch, D. 2003. "A reconsideration of the native status of *Linnaea borealis* L. (Caprifoliaceae) in lowland Scotland." *Watsonia* 24: 427–432.

Wells, T.C.E., S.A. Bell, and A.J Frost. 1981. *Creating attractive grasslands using native plant species.* Shrewsbury: Nature Conservancy Council.

Wesche, S., K.J. Kirby, and J. Ghazoul. 2006. "Plant assemblages in British beech woodlands within and beyond native range: implications of future climate change for their conservation." *Forest ecology and management* 236: 385–392.

Wheeler, B.D. 1980. "Plant Communities of Rich-Fen Systems in England and Wales: III. Fen Meadow, Fen Grassland and Fen Woodland Communities, and Contact Communities." *Journal of Ecology* 68: 761–788.

Whitehouse, N.J., and D. Smith. 2010. "How fragmented was the British Holocene wildwood? Perspectives on the 'Vera' grazing debate from the fossil beetle record." *Quaternary Science Reviews* 29: 539–553.

Wiberg, R.A.W., A.R. Scobie, S.W. A'hara, R.A. Ennos, and J.E. Cottrell. 2016. "The genetic consequences of long term habitat fragmentation on a self-incompatible clonal plant, *Linnaea borealis* L." *Biological Conservation* 201: 405–413.

Wilcock, C.C. 2002. "Maintenance and recovery of rare clonal plants: the case of the twinflower (*Linnaea borealis* L.)." *Botanical Journal of Scotland*, 54, 121–131.

Wilson, C.J. 2003. "Distribution and status of feral wild boar *Sus scrofa* in Dorset, southern England." *Mammal Review* 33: 302–307.

Wittig, R., and H. Neite. 1986. "Acid indicators around the trunk base of *Fagus sylvatica* in limestone and loess beechwoods: distribution pattern and phytosociological problems." *Vegetatio* 64: 113–119.

Wohlleben, P. 2016. *The hidden life of trees: what they feel, how they communicate – Discoveries from a secret world.* Vancouver: Greystone Books.

Woodland Trust. 2006. *Back on the Map, An inventory of ancient and long established woodland in Northern Ireland.* Grantham: Woodland Trust.

Woodruffe-Peacock, E.A. 1918. "A Fox-Covert Study." *Journal of Ecology* 6: 110–125.

Wormell, P. 1994. Isle of Rum woodlands – progress report 1994. Edinburgh: Scottish Natural Heritage.

Worrell, R., D. Long, G. Laverack, C. Edwards, and K. Holl. 2016. *The introduction of woodland plants into broadleaved woods for conservation purposes: best practice guidance.* Edinburgh: Plantlife Scotland, Scottish Natural Heritage, Forestry Commission Scotland and Scotia Seeds.

Yalden, D. 1999. *The history of British mammals*, London: Poyser.

Zimov, S.A. 2005. "Pleistocene Park: Return of the Mammoth's Ecosystem." *Science* 308: 796–798.

Picture credits

Index

Page numbers in **bold** refer to illustrations.
Page numbers in *italics* refer to tables.